S0-AYW-658

# Work,
## Welfare
### and
## Politics

# Work, Welfare and Politics

*Confronting Poverty
in the Wake of
Welfare Reform*

**Frances Fox Piven,
Joan Acker,
Margaret Hallock
and Sandra Morgen
Editors**

UNIVERSITY OF
OREGON

PRESS

Copyright © 2002 University of Oregon Press
All rights reserved. No part of this book may be reproduced in any form without written
permission from the publisher.

Published in association with the
Wayne Morse Center for Law and Politics

Cover image © Photonica

Published by
University of Oregon Press
5283 University of Oregon
Eugene, OR 97403-5283

Designed by Jeffrey Jane Flowers and Jessica MacMurray
Edited by Cheri Brooks

Book manufactured in the United States

ISBN: 0-87114-301-1

h  g  f  e  d  c  b  a

# Contents

| | |
|---|---|
| Glossary | 7 |
| Introduction | 9 |
| About the Editors | 15 |

## Part I
### The Politics and Ideology of Welfare Reform

1. Welfare Policy and American Politics
— Frances Fox Piven 19

2. Welfare Racism and its Consequences: The Demise of AFDC and the Return of the States' Rights Era
— Ken Neubeck and Noel Cazenave 35

3. Not-So-Rugged Individualists: U.S. Americans' Conflicting Ideas about Poverty
— Claudia Strauss 55

## Part II
### Families, Caregiving and Wage Work

4. What's Wrong with Welfare-to-Work
— Randy Albelda 73

5. "Some of Us are Excellent at Babies": Paid Work, Mothering, and the Construction of Need in a Welfare-to-Work Program
— Stephanie Limoncelli 81

6. What Do Sex and Reproduction Have to Do with Welfare?
— Wendy Chavkin, Diana Romero and Paul H. Wise 95

## Part III
### Work and Wages

7. Welfare Reform and the Low-Wage Labor Market
— Jared Bernstein 115

8. Welfare Reform and Working Poverty: Job Types, Wage Mobility and Post-Exit Earnings of Welfare Recipients in North Carolina, 1995-1999
— Lisa Morris 129

9. The Effect of Welfare Reform on the Incomes and Earnings of Low-Income Families: Evidence from the Current Population Survey
— Laura Connolly 145

10. Struggling to Live and to Learn: Single Mothers, Welfare Policy and Post-Secondary Education in Michigan
— Peggy Kahn and Valerie Polakow 157

**Part IV**

**Welfare Reform as Social Control**

11. Job Training for Welfare Recipients: A Hand Up or a Slap Down?
— Gordon Lafer 175

12. Opportunity and Control: Living Welfare Reform in
Los Angeles County
— John Horton and Linda L. Shaw 197

13. Talking Across the Welfare Divide
— Chariti Gent 213

14. Ties that Bind: Child Support Enforcement and
Welfare Reform in Wisconsin
— Renee Monson 227

**Part V**

**The Impact of Welfare Reform on Family Wellbeing**

15. The Impact of Welfare Restructuring on Economic
and Family Wellbeing
— Joan Acker and Sandra Morgen 243

16. Making the Transition to Self-Sufficiency in Oregon
— John Tapogna and Tara Witt 259

17. From War on Poverty to War on Welfare: The Impact of
Welfare Reform on the Lives of Immigrant Women
— Doris Ng. 277

18. Integrating Meaningful Health and Welfare Reforms
— Karen Seccombe 289

19. The Effects of Welfare Reform on the Characteristics
of the Food Stamp Population
— Phil Gleason, Carole Trippe and Scott Cody 301

**Part VI**

**The Structure of Welfare Reform**

20. Is Welfare Reform Working in Arizona and Oregon?
— Mary Ann Steger 321

21. Welfare Reform Strategies and Community-based
Organizations: The Impact on Family Wellbeing in an
Urban Neighborhood
—Michael Reisch and Ursula Bischoff 333

**Part VII**

**Conclusion**

22. Toward a New Politics
— Joan Acker, Sandra Morgen, Frances Fox Piven and Margaret Hallock 349

Acknowledgments 358
Index 359

## Glossary

| | |
|---|---|
| ABAWD | Able-bodied adult without children |
| AFDC | Aid to Families with Dependent Children |
| AFS | Division of Adult and Family Services (Oregon) |
| CalWORKs | California Work Opportunity and Responsibility to Kids |
| CBO | community-based organization |
| CCTC | Child Care Tax Credit |
| CNA | Certified Nursing Assistant |
| CPS | Current Population Survey |
| CSEA | California School Employees Association |
| DES | Department of Economic Security (Arizona) |
| EITC | Earned Income Tax Credit |
| EMPOWER | Employing and Moving People Off Welfare and Encouraging Responsibility (Arizona welfare reform program) |
| EDP | Employment Development Plan |
| ERDC | Employment-Related Day Care |
| ESC | Employment Securities Commission |
| ESL | English as a Second Language programs |
| FMR | Fair Market Rent |
| FSA | Financial Services Authority |
| FSP | Food Stamp Program |
| FSPQC | Food Stamp Program Quality Control |
| GAIN | Greater Avenues for Independence (mandatory program for welfare parents in Los Angeles County, its version of CalWORKs) |
| GAO | General Accounting Office (U.S. Congress) |
| GNP | Gross National Product |
| HUD | U.S. Department of Housing and Urban Development |
| JOBS | Job Opportunities and Basic Skills program (Oregon) |
| JSS | Job Search Specialist |
| JTPA | Jobs Training Partnership Act |
| LACOE | LA County Office of Education |
| LA DPSS | LA Department of Public Services |
| NLSY | National Longitudinal Survey of Youth |
| NMES | National Medical Expenditure Survey |
| OECD | Organisation for Economic Co-Operation and Development |
| OHP | Oregon Health Plan |
| PSID | Panel Study of Income Dynamics |
| PRWORA | Personal Responsibility and Work Opportunity Reconciliation Act |
| SIC | Standard Industrial Code |
| SIPP | Survey of Income and Program Participation |
| S-CHIP | State Children's Health Insurance Program |
| TANF | Temporary Aid for Needy Families (replaced AFDC under PRWORA) |
| UI | Unemployment Insurance |
| WtW | Welfare-to-Work |

# Introduction

Is low-wage work the solution to poverty? Should work trump caregiving for low-income mothers? How are states dealing with low-income people after the "end of welfare as we knew it?" Can a new politics of welfare emerge?

These and other questions were posed at a conference in February 2000 hosted by the Center for the Study of Women in Society and the Wayne Morse Center for Law and Politics at the University of Oregon. The strength of the conference lay in its multidisciplinary focus and explicit attention to three key themes referred to in its title — Work, Welfare, and Politics. This volume presents a set of essays that discuss these issues and how they interrelate. Focusing on the history, ideology, politics, impacts, and prospects of welfare reform in the United States, we shed light on aspects often ignored and also question the assumptions and ideology of the Welfare-to-Work nexus.

When the conference was held, the American economy was booming, allowing many of the women confronting the Work First policies of the new welfare regimen to find jobs — albeit, as the papers that follow show, usually low-wage jobs and often irregular jobs. At the dawn of the twenty-first century, however, the United States is in the midst of recession. Employment in the service sector, where many former recipients found jobs, is plummeting. And this economic downturn is occurring just as federal and state lifetime limits on welfare utilization are taking effect. The proponents of welfare reform talked as if the American economy would expand forever, as if the prospect of a recession would never cast a shadow on their proposals to cut entitlements for the poor. Now the recession may be derailing the much ballyhooed "success" of welfare reform, making the questions raised in the papers that follow all the more urgent.

The Work, Welfare, and Politics Conference emerged out of the politics of the 1990s, a decade that saw a sharp reversal in the slow progress the United States was making toward developing social policies that would provide, at least, a subsistence income for the poor. The capstone of this reversal was the Personal Responsibility and Work Opportunity Reconciliation Act of 1996 (PRWORA), which effectively revoked federal responsibility for providing income to impoverished families. The open-ended federal funding of the Aid to Families with Dependent Children (AFDC) program was replaced by a program of state block grants, fixed at roughly the level of the federal share of state AFDC spending in 1994.

Along with these block grants, PRWORA gave states wide discretion to administer the disbursement of aid, including the discretion to use federal monies for other programs if they could be considered to be related to the broad purposes of the new legislation. The main limits imposed on the states were caps on generosity—a lifetime limit of five years on the receipt of welfare benefits and the requirement that beneficiaries work in exchange for their checks. States would be penalized if they did not reach federal quotas for work relief. The legislation also explicitly allowed states to tie a range of behavioral conditions to the receipt of aid.

Consistent with these policy directions, welfare reform also tightened eligibility for Food Stamps and introduced work requirements into that program as well. PRWORA also sharply restricted the eligibility of legal immigrants for either cash assistance or Food Stamps. And it introduced new restrictions on the eligibility of poor children for Supplemental Security Income (SSI). The rhetorical thrust of the legislative language justifying these measures was clear: Welfare policy would heretofore be directed toward enforcing waged work and discouraging out-of-wedlock childbearing.

The states acted rapidly to redesign their welfare programs to wield the discretion they had been granted and to implement the new federal restrictions. This was hardly surprising. The states, in fact, had been in the forefront of agitation for "ending welfare as we know it," and many already had been taking advantage of a legislative loophole, which permitted waivers of the terms of the Social Security Act governing AFDC, to introduce many of the features later instituted by PRWORA. After national welfare reform passed, states moved rapidly to introduce further restrictions.

In part, this reflected the political animus toward welfare that had been building for two decades, one encouraged by regular bashing of welfare mothers by politicians in both major parties. But the eagerness with which the states moved to revamp their welfare programs also reflected the fiscal incentives built into the block grant arrangement. What the states did not spend on cash assistance, they could use for other programs that presumably would benefit the poor. In the process, a good deal of state spending came to be replaced with federal dollars. The fiscal windfall was estimated by the Center for Community Change at roughly $7 billion.

The new welfare programs that emerged emphasized work requirements, time limits on assistance (which were often far shorter than the federal limits), behavioral rules and sanctions, diversion (which meant that poor women were often turned away when they attempted to make formal application for assistance), and privatization. This last deserves a brief comment, for when states turned aspects of the administration of assistance over to private companies they replicated the pernicious fiscal disincentive against providing assistance that the block grant contained. Companies profit when they provide less assistance to fewer people, just as states profit when they provide less assistance to fewer people.

Descriptions of how the administration of welfare works frequently invoke the contract metaphor. "If you work hard and play by the rules, you shouldn't be poor," was Bill Clinton's way of stating the terms of the contract. Presumably, this means that if poor mothers obey the rules of the new welfare regime and try hard, they will be on their way out of poverty. But contract talk is a poor guide to the realities of power in the new welfare regime, where agencies are free to multiply rules and to decide which of them to obey. Meanwhile, poor women are easily subjected to stiff sanctions for behaviors deemed to be in violation of "the contract."

Now, several years into the implementation of the new policies, some assessment of the consequences is possible: Most obviously and most loudly trumpeted, the rolls have fallen by more than half. Data suggest that about half of the leavers are working. Indeed, politicians compete to claim credit for this result, and press coverage has been nothing short of triumphal, featuring personal portraits of beaming women who have managed, as a result of the new "tough love" regime, to break the habit of "welfare dependency."

In fact, data on the consequences of welfare reform are far from complete. And it is important to keep in mind that the welfare experiment was conducted in an unusual economic context, when unemployment had fallen to its lowest level in more than forty years and wages were rising, even for the lowest-paid workers. Even in this context, the earnings of former recipients who began working remained low. For those not working, there is not much good data, in part because neither the federal government nor the states have been seriously interested in tracking them. The impoverished and often disorganized circumstances of the non-working poor (they are less likely to have telephones, for example) mean they also tend to fall out of the net of independent surveyors. Meanwhile, there is disturbing evidence that, even during the boom times, hunger and homelessness rose.

In Wisconsin, the state that pioneered most of the features of the new regime, welfare rolls have fallen by two-thirds, and the former governor was rewarded with an appointment as Secretary of Health and Human Services by the Bush administration. But Wisconsin's pioneering policies have been accompanied also by a sharp rise in foster-care placements and the reversal of long-term downward trends in black and Hispanic infant mortality.

Given the huge amount of funded research spurred by welfare reform, the paucity of knowledge about the potential casualties of the experiment should be explained. Partly, it is a consequence of the reluctance of federal and state politicians to learn uncomfortable facts. Senator Paul Wellstone, a Democrat from Minnesota, repeatedly has attached to other legislation amendments requiring full reports to the Congress, but these amendments are eliminated in conference. The states have shown comparable disinterest in discomfiting findings. When Wisconsin's scheme to reduce adolescent truancy by docking family benefits was shown to increase truancy, the state government terminated the research contract that produced these findings.

Even more important because of the scale of the potential impact, we know virtually nothing about the large numbers of people who are simply turned away from welfare centers, or who never even take steps to seek assistance because the campaign against welfare has so intensified the stigma of welfare status. Data from the 2000 census provide reason to be concerned, however. Consistent with the economic boom, overall poverty rates declined, albeit modestly. However, the so-called poverty gap — the amount of money required to bring the average poor household up to the poverty line — increased. This indicates that substantial numbers of the poor are in increasingly desperate straits.

We hope this book will broaden the investigation of the impacts of welfare cutbacks. It is divided into seven sections. The first explores the politics and ideology of welfare reform. The lead chapter by Frances Fox Piven describes the history and politics that informed the welfare reform movement of the 1990s. Piven confronts arguments that globalization required a reduction in welfare and, instead, describes a "politics of greed" that drove the campaign for welfare reform and dictated its specific nature. Based on their 2001 book, *Welfare Racism: Playing the Race Card Against America's Poor*, Ken Neubeck and Noel Cazenave explain, in Chapter 2, how welfare racism acts as a systemic phenomenon that serves to reinforce racial inequities and argue that racism is central to the demise of AFDC and the passage of the federal welfare reform bill. In Chapter 3, Claudia Strauss suggests that, with proper framing, support for progressive welfare reform is still possible. Her research shows that, although the public wanted a change in welfare in the 1990s, they did not necessarily want the "rugged individualist" model promoted in the federal campaign.

Section II examines the central issues of motherhood and sex inherent within the welfare reform ideology. In Chapter 4, Randy Albelda maintains that the new emphasis on Welfare-to-Work devalues caregiving and provides inadequate support to mothers. Rather than ask if low-income mothers are "job ready," she argues, we should be asking if low-wage jobs are "mother ready." Stephanie Limoncelli expands on this theme in Chapter 5, detailing research that shows that Work First policies view women primarily as workers, without acknowledging that domestic work is gendered and that many participants identify themselves primarily as caregivers. In Chapter 6, researchers from the Finding Common Ground Project argue that welfare reform was not aimed at reducing poverty but at altering individual sexual and reproductive behaviors. The research of Wendy Chavkin and her colleagues critiques family caps, immunization requirements, family planning, and out-of-wedlock births.

Section III moves from the ideology of welfare reform to a scrutiny of one of its main planks—Work First. Jared Bernstein, in Chapter 7, provides an excellent overview of the problems of welfare reform in the context of the low-wage labor market. He summarizes a broad range of research on the impact of sending welfare recipients into this labor market, including their wages, labor market mobility, and living standards. In Chapter 8, Lisa Morris provides evidence that most recipients find jobs in service, retail, and manufacturing industries, where entry-level jobs tend to be low-wage with little chance for upward mobility. Her innovative use of firm-level employment data provides one of the first examinations of the welfare reform premise that upward mobility in the labor market justifies low-wage entry-level jobs. The obvious problem, as Morris points out, is that upward mobility is so limited, few can maintain steady earnings over time. Similarly, in Chapter 9, Laura Connolly uses data from the Current Population Survey to show that work requirements have no effect on incomes. Indeed, incomes may actually fall if work is required, and families are not better off and may be worse off. One of the most controversial aspects of the push to low-wage work is its negative impact on education opportunities for recipients. In Chapter 10, Peggy Kahn and Valerie Polakow argue that, in practice and design, Work First restricts access to post-secondary education in Michigan and elsewhere, despite strong evidence that education is the key to higher earnings and job stability.

Section IV examines the ugly underside of welfare reform, specifically its thrust for control and repression of clients. Building on the seminal analysis of Piven and Cloward (1971), these papers show how current policies continue to control and regulate poor people. In Chapter 11, Gordon Lafer critiques Work First, Workfare, and job training initiatives as Orwellian policies designed to control and demobilize recipients. In Chapter 12, John Horton and Linda Shaw examine how clients are disciplined and controlled in Job Clubs, likening them to boot camps that plays on clients' internalized societal images of themselves. Likewise, Chariti Gent's detailed analysis, in Chapter 13, of the dialogue of welfare reform shows that the players are talking past each other, each group with a different agendas. Chapter 14 continues the earlier thread that welfare reform is based on an attack on women and motherhood. Renee Monson presents a feminist critique of mandatory child support enforcement and paternity policies as punitive and potentially in conflict with women's economic interests, their interests as mothers, and their personal safety and autonomy.

While Section III demonstrates the problems of requiring welfare recipients to find jobs in the low-wage labor market, Section V asks a slightly different question: Does welfare reform, as a whole, enhance family wellbeing? Are families better off with a combination of work and support services, compared with the welfare benefits of the past? In Chapter 15, Joan Acker and Sandra Morgen present the results of research that examined the status of people who left or were diverted from TANF and Food Stamps in Oregon, one of the first states to embrace changes to its welfare system. Using surveys and interviews, they draw a complicated picture that shows, despite high employment among former recipients, the goal of self-sufficiency has not been met in Oregon. The pernicious disincentives of previous welfare programs were not entirely eliminated in the current policy. In Chapter 16, John Tapogna and Tara Witt show what happens to family income and assistance levels as recipients move from welfare to different levels of work. Surprisingly, although minimum-wage workers may be better off working, they can face financial penalties when they move into higher-wage jobs. Some welfare recipients face extraordinary obstacles in the transition required by new welfare policies. In Chapter 17, Doris Ng presents a case study of a community organization serving immigrant women in Santa Clara, California, documenting barriers to work and the resulting impact on families. Welfare and health care are critically linked, as Karen Seccombe explains in Chapter 18. And researchers at Mathematica, Inc. suggest, in Chapter 19, that welfare reform has had an unexpected impact on the Food Stamp population, with the biggest impacts on the most disadvantaged recipients.

Welfare is administered at the state level, and the federal reform "devolved" even more authority to states. What are the institutional effects? Section VI looks at the impacts of welfare reform on state and local systems. In Chapter 20, Mary Ann Steger compares Oregon and Arizona and finds that the degree of centralization, as well as the goals, of state bureaucracies have an impact on the nature of the reform. In Chapter 21, Michael Reisch and Ursula Bischoff present research on impacts to community-based organizations involved in welfare reform in Philadelphia. Organizations have little support to deal with the enormous changes, even though society is asking much of them in this new era of public assistance.

The final section captures the many voices of advocates and policy makers who attended the conference, who call for a reversal of the ideological assault on caregiving and a renewed emphasis on reducing poverty, rather than welfare caseloads. These voices emphasize the wellbeing of families, needed reforms to the low-wage labor market, access to education and meaningful training, and a reweaving of the safety net. The concluding section, thus, calls for a new national discussion as PRWORA comes up for reauthorization. Achieving meaningful welfare reform requires changing the ideology of Work First, even more important in this era of economic recession. The obstacles are obvious, as is the need for a new and bold politics that attract workers and poor people to a vibrant new movement.

**Frances Fox Piven, Joan Acker, Margaret Hallock and Sandra Morgen**
**January 2002**

## References

Piven, Frances Fox, and Richard A. Cloward. 1971. *Regulating the Poor: The Functions of Public Welfare.* New York: Random House.

## About the Editors

### Frances Fox Piven

One of the foremost scholars of poverty and politics in the United States, Frances Fox Piven's critique of social welfare policies has been the impetus for hundreds of other scholars seeking to improve our understanding of the welfare system, economic inequality, and the central role of protest in American politics. Piven changed the thinking of a generation of scholars and activists with her 1971 seminal book, *Regulating the Poor: The Functions of Public Welfare*. With Richard Cloward, she revolutionized popular thinking about welfare, showing how it functions as a mechanism of political and social control. With welfare recipients and other activists, Piven helped create the welfare rights movement of the 1960s and 1970s. Piven is currently Distinguished Professor of Political Science and Sociology at the Graduate School, City University of New York. She served as the University of Oregon's Wayne Morse Chair Professor in 1999 and keynoted the Work, Welfare, and Politics Conference. Piven's other award-winning books include *Why Americans Don't Vote* and *Poor People's Movements: Why They Succeed, How They Fail*, both with Richard Cloward.

### Joan Acker

Joan Acker was a founder and the first director of the Center for the Study of Women in Society at the University of Oregon and has dedicated her scholarship to issues of social and economic equity. A professor emeritus of sociology at the University of Oregon, Acker has authored books and articles on feminist theory in sociology, gender and work, welfare reform, issues of class, gender, and race, labor and workplace issues, and gender and organizations. She has had a particular research interest in Scandinavia, and has held teaching and research positions in Sweden, Norway, and Finland. Acker has also taught in Germany, Australia, Canada, and England. She has received the Career of Distinguished Scholarship Award and the Jessie Bernard Award for feminist research from the American Sociological Association, as well as other fellowships and awards.

### Margaret Hallock

Margaret Hallock is director of the Wayne Morse Center for Law and Politics, an independent center at the University of Oregon dedicated to interdisciplinary research, discussion, publication and teaching on critical topics in the fields of law and politics. From 1988 to 2000, she served as director of the UO Labor Education and Research Center. With a Ph.D. in economics, Hallock specializes in the role of women in the economy, as well as workforce development and public policy issues. During the 1980s, she chaired the pay equity commission for the state of Oregon and led the successful battle for pay equity for state employees. She writes and lectures on a broad range of policy issues affecting women workers, including welfare reform and economic inequality. She also teaches collective bargaining, labor and the economy, and leadership.

## Sandra Morgen

Sandra Morgen, an anthropologist, is director of the Center for the Study of Women in Society (CSWS) at the University of Oregon, where she also is a professor in the sociology department. For the past two decades her research has focused on women and the State, women's political activism, and the intersection of gender, race, and class in women's lives. For the past three years Morgen has been the co-director of the CSWS Welfare Research Team, which completed an ethnographic study of three welfare offices in Oregon in addition to the study of families who left or were diverted from TANF or Food Stamps, which is discussed in this volume. Her book *Into Our Own Hands: The Women's Health Movement in the U.S.* will be published by Rutgers University Press in 2002. In addition to her scholarly work on welfare, Morgen has been involved in efforts to influence public policy on both the state and national level.

## PART I

# The Politics and Ideology of Welfare Reform

Frances Fox Piven

Ken Neubeck

Noel Cazenave

Claudia Strauss

# Welfare Policy and American Politics

*Frances Fox Piven*[1]

I t is useful to look at the changes in American welfare policy in the context of developments occurring in other rich, democratic countries. At first glance, the pattern seems similar. All Western countries have income protection programs, won in response to the political mobilization of poor and working people over the course of the twentieth century. And efforts to roll back these programs — old age pensions, disability allowances, unemployment insurance, social assistance or poor relief programs, and a range of other public services — are underway everywhere.

In all of these countries, a similar argument is being made about the economic imperatives that are forcing changes in social policy. The argument goes like this: The social programs to which we have become accustomed made sense in an industrial era. But now we are in a new era. The economies of industrial countries have been transformed by globalization and by the electronic and transportation networks that make globalization possible. The capital mobility and accelerated trade that are the signposts of globalization mean that domestic producers, and entire domestic economies, confront intensified worldwide competition. Workers in the mother countries, whether Germany, France, or the United States, must compete with workers across the globe. The goods produced by the relatively well-off workers in the First World compete with the goods made by potentially billions of poor workers in the Southern Hemisphere. Otherwise, lower-cost goods produced offshore will crowd out goods produced at home, or workers from low-wage countries will flood into high-wage countries where they will undercut prevailing wages. Because globalization means that capital races around the globe at the click of a mouse to take advantage of low wages and low taxes, governments themselves are pitted against each other in the contest to attract investors.

Under these conditions, the argument goes, the relatively generous social programs of the industrial era have become dysfunctional. Income-support programs increase wage costs and interfere with competitiveness. They do this both because they require high taxes, whether payroll taxes or taxes on capital, and because they create a reservation wage, a floor below which wages cannot fall. The conclusion seems inescapable: generous social programs make domestic production uncompetitive and drive investment elsewhere. Hence, the programs must be refashioned so that they are more "market-friendly," which means rolling back benefits, narrowing eligibility, and imposing stricter work requirements as a condition for access to those benefits that are still available.

This argument is made in all of the rich democracies, but it is not equally successful everywhere. In continental Europe, the actual program cuts have been modest, despite the vigor with which the OECD has called for rollbacks in social programs to promote what is called "wage flexibility." The reason is simply that politicians do not dare! Popular resistance is too vigorous — a popular resistance rooted in political traditions that support state policies that intervene in markets in the interest of poor and working people, that support an expanded public sector. Moreover, in many of these countries, unions have remained strong, and unions understand the role of generous social programs in undergirding wage levels (ILO 1997, tables 1.2 and 3.2). Consequently, wages in continental Europe have not fallen as they have in the United States over the past twenty-five years, and poverty levels have not risen (Gottschalk and Smeeding 1997).[2]

Still, the campaign to "reform" the European welfare state continues, and it is strident, insistent, and has powerful backers. In that campaign the United States is regularly pointed to as the exemplar, as the nation on which other rich democratic nations should model themselves. ("Model USA" was the title of a recent well-attended conference in Berlin.) First, the story is told of America's apparent economic success. We have lower unemployment levels, higher rates of economic growth, and extraordinary rates of growth in profits, all this in contrast to Western Europe. Why? Because our wages are lower and more "flexible."

Wage flexibility, in turn, is traced to our different social policies.[3] Not only did the United States enter the era of globalization with less generous social programs, it has since made big cuts in these limited programs. Not unexpectedly, big cuts in social protections have been accompanied by declining wages. This of course is exactly what the OECD means by its call for "wage flexibility." When public income supports that undergird wages are rolled back, workers are inevitably less secure, and it becomes easier for employers to roll back wages and restructure work.

The implications of this argument are chilling. For one thing, the logic of the argument means that workers everywhere must now accept wages driven down toward the level of the wages paid to the poorest workers in the world. The implications are especially chilling for democratic politics, because the argument asserts that governments are helpless in the face of the threat of capital flight, and if governments are helpless, so are their citizens. Indeed, citizenship loses much of its meaning if governments cannot act on matters crucial to the economic wellbeing of ordinary people. In this sense, democratic rights are rolled back along with the social programs.

This argument has played a large role in the politics of U.S. social policy. But is it true that the anonymous logic of economic globalization has made the welfare state dysfunctional? Of course, the evidence of accelerating international trade is all around us — in the clothes we buy that are made in Korea or China, in the electronics we buy made in Japan or Taiwan. But although the argument that the welfare state impedes a global economy is louder and shriller in the United States, and although the United States has been the leader in actual social program cutbacks, the United States is far from a leader in economic globalization. Because imports and exports account for a smaller share of our GNP, the American economy is in fact less exposed to international trade than most European countries with export-oriented "open economies."

Moreover, while U.S. multinationals are indeed leaders in overseas investments, most of their investments are in Western Europe (Tabb 1997). On its face, the economic argument against social expenditures is dubious. The United States lags behind Western Europe in terms of the internationalization of its economy, yet is the world leader in social policy reforms that are attributed to internationalization. If competitive pressures were the underlying reason for social program cutbacks, we would expect American investors to be seeking out locations with lower taxes and lower wages. In fact, when our big corporations invest abroad, it is mainly in Western countries with higher wages and higher tax levels. So the least globalized country is the pioneer in the policy cutbacks, falling wages, and rollbacks in workplace protections that are said to be the inevitable result of globalization (Page, Simmons, and Greer 2000).

What the American example actually suggests is not a model of a country adapting to globalization, but rather the impact of *politics* — class politics — specifically, the impact of a business class moving to use public policy to shore up private profits.[4]

Of course, business is not the whole story. The path for business's political mobilization was smoothed by the weakness of popular opposition, especially during the past three decades. That weakness is partly owed to longstanding features of American politics: fragmented, weak political parties that privilege interest groups; the feebleness of organized labor; a political ideology with which an updated version of *laissez-faire* resonates easily; and a popular political culture deeply infused with racism and sexual obsessions.

## The Politics of Greed

There is an economic logic to these changes in American social policy — not the anonymous logic of competitive global markets but rather the logic of unfettered greed. The mobilization of the business community toward aggressive class politics began in the early 1970s. It unfolded first in the workplace, with a direct attack on unions, wages and benefits, and workplace protections. This campaign largely succeeded. Union organizing efforts were halted, and established unions were rolled back, sometimes in unprecedented business campaigns for union decertification. With unions on the defensive it was easier to restructure employment, through the introduction of two-tiered employment, the shift from permanent to contingent workers, and the massive downsizings and speed-ups called "lean production." No longer was a job at the auto plant a job for life and a job for your kids. The resulting insecurity among workers contributed to successful efforts by business to reduce wages and benefits.

Business also mobilized to push for public policies that would shore up profits (Edsall 1985; Ferguson and Rogers 1986; Greider 1992; Judis 2000). By the late 1970s it was able to halt most of the Carter administration's regulatory or labor-oriented initiatives, and in the 1980 election business threw its weight and money behind the candidacy of Ronald Reagan. When Reagan took office, the business agenda unfolded its campaign of tax cuts, military buildup, and the rollback of regulatory controls and social program expenditures. The tax cuts of 1981 began a process that slashed the effective rate of taxation on the American rich from about 50 percent in 1980 to about 28 percent today. The military buildup was also a business grab, benefiting mainly our huge defense industry. Together, tax cuts and rising defense expenditures inevitably produced a large deficit, and initiated the long period during which the growing deficit was regularly used as a club against social spending.

During the 1980s, this agenda met only mixed success. In particular, Congress resisted the cuts in social spending. But the business-Republican alliance persisted and persists. Even the minimum wage bill was loaded with special interest tax cuts. The argument is incredible: If poor workers are insured a $5.15 minimum wage, the government has to make it up to businesses by reducing their taxes. And huge tax cuts again are at the top of the agenda of the new Bush administration.

Meanwhile, government income-support programs are steadily being whittled back. Unemployment insurance benefits reached more than half of the unemployed during the 1970s and more than two-thirds during the mid-decade recession. By the 1980s only a third of the unemployed were protected. The disability insurance rolls were also slashed in the early 1980s. Largely unnoticed and unopposed, eligibility for social security was narrowed by raising the age at which seniors become entitled to full benefits to sixty-seven. And means-tested benefits were slashed (Piven 1997; Piven and Cloward 1993).

Public attention mainly has focused on cuts in the programs that provide income supports to women and children, especially on the changes in welfare initiated by the Personal Responsibility and Work Opportunity Reconciliation Act of 1996 (PRWORA). In fact, the rollback of means-tested benefits began in the early 1970s and took the form of allowing inflation to erode the real value of benefits — by one-third between the early 1970s and the mid-1990s — while politicians began the assault on welfare mothers for their sexual and work behavior. Passage of the PRWORA was the capstone of this development.

PRWORA shifted administrative authority to the states, imposed time limits on assistance, required work as a condition for cash assistance, increased the behavioral monitoring of women as a condition for assistance, and reduced in-kind food and medical assistance.

The devolution of authority to the states in the PRWORA was important, particularly since a similar pattern of devolution has characterized other recent policy initiatives. The argument for devolution was that state governments were both closer to the people and more flexible, and therefore would design more flexible, responsive programs. More likely, the reasons for devolution has to do with the political advantages that state responsibility yields to the campaign against welfare.

For one thing, many state capitols are now presided over by Republican governors. Even if that changes, other features of state politics disadvantage the less powerful. The politics of the state capitols are even murkier than the politics of Washington. There is less scrutiny from the press, for example. Even more important, state governments are inevitably more responsive to business, not only because they are shielded from public scrutiny, but also because officials are acutely sensitive to the threat that mobile businesses will leave the state if they fail to win their demands from the state government. Thus, for structural reasons, the new state-run welfare programs are likely to be more responsive to the labor-market interests of business and less responsive to the interests of the poor.[5]

Given these developments, we should look a little more closely at the American economic success story. During the 1990s, American unemployment levels were lower than those in Western Europe (although unemployment is now declining in Europe). And American profit levels were up, by more than 100 percent since 1990. The earnings of CEOs were up much more, by more than 500 percent (Straus 2000; Wolman and Colemosca

1997). And of course, the stock market was booming. Overall, the top 1 percent of Americans now controls 42 percent of American wealth, a pattern familiar in the so-called banana republics (Wolf 1995). Sixty percent of all gains in after-tax income have also gone to the top 1 percent.

But in terms of the economic wellbeing of ordinary people, the picture is quite different. Average workers' wages are down by about 10 percent since the 1970s, despite the boom. Low-wage workers are, to be sure, now seeing an increase in their take-home pay, but the rise is still quite modest. Despite the unprecedented length of the economic recovery, they have not fully recovered from a two-decade pummeling, which especially affected wages among low earners (Bernstein and Greenberg 2000). The real value of the minimum wage is lower than it was in the 1960s, when a family of three supported by a minimum-wage earner was comfortably above the poverty line. Today, that family is below the poverty line, and 20 percent of those families have no benefits at all.[6] Western Europe presumably lags in the social policy adjustments necessary for economic success in a global world. Perhaps it is for just this reason that Western Europe has not experienced widening income inequality and stagnating wages comparable to the American pattern.

## The Arguments Against Welfare

If so many people were harmed by these new policies, why was there so little protest? Though welfare benefits were only one piece in a pattern of rollbacks, they had the effect of obscuring and justifying larger cutbacks. Welfare "reform" became the symbolic core of a broad ideological campaign against government income-maintenance programs. We all remember the deafening political roar generated by the campaign against welfare. Arguments that had been bubbling on the cook stoves of right-wing think tanks for two decades burst onto the talk shows, dominated the editorial pages, were seized upon by state governors and then blasted forth by the Congress and the president.

The arguments were not new. They were dug up from nineteenth-century attacks on poor relief, although no one who mattered knew or remembered that. The critique of welfare was treated as insightful and original. We were told again and again that while our so-generous welfare system spoke well of the kindly spirit of the American people, it was nevertheless bad for our society. A too-generous welfare system was leading people to become slackers. OECD is now making the same argument when it maintains that generous European social programs create wage inflexibility with deleterious consequences for competitiveness. But in Europe the argument is mainly about unemployment insurance and old-age pensions. In America, the argument was mainly about welfare and the single moms who received it. Because these women were too comfortable on welfare, talk show guests and politicians explained endlessly, they were shunning waged work.

The argument was made with a good deal of animus, evidenced by the reiteration of the phrase "welfare dependency," as if welfare were addictive. But there was a certain logic that a relationship exists between work and welfare.[7] If women and their children could survive on welfare, they would not have to take low-wage work that didn't improve their circumstances. But this logic also makes room for a more benign policy alternative than slashing welfare. If the concern is that welfare creates a work disincentive, then the crusaders against welfare dependency could propose making work more rewarding — by raising wages, for example. Or they could propose that we provide health care to low-wage workers, or that we guarantee reliable childcare to ease the anxiety of poor, working women. These reforms can be justified by the same logic as cutting welfare to enforce work. But nobody talked about these benign reform possibilities. Instead, the focus was on the "tough love" measures of benefit cuts, sanctions, forced work, and behavioral controls.

Even more heated than talk about the work-disincentive effects of welfare was talk about the perverse effects of welfare on sexual and family morality. The availability of welfare, it was said, encouraged women, especially teenagers, to have out-of-wedlock babies. This argument seemed to dominate discussion in Congress, especially the Senate. But the political talk ignored virtually all of the data that we have about out-of-wedlock births.[8] It ignored the fact that out-of-wedlock births have been increasing across the globe and in countries where women have no prospect of a welfare check. It ignored the fact that out-of-wedlock births were increasing among all income strata in the United States, not just among poor women. It ignored the fact that out-of-wedlock births continued to increase even when welfare benefits fell sharply in the 1970s and 1980s. It ignored the fact that there was no correlation between the rate of out-of-wedlock births and state welfare grant levels. And finally, it ignored comparative international evidence that shows no correlation whatsoever between rates of out-of-wedlock births and the generosity of welfare or social assistance. In the United States where benefit levels are very low, teenage out-of-wedlock birth rates are very high — two to six times higher than in the much more generous European welfare states. How then can the availability of generous benefits be to blame for out-of-wedlock births?

The premise of this charge was built on a statistical sleight-of-hand. Overall teenage birth rates were not increasing, they were falling. However, marriage rates among teens were falling even faster. As a consequence, the percentage of in-wedlock births among teens fell, causing the percentage that were out-of-wedlock to increase. A wise observer might suspect that changed attitudes had reduced the stigma of births to the unwed, so there were fewer shotgun marriages, which might not be a bad thing at all.

These arguments were made so loudly, so insistently, and resonated so strongly in the American mind, the opponents of welfare retrenchment were pinned to the wall. Feebly, we tried to answer by showing that the facts being bruited about were wrong. But facts alone are a weak weapon in the face of a propaganda campaign tapping deep cultural antipathies and fueled by powerful economic and political interests.

### The New Welfare Regime

Some of the consequences of the new social policy regime are now becoming apparent. The lower tiers of the labor market already are characterized by growing instability and insecurity, as a result of job restructuring and an increasing reliance on contingent workers. To this mix add several million desperately poor women who have lost their welfare benefits and must compete with other low-wage workers for jobs that are already insecure.[9] As a consequence, despite low levels of unemployment, insecurity is increasing at the bottom of the labor market.

Put another way, welfare cutbacks counter the healthy effects of low unemployment levels to increase the leverage of low-wage workers. Low unemployment is always good for working people because it increases their bargaining power in their dealings with employers. It is especially good for low-wage workers, because now the boss has to pay them a little bit more than they need for bare subsistence to get them to keep or take a particular job. Workers have options. But if insecurity increases at the bottom tiers of the market by a flood of desperate people who have lost their welfare benefits and, perhaps, their food stamps and their Medicaid, the healthy effects of low unemployment levels are reduced.

Then there are the work requirements of the new welfare law. Indeed, work requirements have been extended to some food stamp recipients, and even to public housing tenants. In some places, the welfare work programs are creating a virtually indentured labor force. In Baltimore, for example, welfare recipients were used to break a strike of housekeepers in the Baltimore Omni Hotel. In New York City some 45,000 welfare recipients are now cleaning the streets and the subways, doing jobs previously held by unionized public workers. In Mississippi welfare recipients are assigned to chicken-processing and catfish plants, and one manager told the press cheerfully that he had been assured by welfare officials that women who did not work out at the plant would not be given welfare again.[10]

Consider also the implications of the public spectacle created by the new welfare regime. Until it became clear that the practice was too outlandish, New York City workfare recipients were made to wear Day-Glo orange vests as they went about the streets and subways with their brooms and trash baskets. This public spectacle is important. A few years ago Mickey Kaus (1986), writing in *The New Republic*, called for putting welfare recipients to work in the streets, scrubbing cobblestones, for example. The reason he gave for making Betsy M. get down on her knees with a scrub brush was not only to punish her, but to give those who saw her a lesson in the degradation awaiting anyone who had an out-of-wedlock birth and did not work for wages.

The provisions barring legal immigrants from a range of benefits have similar work-enforcing effects. Most of the people who listened to the tirades against welfare, who heard Senator Phil Gramm from Texas call for getting those people out of the wagon so they could help pull the wagon, probably thought that without welfare or food stamps or Medicaid fewer immigrants would enter the country to compete for American jobs. But the American public had it completely wrong. Very few immigrants, especially Latino immigrants who everyone has in their mind's eye during this sort of discussion, come into the country to go on welfare or SSI. They come for jobs. And the politicians cheering for welfare cutbacks, including cutbacks that single out legal immigrants, were generally in favor of relatively liberal immigration policies, as American business and its political allies have been since the nineteenth century. A plentiful flow of immigrants means, after all, plenty of vulnerable people willing to take low-wage jobs. By denying those people any recourse to government benefits, they are kept even more vulnerable, ensuring that their wages will remain low.

### What Happened to Democratic Politics?

The rise of business's power was made easier by longstanding obstacles to the influence of ordinary Americans. That surely includes obstacles to influence by ordinary people through elections. Still, since the New Deal, pundits and political scientists have argued that in at least one very important way, election outcomes were driven by economic conditions. When things were a bit better, people voted for the incumbent; when they weren't, they voted against the incumbent. The emergence of this "pocket-book" politics in the 1930s was a kind of progress, for it displaced to some extent the tribalist and clientelist appeals that had dominated elections until then. It meant that incumbents facing elections had to produce the policies, or at least to claim to produce the policies, that improved the economic wellbeing of the people going to the polls.

But in the 1990s this sort of pocket-book politics weakened. Both Republicans and Democrats actually ran on an agenda that promised to make conditions worse for a broad swath of the American people. When income supports were slashed not only did women on welfare suffer, so did large numbers of people whose wages and working conditions deteriorated as an indirect consequence. Even the direct consequences are substantial. The Public Policy Institute of California, for example, estimated that one-third of the families in California would lose income as a result of the new welfare regime. Yet there was overwhelming public support of PRWORA. How is this possible?

I think public attitudes were influenced, in part, by the force of the big argument about the rise of markets and the helplessness of government. These nineteenth-century laissez-faire themes gained new credibility because they were tied to globalization: Markets were now international, and government had to get out of the way.

Another factor was the feebleness of the Democratic Party's efforts to resurrect popular economic issues. Bill Clinton's slogan in 1992 was, "It's the economy, stupid," and people responded. But once in office, he didn't follow through. Cowed by Federal Reserve Chairman Alan Greenspan, by investor-banker allies like Robert Rubin, and by fat-cat contributors, Clinton allowed his very modest economic stimulus package to fail. He proceeded to lead the Democratic Party with talk of family values and calls for V-chips and school uniforms, even while championing free trade and social-program cutbacks. No wonder the usual economic indicators failed to predict the outcome of the 2000 election.

But there was another political strategy at work to win votes. Everywhere in the world, when people are blocked from a politics that deals with the material problems of their daily life, they become susceptible to extremist and fundamentalist appeals. When institutional reforms seem impossible, people respond more readily to the appeals of "strong men" who promise to set the world right again by the force of their character — men like the Ayatollah Khomeini or Rudolph Giuliani. They also become susceptible to appeals based on resentment, to political arguments that point to vulnerable groups in the society, groups that are demarcated in some way by the culture. They say that those people are to blame — they are the source of your troubles, they are polluting our community. Frustrated from acting on rational and material needs, people become susceptible to politics that creates "the Other." Because this Other is marginalized and vulnerable, something can indeed be done about them.

This kind of change has been noticeable in American election campaigns of the last two decades. We've seen the rise of a politics calling for moral rejuvenation, a politics for which there really cannot be a program. The invoking of values does tap real cultural anxieties in American society, anxieties provoked by large changes in sexual mores and in race relations. Family life is changing dramatically, in part undermined by the increase in wage work. Overall, two-parent families are working four months per year more than they were two decades ago (Bluestone and Rose 1997).[11] An increase of this scale in wage work inevitably means that there is less time for the mother to work — the family meals, holiday celebrations, visits to the school or the scout club — that was the very stuff of family life. The world as people knew it has become unsettled.

The arguments of the Right, of the new think tanks, and the public intellectuals they support — people like Martin Anderson (1978), George

Gilder (1981), Charles Murray (1984), and Larry Mead (1984) — are attempts to substitute calls for moral rejuvenation, coupled with castigation of the Other, for politics that hinge on popular economic wellbeing. Hence, we are told that government programs undermine not only our competitive position in the world economy, but also our moral fiber. Generous social policies cause worklessness, social disorganization, family breakdown, and so on.

It is not a coincidence that such arguments are laced with racial allusions that take advantage of deep-seated resentments. Nor is it an accident that they are steeped in the strange preoccupations with sexual behavior that characterize American culture, which were the basis for the alliance of the Christian Right with the business-led political mobilization of the past two decades.

Thus, the campaign for welfare reform told a story with pernicious effects for American politics. In a way the story was about the nation's travails, about economic insecurity, about hard work and too much work, about rising inequality. But the main actors in this story were not the corporations who dominate our economy and our politics. Rather, the main actors were poor women, especially poor women of color. In the story these women were to blame for poverty, social disorganization, family breakdown, the weakening of morality in America, for all of the economic anxieties Americans feel. It is a powerful story because it evokes the demons of our culturally informed imagination, the demons of poor people and dark-skinned people and our insane preoccupation with the sexual license of women.

But this was not just a right-wing strategy. Even as Clinton was campaigning in 1992 on "it's the economy, stupid," he also raised the slogans of "end welfare as we know it" and "two years and off to work." His pollsters told him the slogans struck a chord. Clinton had stumbled on the uses of the angry politics of resentment. The result was a contest between Republicans and Democrats and between national and state politicians to "own" the welfare issue. And welfare reform is the consequence.

The welfare reform legislation is up for renewal in 2002. Is it possible to undo its most pernicious features, including time limits and work requirements, and the license it gives the states to refuse aid to poor women and to freely use sanctions to slash benefits to those already on the rolls? At first glance, the prospects seem grim. Politicians and the media seem never to tire of applauding the new welfare regime's success at lowering the numbers of women and children who receive aid. By contrast, the hardships that result receive little or no attention.[12]

The new Bush administration and the cabal of businessmen it has elevated to power surely is unlikely to propose any reversals of the new practices.[13] Indeed, they appointed Tommy Thompson, former governor of Wisconsin and renowned as a pioneer of state-level welfare reform, to head the Department of Health and Human Services. Thompson is applauded for the dramatic decline in Wisconsin's welfare rolls. There is less attention to the increase in extreme poverty in Wisconsin that has accompanied that decline.

In the short term, a kinder welfare policy seems unlikely. But we should remember that all this is unfolding in the realm of politics, and it is not a politics predetermined by immutable and exogenous economic developments. The propelling force behind the campaign against welfare arises not from some quasi-mystical economic globalization, but from business politics and the political ideas and political strategies conceived by business and the political Right.

They are not likely to dominate the political stage forever. After all, even the Malthusian-inspired "poor law," which PRWORA so much resembles, a law promoted by the rising English manufacturing class in 1834, was ultimately defeated by popular opposition. As the consequences of the new regime unfold, and especially as the business cycle turns, ordinary people and especially poor people are likely to regain their footing, and their common sense. They will begin to penetrate ruling class propaganda and develop their own assessments of their situation. This capacity for a measure of independence, of invention, of defiance, and the protest movements that result, has always been the real source of reform in American politics.

In the meantime, it is important to keep alive and to nourish the understandings about a gentler and more protective society that undergirded the development of social programs, however flawed particular programs might have been. To destroy these programs and leave so little in their stead is to allow life to become a jungle for our most vulnerable people.

## References

Andersen, Martin. 1978. *Welfare: The Political Economy of Welfare Reform in the United States.* Stanford, California: Hoover Institution.

Bernstein, Jared, and Mark Greenberg. 2001. "Reforming Welfare Reform." *The American Prospect* 12 (January 1-15): 10–17.

Bluestone, Barry, and Stephen Rose. 1997. "Overworked and Underemployed." *The American Prospect* 31 (March/April).

Danziger, Sheldon, Robert Haveman, and Robert Plotnick. 1981. "How Income Transfer Programs Affect Work, Savings, and the Income Distribution: A Critical Review." *Journal of Economic Literature* 19.

Edsall, Thomas Byrne. 1984. *The New Politics of Inequality.* New York: W.W. Norton.

Ferguson, Thomas, and Joel Rogers. 1986. *Right Turn: The Decline of the Democrats and the Future of American Politics.* New York: Hill and Wang.

Gault, Barbara, and Annisah Um'rani. 2000. "The Outcomes of Welfare Reform for Women." *Poverty & Race* 9 (July/August).

Gilder, George. 1981. *Wealth and Poverty*. New York: Basic Books.

Gottschalk, Peter, and Timothy Smeeding. 1997. "Cross-National Comparisons of Earnings and Income Inequality." *Journal of Economic Literature* 35 (June).

Greider, William. 1992. *Who Will Tell the People: The Betrayal of American Democracy*. New York: Simon and Schuster.

Haveman, Robert. 1997. "Equity with Employment." *Boston Review* (Summer).

Helleiner, Eric. 1994. *States and the Reemergence of Global Finance: From Bretton Woods to the 1990s*. Ithaca, New York: Cornell University Press.

———. 2000. Markets, politics and globalization: Can the global economy be civilized. Tenth Raul Prebisch Lecture, December 11, Geneva, Switzerland.

International Labor Organization (ILO). 1997. *World Labor Report 1997–98*. Geneva: International Labor Organization.

Judis, John B. 2000. *The Paradox of American Democracy*. New York: Pantheon Books.

Kaus, Mickey. 1986. "The Work Ethic State." *The New Republic* (July 6).

*Left Business Observer*. 1997. (No. 77, May 14).

Mead, Lawrence. 1985. *Beyond Entitlement: The Social Obligations of Citizenship*. New York: Free Press.

Moffitt, Robert A. 1995. "The Effect of the Welfare System on Nonmarital Fertility." In A Report to Congress on Out-of-Wedlock Childbearing. Washington D.C.: US Department of Health and Human Services, National Center of Health Statistics.

Murray, Charles. 1984. *Losing Ground: American Social Policy, 1950–1980*. New York: Basic Books.

Page, Benjamin I., James R. Simmons, and Scott Greer. 2000. "What Government Can Do About Poverty and Inequality: Global Constraints." Paper prepared for delivery at the annual meeting of the American Political Science Association, Washington, D.C.

Palast, Gregory. 2000. "Best Democracy Money Can Buy." *The Guardian* (November 25).

Peck, Jamie. 2001. *Workfare States*. New York: Guilford Publications.

Piven, Frances Fox. 1997. "The New Reserve Army of Labor." In *Audacious Democracy*, ed. Steven Fraser and Joshua B. Freeman. New York: Houghton Mifflin Co.

Piven, Frances Fox, and Richard A. Cloward. 1985. Chap. 3. In *The New Class War*. New York: Pantheon Books.

———. 1993. Chap. 11. In *Regulating the Poor*. New York: Pantheon Books.

Straus, Tamara. 2000. "Study Finds Dangerous Rise in Corporate Power." AlterNet.org, http://www.alternet.org/beta/story.html?StoryID=10184 (December 7).

Tabb, William. 1997. "Globalization is *an* Issue, the Power of Capital is *the* Issue." *Monthly Review* (June).

Therborn, Goran. 2000. "Social Democracy in One Country?" *Dissent* (Fall).

Vulliamy, Ed. 2000. "Ed Vulliamy in Washington." *The Observer* (December 3).

Wolf, Edward N. 1995. "How the Pie is Sliced: America's Growing Concentration of Wealth." *The American Prospect* (Summer).

Wolman, William, and Anne Colamosca. 1997. *The Judas Economy: The Triumph of Capital and the Betrayal of Work*. Reading, Massachusetts: Addison-Wesley Publishing Co.

## Notes

[1] One of the foremost scholars of poverty and politics in the United States, Frances Fox Piven's critique of social welfare policies has been the impetus for hundreds of other scholars seeking to improve our understanding of the welfare system, economic inequality, and the central role of protest in American politics. Piven changed the thinking of a generation of scholars and activists with her 1971 seminal book, *Regulating the Poor: The Functions of Public Welfare*. With Richard Cloward, she revolutionized popular thinking about welfare, showing how it functions as a mechanism of political and social control. With welfare recipients and other activists, Piven helped create the welfare rights movement of the 1960s and 1970s. She is currently Distinguished Professor of Political Science and Sociology at the Graduate School, City University of New York. Her other award-winning books include *Why Americans Don't Vote* and *Poor People's Movements: Why They Succeed, How They Fail*, both with Richard Cloward.

[2] Nor is there good evidence for the main argument that social spending interferes with international competitiveness. The Scandinavian countries, for example, are both leading welfare state spenders, and world leaders in exports (see Therborn 2000).

[3] Haveman (1997) points out that in countries with narrow and narrowing income protections, the relative wages of low-skilled workers fell during the 1980s by 10 to 15 percent. Where income protections remained stable, the relative wages of the unskilled remained stable, and measures of income inequality were substantially lower than in the United States.

[4] Helleiner (1994; 2000) distinguishes between the technological changes in transportation and communication, which may facilitate globalization, and the *policies* that lead to accelerated international competition. He further argues that internationalization is significantly the result of policies promulgated by major national governments.

[5] For a fuller discussion of the influence of governmental decentralization on class power, see Piven and Cloward (1985).

[6] Interestingly, the Conference Board, a prestigious business organization, recently concluded that despite an increase of 25 percent in the gross domestic product between 1986 and 1998, the poverty rate among fulltime workers has actually increased by 7.4 percent. See www.conference-board.org.

[7] This issue has been subject to a good deal of empirical research. For a review, see Danziger, Haveman and Plotnick (1981).

[8] There is a large volume of research on this question as well. For a summary, see Moffitt (1995).

[9] According to Current Population Survey data, single mothers in the lowest earnings quintile had been doing better in the 1993–1995 period. But after passage of PRWORA, they experienced a sharp decrease in overall income, and an even sharper decrease in earnings in the 1995-1997 period. See Gault and Um'rani (2000).

[10] Peck (2001) reviews U.S. workfare programs and compares them to developments in Canada and the United Kingdom.

[11] According to the U.S. Bureau of Labor Statistics, between 1976 and 1993 the average employed man added 100 hours of work per year, while the average employed woman increased her working time by 233 hours. See Left Business Observer (1997).

[12] Schram and Soss (2001) looked at 250 news stories on caseload decline that appeared between January 1, 1998, and September 1, 2000, in the top fifty highest circulation newspapers. They found that three-quarters of the stories were positive or neutral on welfare reform, and that only seven stories even mentioned the new practice of "diverting" people from making application for aid.

[13] For revealing reports on the new Washington power elite, see Vulliamy (2000) and Palast (2000).

# Welfare Racism and Its Consequences

## The Demise of AFDC and the Return of the States' Rights Era[1]

### *Kenneth J. Neubeck[2] and Noel A. Cazenave[3]*

For decades now, public opinion polls have revealed a carefully forged link between "race"[4] and "welfare," a link that political elites and the mass media have helped hammer into the public mind (Gilens 1999). Today, politicians are adept at playing the welfare "race card." When they wish to tap into white racist sentiment to bolster their political fortunes, they need not say the racially offensive N-word or other racial slurs; they need only excoriate "welfare" and its recipients. Yet despite the preponderance of evidence regarding the racialization of welfare discourse and its policy impact, most academicians and poverty policy analysts typically act as if they have no clue as to what seems obvious to almost everyone else.

Mainstream academicians and policy analysts stood by quietly over the years as the Aid to Families with Dependent Children (AFDC) program was subtly framed as a "black program" by the media and political elites, and then abolished with passage of the Personal Responsibility and Work Opportunity Reconciliation Act of 1996 (PRWORA). Today, when individual states' discretion over welfare polices and practices is reminiscent of the states' rights era of U.S. race relations, they remain largely silent about the racially differential impact welfare reform is having on millions of poor people of color. They seem equally oblivious to the fact that racism-driven welfare "reform" policies (e.g., the abolition of AFDC) are having a devastating effect on *all* of this nation's impoverished people to varying degrees.

In order to fully understand U.S. welfare policy, including the recent welfare reform legislation of the 1990s and its consequences, we believe that it is imperative to adopt a "racism-centered" perspective. Racism is a socially structured and systemic phenomenon in highly racialized societies such as the United States (Bonilla-Silva 1997). Consequently, it cannot be reduced simply to the attitudes and actions of racially bigoted individuals. In the United States, racism-driven disparities in power and privilege both reflect and reinforce an ongoing system of society-wide white racial hegemony in which European Americans have exercised dominance over racially subordinated groups for hundreds of years.

This white racial domination has shifted and changed in its mechanisms and manifestations. Today, it is normally maintained not so much through coercion or force, but by exercising control over cultural beliefs and ideologies, as well as over the key legitimizing institutions of society through which they are expressed, such as the state and mass media (Wilson 1996). Consequently, European Americans have occupied a position of political, economic, and social privilege over African Americans, Latino/a Americans, Asian Americans, and Native Americans.

The state — operating within the context of this racialized social system — has more often than not functioned historically as the political arm of white racial hegemony. Its actions and inactions have helped to protect and reinforce racial equalities, during both the United States' long-term history of overt white racial supremacy and into the contemporary period, when there is much denial on the part of European Americans that racism is any longer a serious social problem. Yet even today, in social arenas ranging from employment to housing, from education to politics, and from law enforcement to health care, African Americans and other people of color continue to suffer collective disadvantages, albeit often subtle, associated with institutionalized racism (Feagin 2000). The absence of racism in welfare policy — given its presence in these other areas — would be an exceptional situation indeed.

In actuality, the formation, implementation, and outcomes of welfare policy are rife with what we term *welfare racism*. We use this umbrella concept to refer to the various forms and manifestations of racism associated with means-tested programs of public assistance for poor families. Welfare racism is the organization of racialized public-assistance attitudes, policy making, and administrative practices. Racialization is not a discrete historical event but a continuous process. U.S. welfare policy has been racism driven since its origins early in the twentieth century (Neubeck and Cazenave 2001).

We hope that those who read this chapter will challenge others to open their eyes and examine the role that welfare racism played in the demise of the AFDC program and continues to play in producing the harmful consequences of welfare "reform" under PRWORA. There is a need for those committed to the elimination of poverty and racism to speak loudly and clearly in the upcoming debate over PRWORA reauthorization.

### Welfare Racist Attitudes and Politicians' Attacks on AFDC

In the 1990s there was a great deal of welfare racist sentiment among members of the public. Many European Americans believed that African Americans as a group preferred to live off welfare instead of working. One survey, commissioned by the Anti-Defamation League, found that 35 percent of those who identified themselves as "white" believed that "blacks" preferred welfare to work (Anti-Defamation League 1993). Data from the National Opinion Research Center showed that, when asked to directly compare themselves with blacks, fully three-fourths of white respondents rated blacks as less likely than whites to prefer to be self-supporting (Bobo and Kluegel 1991). Similar sentiments were expressed by many whites when comparing themselves with Latinos/Latinas.

Prior to the abolition of AFDC, black people and white people were about equally represented on the welfare rolls for many years (U.S. Department of Health and Human Services 1998, 57). Yet a CBS News/*New York Times* poll found, in 1994, that almost half of the respondents — the vast majority of whom were white — held erroneous beliefs that most people who are poor are black, and that most people who are on welfare are black (Dowd 1994, A1). Most of those polled believed that lack of effort was to blame for people being on welfare, and that most welfare recipients really did not want to work. These beliefs were found most often among poll respondents who believed that most people on welfare were black. Based on his analysis of still other survey data, political scientist Martin Gilens has argued that the most important source of whites' hostility toward public assistance is their stereotypical view of black people, including the racist belief that African Americans are lazy (Gilens 1999).

Political elites have fueled and exploited such racist sentiments about African Americans and other people of color for their own political gains and their parties' agendas. Prior to the passage of the PRWORA, political elites routinely linked "race" and "welfare" in their attacks on AFDC by employing code terms like "welfare chiselers" and "welfare queens" that thinly camouflaged racist sentiments. Political discourse on welfare reform routinely exploited racist stereotypes that the AFDC recipient population was synonymous with the nation's "underclass," a code term for undeserving, poor people of color. Welfare-racist attitudes were not only central to the demise of AFDC,[5] but also to the initiation and passage of the behavior modification–targeted reform policies that were institutionally enshrined by PRWORA.

A great deal of attention has focused on the "welfare-to-work" provisions of PRWORA, wherein impoverished mothers who must rely on welfare assistance are subjected to mandatory work requirements. The political elites who constructed and argued for these provisions subtly played upon (and reinforced) racist stereotypes concerning the alleged slothfulness and "welfare dependency" of African Americans, such as those revealed by public opinion polls. We will address some of the barriers facing impoverished women of color as they struggle to meet these mandatory work requirements. But first we wish to examine a much less discussed dimension of PRWORA — the provisions initiated by political elites seeking to alter the procreative and immigration behaviors of poor people of color.

## Welfare Reform Legislation as Race Population Control

An important way that racial control is maintained by dominant groups in any highly racialized society is through the ability of the state to determine who — racially — is allowed to be there and in what numbers. Political actors in this nation's "racial state" had two principal race population control concerns in mind when they proposed and later enacted PRWORA. First, politicians wished to implement measures intended not only to force stereotypically lazy, low-income African-American women to work, but also to discourage them from reproducing. Second, they wanted measures that would discourage immigrants of color from coming to the United States and make life less bearable for those who were here already. Through the mobilization of what Patricia Hill Collins (2000, 5, 69) calls "controlling images" of welfare recipients, PRWORA promoted both immigration-focused and procreation-focused race population control.

### Immigration-focused Race Population Control

PRWORA made both legal and illegal "aliens" ineligible for most federal programs. Illegal aliens were declared ineligible for welfare assistance. Legal aliens were deemed not eligible for such assistance until five years after they entered the United States. It was also mandated that the individual states and public housing agencies report names, addresses, and other pertinent information regarding noncitizen recipients to the U.S. Immigration and Naturalization Service.

Both the tone of the PRWORA and the rhetoric surrounding it implied that large numbers of aliens were coming to the United States (especially from Latin America and the Caribbean) ill-prepared or unwilling to work, expecting public assistance and other governmental benefits, and with the goal of being dependent on the government and hard-working taxpayers for their livelihood. Recent immigration-focused race-population-control policies typically have been justified through selected facts and arguments regarding the benefits of restricting "our" borders. However, they are ultimately based largely on white racist sentiment toward people of color, such as that expressed in Peter Brimelow's influential and overtly racist book, *Alien Nation* (1995). As applied to certain groups of racial "aliens," that sentiment can be summed up as follows: "We don't want them here!" That sentiment has affected the treatment that immigrants of color have received in welfare offices since the passage of PRWORA.

## Procreation-focused Race Population Control

An examination of the evolution of the text language of various versions of what ultimately became the Personal Responsibility and Work Opportunity Reconciliation Act of 1996 suggests that another major goal of that bill was procreation-focused race population control. What was being proposed was a bill to reduce not simply "dependency" on welfare, but also out-of-wedlock births among poor African Americans.

The most overt expression of the intent to regulate reproductive activity was made in the first welfare reform bill introduced by the Republican members of the U.S. House of Representatives, the Personal Responsibility Act of 1995. The stated rationale of that bill was, "To restore the American family, reduce illegitimacy, control welfare spending and reduce welfare dependence" (U.S. House 1995). Indeed, its very first title was Reducing Illegitimacy. The bill began with a "Sense of Congress" section that listed more than three pages of statistics and other findings about the prevalence, correlates, and consequences of "illegitimacy"[6] (U.S. House 1995, 2, 3, 4–7). Moreover, the first set of statistics cited in this 1995 bill referred to the "illegitimacy" rate of "black Americans."

Not surprisingly, the *Personal Responsibility Act of 1995* contained a number of reproduction control–related provisions. These included federal mandates to deny welfare benefits to unwed teenage mothers and to prohibit benefits for any additional children born while a mother was receiving welfare. In addition, the individual states were given the option to deny benefits to mothers aged eighteen through twenty. The states were also to receive funds to implement their own programs to reduce "illegitimacy." The House bill specified that funds could be used by states to remove children from financially destitute mothers and place them up for adoption or in orphanages. From its rationale statement, "illegitimacy" statistics, and provisions, it is clear that a major goal of the Republican bill was to reduce births among poor women, with particular emphasis on impoverished African Americans.

Most of the procreation-focused race-population-control language was deleted or modified as various versions of the House bill moved deeper into the legislative enactment process and faced more public scrutiny. However, the finally enacted welfare reform legislation that President Bill Clinton signed did provide the states with financial bonus incentives to reduce out-of-wedlock births. PRWORA also gave states the freedom to deny benefits to teenage mothers and allowed states to impose family caps barring additional aid to families in which children are born to women receiving welfare assistance.

**Charles Murray's Influence on PRWORA's Reproduction Provisions**

Politicians preoccupied with controlling the procreative behaviors of poor women of color received a great deal of support from prominent conservative policy analysts such as George Gilder, Lawrence W. Mead, and Charles Murray. Perhaps no single individual was more influential in framing the contemporary welfare-reform discourse that led to PRWORA than Murray. His success came from an ability to simultaneously exploit racist, patriarchal, and class-elitist sentiments about who should be allowed to reproduce.

In 1993 Murray published a widely discussed newspaper essay that provided an ideological and policy blueprint for the House Republicans' proposed *Personal Responsibility Act of 1995*. As was true for that House bill, Murray focused in on race-specific statistics on "illegitimacy." In his essay, however, Murray dismissed the high rate of out-of-wedlock births for black mothers as "old news." The "new news" he wanted to stress was the growing increase in the "illegitimacy" rate for white women. This development, he argued, "threatens the U.S." with the emergence of a "white underclass" (Murray 1993).

Like his argument in *The Bell Curve*, a book alleging the existence of a genetic link between race and intelligence that Murray co-authored (Herrnstein and Murray 1994), his article offered a social-Darwinist solution to the "illegitimacy" crisis, which he suggested was spreading from blacks to whites. In his view, solving the problem of out-of-wedlock births required that "the state stop interfering with the natural forces that have done the job quite effectively for millennia."[7] Murray urged the use of economic penalties to discourage single motherhood, including an end to all economic support for poor mothers (Murray 1993).

The essay made proposals and cited statistics that later emerged in the Republicans' proposed *Personal Responsibility Act of 1995*. The proposals included an end to AFDC payments and a withdrawal of subsidized housing and any other benefits for which single teenage mothers were eligible. Members of Congress anticipated that such cuts in economic support would result in many single mothers placing their babies for adoption. Murray also suggested, "The government should spend lavishly on orphanages."

### Discriminatory Policies and Practices Under PRWORA

There is ample evidence of welfare racism in states' implementation of welfare reform policies and practices (Neubeck and Cazenave 2001). While the PRWORA pushes states to subject impoverished women to mandatory work requirements as a condition of welfare assistance, many women of color face racial barriers to labor-force participation. States' restrictive and punitive welfare policies and practices disregard these barriers.

**40**

### Racial Barriers to People of Color Leaving Welfare

One of the most significant outcomes of PRWORA is the changing racial composition of the nation's welfare rolls. Welfare reform researchers have taken little notice of this phenomenon,[8] leaving it to journalists to bring the matter to public attention. The "darkening" of the welfare rolls and the increasing concentration of welfare caseloads in large cities was addressed in a 1998 article in the *New York Times*, two years after PRWORA's passage. The *Times* surveyed fourteen individual states and New York City, whose welfare caseload was larger than every state except California. Together these states and New York City accounted for almost 70 percent of the nation's welfare recipients (DeParle 1998).

Calling its survey findings "new, little-noticed, and as yet largely unexplained," the *Times* reported the gist of its findings:

> As the welfare rolls continue to plunge, white recipients are leaving the system much faster than black and Hispanic recipients, pushing the minority share of the caseload to the highest level on record.... Some analysts warn that the growing racial and urban imbalance could erode political support for welfare, especially when times turn tight.

The article implies that the erosion of (already low) "political support for welfare" could be tied to welfare racist attitudes, and that such attitudes can be expected to *increase* in the post-AFDC future.

A follow-up by the Associated Press in March 1999 described the results of an AP survey of the changing racial composition of individual states' welfare rolls (Meckler 1999). Citing caseload declines by race, the survey noted that in thirty-three of the forty-two states studied, there had been a drop in the proportion of white (as compared to black and Latino/Latina) welfare recipients since 1994, a year when AFDC caseloads peaked nationally. The AP survey likewise indicated that in fourteen out of sixteen "big states," which together contained 76 percent of the nation's welfare recipients, whites had left faster than blacks and Latinos/Latinas.

It is likely that mothers of color have indeed been pressured to abandon welfare for employment, but that — given the racist nature of U.S. society — they face more obstacles to obtaining employment than whites. Women of color contend with racial barriers that are erected by many white employers (Browne 1999). Their increased presence on the rolls also may reflect the fact that mothers of color are more likely than white mothers to return to welfare within a year. The role that racial discrimination plays in hindering women of color from supporting their families while off welfare has yet to be assessed by academicians or policy analysts.

## Race-based Sanctions and Family Caps

Punitive welfare policies make it difficult for mothers who rely on public assistance to avoid benefit reductions and even benefit loss. Joe Soss and his colleagues (1999) take note of the "devolution revolution" that occurred in the 1990s, wherein the federal government granted individual states discretion in formulating and administering their own welfare reform policies.[9] Under PRWORA individual states have been encouraged to fashion sanctions that punish recipients of TANF who violate the rules.

Individual states' approaches to these sanctions has varied. But many have adopted "family caps" that deny or restrict additional aid to families in which mothers become pregnant and bear children while on the welfare rolls. Family caps are especially punitive because they mean less TANF aid per capita in a family, because the aid provided must be shared by more family members (Roberts 1997, 210–211).

Soss and his colleagues (1999) asked what factors determined the likelihood that an individual state would adopt strict sanctions such as the family cap. For instance, was there "a systematic relationship between race and the adoption of welfare reforms"? After examining various factors, the researchers found that a state's adoption of the family cap "is most strongly associated with the percentage of recipients who were African-Americans." The higher the proportion of African Americans on its rolls, the more likely a state was to have a family cap policy (Soss et al. 1999, 13):

> [A] recipient population that is disproportionately com-
> posed of African-Americans will be a more vulnerable
> population, more likely to be subject to the imposition of
> the harshest sanctions policies. The connection between
> the racial composition of the recipient population and the
> adoption of the family cap also suggests that racial
> hostility and vulnerability are factors affecting whether
> this particularly harsh policy will be adopted.

In subsequent research Soss and his colleagues found that not only was the racial composition of states' welfare rolls correlated with harsh sanctions and family cap policies, but also with shorter time limits on cash assistance. Short time limits and their strict enforcement is a way of pushing mothers of color into the labor market regardless of their ability to find decent jobs (Soss et al. 2000).

Moreover, they found that the presence of Latinos/Latinas on the welfare rolls, as well as African Americans, had a distinct effect on individual states' adoption of harsh policies: "Indeed, the effects are independent and additive, suggesting that restrictive TANF policies are most likely to be adopted in states where *both* Hispanics and African Americans receive aid in large numbers" [italics theirs] (Soss et al. 2000, 28).

Soss and his colleagues (2000, 32) went on to conclude, "The TANF system has returned authority over public assistance to the states, and the states have returned to some very old and troubling patterns of behavior." Other researchers have documented the long history of racial control efforts aimed at exploiting the labor of mothers of color and restricting their reproductive behavior (Amott and Matthaei 1996; Roberts 1997).

### Poor People's Experiences with Welfare Racism

Mainstream academicians and social policy analysts have by and large paid little attention to what poor women have to say about discriminatory policies and practices under welfare reform.[10] However, discrimination is a major concern of the Applied Research Center (ARC), an organization that provides direct support for groups who work with and organize poor people at the grassroots level. In the summer of 2000, ARC collaborated with fifteen local community-based organizations in thirteen states to conduct the Welfare Race and Gender Equity Survey (Gordon 2001). The survey's purpose was to test for discrimination in four areas: race, gender, language, and national origin.

Researchers from the local community organizations administered detailed questionnaires to more than 1,500 people who had contact with the welfare system under their states' welfare reform laws. They approached people in welfare offices, public health clinics, and other places where those having contact with the welfare system could most easily be found. Those who filled in the questionnaires were almost all adult women heading families with children. Approximately four-fifths of the respondents were people of color.[11] Some were immigrants. When necessary researchers conducted the surveys in respondents' own languages.

ARC summarized its survey findings on discrimination as follows:

> People of color routinely encounter insults and disrespect as they seek to navigate the various programs that make up the welfare system. Women are subject to sexual inquisitions in welfare offices and sexual harassment at their assigned work activities. People whose first language is not English encounter a serious language barrier when they have contact with the welfare system.... Eligible immigrants and refugees are often told to go back where they came from when they try to get help for themselves or their U.S. citizen children (Gordon 2001, 4-5).

In its report ARC noted that the U.S. Department of Health and Human Services' Office of Civil Rights (OCR) has not been effective in combating these rampant forms of discrimination. The report stated that OCR takes too long to investigate the complaints it receives and does too

**43**

little to enforce and oversee change when law violations are confirmed (Gordon 2001, 7). The problem of ineffective enforcement of civil rights protections is clear, for example, in the case of language discrimination against immigrants of color.

**Welfare Racism and Attacks on Immigrants of Color**

As noted, an important goal of the architects of PRWORA was to discourage immigrants of color from coming to the United States, and to make those already here think about leaving by decreasing their ability to rely on welfare as a safety net. Federal actors stripped many immigrants of eligibility for PRWORA's Temporary Assistance for Needy Families (TANF) or set strict conditions under which they may receive it, such as tying benefit eligibility to residency and citizenship status. Nonetheless, many immigrants, including refugees and asylum seekers, are on the welfare rolls (Zimmerman and Tumlin 1999). Reflecting the composition of the vast majority of the immigrant population in recent years, many are women and children of color from Latin America, the Caribbean, and Asia. As the Applied Research Center's survey showed, many are subjected to racially discriminatory practices.

In 1999 an advocacy organization called Make the Road by Walking issued a scathing report on the hostile treatment of immigrants by the New York City welfare system (Make the Road by Walking 1999). This system is but one of many that have been afflicted with "government lawlessness" under PRWORA (Houppert 1999). Interviewing welfare recipients in various neighborhoods around the Brooklyn area, Make the Road by Walking found that the most pressing concerns of people were inadequate translation services and the lack of respect showed by staff members of the Human Resources Administration, which implemented welfare reform policies.

Many Spanish-speaking recipients had problems communicating with their caseworkers about benefits, and most recipients felt frustrated by the treatment they received at welfare offices. Even those who spoke English reported that caseworkers often were unreachable by telephone, rude, or absent. Among the welfare racist practices recipients reported were "being verbally abused by their caseworkers, misinformed about their legal rights, and unable to obtain attention or assistance from their caseworkers in emergency situations" (Make the Road by Walking 1999, 6). Language discrimination posed another barrier, for the majority of those on New York City's welfare rolls — some 59 percent — were Latino/Latina.

Growing press coverage, especially in the Spanish language media, put pressure on the OCR to respond to this expression of welfare racism. In October 1999 OCR "validated all of the issues raised by Make the Road by Walking," according to the grassroots Center for Community Change. But even though OCR, in the face of continued pressure, prodded New York

City officials to conform to federal civil rights law regarding language access, the problems remained. The Center for Community Change newsletter reported, "Some Make the Road staff called welfare offices speaking Spanish, and of the few instances they got through to a worker, half the time they were hung up on" (Lawlessness 2000, 15).

## The Denial of Racism in "Race Blind" Welfare Reform Outcome Studies

Under PRWORA, racism-driven welfare attitudes, policies, and practices are widespread across the United States. Their negative impact is exacerbated insofar as impoverished women of color must deal with the demands of welfare caseworkers while also facing employer discrimination and the isolation of residential racial segregation. It is thus extremely disturbing that few mainstream academicians or social policy analysts have even acknowledged the existence of racism in their research on the outcomes of welfare reform. In our view, recent studies on welfare reform are so limited by the dominant racial politics of the United States that this research itself can be viewed as a dimension of racial control.

Most research on the outcomes of welfare reform has sought to measure the government's success in affecting, and thus controlling, what welfare recipients are doing. The bulk of this research has been conducted without any attention to "race" or racism, gender or sexism, or class relations, as if the simultaneous oppression of racial inequality, patriarchy, and class exploitation were simply irrelevant to poor women's lives. In effect, the subjects of welfare reform research have been de-raced, de-gendered, and de-classed.

Here we wish to comment on the flood of welfare-reform "outcome studies" and outcome research overviews that have appeared since the passage of PRWORA in 1996. Such studies have been issued by government agencies, university research centers, policy research organizations, and advocacy groups. What have these studies had to say about racism and the impact of welfare reform on impoverished mothers of color?

### 1. Is the possible effect of "race" on welfare reform outcomes recognized?

Those conducting welfare reform research rarely use the "race" of welfare applicants, recipients, or those who had left welfare as a key variable when tracking the outcomes of reform. Although some research reports mention the racial composition of the study population (or sample) — usually in the context of introducing the research that was undertaken — the attention researchers devote to the race variable is typically brief. Nor does it carry over into the analysis of welfare reform's outcomes. The race of recipients or former recipients is rarely accorded any recognition in these reports, leaving the overall impression that all of those under study are interchangeable or "universal" poor people whose

**45**

biographies and lived experiences are unaffected by any race-based disadvantage or privilege.

**2. Does welfare reform outcome research address barriers faced by people of color?**

We know that the probability of being poor, and especially of being extremely poor, is much higher for people of color than for whites. According to the U.S. Bureau of the Census (1999), in 1998 only 3.2 percent of whites had family incomes of less than half of the official poverty line, as opposed to 11.2 percent of African Americans and 9.8 percent of Latinos/ Latinas. Indeed, the proportion of the welfare rolls comprised of people of color has actually increased in conjunction with the welfare reforms of the 1990s, raising the important question of whether racially discriminatory barriers to leaving welfare and achieving economic self-sufficiency exist. Most outcome research reports, however, do not shed light on this phenomenon, since they fail to address racism or to attach any special significance to racial differences among those they are studying.

**3. Are special or unique problems faced by poor women of color addressed?**

Even as they are overrepresented in the poverty population, poor women of color bear the additional burden of being both of color and female in a society dominated predominantly by white males. Thus, they face somewhat different problems in daily life than poor white women, particularly because women of color have to contend with the past consequences and present effects of racism. Outcome studies fail to look at how poor women of color are socially positioned. Nor do they address whether the status of those studied — disadvantageously situated as they are within the social matrix of racial, gender, and class inequalities — poses special obstacles to attaining family "self-sufficiency" and rising above the poverty line. Researchers seem to assume a level playing field in which all poor women are basically the same and face the same obstacles in terms of these goals.

**4. Is racism a concern of welfare reform researchers and policy analysts?**

Racism in the realm of welfare reform is typically not made a subject in outcome studies. Indeed, it is extremely rare to even see the word "race" mentioned. The typical outcome study leaves the impression that welfare reform has been implemented in a racism-free society, without racial bias or discrimination, and that it is therefore being experienced — for better or worse — across color lines in the same ways.

Treating impoverished women of color as if they had no racial designations or gender serves to obscure the role that welfare reform plays as an expression of "gendered racism" (Essed 1991). This type of research also diverts us from asking how welfare reform contributes to white racial hegemony. Considering the role that gendered racism played in rallying support for punitive welfare reform measures, the assertion that research can be somehow "race" and gender blind seems like some perverse accountability "shell game."

Welfare reform research is "race blind" only in the sense that policy analysts have largely ignored racism and focused their inquiries on supposedly race-neutral topics, such as welfare "dependency." But in focusing on such topics, researchers have in effect aligned themselves with prevailing racist stereotypes regarding African Americans' alleged lack of work ethic. In reporting on trends in welfare "dependency," researchers cannot help but implicitly objectify and reify the stereotypes and controlling images of welfare-reliant mothers' assumed laziness and irresponsibility — behaviors that welfare reform is presumably there to alter. Racist stereotypes and controlling images are likewise subtly raised and reinforced whenever "race-blind" researchers address the impact of welfare reform on "illegitimacy," a code term for African Americans' sexual promiscuity. At the same time, researchers' choice of research topics, as well as their choices of terminology, methods, forms of data, and variables, avoid addressing the issues of how patriarchy, racial inequality, and class exploitation contribute to the maintenance of a seemingly permanent population of poor families with dark skin.

While most welfare reform analysts would probably be shocked to hear their efforts described in this way, we believe that much of their research has functioned to reinforce the media's and political elites' portrayal of welfare recipients as the deviant, threatening, slothful, promiscuous "Other" in need of the controls provided by welfare reform.

### How "Race" and Racism are Ignored in Welfare Reform Assessment

How are we to understand the marked tendency of welfare reform monitoring organizations and groups to ignore race and racism and their failure to address the ramifications of welfare policy for the daily lived experiences of people of color? Sanford E. Schram (1995, xxvii) asserts, "The microdiscourse of the social science of poverty is influenced by the macrodiscourse of the broader society."

The denial among European Americans of racism's salience is so widespread and pervasive — and so unsuccessfully challenged by racially subordinate groups and their supporters — we should not be surprised if race and racism are "out of mind" and thus "out of sight" to most researchers (Steinberg 1995; Thomas 2000). Moreover, welfare reform research is typically conducted in conformity with the ways in which problems are framed by the state, which generally only acknowledges racism episodically, when under pressure to do so, and with caution and reluctance.

In Schram's words, "All the while aspiring to scientific impartiality, welfare policy research achieves political credibility not by its objectivity, but by its consistency with the prevailing biases of welfare policy discourse" (Schram 1995, 6). For decades these biases have reflected a preoccupation with the alleged cultural deficiencies of poor people of color, whose supposedly pathological behaviors in the areas of work, family, and reproduction are said to be responsible for their poverty. It is thus no accident that the bulk of welfare reform research focuses upon tracking the behavior of impoverished persons without due regard for the varied social, economic, and political contexts within which they struggle to function.

Most welfare reform research is profoundly conservative, for it uses outcome measures that produce findings that do little more than reinforce the status quo. By continuing to conform their inquiries to the limited "success" criteria embedded in the goals of punitive welfare reform legislation, thus ignoring gender and racial inequalities, welfare reform researchers are unlikely to find reason for the radical policy changes that would be necessary to eliminate poverty. Rather, by limiting the realm of discourse within which research findings are sought and interpreted, all they can recommend is modest fine-tuning of present welfare reform policies to better exercise control over poor mothers.

Much debate is likely to revolve around how to better provide incentives to change poor people's work and reproductive behaviors and whether it would be more effective to increase the carrot or the stick. This fine-tuning is likely to occur with little knowledge or understanding of how it will affect mothers and children of color. The greatest bias here is in the questions that go unasked, and therefore unanswered.

While outcome studies are certainly racism-blind, they do indirectly reveal crucial problems that welfare reform has created or left unaddressed for poor people *regardless* of their skin color. Taken as a whole, such studies show that welfare reform has moved relatively few families out of poverty, exacerbated income difficulties for many, placed increased stress on mothers and other family members, and inadequately addressed impoverished families' needs for childcare, transportation, housing, health care, and nutrition. While welfare reform researchers generally fail to address the degree to which these problems are distributed along the lines of "race," it is safe to conclude that people of color are hurt disproportionately. Moreover, so long as the current states' rights approach to welfare policy continues, we should expect expressions of welfare racism to increase.

## Exposing and Challenging Welfare Racism in the Public Policy Arena

What must be done in order to place welfare racism on the public policy agenda? A good place to begin is by examining the public policy response to racism in the United States.

Conceptually, welfare and other poverty-focused policies and programs may be placed along a continuum of racism-related responses. *Racism-driven* policies and programs are significantly influenced by racist sentiments, attitudes, and goals. *Racism-blind* policies and programs do nothing to challenge welfare racism. Indeed, as a policy ideology of denial, they reenforce it (Roberts 1997, 5-6). *Racism-cognizant* policy and programs acknowledge racism as a cause of poverty and punitive welfare policies, but offer little if anything to specifically challenge that racism. *Racism-sensitive* **safeguards**, such as the inclusion of strong preventive antidiscrimination provisions as part of public assistance legislation, can challenge welfare racism. Finally, *racism-targeted* **interventions** are needed to address the racism-specific causes of poverty and to challenge existing racialized poverty policies when there are no racism-sensitive safeguards in place, or when they do not work effectively. Challenges to welfare racism cannot be racism-blind. Racism-cognizance is merely a start. Effective challenges to welfare racism must be either racism-sensitive or racism-targeted.

In anticipation of the possible reauthorization of the PRWORA in 2002, the Women's Committee of 100, a group of prominent feminist scholars, professionals, and activists, prepared "An Immodest Proposal: Rewarding Women's Work to End Poverty." As the following racism-cognizant excerpt from that legislative proposal makes clear, that proposal is not blind to the existence of welfare racism:

> Poverty in the United States is not color-blind. The debate preceding the 1996 welfare law made the color of poverty the fault of the poor. We insist that the color of poverty is the consequence of racism and related forms of discrimination.... We call for policies that address the shared vulnerabilities of the poorest caregivers, especially poor women of color (Women's Committee of 100 2000).

However, the ultimate goal of legislation-focused antiracist initiatives must be to move beyond racism-cognizant discourse to legislation that is explicitly racism-sensitive and racism-targeted.

The expiration of the PRWORA in 2002 will be preceded by Congressional hearings and debates on whether that racist bill should be abolished, renewed, reformed, or replaced. The consequences of that debate will be felt by millions of this nation's poor. It is therefore urgent that progressive academicians and policy analysts collect, analyze, and disseminate race-specific welfare-reform-outcome data immediately.

As Gary Delgado of the Applied Research Center (ARC) suggests, if the negative consequences of welfare reform are to be challenged using a civil rights strategy (Delgado 2000), what could be called the *racial data deficit* created by the racism-blindness of earlier outcome studies must be overcome in a hurry. ARC has been collaborating with grassroots community organizations across the nation to assist them in the collection of such data (Gordon 2001).

Once race-specific welfare reform outcome data are collected and made public, pressure can be applied to politicians for legislative action that mandates appropriate government agencies to conduct their own research and monitoring. Relevant government agencies, and those organizations with which they enter into contracts for welfare recipient services, should be required to conduct "racial audits" to demonstrate that different racialized ethnic groups are benefiting from programs equally and making equal use of services.[12]

There is a great need for racism-sensitive monitoring safeguards, which include building antidiscrimination provisions into all public assistance–related legislation, and racism-targeted actions, such as the extensive use of antidiscrimination testers in welfare offices and in places of employment to which welfare recipients are referred. Appropriate government agencies should be made to take racism-targeted actions to insure that current public assistance policies do not violate existing laws against racial discrimination. New antidiscrimination laws should be enacted as needed. Similar actions to monitor and eliminate welfare racism should be the subject of advocacy group efforts at the state and local levels.

## Conclusion

We conclude this chapter by reiterating three major points. First, in the United States racism is a major determinant of both who is poor and the public policy response to poverty. Second, such racism works best when it is invisible, as it currently is now in most academic research and social policy analysis. Finally, only by "seeing" welfare racism's impact in shaping both punitive welfare reform legislation and its consequences can welfare racism be effectively challenged, and the ideal of economic justice for all brought closer to reality.

## References

Amott, Teresa, and Julie Matthaei. 1996. *Race, Gender, and Work: A Multi-Cultural Economic History of Women in the United States*. Boston: South End Press.

Anti-Defamation League. 1993. *Highlights from an Anti-Defamation League Survey on Racial Attitudes in America*. New York: ADL.

Applied Research Center. 2000. *Putting Welfare Reform to the Test: A Guide to Uncovering Bias and Unfair Treatment in Local Welfare Programs*. A publication of the Applied Research Center's Grass Roots Innovative Policy Program (www.arc.org/gripp).

Bobo, Lawrence, and James R. Kleugel. 1991. "Modern American Prejudice." Paper presented at the Meetings of the American Sociological Association, Cincinnati, OH.

Bonilla-Silva, Eduardo. 1997. "Rethinking Racism: Toward a Structural Interpretation." *American Sociological Review* 62 (June): 465-480.

Brimelow, Peter. 1995. *Alien Nation: Common Sense About America's Immigration Disaster.* New York: Random House.

Browne, Irene, ed. 1999. *Latinas and African American Women at Work: Race, Gender, and Economic Inequality.* New York: Russell Sage Foundation.

Collins, Patricia Hill. 2000. *Black Feminist Thought: Knowledge, Consciousness, and the Politics of Empowerment.* New York: Routledge.

Delgado, Gary. 2000. "Racing the Welfare Debate." *ColorLines* 3 (Fall): 13–17. Available at www.arc.org/C_Lines/CLArchive/story3_3_04.html.

DeParle, Jason. 1998. "Shrinking Welfare Rolls Leave Record High Share of Minorities." *New York Times* (July 28): A1.

Dowd, Maureen. 1994. "Americans Like G.O.P. Agenda But Split on How to Reach Goals." *New York Times* (December 15): A1.

Essed, Philomena. 1991. *Understanding Everyday Racism: An Interdisciplinary Theory.* Newbury Park, CA: Sage Publications.

Feagin, Joe R. 2000. *Racist America: Roots, Current Realities, and Future Reparations.* New York: Routledge.

Gilens, Martin. 1999. *Why Americans Hate Welfare: Race, Media, and the Politics of Antipoverty Policy.* Chicago: University of Chicago Press.

Gooden, Susan T. 1997. "Examining Racial Differences in Employment Status Among Welfare Recipients." Available at www.arc.org/gripp/researchPublications/reports/goodenReport/reportTitlePg.html.

––––––. 1998. "All Things Not Being Equal: Differences in Caseworker Support Toward Black and White Welfare Clients." *Harvard Journal of African-American Public Policy* 4 (4): 23–33.

––––––. 1999. "The Hidden Third Party: Welfare Recipients' Experiences with Employers." *Journal of Public Management and Social Policy* 5 (1): 69–83.

––––––. 2000. "Race and Welfare: Examining Employment Outcomes of White and Black Welfare Recipients." *Journal of Poverty* 4 (3): 21–41.

Gordon, Rebecca. 2001. "Cruel and Usual: How Welfare "Reform" Punishes Poor People." Oakland, CA: Applied Research Center (www.arc.org).

Herrnstein, Richard, and Charles Murray. 1994. *The Bell Curve: Intelligence and Class Structure in American Life.* New York: Basic Books.

Houppert, Karen. 1999. "You're Not Entitled! Welfare 'Reform' is Leading to Government Lawlessness." *The Nation* 269 (October 25): 11–13.

"Lawlessness." 2000. *Organizing* (February). (Available at www.communitychange.org under "Jobs and Economic Development," "Organizing Newsletter.")

Lower-Basch, Elizabeth. 1999. 'Leavers' and diversion studies: Preliminary analysis of racial differences in caseload trends and leaver outcomes. Paper presented at Fall Meeting of the Office of the Assistant Secretary for Planning and Evaluation Outcomes Grantees. U.S. Department of Health and Human Services, Washington, D.C.

Make the Road by Walking. 1999. *System Failure.* Brooklyn, NY: Make the Road by Walking (www.maketheroad.org).

Meckler, Laura. 1999. "Whites Beat Minorities Off Welfare." Associated Press Online Report (March 29): 1-3.

Murray, Charles. 1993. "The Coming White Underclass." *Wall Street Journal* (October 29): A14.

Neubeck, Kenneth J., and Noel A. Cazenave. 2001. *Welfare Racism: Playing the Race Card Against America's Poor.* New York: Routledge.

Roberts, Dorothy. 1997. *Killing the Black Body: Race, Reproduction, and the Meaning of Liberty.* New York: Pantheon.

Schram, Sanford F. 1995. *Words of Welfare: The Poverty of Social Science and the Social Science of Poverty.* Minneapolis: University of Minnesota Press.

————. 2000. *After Welfare: The Culture of Postindustrial Social Policy.* New York: New York University Press.

Soss, Joe, Erin O'Brien, Sanford F. Schram, and Thomas P. Vartanian. 1999. Predicting welfare reform retrenchment: race, ideology, and economy in the devolution revolution. Unpublished paper made available by co-author Sanford F. Schram, Bryn Mawr College.

Soss, Joe, Sanford F. Schram, Thomas P. Vartanian, and Erin O'Brien. 2000. Setting the terms of relief: political explanations for state policy choices in the devolution revolution. Unpublished paper made available by co-author Sanford F. Schram, Bryn Mawr College.

Steinberg, Stephen. 1995. *Turning Back: The Retreat from Racial Justice in American Thought and Policy.* Boston: Beacon Press.

Thomas, Melvin. 2000. "Anything But Race: The Social Science Retreat from Racism." *African American Research Perspectives* 6 (Winter): 79–96.

U.S. Bureau of the Census. 1999. *Poverty in the United States, 1998.* Washington, D.C.: U.S. Government Printing Office, 1999.

U.S. Department of Health and Human Services. 1998. *Aid to Families with Dependent Children: The Baseline.* Washington, D.C.: DHHS.

U.S. House. 1995. *Personal Responsibility Act.* 104th Cong., 1st sess., H.R. (March 24).

Wilson, Carter A. 1996. *Racism: From Slavery to Advanced Capitalism.* Thousand Oaks, CA: Sage.

Women's Committee of 100. 2000. "An Immodest Proposal: Rewarding Women's Work to End Poverty." *Survival News* (Summer): 18. (Available also at www.welfare2002.org.)

Zimmerman, Wendy, and Karen C. Tumlin. 1999. *Patchwork Policies: State Assistance for Immigrants Under Welfare Reform.* Washington, D.C.: The Urban Institute.

# Notes

[1] Portions of this chapter are adapted from Chapters 2,6,7, and 8 of Neubeck and Cazenave (2001).

[2] Kenneth J. Neubeck is associate professor of sociology at the University of Connecticut. His publications include *Social Problems: A Critical Approach* (with Mary Alice Neubeck), *Welfare Racism: Playing the Race Card Against America's Poor* (with Noel A. Cazenave), and articles on racism, urban political economy, and the politics of U.S. poverty policy. He can be contacted at kenneth.neubeck@uconn.edu.

[3] Noel A. Cazenave is associate professor of sociology at the University of Connecticut. The co-author (with Kenneth J. Neubeck) of *Welfare Racism: Playing the Race Card Against America's Poor*, he is writing a book on professional turf battles and grassroots democracy in program precursors to the "War on Poverty" community action programs. Cazenave has published articles on the War on Poverty in the *Journal of Policy History*, *Civil Rights In the United States*, and the *Journal of Urban History*. He can be reached at cazenave@uconn.edu.

[4] In our view, "race," "white," and "black" are erroneous and injurious ideological constructs. Whenever they are used in this paper they should be read as if they appear in quotation marks.

[5] Historical material on the roots of welfare racism and its impact on AFDC's demise are further developed in Neubeck and Cazenave (2001).

[6] We do not believe that any children should be labeled as being "illegitimate." We prefer the term "out-of-wedlock" or "nonmarital" births to "illegitimacy."

[7] Noting what they saw as the dangers of government efforts to affect fertility, Herrnstein and Murray complained that "American fertility policy ... subsidizes births among poor women, who are also disproportionately at the low end of the intelligence distribution" (Herrnstein and Murray 1994, 548–549).

[8] An exception is Lower-Basch (1999).

[9] See also Schram (2000, Chapter 4).

[10] For a notable exception, see Gooden (1997; 1998; 1999; 2000).

[11] They were 46 percent black, 21 percent Latino/Latina, 5 percent Asian, and 5 percent Native American.

[12] Guidelines for such audits have been developed by the Applied Research Center's Grass Roots Innovative Policy Program (Applied Research Center 2000).

# Not-So-Rugged Individualists

## U.S. Americans' Conflicting Ideas about Poverty

*Claudia Strauss*[1]

What values and beliefs do U.S. Americans draw upon to think about antipoverty policies? The dominant view is: *Americans share a culture of rugged individualism.* For rugged individualists, the cause of poverty is the failure of poor people to work hard, and the remedy is the elimination of government assistance. The research reported below[2] shows that this interpretation of American culture is wrong. Most Americans believe that poverty has multiple causes and that the government should do more to alleviate it. For example, a July 2000 Harris poll found 67 percent of Americans in favor of "devoting significantly more federal resources to help the poor."

If Americans favor devoting more federal resources to help the poor, why have they been supportive of cutbacks to welfare programs? This chapter explains that Americans have multiple cognitive frameworks or "schemas" for thinking about poverty and antipoverty policy. These differing schemas mean that they are capable of supporting a wide range of antipoverty policies, from cutbacks to a large-scale expansion of government programs that most analysts would judge to be politically infeasible at this time. Thus, the research reported here challenges the conventional wisdom that there is little popular support in this country for generous anti-poverty programs.

The major findings from this research are as follows:

▶ Most Americans have multiple schemas for thinking about the causes of poverty. Sometimes they say poverty is the result of lack of effort and poor choices; at other times the same people say poverty is the result of behaviors learned from social environments, psychological or medical problems, the unequal burden of childcare for women, or economic structures.

▶ In the mid-1990s most Americans favored welfare reform because they felt welfare, especially AFDC, gave money to people who "just sit around." Thus, for the most part, Americans were supportive of time limits and work requirements. However, most Americans feel: (a) the issue is not self-reliance but whether individuals are "doing something;" (b) education and community service count as doing something; (c) the government also has a responsibility to do something about poverty; and (d) we should make allowances for individual situations because poverty has multiple causes.

▶ Different political discourses can create overarching *morality, charity,* or *equity* frameworks. The experimental research described in the final section of this chapter shows that a charity framework induced by "helping" language strengthens support for time limits, while an equity framework induced by populist language produces strong public support for expanded social welfare programs.

Overall, this research shows that there is potential support among the public for both progressive *and* regressive antipoverty policies. Antipoverty advocates and lawmakers concerned with this issue should not retreat defensively, assuming that the whole weight of American political culture is against them, nor should they preach only to the choir of diehard liberals and the poor themselves. With the right framing, public opinion can be mobilized to support policies that truly fight poverty.

### Overview of Research

It has been known for some time that U.S. Americans must have multiple cognitive frameworks for thinking about poverty. National surveys in the 1980s and 1990s repeatedly found that most Americans felt we were spending too much on "welfare" but too little on "assistance to the poor" (Smith 1987; Weaver, Shapiro, and Jacobs 1995).[3] Responses to the following survey question are particularly striking:

> Some people think that the government in Washington should do everything possible to improve the standard of living of all poor Americans; they are at point 1 on this card. Other people think it is not the government's responsibility, and that each person should take care of himself; they are at point 5.[4]

Table 3.1 summarizes the results. From 1986 through 2000,[5] a plurality of respondents chose the middle point of this scale: "Agree with both." Among those who did not place themselves in the middle, the percentage leaning toward one of the positions has nearly equaled the percentage leaning toward the other in recent years.

**Table 3.1**

**Government versus individual responsibility for poor people's standard of living**

| | 1986 | 1988 | 1990 | 1993 | 1996 | 1998 | 2000 |
|---|---|---|---|---|---|---|---|
| Government should improve living standards: | | | | | | | |
| | 30% | 30% | 34% | 26% | 25% | 25% | 27% |
| Agree with both answers: | | | | | | | |
| | 45% | 44% | 43% | 47% | 45% | 43% | 42% |
| People should take care of themselves: | | | | | | | |
| | 22% | 23% | 20% | 24% | 26% | 29% | 28% |

The research described here was undertaken to understand this pattern of results. In 1995 I conducted a random sample survey in Rhode Island and North Carolina on the topic of welfare policies. (Those two states were chosen in part because they diverge in their political leanings.) The survey was an experiment to investigate whether priming respondents with different political discourses would affect how favorably they responded to various options for welfare reform. Following the survey, I contacted a subsample of the survey respondents for in-depth semistructured interviews (two interviews per person, each interview approximately ninety minutes). The interviewees were sixteen Rhode Islanders chosen for diversity of gender, ethnicity, class, welfare experience, and opinions about welfare.[6]

In addition to this series of individual interviews, I organized two focus groups on the topic of welfare in 1994.[7] Also reported below are preliminary results of a series of interviews I conducted in the spring of 2000 with twenty-eight North Carolinians, half of whom lived in the former mill town of Burlington and surrounding rural Alamance County, the other half in the affluent suburbs of Research Triangle Park (Strauss n.d.[a] ;[b]).

## Findings (1)

### Most U.S. Americans have multiple, inconsistent schemas for thinking about the causes of poverty

One only has to talk to Americans about poverty and the welfare system to see that their views can be hard to categorize. The following are verbatim quotes from my interviews. The first speaker, Marlene Randall, is white and working-class:[8]

> It isn't fair for them to have my mom…*pay* for pills when she *can't* work and these young girls…sitting on their butt…You know what I mean—having—you can make a mistake, yeah. But when you have child, and child, and child…I have an acquaintance whose daughter has three children. Three different fathers, and she's on *welfare*. You know?

At this point, however, Randall's comments veered in a different direction:

> And so the girl *tries* to get off of welfare. Right? She gets a job. The child gets sick. So the… calls up, the babysitter says, "You have to come *home*. The child has *measles*." Oh, so you say to your boss, "Oh for two weeks, I'm not going to be in." And he says, "Well, excuse me, but I don't need you." So where are you? Right back on welfare. So it's the system too, there's no help. You have to pay someone to watch your children. And now they don't want 25 bucks a week. They want 125 dollars per child. [*Randall continues with how this woman made a good-faith effort.*]

Mason Carter, an African-American storefront minister, had earlier in his life fallen ill, lost his job, and become homeless. Now he devotes his ministry to raising money for homeless shelters. The dominant tone of his comments was very sympathetic:

> I used to pass by people—homeless people—before I got sick, and I used to look and say, "Why don't these people get up and do this? Why don't these people get up and do that?" Some people just not able. [*sic*]

Yet, at other times he stressed instead the importance of making the right choices:

> God gave us a will to choose between good and evil. I'm not a drug addict, I'm not a drunk, but if I wanted to choose to do that, I can be. [...] It's not the government's fault because we're in poverty; it's not the government's fault that the man down the street is an alcoholic, that somebody's on welfare. A lot of people are blaming the government for something because they are being irresponsible themselves.

Vincent Rocha came to this country from Portugal when he was thirteen, worked his way through college, and is now a successful engineer. When I asked him why most people go on welfare, he said,

> Sometimes there's no choice but I'd say 60 percent of the time that person is going in [*the system*] because they don't care. Maybe 30 percent is forced into it, and the other 10 percent is miscellaneous.

Yet, much later in the interview when I asked if welfare is related to women's place in society, he replied:

> Ninety-five percent of the time it's the woman caught in this situation. The husband takes off and she's stuck with the kids. There's no way of getting out other than financial assistance, because she cannot work due to small children—sometimes sickness—and that's the reason probably 95 percent [*of the time*].

Linda Fuller is white and upper-middle class. She felt torn between her conflicting ways of thinking about poverty:

> I think I let, with things like *welfare*...to me it's... it's a hard thing to justify. You know in terms of the whole capitalist, you know you work hard and I am a Midwesterner, and I was raised with this *very* strong work ethic. One thing I remember my father telling me is [*louder voice*] "Always do work," you know, "Work more than you have to. Always do a little bit *more* than you have to." And "*Find new ways.*" [*resuming her normal voice*] And it's hard for me to *justify* that. On the other hand...you know there is the social issue of ...not having enough work and people and

children going hungry…and…and it's something that's very *frustrating* to me…overall.

Usually my interviewees' first response highlighted individual causes of poverty, such as poor people's bad choices or lack of effort ("hav[ing] child, and child, and child;" "they are being irresponsible themselves;"[9] "that person is going in [the system] because they don't care;" "you know you [should] work hard"). However, typically this first response was followed immediately or later on by discussion of causes of poverty beyond the individual's control ("So it's the system too, there's no help;" "Some people just not able;" "Ninety-five percent of the time it's the woman caught in this situation. The husband takes off and she's stuck with the kids;" "You know there is the social issue of not having enough work"). Quick person-on-the-street interviews would most likely capture only the individualist first layer of Americans' conflicting ideas on this subject (Strauss 2000).

The particular reasons that were frequently cited as explanations of why poverty is not simply a matter of individual effort and choices were *social conditioning; women's unfair childcare burden; psychological or medical problems and addictions;* and *economic constraints.*

## Social conditioning

Part of the conventional wisdom about Americans' views about poverty is that during the Reagan years they turned away from social environment explanations for poverty (e.g., Ellwood 1988, 41). That is quite wrong. Explanations for poverty as the result of social learning are commonplace, invoked by conservatives as much as liberals. The difference is that those sympathetic to the poor invoke these explanations by way of excuse, while those who are unsympathetic use it to indict poor mothers for raising irresponsible children.

> Tommy Marino, self-described conservative, responding to the question of why most people go on welfare: Well, for a variety of different reasons, but most of them go on because they have been conditioned that way because of the modeling.

> Rick Reynolds, self-described liberal: [I]t's not you, you know, you had this tremendous, as a five-year old, this burning desire to aspire in life and that's what drove…It was a lot of what your surroundings were. And a lot of what growing up you were exposed to. And who you were around and what thoughts you were shared with you [sic] from people that were around you.

**Women's unfair childcare burden**

We saw one example of this in Vincent Rocha's comments, above. These views are also quite widespread.

> Greg Lloyd, dishwasher: Normally most of the girls ain't getting child support, that's probably it. [...] If they got their child support probably things wouldn't be so hard.

> Kathy Costa, nurse: I think society persecutes women when they have children. Financially.

**Psychological or medical problems and addictions**

Psychological explanations were given more frequently by those born after than before World War II. In the former group, they appeared at every socioeconomic level.

> Esther Black, secretary-clerical temp: When you go to interview and the people don't hire you, you (get your?) confidence down. You get depressed. Some people are not strong, like other people. Where some people let it affect them to the point that they are so depressed that they can't even get themselves back on track.

**Economic constraints**

Most interviewees were quite cognizant of the facts that the minimum wage is too low, childcare is very expensive, and health insurance can be unaffordable. Thus, even Tommy Marino, my most conservative interviewee, observed,

> Many people feel if they're unskilled and they can only earn $6 or $5 an hour, whatever the minimum wage is, they're better off going on welfare. And there again, the system *encourages* people to go on welfare because...the minimum wage is so low that...by having a minimum wage what it is, that encourages people to go on welfare.

In Rhode Island in 1995 they frequently referred to the shortage of good jobs. As the economy takes a downturn, job opportunities will very likely be on voters' minds again. The popular wisdom is that Americans are less inclined to support generous social welfare programs during economic downturns. Gilens (1999) shows that the reverse is the case, because the worse the economy, the more obvious it becomes that hard work alone is not sufficient to guarantee an adequate standard of living.

## Findings (2)

### The issue is "doing something," not self-reliance or the size of the government.

My interviewees, like most Americans in the mid-1990s, wanted to see changes to the welfare system. Most of them favored time-limited assistance for the majority of recipients and work requirements of some sort. However, they would also have been much more generous than the 1996 Personal Responsibility and Work Opportunity Reconciliation Act in allowing education or community service to count as work activities, permitting exceptions to the limits, and providing supportive government programs for those in need. To understand this, it is necessary to appreciate the interpretive frameworks that come into play as they discuss policy solutions. The defining symbol for them was the importance of "doing something," not self-reliance or shrinking government.

### The importance of "doing something"

The prime complaint I heard about welfare recipients, aside from having too many children, was that they "sit around," or "get something for nothing," and should be "doing something." For example, one man in his twenties, a dishwasher in a local restaurant, complained, "You just want to sit there and get the money for free, you're not doing nothing." A mid-level state worker commented, "I don't care if you have a kid in day care for three hours a day, well for three hours a day you can do something. If you do nothing—for no other reason than for your own self-esteem you do something, you just don't sit there and get money." (Note the implicit assumption that fulltime parenting is "nothing." This view was not shared by all interviewees. For example, while the women in the twenty-something focus group expected mothers to work outside the home, the women in the forty-something focus group debated whether this is good for children.)

### Education and community service count as "doing something"

Thus, the dominant concern is whether someone who is poor is taking the initiative to improve his or her circumstances and keeping busy in a socially approved way. A few interviewees explicitly mentioned volunteer work as examples of doing something, and many favored encouraging welfare recipients to get further education. I found middle-class interviewees particularly supportive of subsidized higher education and other measures that would help former welfare recipients get good jobs (i.e., with high wages and good benefits) rather than just any job. This is not because middle-class interviewees were more liberal overall. Rather, it was because their idea of an adequate standard of living could not be attained without a college education.

## The government should also be "doing something"

My interviewees were not particularly interested in shrinking the size of government. Three interviewees (all in their twenties and working-class) did not even know what I was talking about when I raised the issue:

> CS: Some people relate this issue to the size of the government. Government bureaucracy or the amount of government programs or — this is what some people relate.

> Anna Monteiro: I never heard that one. I couldn't relate to that. I wouldn't know how to relate welfare to the size of government.

With few exceptions, their approach to welfare policies was not shaped by neo-liberal ideology but rather by the key symbol of "doing something." This meant that they favored both individual and government initiative to deal with poverty.

On the one hand, each person should try to take care of him or herself. Thus there was little support for programs, like AFDC, that had the reputation of encouraging passivity. My interviews showed this to be a greater concern, voiced by interviewees of all races, than white antipathy to blacks and Latinos. (See also Gilens 1999.)[10]

On the other hand, "the government in Washington should do everything possible to improve the standard of living of all poor Americans" because the government, like the good person, should not just "sit around" but should "do something." It is interesting in this connection that the main complaint some of my interviewees had about the federal government was not that it does too much, but that it is inefficient. They longed for a strong leader who would take charge and get something done.

Similarly, I found that given three options for welfare reform, 44 percent of my North Carolina and Rhode Island survey respondents agreed *both* that "the best way to reform the welfare system is for the government to provide welfare for two years, then expect recipients to work" and that "the best way to reform the welfare system is to replace welfare with a system of government-subsidized child care, health insurance, and jobs for all Americans who need them." People should be working, but it is also seen as important that the government help people to meet their basic needs. Overall, 64 percent of my NC and RI survey sample agreed with the proposal to replace welfare with government-subsidized childcare, health insurance, and jobs "for all Americans who need them," including majorities of men and women, blacks and whites, and respondents at every income level up to household incomes of $75,000 or more in 1995. It probably helped to use the wording "all Americans who need them." This does not sound as expansive as subsidized childcare, health insurance, and jobs for every American, yet it clearly applies to anyone who feels they could benefit from such programs.

Certainly there are Americans who reject government programs in principle. One interviewee was an evangelical Christian who advocated abolishing all government social programs and replacing them with a generous system of faith-based charity. I found that older white interviewees in semi-rural Alamance County, North Carolina, were more likely to oppose government social programs than were interviewees in the suburban Research Triangle Park area of North Carolina or in Rhode Island. My interview results are consistent with a national survey that found that only Americans in rural areas and those sixty or older are on the whole more critical than supportive of government powers and programs (Cantril and Cantril 1999).

## Programs should recognize the multiple causes of poverty

The first section of findings described my interviewees' recognition of the multiple causes of poverty. This awareness affected the way they thought about policy solutions. Even the evangelical Christian interviewee referred to above had found a way to integrate religious teaching and modern psychology to justify the extensive assistance programs run by her church:

> So the scripture clearly says if you don't work you don't eat. [...]Well, nobody's taught them, they've got to be taught. [...]People who are healthy will *risk* having a failure because their self-image is not tied up into their success. [...]You can't mass lecture people into having a good self-image, that doesn't make any sense. So you one-to-one take care of it, you do one family at a time, one person at a time...you know, get them the job, get them the house, get them the training.

Several interviewees noted that sick children or mental illness could keep people from working for a long time. Still others recommended that low-wage work be supplemented with income supports:

> Peter Vieira, discount store management trainee: [G]o into a McDonalds and start working. I don't see a problem with that. I mean, it is some type of work. You're doing something, you're making some kind of money. Grant you,

it might not be enough money for you to live on, and at that point, yes, your assistance would still be provided.

## Findings (3)

**Individualist, humanitarian and populist rhetoric have different effects on public support for various antipoverty programs.**

Given the analysis presented so far, it should not be surprising that public opinion can be mobilized in favor of a variety of antipoverty policies. The following experimental findings show that the language used to frame antipoverty policy proposals strongly affects how favorably they are viewed.

The experiment was a random-sample telephone survey on welfare reform conducted January 12–24, 1995. The sample consisted of 143 adult U.S. citizens in Piedmont (central) North Carolina and the greater Providence area of Rhode Island.[11] All respondents were told that this was a survey of attitudes about welfare reform. Those randomly chosen for the experimental manipulation were then told, "First, before I get to welfare reform, I will read a statement. Please tell me whether you agree or disagree." One quarter of the sample heard a statement full of individualist language ("too many people avoid taking responsibility for their lives"). Another quarter heard a statement phrased with humanitarian language (emphasizing "help" for the poor).[12] Another quarter heard a populist statement ("the average person pays too much in taxes and doesn't get enough in return from the government"). The last quarter served as a control group and heard none of these statements. Then all respondents were asked how favorably they viewed three proposals for welfare reform and which of these proposals they preferred overall — eliminating welfare for out-of-wedlock births to teenage mothers; instituting a two-year time limit; or replacing welfare with government-subsidized childcare, health insurance, and jobs.

The effect of the rhetorical priming was dramatic. The individualist rhetoric tapped into *morality* schemas that led to increased support for eliminating welfare for single teenage mothers. The humanitarian rhetoric tapped *charity* schemas that led to an overall preference for time-limited assistance. The populist rhetoric tapped *equity* schemas that led to preference for replacing welfare with expanded social benefits. These effects occurred regardless of whether those primed with the rhetoric agreed or disagreed with the priming statement. Simply being asked to think about the statement was enough to affect the way the proposals were viewed.

Some of these effects were statistically significant for the full sample. Other effects were strongest for the less opinionated respondents (i.e., those who agreed or disagreed "not so strongly" with one or more proposal). These "moderate-certainty" respondents comprised 71 percent of the sample.

### Effect of individualist rhetoric

Among the moderate-certainty respondents, 46 percent of those primed with the individualist personal responsibility rhetoric favored the proposal to eliminate welfare for teenage single mothers, compared to only 11 percent of the control group.[13] While this is unsurprising, it could explain why the Clinton task force's original proposals for welfare reform failed to gain support. Clinton used individualist rhetoric to build support for what was, in effect, a government jobs program. That rhetoric, instead, probably led to increased public support for welfare cutbacks.

### Effect of humanitarian rhetoric

Priming respondents with rhetoric about the need to help the poor (charity framework) led at first to significantly increased support for expanded government provision (by 31 percentage points over the control group and 27 percentage points over all other respondents among the moderate-certainty respondents).[14] However, these respondents were also the most favorably disposed of all three experimental groups to time-limited assistance, and when they were then asked to choose which proposal they preferred overall, 54 percent chose the two-year time limit while only 34 percent chose expanded social welfare programs. When the stress is on the importance of helping others in need, Americans will give, but they want limits to their giving.

### Effect of populist rhetoric

One might assume that thinking about the statement, "The average person pays too much in taxes and doesn't get enough in return from the government," would lead to diminished support for all government social programs. It didn't. Instead, it seemed to create an equity framework, leading respondents to weigh whether there was a fair balance between taxes paid and government services rendered. This concern with a fair social exchange is probably what led some of my interviewees to complain that welfare recipients are "getting something for nothing." Accordingly, a negative effect of this equity framework in the experiment was increased support for eliminating welfare for teenage single mothers.[15] Strikingly, however, the populist experimental group was the only one in which a majority preferred government-subsidized jobs, childcare, and health insurance over time-limited assistance. The preferences of those primed with the populist rhetoric were almost the reverse of those primed with the humanitarian rhetoric: 58 percent picked expanded social provision as their top choice, while 33 percent chose the two-year time limit. Unlike humanitarian rhetoric, which makes listeners feel guilty for not giving

**66**

more, but possibly resentful that *they* have to give, populist rhetoric turns resentment toward the powers that be who are not doing enough for *us*.

## Conclusions

It is natural for welfare activists to look for the core of their support from welfare recipients, sympathetic religious leaders, and those on the left politically. Yet, as the welfare reform battles of the 1990s show, that is not a large enough base to convince politicians and policymakers to protect and expand programs to help lift more Americans out of poverty. For the battles ahead it is crucial to mobilize a large, diverse coalition of Americans. This is a realistic goal, because most U.S. Americans believe that poverty has multiple causes, that being self-reliant is less important than trying to improve one's situation, and that society should take the initiative, just as individuals should, to deal with poverty. Americans are even more favorably disposed toward expanded social provision if the issue is framed as one of equity (the government owes us all more benefits in relation to the taxes we pay) rather than charity (the better off should help the less well off).

In sum, most U.S. Americans are considerably more open to government antipoverty programs than those who stress American individualism, or partisan differences, would allow. The dismal state of U.S. antipoverty policies is due to a failure of political leaders in this country to call upon the best of what Americans believe, not intractable resistance endemic to our political culture.

## References

Cantril, Albert H., and Susan Davis Cantril. 1999. *Reading Mixed Signals: Ambivalence in American Public Opinion about Government.* Washington, DC: Woodrow Wilson Center Press.

Ellwood, David T. 1988. *Poor Support: Poverty in the American Family.* New York: Basic Books.

Feldman, Stanley, and John Zaller. 1992. "The Political Culture of Ambivalence: Ideological Responses to the Welfare State." *American Journal of Political Science* 36:268–307.

Gilens, Martin. 1999. *Why Americans Hate Welfare.* Chicago: University of Chicago Press.

Hochschild, Jennifer. 1981. *What's Fair? American Beliefs about Distributive Justice.* Cambridge, Mass: Harvard University Press.

Kluegel, James R., and Eliot R. Smith. 1986. *Beliefs About Inequality: Americans' Views of What Is and What Ought to Be.* New York: Aldine de Gruyter.

Smith, Tom W. 1987. "That Which We Call Welfare by Any Other Name Would Smell Sweeter: An Analysis of the Impact of Question Wording on Response Patterns." *Public Opinion Quarterly* 51: 75–83.

Strauss, Claudia. 2000. "The Culture Concept and the Individualism-Collectivism Debate: Dominant and Alternative Attributions for Class in the United States." Pp. 85–114 in *Culture, Thought, and Development*, ed. L. P. Nucci, G. B. Saxe, and E. Turiel. Mahwah, NJ: Lawrence Erlbaum Associates.

———. n.d. [a] Engendering Public Support For Different Welfare Reform Options: The Effects of Individualist, Communitarian, and Populist Political Rhetoric. Unpublished manuscript. (Available from the author.)

———. n.d. [b] Welfare Reform, Misrepresentations of American Culture, and Social Science. (Available from the author.)

Weaver, R. Kent, Robert Y. Shapiro, and Lawrence R. Jacobs. 1995. "The Polls-Trends: Welfare." *Public Opinion Quarterly* 59: 606–627.

Wolfe, Alan. 1998. *One Nation After All: What Middle-Class Americans Really Think About: God, Country, Family, Racism, Welfare, Immigration, Homosexuality, Work, the Right, the Left, and Each Other*. New York: Viking.

## Notes

[1] Claudia Strauss is an assistant professor of anthropology at Pitzer College. Co-author of *A Cognitive Theory of Cultural Meaning* (Cambridge University Press, 1997) and co-editor of *Human Motives and Cultural Models* (Cambridge University Press, 1992), she studies how Americans think and talk about class issues.

[2] Partial funding for this research was provided by an American Council of Learned Societies Fellowship and Duke University Arts and Sciences Research Council Grants. I am grateful for helpful comments by Margaret Hallock, Lee Strauss, and by members of the audience when this material was presented at the Welfare, Work, and Politics Conference, the American Anthropological Association 98th annual meeting, and at Rollins College, SUNY-New Paltz, the University of Wisconsin-Milwaukee, Boston University, the University of Minnesota, and Queens College.

[3] For further discussions of what is often termed "ambivalence" in attitudes about poverty and social redistribution, see Feldman and Zaller (1992); Hochschild (1981); Kluegel and Smith (1986); and Wolfe (1998).

[4] Source: NORC-GSS poll in Weaver, Shapiro, and Jacobs 1995 and at http://www.icpsr.umich.edu/GSS99/codebook/helppoor.htm.

[5] The 2000 figures are preliminary. I am grateful to Tom Smith for providing them.

[6] There were nine women and seven men. Four were Portuguese-American; the rest were English-, Irish-, Italian-, Polish-, and African-American, as well as one Afro-Caribbean. Nine had household incomes under $55,000 per year.

[7] Eight white women, 20–31 years old, and nine white women, 39–56 years old.

**68**

[8] The following transcription conventions were used:

[*italics*]=contextual information
*italics* = emphatic intonation
**boldface** = highlighted for analysis
… = pause of half second or more
[…] = deletion
(words?) uncertain transcription

Some interviewees repeated words or phrases. Those and some verbal fillers have been omitted. All interviewee names are pseudonyms.

[9] In Mason Carter's case, his individualist explanations of poverty *followed* his alternative explanations. That was typical of interviewees who had been recipients of public assistance.

[10] Racial antipathy is not the same as stereotyping. My findings concur with those of Gilens (1999) that U.S. Americans of all races share the racial stereotype that African-Americans tend not to try hard enough to improve their situation.

[11] The survey had a 70 percent participation rate.

[12] The actual wording was: "One of the biggest problems in America today is that we have forgotten that all of us, rich and poor, are in the same boat. Giving help to some people now will eventually help other people later." It was intended as a communitarian message, but it was probably interpreted as a humanitarian or charitable appeal. All three priming statements began with the phrase, "One of the biggest problems in America today is…" All three welfare reform proposals began with the phrase, "The best way to reform the welfare system is…"

[13] Only 18 percent of all moderate-certainty respondents favored this proposal (Pearson chi-square, p=.01 for difference between individualist and other respondents).

[14] Pearson chi-square, p=.03 for the difference between humanitarian and all other respondents in the moderate certainty subsample.

[15] 32 percent of the moderate-certainty subsample of the populist group favored this proposal, which was less than those primed with the individualist rhetoric but more than the control group.

[16] The difference between the populist and humanitarian groups was significant (Pearson chi-square, p=.05).

## PART II

# Families, Caregiving and Wage Work

Randy Albelda
Stephanie Limoncelli
Wendy Chavkin
Diana Romero
Paul H. Wise

# What's Wrong with Welfare-to-Work[1]

## *Randy Albelda*[2]

"Ending welfare as we know it" has rapidly become ending welfare. Time limits virtually assure that the majority of families who receive welfare will be cut off at least from federal funding. The current trend is to replace welfare with earnings, best summed up by the ever-present term "Welfare-to-Work."

The Welfare-to-Work "solution" can be thought of as a match made in hell. It puts poor mothers who need the most support and flexibility into jobs in the low-wage labor market, which often are the most inflexible, have the least family-necessary benefits (vacation time, health care, sick days), and provide levels of pay that often are insufficient to support a single person, let alone a family. This mismatch is not going to be resolved by providing short-term job training, work vans, poor-quality childcare, or even refundable earned income tax credits. It is a political, social, and economic problem that must be addressed in our policies but also in our national psyche. It starts with valuing the work that families do. Raising children — in any and all family configurations — is absolutely vital work to our individual and collective wellbeing. And it is deserving. Recognizing this will not only transform how we think about welfare, it can and must change how we think about the structure of paid work. We must have access to paid work that allows us to take care of our families and have a family life without relegating all women to the home.

## Been There, Done That

Ending welfare poses some historically familiar alternatives for women. Getting married and staying married — thus being dependent on a man — was of course the fond hope and major inspiration for conservatives who sponsored the 1996 Personal Responsibility and Work Opportunity Reconciliation Act (PRWORA). The act leads with these two "findings": 1) Marriage is the foundation of a successful society; and 2) Marriage is an essential institution of a successful society which promotes the interests of children.

The path most proponents of welfare reform promote publicly, however, is Welfare-to-Work. There is a wide range of methods for promoting paid work instead of welfare, from the punitive Work First strategies pursued by over half the states to the more liberal strategies (which include a generous package of training and education options, day care, transportation, and health care) put forth by Mary Jo Bane and David Ellwood when they were welfare reform policymakers in the Clinton Administration. Despite its current popularity, the notion of putting welfare mothers to "work" is hardly new. Work requirements have long been part of AFDC, and were seen as an important way to get women, particularly black women, off the welfare rolls. It was only in the early 1990s, however, that paid work became the main alternative in light of benefit time limits.

Most states, as well as the ancillary not-for-profit agencies and for-profit companies that get lucrative welfare-related contracts, are putting significant energies into getting adult welfare recipients to "work." Work in this case means paid employment or unpaid community or public-service placements (workfare). But there are problems with Welfare-to-Work, some of which states readily recognize and are working to cope with (however inadequately), and others which states do not even recognize.

### Inadequate Supports for Welfare-to-Work Moms

One aspect of states' Welfare-to-Work policy has always been their concern with the "job readiness" of welfare mothers. From vast amounts of published research we know many welfare mothers have low educational attainment and many lack recent job experience (although the vast majority have been employed at some point). Both of these characteristics impede entry into the labor market and, once there, all but assure low wages. This is too bad since Welfare-to-Work ideology rests on short-term training, which is reinforced by precluding most education from qualifying as "work-related activities" in the work quotas established in PRWORA. This of course means that many state programs will be ineffectual in improving women's skills.

74

More and more research is uncovering another set of barriers to work, including learning disabilities, severe bouts of depression, and experiences with domestic violence. The prediction is that the easy-to-place recipients will soon be thrown out of the welfare system and those who remain will require much more training and support to get paid employment. Ironically, or perhaps cynically, welfare will become exactly how it was portrayed for years — a system that serves very low-functioning women with children who need long-term assistance. Recent studies show that over 41 percent of current recipients have less than a high school diploma, and between 10 percent and 31 percent of welfare recipients are currently victims of domestic violence. Helping women overcome barriers to employment will take time, quality counseling, and long-term training, something welfare reform is discouraging or prohibiting.

What distinguishes welfare recipients from other poor people is that two-thirds of them are children being raised, most often, by a mother on her own. Welfare has always been a program for families with young children. Therefore, Welfare-to-Work requires a substantial set of ancillary supports that mothers with small children need to get to work, such as health insurance, transportation, and childcare. Since many jobs available to Welfare-to-Work mothers do not provide health insurance, states allow women to stay on Medicaid, but typically only for one year after leaving welfare. Then they're on their own. Some states have recognized the transportation challenge mothers face — efficiently getting children to and from day care and school, and getting themselves to and from work in a timely fashion — and some are trying to solve this problem with loaner cars, work vans, and public transportation vouchers. In rural and suburban areas, however, the problems are much more difficult because adequate transportation is just not there. Regarding childcare, policymakers recognize the need for it, but their solutions should make us shiver. Very few states pay any attention to the quality of care. Any care seems to do for poor mothers. In Massachusetts, for example, the state encourages mothers to find low-cost caretakers with reimbursements of $15 per day. Assuming you get what you pay for, such childcare is a disaster for mothers and children. Moreover, it impoverishes and exploits the caregivers.

### And What about the Problems with No Name?

Will Welfare-to-Work actually ensure economic "independence"? Many are avoiding this question because the economic expansion, which has both accompanied and accommodated Welfare-to-Work, has at least fulfilled one premise of welfare reform — moving women from the rolls to a job. However, come the downturn, many who did get jobs will lose them, and caseloads will creep back up. Further, the expansion has allowed

**75**

states to be slack, if not entirely unimaginative, in their training and education efforts, relying on the economic expansion to reduce rolls and thereby claim victory in the welfare reform battle.

Will finding a job mean earning a living wage? Not likely. What is almost always ignored or conveniently forgotten in the blind faith that all too often accompanies the Welfare-to-Work mentality is that the U.S. labor market has always failed women who have little formal education and sporadic job experiences. Women have a very hard time supporting themselves, let alone families, on wages from waitressing, sales clerking, cleaning hotel rooms, or even assisting administrators. Yet these are exactly the kinds of jobs Welfare-to-Work mothers are likely to get.

In addition to the problems of a fickle labor market and chronically low wages, women in the Welfare-to-Work pipeline must cope with the fact that most jobs are not "mother ready." That is, they do not accommodate mothers' needs, even when training, work, and childcare arrangements are in place. These are not unknown or new needs. They include the remarkably mundane events such as children getting sick, school and medical appointments, school vacations, and early-release school days. Employers, especially those who employ low-wage workers, do not want workers who come in late because a school bus didn't show up, miss days because there was no childcare, or worry about their children at 3:00 P.M. — instead of doing their tedious low-wage-earning tasks. Unfortunately, low-wage employers of current and former welfare recipients are least likely to grant sick leave and vacation time. According to a report in the *American Journal of Public Health* (Heymann and Earle 1999), 46 percent of women who had never been on welfare got sick leave and vacation pay at their jobs, as compared to 24 percent of women who had been on welfare less than two years, and 19 percent of women who had been on welfare more than two years.

Most state administrators, politicians, journalists, and researchers see the work of taking care of children as a cost of Welfare-to-Work, but not as an important and valuable family activity. Devaluing women's unpaid work in the home is clearly evident in studies of welfare reform. Typically, researchers compare welfare families' and employed families' material wellbeing without imputing any value to women's time. In short, the value of a woman's unpaid labor in the home when she is receiving welfare is zero. As a policy, Welfare-to-Work fails to grapple with the fact that adults responsible for children cannot (and probably should not) put their jobs — especially low-wage ones — before the needs of their children.

### Family Values/Valuing Families

The ideologues who concern themselves with poor mothers exhibit split personalities when it comes to getting women to work. The conservative architects of welfare reform who want to force poor mothers to do lousy jobs are now busy enacting tax cuts to encourage middle-class moms to stay at home and trying hard to eliminate the "marriage penalty" in the tax code. Liberals, on the other hand, seem preoccupied with providing inadequate supports for full-time employment for poor mothers. What's going on?

One way to make sense of the obsession with employment for poor mothers is to see the emphasis on paid work in welfare reform as a major change in thinking about women and public assistance. Indeed, it is a major value shift. The Social Security Act of 1935 made all poor single mothers entitled to receive Aid to Families with Dependent Children (AFDC), although the levels received were far lower than the other two major programs (Social Security and Unemployment Insurance) in that historic legislation. At that time, the notion of having to "work" for one's benefits was not an expectation of most single mothers. Women who were not attached to male breadwinners received income, but not much.

Another old value set guiding single mothers' receipt of cash assistance pivoted on how women became single mothers. Widows were seen as deserving, while divorced, separated, and never-married mothers were not. Benefit levels reinforced these "values."

What makes a single mother "deserving" today has changed. The salient factor is no longer how she happened to become a single parent, but rather if she is engaged in paid labor. This sentiment is only possible in an age when most women are in the paid labor market and when the moral repugnance of women without men has dissipated. Ironically, both of these accomplishments can be attributed in part to the successes of the women's movement, coupled with modern industrialization. As more and more women are drawn into the labor force, they tend to have fewer children and are not as likely to get or stay married. Interestingly, both conservatives and liberals have lent weight to the idea that working single mothers are more deserving.

The positive value of employment was accompanied by the negative value placed on receiving welfare. Led by Ronald Reagan and conservative thinker Charles Murray in the 1980s, welfare opponents referred to AFDC recipients as "welfare queens." They were presumed to have loads of children, leech resources from the state, and then pass their dysfunctional behavior on to their children. In the mid-1980s through the 1990s, many "liberal" poverty researchers carried this banner as well. "Underclass" authors, notably William Julius Wilson and Christopher Jencks, as well as their left detractors, such as William Darity and Samuel Myers, discussed welfare receipt as a pathology — one of the many "bad" behaviors that helps reproduce poverty. Jencks even referred to women receiving welfare as the "reproductive underclass." Further, when adult recipients have earnings, even if they receive hefty supplements, they are not perceived as receiving "hand-outs" and hence are deserving. It would seem, then, that putting welfare mothers to work solves the problem of growing welfare rolls and plays into American values that will help restore safety nets for the poor. On both the Right and the Left, putting poor mothers to work is the prescribed cure to their "dysfunctional" tendencies.

## A Progressive Agenda

I do not want to argue here that paid work is bad. Indeed, earnings can and do buy economic security and some independence from men, especially from abusive relationships. In a society that values paid work, doing it can build your self-esteem as well. However, Welfare-to-Work is a setup. The types of jobs poor mothers get and can keep provide neither much dignity nor sufficient wages. Working enough hours at low wages to support a family is often untenable. Women fail too often. This is not only demoralizing, but economically debilitating. If we don't think both about valuing women's work at home as well as when they do paid work, Welfare-to-Work is a cruel hoax that makes legislators feel better about themselves, but leaves poor families in the lurch.

Instead of trying to reform poor mothers to become working poor mothers, we need to take a closer look at job structures and what it will take to make work possible for mothers who support families. This might include a shorter work week or at least income supplements to those who take a part-time job so that families can still pay for basic needs like housing, health insurance, childcare, food, and clothing. Paid family and medical leave and expanded unemployment insurance to cover less continuous and low-paying part-time work must also be in place. A mother shouldn't lose her job or her weekly pay because her child gets chicken pox. Herein lies the true opportunity of Welfare-to-Work welfare reform.[3]

A national discussion about the value of women's work in the home is much needed for all women, not just those who turn to public assistance. It would raise several important sets of policy issues, including:

> ❯ seriously considering the provision of publicly funded family care, such as childcare centers, extended day programs, and child allowances;

> ❯ working to make sure that welfare is not punitive and is at least comparable to social security and unemployment insurance; and

> ❯ focusing not just on making mothers "job ready," but promoting policies that make paid work "mother-ready" — in other words, conducive to mothers' needs, paying a living wage, and offering opportunities for advancement.

If we as a nation recognized the value of women's work, we wouldn't have welfare reform that merely replaces public assistance with forcing mothers into working jobs at low wages and a shallow set of supports that vanishes quickly. Seeing the work of raising children as a benefit to society, not merely a cost of going to work, would mean developing a Welfare-to-Work regime that truly supports part-time waged work. Further, it might make us more cognizant that for some families at some points in their lives, having the sole adult in the labor force is not possible or desirable. Public income supports for poor single mothers will always need to exist precisely because we value the work of mothers taking care of their children.

## References

Darity, William A. Jr., and Samuel Myers. 1994. *The Black Underclass: Critical Essays on Race and Unwantedness*. New York: Garland Publishers.

Heymann, Jody, and Alison Earle. 1999. "The Impact of Welfare Reform on Parents' Ability to Care for Their Children's Health." *American Journal of Public Health* 89 (April): 502–505.

Jencks, Christopher, and Paul E. Peterson, eds. 1991. *The Urban Underclass*. Washington, D.C.: Brookings Institution.

Murray, Charles. 1984. *Losing Ground: American Social Policy 1950–1980*. New York: Basic Books.

Wilson, William Julius. 1987. *The Truly Disadvantaged: The Inner City, the Underclass, and Public Policy*. Chicago: University of Chicago Press.

Women's Committee of 100. 2000. "An Immodest Proposal: Rewarding Women's Work to End Poverty." *Dollars & Sense* (September/October): 36–. (Also available at http://www.welfare2002.org/.)

## Notes

[1] Reprinted with permission from *Dollars & Sense*, September/October 2000, pp.32-35.

[2] Randy Albelda is a professor of economics at the University of Massachusetts in Boston. Her research and teaching focus is on poverty, women's economic status, welfare reform, income inequality, and state and local finance. She is the author of *Economics and Feminism: Disturbances in the Field* (Twayne Publishers), coauthor of the books *The War on the Poor: A Defense Manual* (with Nancy Folbre, the New Press) and *Glass Ceilings and Bottomless Pits: Women's Work, Women's Poverty* (with Chris Tilly, South End Press), and the recent reports *Choices and Tradeoffs; The Parent Survey of Child Care in Massachusetts* and *In Harm's Way? Domestic Violence, AFDC Receipts, and Welfare Reform in Massachusetts*. Professor Albelda is currently engaged in a research project estimating the costs of paid family and medical leave in Massachusetts. She is an active participant in legislative and educational efforts to improve policies and our understanding of welfare and employment policies that affect low-income women and their families.

[3] For more policy initiatives, see Women's Committee of 100 (2000).

# "Some of Us Are Excellent at Babies"

## Paid Work, Mothering, and the Construction of "Need" in a Welfare-to-Work Program

### Stephanie A. Limoncelli[1]

With the passage of PRWORA in 1996, all women receiving TANF have been required to engage in paid work. This represents a shift from early twentieth-century maternalistic welfare policies and more recent voluntary work programs for low-income women receiving cash assistance. PRWORA universally constructs all women as "female breadwinners," tying entitlement to women's status as workers and requiring them to participate in Welfare-to-Work (WtW) programs. The WtW programs that states developed or expanded in response to PRWORA reflect this universal construction of women. In California, for example, the WtW program curriculum is focused mainly on teaching participants who are presumed to be lacking the psychological and practical skills necessary to secure waged work, how to obtain immediate employment. Program materials are replete with "needs talk" — participants *need* to learn how to be self-reliant, they *need* to be motivated to engage in paid work, and their self esteem *needs* to be fostered through such work.[2] These assumptions have been encoded into WtW practice as programs have adopted Work First models and hired expert "facilitators" and "job search specialists" to help meet these "needs". Policymakers tout the decrease in welfare rolls as evidence that programs have been successful in this regard.

Though the Work First philosophy advocates female empowerment and emancipation through employment, the lived experiences of low-income women often foster a different view of the importance of paid work relative to other aspects of their lives. For example, many low-income women in the United States embrace the ideal of mothering their children in the home as important work; this is part of the cultural practice of many women of color (Hondagneu-Sotelo and Avila 1997). However, in welfare rhetoric, unemployed low-income women are characterized as neglectful of or even harmful to their children, as failing to instill a work ethic in them, and as creating the next generation of the underclass through this failure.[3]

It is the disjuncture between the assumptions of a Work First program and the lived experiences of participants in the program that is the focus of this paper. Using participant observation, I question how paid work and mothering are constructed in program policy and how women respond to program messages: Do staff follow program rhetoric in their interactions with participants? Do participants identify primarily as mothers, workers, or both? By examining the interactions of staff and participants in a Work First program, I explore the extent to which low-income participants see it as creating opportunities for them to resist traditional gender roles or impeding them from roles they wish to claim.[4] I show that staff, constrained by the institutional structure of the program but generally supportive of the Work First curriculum, mediate between the assumptions of program policies and the reactions of participants. Thus, a process of needs contestation occurs: Staff articulate Work First messages, while participants express a child-first perspective, asserting their values as mothers.

## Background

State policies affect women in their everyday lives, but they are not simply imposed by bureaucratic actors onto unsuspecting women. Rather, they are implemented in local contexts by actors who may or may not follow the intentions of policymakers. The actions of bureaucrats are interpreted by female clients who may resist, negotiate, or comply with various policy requirements in order to meet their own ends. Those interested in doing an "ethnography of the state" seek to understand the rhetorical and institutionalized practices of the state within the public sphere and the ways in which these practices are integrated into everyday life (Kligman 1998). In keeping with such an approach, I began with a notion of the welfare state as a process, both structuring and being structured by interaction. In the summer of 1999, I observed this interaction during my participation in a Work First program in California.[5]

The program, which served primarily Black and Latina clients, was structured into three sections. First, participants attended a one-day orientation that was intended to motivate them to look for work, bolster their self esteem, and foster a positive attitude about themselves and the program. Within one to three weeks of attending an orientation workshop, participants attended a week-long job club, intended to help them improve their job search skills. Here, a Job Search Specialist (JSS) held class with participants for four hours each day. She taught them to "dress for success," generate their own job leads, fill out applications, and present themselves in interviews. Further motivational exercises were included in the curriculum, and the emphasis was on encouraging participants to find immediate paid, full-time employment.

After successfully completing the job club component of the program, participants took part in a two-week "job search" at the same location. They spent a certain amount of time each day "pounding the pavement" for employment and were required to bring back evidence of their efforts to the JSS on a daily basis. If participants failed to adhere to program requirements, or were not able to obtain a job despite compliance, they were often sent back through these components of the program and allotted a longer period for a job search. However, many of the participants dropped out of the program prior to completion. In two of the job clubs that I attended, for example, about a quarter of the class disappeared after the first day. In the remaining three weeks, participants dropped off one by one, most often because they chose to leave despite the sanctions that they would receive or because the JSS dropped them for noncompliance with program requirements, such as being consistently late for class or, more commonly, failing to provide evidence of the required number of job search contacts.

### Findings

Much of the curriculum of the Work First program was dedicated to helping participants gain a sense of themselves as workers capable of obtaining employment and teaching them to see any type of paid work as a means for becoming "self-sufficient." Considered progressive by policymakers because of its incorporation of motivational psychology to help foster enthusiasm for paid work, the program curriculum focused on teaching participants to tailor themselves around employer expectations and needs. This entailed viewing and presenting themselves as individuals whose primary identity is that of a paid worker who does not "allow" any other responsibilities to interfere with employment. Because of this focus on the individual worker, participants' ties to families were made invisible in the program exercises. In addition, the program purposely operated like a workplace in that participants were expected to manage family conflicts or demands privately before they appeared at the program ready to present a "public" self fully committed to the activities at hand.

The way that work was framed in the program and the division between work and family that was assumed created problems for staff and participants from the outset. For example, participants were told to arrange childcare prior to coming to the orientation for the program, but several appeared with children by their side and were sent home. Participants, many of whom had young children, did not accept the program view of paid work nor the separation of work and family so easily. Consequently, I observed three main issues that were contested by participants: (1) the meaning of paid work and its importance for independence; (2) efforts to combine work and family; and (3) the importance and meaning of mothering.

## Paid Work

There were several messages about paid work that were articulated frequently by staff: any type of paid work is better than receiving assistance; women receive self-esteem through paid work; and paid work is the only means of attaining economic independence. Clients countered these messages by arguing that they wanted living wage jobs; that they saw paid work as a practical means to an end (i.e., they did not articulate employment as a means by which they gained self-esteem); and that receiving assistance did not necessarily make them dependent.

Many of the participants had worked in typically female-typed jobs, such as certified nursing assistants (CNAs), childcare providers, retail clerks, telemarketers, warehouse staff, receptionists or other administrative support staff, and fast-food employees. Some were currently working under the table at places such as swap meets or doing one-time work, such as delivering phone books, conducting food demonstrations in stores, or cleaning houses in order to gain a little extra money. The participants understood that they would never have a stable economic situation working in such jobs and repeatedly expressed the desire for education and training so that they could obtain the skills necessary to make a living wage.

Even so, the jobs they were envisioning were not described as emotionally fulfilling. Rather, they were seen as a practical means to make ends meet. It was common for women to aspire to positions just above the ones in which they had already worked. CNAs wanted to become licensed vocational nurses, for example, or women with some office experience wanted to learn to use computers. Brenda, a young white woman with one son, spoke with me on a break from class one day:

> If they would let me go to school for six months, I could
> be a dental assistant and make enough money to get off
> of aid. But if they make me do Job Search, I won't be able
> to start school on time and six months of being on aid is
> going to turn into a year. If they want to save money,
> they should let me go to school; but my caseworker told
> me I have to get a job. I could get a $6 or $7 an hour job;

see, I don't think it's hard to get a job [that doesn't pay well]....

Brenda viewed dental assistance work in primarily financial rather than career terms and pointed out the contradiction of the program denying her the possibility of training that would allow her a living-wage job. However, from the perspective of the program and the personal experiences of the staff, any work, including minimum-wage jobs, could afford women self worth. Once women are working, the staff believed, they have made the first step toward increasing confidence, better jobs, and eventual economic independence. Yolanda, the JSS at the first job club I attended, said in an interview that she understands the program to be teaching women that:

> You will be better off if you work, not just financially, but you'll feel better too. You're showing an example to your family, you're accomplishing something, you're doing more than just taking care of your kids, where you might get a thank you and you might not.

In espousing the value of paid work here, Yolanda is at once promoting it as a means of emotional self-worth ("you'll feel better too"); devaluing mothering (you are "accomplishing" something only if you are involved in paid work); and expressing the emotional dissatisfaction resulting from childrearing ("you might get a thank you and you might not").

This view did not fit the experiences of the participants. Having raised their families in (and out of) poverty and worked at low-waged and temporary jobs, they were dubious about the stepping-stone philosophy. Elena, a twenty-four-year-old Latina mother of two, pointed out the reality of low-wage work during an interview:

> [The staff] say go out and get a job. They don't care if you're walking the sidewalk, as long as it's for minimum wage. But there is no way you can make it on minimum wage.

Like many of the participants, Elena relied on living arrangements with parents or other relatives in order to survive on a minimum-waged job.

Participants also were taught that economic security should come from paid work and not through government assistance, but this message was not uniformly accepted by participants. Yolanda asked the class if there was anyone who felt self-sufficient and independent even though they receive a welfare check. This particular question elicited a determined response from participants: "Yes!"

The interchange proceeded as follows:

> PARTICIPANT 1: I do [feel self-sufficient]. I have other trades, other things to fall back on.
> YOLANDA: So you feel a sense of self-sufficiency?
> PARTICIPANT 1: Yes I do! I'm not the first in line when the checks come.
> PARTICIPANT 2: I understand what she is saying because the check covers my rent [only].
> PARTICIPANT 3: I understand what she, back there, is saying. I'm independent and self-sufficient. I don't need the check, but I want the check every month. But if I go look and it's not there, I'm still okay.

The participants frequently described themselves as resourceful and able to make ends meet in creative ways, much as Edin and Lein (1997) describe. This may entail exchanges with family and friends, underground work, or income from boyfriends. Rather than defining government assistance as a *need*, they spoke of support in some sense as an *entitlement*, something they deserved as long as they are attempting to better their own lives.

## Combining Work and Family

When staff are faced with participants' resistance to low-wage work, they advise them to work on their attitudes and behaviors. Attitude adjustment is a large portion of the curriculum. The women are presumed to suffer negative self-talk (e.g., telling themselves they *cannot* do something rather than telling themselves they *can* and *will*), which interferes with their ability to obtain paid work and support themselves and their children. This message was not well-received by many participants who felt that the JSS was not realistic about the barriers they face.

One woman explained it to the class this way:

> I had a job where I commuted four hours on the bus [she holds up four fingers for emphasis] ... I took my kids on the bus to my mom's and then went to work. I was giving my paycheck to my mom for watching my kids, so I quit!

While the participants frequently used examples of personal experience to counter the idea that combining paid work and mothering was a realistic goal, the staff used various strategies to respond. One strategy was to counter with their own personal experiences. For example, Yolanda, twenty-eight years old and African-American, had lived at home until two years before, when she married her husband, became a parent to his two children, and later had a son with him. Though she did not divulge all of this information to the class, she did talk about her nine-month-old child:

> When I was at home, after I had my son, I couldn't wait to get back to work. Being at home was a job you can't clock out of. It's easier to work.

Yolanda exemplified the middle-class mothers that Hochschild (1997) suggests are fleeing Taylorized family lives and embracing home-like work settings. These women find meaning and support through their work relationships and are increasingly finding home life less than satisfying. In an interview I asked Yolanda if she believed that the family barriers clients raised were real to them or just a good excuse not to participate. She responded:

> Oh, they really *do* see family issues as barriers, but I tell them, Do your *kids* want you to stay home with them or do *you* want to stay home with them? It's a real issue, but it's a false reality. They need to recognize that.

For Yolanda, participants who wanted to mother were attending to their own desires rather than responding to the needs of their children.

Staff without children could not draw from personal experience to counter the family concerns of the participants. They tended to appeal to participants by sympathetically acknowledging their family responsibilities while reiterating the message that such responsibilities have little to do with program or employer requirements. During one class I noted how Sheila, a single African-American JSS in her late twenties, laid out the rules for attendance: "Your child is your first priority, so you take care of your children." In her next sentence she followed with, "Children get sick, I understand that, but you have to be here every day the first week or else you will be dropped." Domestic labor, including caretaking, is relegated to the private sphere in program interactions.

Participants, who did not experience such clear divisions between their private and public responsibilities, frequently sought ways to combine paid work and family activities. Carmen, for example, was working hard on a correspondence course to become a medical billings clerk so that she could work out of her home and care for her children and her chronically ill husband. Angelique, who had separated from her husband, was searching in vain for a nanny position that would allow her to "live in" with her little girl, but was having little luck. Such opportunities for combining work and family responsibilities were rare but valued by the participants.

## Mothering

> It's the third day of Job Club #2. We've just come back
> from a short break, but the class is still restless. Sheila,
> the JSS, is trying to motivate the class: "You're here a
> whole forty-five minutes ... so work with me for forty-five
> minutes. Do you think you could make it?" She begins
> discussing the practice applications the class filled out
> the day before and how to play up strengths to employers.
> She advises, "We all have subjects that we're good at.
> Some of us are good in math, some of us are good
> in reading. Not many of us are good at both...."
> Estella, a participant sitting near the front of the class,
> interrupts: "Some of us are excellent at babies!" She
> smiles and laughs.

Estella, who wished to have more children but had a medical
problem that would likely prevent her from doing so, believed she was
good at mothering. She was one of many participants who, in response to
the Work First message of the program, expressed a child-first philosophy.
These participants depicted mothering as an important responsibility that
involved protecting and nurturing children, an arena where they enjoyed
accomplishment and competence, and a central part of their identity.
These constructions of mothering did not seem to vary according to the
racial or ethnic backgrounds of the women. Rather, what seemed to
unite the women in their perspectives was their shared experience as
low-income mothers.

Many participants articulated their desire to stay home with their
young children and care for them personally. They often voiced a deep
mistrust of childcare providers. One orientation facilitator tried to counter
this apprehension by telling participants that more child abuse occurs in
families than in daycare. This did little to ease participants' concerns that
many childcare providers are unskilled, unable to deal with particular
medical conditions, or more concerned with monetary reward than the
welfare of the children in their care. Roseanna, a Latina mother of three
with eight years of experience as a receptionist, had a son with asthma:

> After I worked at the oil company I worked at a hospital,
> but I had to quit because my son has attacks and no one
> knows how to care for him.... The childcare staff don't
> know what to do. They aren't trained for that. They don't
> deal with medical problems. I have a friend whose
> daughter has diabetes. She has to have a shot every day.

You can't expect childcare staff to deal with that. What if they give her too much [insulin] or not enough?

In addition, many women feared that their children could be molested by childcare providers. For example, Deborah, a twenty-three-year-old African-American mother of a four-year-old son told me:

> When I had my son, I didn't want to leave him with nobody else.... I just don't trust anyone else to watch him, there's too much stuff that can happen [shakes her head].... [My caseworker] wanted me to leave my son with someone else, to pay someone else to watch him, but I wanted to stay home with him.... Now that he is four and about to start school, it's different. He can talk now, he can tell me if someone tries to touch his privates, or if someone hits him.

If participants could not care for their own children, they often sought childcare from mothers, husbands, or close female friends. The participants found paid childcare acceptable only when children were old enough to communicate their experiences.

In addition to their role as protector, participants often voiced their belief that they were competent mothers in charge of their children. While motivational exercises sought to teach women that the only thing a person can control is herself, the participants saw themselves as influential in their children's lives. For example, during the first orientation workshop I attended, the facilitator led us through an exercise to list things over which we had control. Members of the class began naming items: our bodies, our attitudes, our choices of whether to marry. When one person suggested "children," a debate unfolded between the class and Michelle, the single, African-American facilitator:

> MICHELLE: You think you have control over your kids?
> PARTICIPANT 1: I don't know about other people's kids, but I have control over my kid! If I say something, he does it!
> PARTICIPANT 2: [sitting next to participant 1, nods in agreement]
> PARTICIPANT 3: You at least have control over your kids when they are babies.
> MICHELLE: Do you ever have to ask your child to do something more than once? Then you are not controlling your child.

Though the participants were not convinced by this reasoning, Michelle had the final word when she wrote "children" on the "no control" side of the flipchart she was using for the exercise.

This insistence on competence was reflective of the participants' assumption that mothering was their most important responsibility. For example, Carmen, a forty-one-year-old Latina mother of three with a chronically ill husband, emphatically expressed the importance of mothering her children in her interview:

> It would be okay if [work] was just four to five hours a day, but nine hours a day? It's really hard to see that. See, I was never a mom before [with my two older children], but now I am. Do you understand that part? There's nobody else but me.

In another example, Angelique, a twenty-seven-year-old African mother of one young daughter, who has worked as a live-in nanny, explained:

> If you have to work from six in the morning to two or three at night, what kind of education you gonna give her? You have a role like a mother and a father and you have to do all that stuff by yourself. Even if you have the father, it's the mother, not the father, it's the mother that teach everything to the child. It's very important for the child.

Bolstered by the belief in the value of mothering, the participants frequently found commonality by discussing their children. They shared pictures and stories. They asked other participants to come outside and meet their children, who had often tagged along with a participant's ride home.

Motherhood was such a salient part of the participants' identities, they often had trouble thinking of themselves in other terms. Many program exercises were intended to teach the participants how to present themselves appropriately to employers, and making their mothering role invisible was an important lesson imparted by the staff. They advised, for example, never to admit to leaving a job because of pregnancy, and they asked participants to come up with "something special about yourself" that had nothing to do with family so that they would appear to be unencumbered applicants during job interviews. If participants were not going to make their mothering role invisible, they were supposed to downplay it. One JSS, in advising the class to tell employers personal weaknesses that would be a strength to the employer, suggested that participants say, "I'm a workaholic. I often stay so late that I neglect my family."

Both strategies were difficult for the women to implement in classroom exercises. When instructed by the JSS to stand up and recount something positive about themselves, but not to mention their families, some of the women asked, "What are we supposed to talk about then?" They proceeded to go against instruction and said that they were good mothers. In mock interviews, which were taped to help participants learn how to interview better, many tended to answer the question, "What do you like to do in your spare time?" with, "Spend time with my children." In one case the exasperated JSS pointedly told one participant not to tell potential employers about her family:

> JSS: Tell [employers] things you like to do in your spare time that show you have energy and that you know how to relax. Taking care of your family is not relaxing. Don't your children stress you out? Therefore you wouldn't want to go home to more stress.
> PARTICIPANT: But I go home and take care of my kids. I teach them. I have patience with that.
> JSS: But there are times when you want to be without your kids.
> PARTICIPANT: Not really, but I guess I'm an overprotective mother.

In this case, the participant's standpoint was completely rejected, so that she reassessed herself as overprotective because she preferred spending time with her children.

Rather than outright denial of participants' views, staff sometimes used a different strategy to deal with participants claims as mothers. For example, they tried to reformulate traditional views of mothering from a focus on caring and nurturing to providing for the financial support of children. Sheila faced a participant who refused to agree that she would put in two applications on a particular day. The participant, a young African-American woman in her early twenties, had an eighteen-month-old son who was sick:

> PARTICIPANT: I won't say I won't ... I'm gonna try, but I gotta take my son to the hospital...
> JSS: You need to do your applications today. Those are the rules. I'm working with you, you have to work with me ... your son is your responsibility, you have to take care of him.

Though participants often articulated a view of mothering as nurturing, the staff attempted to reinforce a notion of participants as material providers. To the participant, a good mother took her son to the hospital herself. To the JSS, a good mother found employment in order to provide for him.

### Conclusion

If social welfare advocates in the early-twentieth-century United States found themselves in the awkward position of "defending the value of women's traditional domestic labor in a capitalist-industrial context," as Gordon (1992) so concisely points out, the administrators and staff of Welfare-to-Work programs today are faced with the opposite task. With welfare reform formalized and implemented across the nation, program administrators and staff support a universal "female breadwinner" ideology, while low-income women express interest in having their mothering activities valued. Partly this has played out between staff and low-income participants in WtW programs in the scuffling around the place and meaning of paid work and motherhood. For participants, motherhood was an arena of expertise that was meaningful to them. They saw the Work First program as discounting their mothering contributions and personal lives, even as they expressed an interest in living-wage employment that they could tailor around their family responsibilities.

While middle-class women flee domestic labor for careers, or cut back on careers in response to concerns over what is best for children, low-income women have little opportunity to make such choices. Motherhood is stratified by class and race. Paid work in low-wage jobs offer little in the way of "economic independence" and it is this reality that led participants in the Work First program to evoke claims as mothers rather than as workers. Ironically, participants articulated the exact vision of mothering that conservative politicians advocate for white, middle-class, married women. Yet participants who fail to work full-time outside of the household are sanctioned and seen as inadequate mothers.

Participants' strategies of claiming the importance of family responsibilities and their competency as mothers did little to counter the assumptions of dependence, personal deficits, and "bad mothering" assumed in welfare policy. The problem is that there is little room for such claims in welfare regimes that function to shore up market needs. As Piven and Cloward (1988) note: "…in the clash with market interests, family interests have consistently given way; and in the clash with market actors, women acting out of family interests have consistently been defeated." While Piven and Cloward were describing welfare advocates, the point is just as valid for the female participants of Work First programs.

The contestation of needs that occurred in the Work First program I observed, however, shows the potential for changing this historical trend through organizing. First, participants' resistance to the program meant that many of them left it before completion, despite the sanctions. Such participants could provide a ready group of women waiting to be mobilized for collective action. Second, the participants' emphasis on mothering provides one basis by which women could be politicized. Participants in the program found shared interests and a common identity as mothers that could help to foster mobilization. Finally, the participants' concern with the value of their mothering work suggests that they might embrace a political movement centered particularly on the issue of caregiving. The concern, of course, is that such a movement would not likely question the responsibility of women for caring work, but it could call for a re-evaluation of its worth. Organizers as well as policymakers would do well to think more carefully about not only how to "make work pay" for women, but also about how caregiving might be incorporated into new definitions of social entitlement.

## References

Butler, Sandra Sue, and Mary Katherine Nevin. 1997. "Welfare Mothers Speak: One State's Efforts to Bring Recipient Voices to the Welfare Debate." *Journal of Poverty* 1 (2): 25–61.

Davis, Diane V., and Jan L. Hagen. 1996. "Stereotypes and Stigma: What's Changed for Welfare Mothers," *Affilia* 11 (3): 319–337.

Edin, Kathryn, and Laura Lein. 1997. *Making Ends Meet: How Single Mothers Survive Welfare and Low-Wage Work*. New York: Russell Sage Foundation.

Fraser, Nancy. 1990. "Struggle Over Needs: Outline of a Socialist-Feminist Critical Theory of Late-Capitalist Political Culture." In *Women, the State, and Welfare*, ed. Linda Gordon. Madison, Wisconsin: University of Wisconsin Press.

Gordon, Linda. 1992. "Social Insurance and Public Assistance: The Influence of Gender in Welfare Thought in the United States, 1890–1935." *The American Historical Review* 97 (1): 19–54.

Hochschild, Arlie Russell. 1997. *Time Bind: When Work Becomes Home and Home Becomes Work*. New York: Henry Holt & Company.

Hondagneu-Sotelo, Pierrette, and Ernestine Avila. 1997. "'I'm Here But I'm There':The Meanings of Latina Transnational Motherhood." *Gender and Society* 11 (5): 548-571.

Kligman, Gail. 1998. *The Politics of Duplicity: Controlling Reproduction in Ceausescu's Romania*. Berkeley: University of California Press.

Piven, Frances Fox, and Richard A. Cloward. 1988. "Welfare Doesn't Shore Up Traditional Family Roles: A Reply to Linda Gordon." *Social Research* 55 (4): 631–647.

Roberts, Dorothy. 1997. *Killing the Black Body: Race, Reproduction, and the Meaning of Liberty*. New York: Pantheon.

## Notes

[1] Stephanie A. Limoncelli is a Ph.D. student in sociology at the University of California, Los Angeles. Her interests are in the sociology of gender, poverty, and political sociology. She is currently pursuing doctoral research on international organizations and women's human rights in a global context.

[2] I draw from Fraser's (1990) notion of needs interpretation and politicization.

[3] This characterization is found not only in popular culture but also in academic work on the culture of poverty. Furthermore, the assumed pathological effect of low-income women's mothering abilities has been particularly focused on Black women, as Roberts (1997) describes.

[4] I do not assume that the interactions of the women with whom I participated in the WtW program reflected a uniform agreement among all the female participants regarding the findings described in this paper, but the common social location of many of the participants seemed to foster common experiences of paid work and mothering.

[5] The findings from this paper are part of a larger ethnographic study of a work-first program. Given the choice by administrators of whether or not to participate anonymously, I chose to announce my purpose at the beginning of each program component. I was expected to adhere to the same rules as clients and to participate in all aspects of program activity. I was not, however, expected to obtain a job by the end of my participation.

[6] There seemed to be some racial/ethnic divisions in the types of work women had engaged in, though I have no statistical evidence to show this is the case. Latina women seemed to more often mention warehouse and factory work, Black women to mention work in hospitals and as CNAs. Concerns about racism preventing Black women from obtaining jobs was a frequently raised issue in the first job club I attended.

[7] See Davis and Hagen (1996) for a similar finding in their focus groups of AFDC clients.

[8] Butler and Nevin (1997) also found this "child first" priority in their survey of AFDC recipients.

[9] At least one California county is now reportedly providing the names of sanctioned TANF recipients to child welfare services, opening the possibility of the state to exert more influence over these families.

# What Do Sex and Reproduction Have to Do with Welfare?[1]

## Wendy Chavkin,[2] Diana Romero[3] and Paul H. Wise[4]

The *Personal Responsibility and Work Opportunity Reconciliation Act of 1996* fundamentally altered some key New Deal and Great Society precepts of American policy towards poor families with children. This legislation ended the entitlement status of income support, emphasized the centrality of work, and shifted responsibility of oversight from the federal to the state level. Equally embedded in the bill is a vision of socially desirable family formation, expressed in terms of individual sexual, reproductive and child-rearing goals. As outlined in Section 401 of the law, the purpose of the legislation is to accomplish the following goals:

> ▶ provide assistance to needy families so that children may be cared for in their own homes or in the homes of relatives;

> ▶ end the dependence of needy parents on government benefits by promoting job preparation, work, and marriage;

> ▶ prevent and reduce the incidence of out-of-wedlock pregnancies and establish annual numerical goals for preventing and reducing the incidence of these pregnancies; and

❯ encourage the formation and maintenance of two-parent families.

The law provided increased flexibility to the states, allowing them to translate these policy aspirations into concrete amendments to their state welfare (now Temporary Aid for Needy Families) programs. Many states have adopted policies intended to mold reproductive and parental decision-making through a series of economic disincentives.

We propose to examine those that do so in the context of health. These policies include family caps on benefits, immunization requirements, family planning mandates, abstinence education, and those directed toward decreasing out-of-wedlock births. Many of these policies had been instituted in the decade preceding the passage of the national legislation when waivers from federal requirements were given to permit state "innovations." The use of waivers became common in the 1980s and early 1990s, increasing dramatically after 1993 when the Clinton Administration granted waivers to a total of forty-three states. The terms of the waiver required evaluation using an experimental research design; however, requirements for such assessment ended with passage of the 1996 legislation.

It is our opinion that the welfare reform law fails to address the underlying issue of poverty. Rather, under the rubric of reform, these policies emphasize changing individual sexual and reproductive behaviors in a manner that raises serious concerns about ethics and efficacy. We will draw on the sparse evaluative data available as we review each of these policies.

### Family Cap or Child Exclusion?

The family cap is a provision that stipulates that when children are born into families already on welfare, the family will not receive increased benefits despite an increase in family size. It is predicated on the notion that welfare recipients have children in order to increase the size of their monthly cash grant, and that economic penalties will encourage "responsible" child-bearing decisions. The basis of this assumption, however, is not clear (Maynard et al. 1998). Although PRWORA is silent on the issue of family caps, in that it neither requires nor prohibits states from adopting the measure, a total of twenty-three states have decided to continue waiver-era policies or create new ones since the passage of the federal law.

During the period preceding passage of the PRWORA, nineteen states had received waivers to implement some version of a family cap (Stark and Levin-Epstein 1999). Of the fourteen states that were first to receive their waivers, only half conducted or completed evaluations. Only two states, New Jersey and Arkansas, completed evaluations using experimental designs comparing outcomes of AFDC recipients subjected to the family cap with those who were not (Turturro et al. 1997; Camasso et al. 1998; Stark and Levin-Epstein 1999). Research in the other early waiver states examined caseworker and client attitudes about the role of the family cap in childbearing, and a few examined the family-planning utilization requirement. Critics of the New Jersey and Arkansas evaluations have charged that the studies were "contaminated"—meaning that there was confusion among the population and caseworkers as to whether or not the family cap applied.

Of even greater significance is the fact that family-cap provisions were embedded in multifaceted program changes and thus were difficult to assess in isolation. For example, the New Jersey Welfare Development Program included the family cap in addition to expanded employment, education, and training services, as well as provisions reducing the marriage penalties and modifications to earnings disregards (Camasso et al. 1998; Maynard et al. 1998). Arkansas reported that the family cap had no effect on birth rates or on other outcome indicators, such as paternity identification, income, exits and entrances to AFDC (Turturro et al. 1997). The investigators found that approximately half of the women were not even fertile, either because of previous sterilization or postmenopausal status (e.g., grandmothers caring for children). The New Jersey analysis revealed a significant decrease in birth rates, especially for those newly joining AFDC, and an increase in both family planning utilization and abortion rates, again especially for new welfare cases (Camasso et al. 1998). At Rutgers University, in their five-year evaluation study, researchers also found that the family cap shaped New Jersey women's decisions on family planning. They estimated that between 1993 and 1996 there were about 14,000 fewer births, almost 1,500 more abortions, and roughly 7,000 more family planning visits in this population of low-income women (Camasso et al. 1999). Levin-Epstein stated in 1999 that some part of the birthrate decline in the New Jersey caseload might be attributable to the fact that fewer women are of childbearing age (Stark 1999).

An additional five of the first fourteen states to implement family cap waivers surveyed AFDC caseworkers and recipients about their attitudes regarding the family cap. In Arizona, Delaware, and Indiana, many caseworkers reported doubts that the cap would influence fertility as they did not believe recipients' childbearing decisions had ever been motivated by the prospect of a grant increase. Client surveys in Arkansas confirmed this, as more than 90 percent said that the AFDC grant was not a factor in their decisions about childbearing. The majority of New Jersey respondents reported that financial insecurity was a reason to avoid pregnancy, but did not see the loss of a grant increment in this light.

Noteworthy policy fillips include earlier return to work requirements when a woman has a "capped" child. Thus, five states (California, Connecticut, Indiana, Massachusetts, and Virginia) require a parent to return to work sooner when she gives birth to a "capped" child. For example, in Indiana, a woman typically is exempt from work requirements if she has a child(ren) under twelve *months* old. However, if a woman gives birth *after* becoming a TANF recipient, she is exempt from the work requirement for only twelve *weeks* (State Policy Documentation Project 1999). It should be noted that eighteen of the twenty-three states with family cap policies do not apply these sanctions to children born within ten months of enrollment in TANF or to children born as a result of rape, incest, or domestic violence.

In a national analysis using cross-sectional state-level (fifty states and Washington, DC) data for 1992 to 1996, the "family cap was associated with reductions in non-marital childbearing among women of all races and ages—including a 9 percent decrease among teens and a 12 percent decrease among older women." Changes in rates of abortion were not reported (Horvath and Peters 2000). According to the Center for Law and Social Policy, more than 83,000 children in sixteen states had been born to families under the family cap provision as of February 1999—meaning that these children and their families have to get by on a reduced per capita income (CLASP 1999).

## Immunization Requirements

Seventeen states (Levin-Epstein 1998) require TANF recipients to document that their children's immunizations are up-to-date or face having a portion of their checks docked.[5] A few evaluations were conducted during the waiver period with disparate results. An evaluation of Maryland's program, which reduced the monthly AFDC check by $25 for families who failed to verify immunization status of children under two, appeared to have no impact (Minkovitz et al. 1999). Overall, vaccination rates stayed low, and no significant differences were found among baseline, control, and experimental groups.

In contrast, Georgia's immunization project between 1992 and 1996, which eliminated AFDC benefits for any child under six years whose immunizations were not up-to-date, appeared to result in immunization rates that were higher for the treatment group than for controls (Kerpelman et al. 2000). However, this study has been criticized for assuming that only parental behavior is important and not addressing other relevant factors such as missed opportunities, health care visits, or practice characteristics (Minkovitz and Guyer 2000). Moreover, there is concern that the younger age of children in the treatment group, for whom records review was conducted, may have biased the findings toward inclusion of children with more visits and greater opportunities for vaccination (Minkovitz and Guyer 2000).

Since the passage of welfare reform legislation and the consequent end of the requirement for program evaluation, there have been some assessments of two programs that bear on this issue. In Chicago, from June

1996 to September 1997, women receiving benefits for children under two years of age through the Supplemental Nutrition for Women, Infants, and Children (WIC) program were given only one month's worth of food vouchers (instead of the usual three-month supply) if they did not bring immunization records with them. The immunization rate among affected children increased significantly over a fifteen-month period from 56 percent to 89 percent (Noble 1998). In Delaware's *A Better Chance Program* (a pre-welfare reform demonstration project involving multiple waivers of federal requirements), failure to document immunization was the third most common reason for sanctions, and 1,300 such sanctions were issued in the first one-and-a-half years (Fein and Lee 1999).

### Family Planning

Thirteen states require TANF recipients to attend family-planning counseling sessions or to be given information about family planning (Chavkin et al. 2000). While TANF recipients are eligible for Medicaid, Medicaid enrollment has been declining and lack of health insurance rising among the poor (Bernstein 1998; Mills 2000).

Our analysis of the relationship between state TANF policy choices and insurance status revealed that efforts to divert women from enrolling in TANF were significantly associated with declines in Medicaid and increases in uninsurance (Chavkin et al. 2000). Similarly, although these did not reach statistical significance, family planning and immunization requirements were associated with declines in Medicaid as well as increases in uninsurance. This potentially creates a circular dilemma: low-income women generally require Medicaid in order to obtain family planning care (whether mandated to the first visit or not), and yet failure to comply leads to sanction, loss of income, and may also involve loss of Medicaid. On the other hand, eleven states obtained Section 1115 waivers from the Health Care Financing Administration, the federal agency that oversees Medicaid, to expand Medicaid eligibility for women needing family planning (Henry J. Kaiser Family Foundation 1999b). Seven states extend the expanded eligibility criteria for pregnant women for up to several years postpartum; four states base eligibility solely on income. As of the end of 1999, six additional states had requested such waivers.

Gold and Sonfield (1999) reported in forty-two states, the District of Columbia and two federal jurisdictions that $41 million was spent on family planning through the MCH program. Most of this money was spent on direct patient care services, predominantly contraceptive services and supplies. In addition to this, outreach and public education provisions were increased through MCH funding. The Alan Guttmacher Institute indicated that family planning spending through the MCH program has remained at approximately 6 percent of the total federal grant as the program grows. MCH programs have moved away from a focus on patient care and have moved toward underwriting a range of supportive services that Medicaid covered pre–welfare reform (Gold and Sonfield 1999).

### Illegitimacy Bonus

The illegitimacy bonus provides a bonus of $20 million to states in which the out-of-wedlock birth rates show the greatest decline, without an increase in abortion rates. It derives from the sentiments expressed in the preamble to the PRWORA and was included in the law, although it does not solely pertain to the TANF population.

In 1999 and 2000, $20 million bonuses were awarded to the top five states (shown in Table 6.1), although the great majority of states experienced increases in out-of-wedlock births ranging from 0.4 to 10.0 percent in 1999, and 0.06 to 9.84 percent in 2000 (National Center for Health Statistics 1999; 2000). Most recently, the bonus winners for 2001 were announced (Department of Health and Human Services 2001). Only two states (Alabama and Michigan) and the District of Columbia had declines (albeit miniscule) in their out-of-wedlock birth rates (0.25 percent, 0.009 percent, and 3.98 percent, respectively); each state received an augmented bonus of $25 million. The remaining forty-eight states had increases ranging from 0.725 percent (New York) to 8.4 percent (Vermont).

### Table 6.1
#### Illegitimacy bonus winners: 1999 and 2000[6]

| 1999 | | | 2000 | | 2001 | |
|------|-------|------------------------------------------|-------|------------------------------------------|-------|------------------------------------------|
| Rank | State | % change in out-of-wedlock births | State | % change in out-of-wedlock births | State | %change in out-of-wedlock births |
| 1 | CA | -5.7 | DC | -4.1 | DC | -3.98 |
| 2 | DC | -3.7 | AZ | -1.4 | AL | -0.25 |
| 3 | MI | -3.4 | MI | -1.3 | MI | -0.009 |
| 4 | AL | -2.0 | AL | -0.3 | – | |
| 5 | MA | -1.5 | IL | -0.02 | – | |

The ratio of out-of-wedlock to marital births could change for a variety of reasons that neither reflect the desired behavioral changes nor any policy-related intervention on the part of the state. As Dye and Presser (1999) explain, potential extraneous variables affecting the out-of-wedlock birth ratio include changes in the number of nonmarital births to state residents, changes in the number of all births, or changes in the age structure of the population. Moreover, abortion reporting and assessment of marital status from birth certificates are known to be very imprecise. Forty-five states actually showed an *increase* in their out-of-wedlock birth rates. The abortion statistics were used to ensure that bonus recipients who did not have an increase in abortions were not included with the birth rates.

Donovan (1999) reported on an Alan Guttmacher Institute (AGI) survey in which thirty-four states and the District of Columbia described specific state-level activities aimed at qualifying for the bonus. However, when we surveyed state maternal and child health directors, however, only nineteen out of fifty-two reported such purposeful activities. According to our survey, three of the five states that were awarded the bonus in the first year did not have policies or programs specifically intended to achieve this goal (Romero et al. 2001).

## Abstinence Education

PRWORA allocated $50 million per year for five years in block grants to states for abstinence-only education programs, which must adhere to specific guidelines advocating sexual abstinence outside marriage and delineating harms to the individual, society, and any children born out of wedlock. These programs must be kept separate from any existing programs that involve contraceptive information or services. Two states—California and New Hampshire—did not accept their first-year allocation. In 1997 Congress allocated $6 million for the national evaluation of abstinence-only education programs conducted as part of PRWORA. The national evaluation is being conducted in six sites and seeks to determine the effects of these programs in achieving several key outcomes, including reduced rates of sexual activity, reduced pregnancy and births, and reduced incidence of sexually transmitted diseases.

States have used the money to fund media campaigns and community-based and in-school programs. According to a survey by AGI of 825 public school district superintendents, the majority (51 percent) of school districts that have a policy on sexuality education have "abstinence-plus" policies, whereby they encourage abstinence but also provide information about contraception and sexually transmitted diseases (STDs) and other reproductive health matters (Landry et al. 1999). About one-third of all public school students in grade six or higher attend schools in districts with "abstinence-only" policies that preclude any information about contraception, or require the information to be framed in terms of its ineffectiveness in preventing pregnancy.

An early analysis of abstinence-only evaluations concluded that none of the programs were able to demonstrate an effect on the onset of intercourse, or on teen sexual activity in general (Kirby 1997). The same review of different approaches to sexuality education supports previous conclusions by the World Health Organization that the programs most effective in delaying intercourse and promoting eventual contraceptive use were those that address abstinence along with contraception for pregnancy and STD prevention (Global Program on AIDS 1993). In 1996, Wilcox et al. stated that they were unaware of any "methodologically sound studies that demonstrate the effectiveness of curricula that teach abstinence-only means of preventing teen pregnancy." This finding was recently supported by Kirby (2001) who found that none of the three programs he evaluated showed a positive effect on sexual behavior.

Critics of abstinence-only education have also expressed concern about the implications of not teaching about barrier contraception and protection against STDs in the context of the HIV epidemic, which is increasingly affecting adolescents, especially girls (Henry J. Kaiser Family Foundation 1999a). In fact, Lee and Fleming (2001) found in a twenty-five-state study, examining new HIV diagnoses in 1998 among women aged nineteen to forty-eight, that the number of cases attributable to heterosexual contact more than doubled since 1994, especially for minority women.

### Changing Demographic Trends

As stated clearly in the preamble to PRWORA, and again in specific provisions, the policies are intended to reduce out-of-wedlock and teen childbearing. By definition, they are directed primarily at the population likely to be TANF eligible, although the illegitimacy and abstinence education policies are more diffusely directed toward the population at large. To better understand the possible motivations behind formulation of such policy objectives, as well as to anticipate their likely efficacy, it is useful to review demographic patterns over the last several decades in the United States and comparable highly developed countries.

There are several dramatic demographic developments that took place over the last several decades (referred to as the second demographic transition): a decline in birth rates overall, and to teens; later age at first childbirth; a decrease in marriage together with an increase in divorce; and a concomitant rise in out-of-wedlock childbearing (Bachrach 1998).

While it is true that these patterns vary somewhat across socioeconomic status and racial/ethnic groupings, it is also true that they pertain to all. To wit, in the United States, while the rate of out-of-wedlock births is higher among poor and black women, the rate of out-of-wedlock deliveries has increased dramatically among white women — and this latter group contributes the greatest absolute number (Bachrach 1998; Ventura and Bachrach 2000). Similarly, as Table 6.2 and Figure 6.1 show, poor black and Hispanic women have higher teen birth rates than do white teens; but the rate of teen births to black women has also declined more steeply than any other group, falling 21 percent between 1991 and 1996 (Annie E. Casey Foundation 1999), and another 7 percent through 1998 (Ventura and Bachrach 2000).

**Table 6.2**
**Births to Unmarried Women, by Race**

| Year | Black Women | White Women |
|---|---|---|
| Rate of births per 1,000 unmarried women[8] | | |
| 1970 | 96.0 | 14.0 |
| 1993 | 84.09 (-13%) | 36.0 (+157%) |
| Number of births to unmarried women[9] | | |
| 1970 | 215,100 | 175,100 |
| 1993 | 452,476 | 742,129 |

**Figure 6.1**
**Teen Birth Rates: United States 1960–1995[10]**

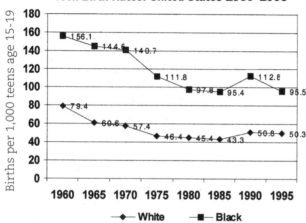

Much of the rise in divorce, deferred childbearing, and out-of-wedlock births has been attributed to women's participation in the paid labor force. In a 2001 North American Agreement on Labor Cooperation analysis of the increase in women's employment in North America, lower fertility, higher education, and need to increase family income were listed among the contributing factors (NAALC 2001).Whatever the complicated socioeconomic causes may be, these are widespread persistent developments affecting all Western industrialized countries. As Table 6.3 shows, out-of-wedlock births rose during the last two decades in the United Kingdom, Germany, and Italy, although Italy's rate remains very low (Chesnais 1996). In fact, since 1990, the United States' out-of-wedlock birth rate practically mirrors that of the United Kingdom, and data for 1998 puts the United States between Ireland, Canada, Finland, and the United Kingdom (Ventura and Bachrach 2000). The Asian industrialized countries have yet to fully experience this change.

**Table 6.3**

**Live births outside marriage as a percent of all births, 1960–1995[11]**

| Year | Italy | Germany | U.K. | Sweden | E.U. | U.S. |
|------|-------|---------|------|--------|------|------|
| 1960 | 2.4 | 7.6 | 5.2 | 11.3 | 5.1 | 5.3 |
| 1970 | 2.2 | 7.2 | 8.0 | 18.4 | 5.6 | 10.7 |
| 1980 | 4.3 | 11.9 | 11.5 | 39.7 | 9.6 | 18.4 |
| 1985 | 5.4 | 16.2 | 18.9 | 46.4 | 14.9 | 22.0 |
| 1990 | 6.5 | 15.3 | 27.9 | 47.0 | 19.6 | 28.0 |
| 1995 | 7.7 | 15.4 | 33.9 | 52.9 | 23.0 | 32.0 |

The profile of formerly Soviet-bloc countries in Eastern Europe had been distinct and is demonstrating rapid shifts in the post-Soviet era. While female labor force participation was high during the Soviet era, so were marriage rates and early childbearing and divorce rates. Since the transition, fertility and marriage rates have plummeted, and out-of-wedlock births now comprise a larger share of the total (The Monee Project 1999).

Although the U.S. profile is similar to that of Western European industrialized nations, some features are exaggerated. The teen pregnancy and birth rates here have been much higher and are currently almost double those of the United Kingdom, despite the fact that levels of teen sexual activity are similar. The high frequency in teen pregnancy and births in the United States has been variously attributed to less access to contraception and to more "religiosity," which in turn constricts education and comfort with sex (Jones et al. 1985).

While these trends have generally prevailed in the last few decades, there was a noticeable blip upward in teen births in the United States in the late 1980s and early 1990s, during the period of economic recession. The teen birth rate has since resumed the previous downward trend, declining each year since 1991 (CDC 2001). It seems highly plausible, however, that this isolated period of increased teen births was taken out of context and used to justify the policies under discussion here. Lack of familiarity with these broad demographic patterns led politicians to form incorrect diagnoses of problems and, consequently, to develop inappropriate solutions.

We assert the critical importance of accurately defining the problem and not mistaking symptoms for causes. For example, what is the problem with out-of-wedlock childbearing? The problem could be a lack of paternal affection, caretaking, and monetary support, which causes hardship for both the child and mother. The logical solution is not necessarily wedlock, as all of these deficits far too often characterize married fathers, and certainly fathers following divorce. The Scandinavian countries tackle this concern very differently by trying to create a series of incentives and infrastructural changes to encourage and sustain paternal participation in childrearing. For example, in addition to other benefits, every couple is allotted 450 days paid parental leave and 30 days of that leave must be taken by the father or is dissolved (Work Life Research Centre 2001).

Similarly, the problem with teen pregnancy (excluding pregnancy and childbearing by teens less than sixteen years old) can be reformulated. The problems accrue to these young women who become mothers and forego completion of their own education and employment opportunities, as well as resources to rear their children. In addition, a large body of evidence indicates that marriages of very young people (i.e., teenagers) are much less stable and successful on average than are first marriages of persons in their twenties and older (Whitehead and Popenoe 2001). An alternative governmental response could be to concentrate on the provision of high school, college, job training, high-quality day care, as well as familiarity and access to contraception and abortion. As Kristin Luker (1996) so eloquently states, "Teen pregnancy is a result, not a cause, of poverty."

### Family and Population Policy

Many societies have policies to achieve desired population levels and certain types of family formation. These have generally been designed to affect families with children (i.e., the elderly retain status as individuals rather than family members). The premise is often that a society needs a specified number of healthy and educated children in order to maintain a productive workforce and standard of living. These policies, therefore, sometimes address the family as an institution, its composition, and the roles of its members, as well as the country's overall health, education, social benefits, labor force participation, and population size.

These policies range from those explicitly designed to curb population growth, such as in India and China, to that of explicitly pro-natalist France to Sweden's efforts to promote gender equity in both the workplace and the home. These countries have employed mixtures of coercive measures, disincentives, and rewards, yet many have not achieved their goals. India's cluster of penalties and incentives (including the notorious vasectomy camps) of the mid-1970s not only led to the downfall of the Gandhi government, but also failed to reduce fertility (Gwatkin 1979).

China's one-child policy, on the other hand, has been associated with curtailment of population growth, as well as of individual choice. France's fertility rate continues to decline, despite its generous paid maternity[12] and parental leave policies (Kamerman 2000). Sweden is distinguished not only by its successful efforts for increasing fertility (highest in Western Europe), but by an ideology that seeks to promote gender equity (Chesnais 1996). This translates into incentives to encourage both men and women to work and care for children, and are well-received by Swedish families.

Singapore's policy is two-pronged—designed to encourage fertility among the more affluent, educated Chinese portion of the population and to reduce the fertility of the poorer Malay and Indian subgroups (Quah 1998).

Though the United States has no explicit family or social policy aimed at addressing population issues, provisions in the welfare-reform law clearly are aimed at altering certain fertility and family patterns. These provisions invite comparison with those of Singapore, in that different policy components are aimed at specific population subgroups. The encouragement of marriage and efforts to reduce out-of-wedlock childbearing is intended for the population as a whole; however, there are no mechanisms, other than rhetorical ones, that might affect the majority of the population. Only those eligible for TANF are exposed to a host of financial penalties if they defy these policy goals.

There are reasons, other than the obvious ethical ones, to be concerned about population-control policies directed toward one segment of the population. As evidenced by the program evaluation data reviewed here, as well as the long-term demographic trends, such policies are not rational. The targeted population subgroup is neither solely responsible for the social changes alarming certain politicians, nor likely to demonstrate change in response to these policies. Though many studies have attempted to analyze whether the welfare system increases nonmarital childbearing, the results of research are inconsistent. Even in studies that found a relationship between welfare and out-of-wedlock births, the effects were modest (Moffit 1995). However, such targeted efforts to reduce poor women's fertility are likely to feed into the smoldering suspicion, distrust, and racial tension prevailing in America.

There is, moreover, an American history of eugenic efforts focused on poor, minority, and vulnerable populations (Roberts 1997). At the turn of the century, many states adopted laws that permitted involuntary sterilization of the mentally retarded, as well as individuals considered to possess inheritable, undesirable traits. In 1927 the Supreme Court affirmed these laws in *Buck v. Bell*, with Justice Oliver Wendell Holmes writing, "three generations of imbeciles are enough" (Isaacs 1981).

In addition to laws that permit involuntary sterilization, the use of coercion to get individuals, particularly poor black and Hispanic women, to agree to sterilization has been well documented (Roberts 1997). Such coercive practices were finally acknowledged in 1973 as a result of the successful litigation of the Relf sisters, who at ages twelve and fourteen, were sterilized through a federally funded family-planning program allegedly without their consent, or that of their parents (Isaacs 1981).

In 1994, 179 countries, including the United States, signed the Programme of Action at the International Conference on Population and Development, in Cairo, Egypt. The document, which outlines principles and objectives for achieving sustainable population development by meeting individual needs, states that reproductive rights:

...rests on the recognition of the basic right of all couples and individuals to decide freely and responsibly the number, spacing and timing of their children and to have the information and means to do so, and the right to the enjoyment of the highest attainable standard of sexual and reproductive health. It also includes their right to make decisions concerning reproduction free of discrimination, coercion and violence....

Reproductive choice, therefore, encompasses the right to have children as well as the right not to. The U.S. welfare reform policies contradict the Cairo consensus by discouraging both abortion and carrying a pregnancy to term — circumscribing reproductive choice in both directions.

The real issue is that too many U.S. women and children live in poverty. The policies outlined here have not redressed the grave income inequalities that typify the United States. Indeed, the number and percentage of children living in severe poverty has grown. Rather than misdirect policies and resources toward constricting individuals' sexual and reproductive choices, we could concentrate on bolstering education and employment opportunities. The European models could serve as guides as they recognize and support the contemporary realities of work and childbearing in the lives of men and women.

### Acknowledgments

We would like to acknowledge the generous support of the following organizations, which has made possible this research: Ford Foundation, General Service Foundation, Moriah Fund, and Open Society Institute. We are grateful to Julia Choe for her assistance with research and manuscript preparation, and to Tammy Draut, MPA, for her work on an earlier version of this paper.

### References

Annie E. Casey Foundation. 1999. *Teen Childbearing in America's Largest Cities*. Report.

Bachrach, C.A. 1998. "Changing Circumstances of Marriage and Fertility." Pp. 9– 32 in *Welfare, the Family and Reproductive Behavior: Research Perspectives*. R.E. Moffitt, ed. Washington, DC: National Academy Press.

Bernstein, N. 1998. "Medicaid Rolls Have Declined in Last 3 Years: Officials Cite Economy and Welfare Reform." *New York Times* (August 17).

Camasso M.J., C. Harvey, R. Jagannathan, and M. Killingsworth. 1998. *A Final Report on the Impact of New Jersey's Family Development Program: Results from a Pre-Post Analysis of AFDC*

*Case Heads from 1990–1996.* Rutgers School of Social Work and Center for Urban Policy Research.

Center for Disease Control and Prevention. 2001. "New CDC Report Shows Teen Birth Rate Hits Record Low: US Births Top 4 Million in 2000." Washington, DC: National Center for Health Statistics, U.S. Department of Health and Human Services.

Center for Law and Social Policy. 1999. "Caps On Kids: Family Cap in the New Welfare Era." Washington, DC: Center for Law and Social Policy. Accessed online (10/01): http://www.clasp.org/pubs/caps_on_kids.htm.

Chavkin, Wendy, Diana Romero, and Paul Wise. 2000. "State Welfare Reform Policies and Declines in Health Insurance." *American Journal of Public Health* 90 (6):900-907.

Chesnais, Jean-Claude. 1996. "Fertility, Family, and Social Policy in Contemporary Western Europe." *Population and Development Review* 22 (December): 729–739.

Donovan, P. 1999. "The 'Illegitimacy Bonus' and State Efforts to Reduce Out-of-Wedlock Births." *Family Planning Perspectives* 31 (2): 94–97.

Dye, J.L., and Harriet B. Presser. 1999. "The State Bonus to Reward a Decrease in "'Illegitimacy': Flawed Methods and Questionable Effects." *Family Planning Perspectives* 31 (3): 142–147.

Family Health International. 1999. *A Framework for the Analysis of Family Planning on Women's Work and Income.* Research Triangle Park, NC No. WP97-01.

Fein, D.J., and Wang S. Lee. 1999. "Executive Summary." In *The ABC Evaluation: Carrying and Using the Stick: Financial Sanctions in Delaware's A Better Chance Program.* Cambridge, MA: Abt Associates Inc. for Delaware Health and Social Services.

Global Program on Aids. 1993. *Effects of Sex Education on Young People's Sexual Behavior.* Geneva: World Health Organization.

Gold, Rachel Benson, and Adam Sonfield. 1999. "Family Planning Funding Through Four Federal-State Programs, FY 1997." *Family Planning Perspectives* 31 (4): 176-181.

Gwatkin, D. 1979. "Political Will and Family Planning: The Implications of India's Emergency Experience." *Population and Development Review* 5 (1): 29–59.

Horvath-Rose, Ann, and H. Elizabeth Peters. 2000. *Welfare Waivers and Non-Marital Childbearing.* Working Paper 128. Joint Center for Poverty Research, Cornell University.

Isaacs, S. L. 1981. *Population Law and Policy, Source Materials and Issues.* New York: Human Sciences Press, Inc.

The Henry J. Kaiser Family Foundation.1999a. "The HIV/AIDS Epidemic in the U.S." Factsheet.

———. 1999b. "State Policies on Access to Gynecological Care and Contraception." Factsheet.

Jones, E. Forrest, Jacqueline Darroch, Noreen Goldman, Stanley Henshaw, Richard Lincoln, Jeanniem Rosoff, Charles Westoff, and Deirdre Wulf. 1985. "Teenage Pregnancy in

Developed Countries: Determinants and Policy Implications." *Family Planning Perspectives* (March/April): 53–62.

Kamerman, S.B. 2000. "From Maternity to Parenting Policies: Women's Health, Employment, and Child and Family Well-Being." *Journal of the American Women's Association* 55 (2): 96–99.

Kerpelman, L., D.B. Connell, and W.J. Gunn. 2000. "Effect of a Monetary Sanction on Immunization Rates of Recipients of Aid to Families with Dependent Children." *Journal of the American Medical Association* 284: 53–59.

Kirby, Douglas. 1997. *No Easy Answers: Research Findings on Programs to Reduce Teen Pregnancy*. Report by the National Campaign to Prevent Teen Pregnancy, Washington, DC.

———. 2001. *Emerging Answers: Research Findings on Programs to Reduce Teen Pregnancy*. Report by the National Campaign to Prevent Teen Pregnancy. Washington, DC.

Landry, D., L. Kaeser, and C. Richards. 1999. "Abstinence Promotion and the Provision of Information about Contraception in Public School District Sexuality Education Policies." *Family Planning Perspectives* 31 (6): 280–286.

Lee, Lisa M., and Patricia L. Fleming. 2001. "Trends in Human Immunodeficiency Virus Diagnosis Among Women in the United States, 1994-1998." *Journal of the American Medical Women's Association* 56 (3): 94-99.

Levin-Epstein, Jodie. 1998. *The IRA: Individual Responsibility Agreements and TANF Family Life Obligations*. Washington, DC: Center for Law and Social Policy.

———. 1999. *Open Questions: New Jersey's Family Cap Evaluation*. Center for Law and Social Policy. Washington DC.

Luker, Kristin. 1996. *Dubious Conceptions: The Politics of Teen Pregnancy*. Cambridge, MA: Harvard University Press.

Maynard R., E. Boehnen, T. Corbett, G. Sandefur, and J. Mosley. 1998. "Changing Family Formation Behavior through Welfare Reform." Pp. 134–176 in *Welfare, the Family and Reproductive Behavior: Research Perspectives*, ed. R. Moffitt. Washington DC: National Academy Press.

Mills, R.J. 2000. "Health Insurance Coverage." Pp. 60–211 in *Current Population Reports*. U.S. Census Bureau.

Minkovitz, C., and Bernard Guyer. 2000. "Letter to the Editor." *Journal of the American Medical Association* 284 (16): 2056.

Minkovitz, C., E. Holt, N. Hughart, W. Hon, L. Thomas, E. Dini, and Bernard Guyer. 1999. "The Effect of Parental Monetary Sanctions on the Vaccination Status of Young Children." *Pediatric Adolescent Medicine* 153: 1242–1247.

Moffit, R.A. 1995. "Report to Congress on Out-of-Wedlock Childbearing." In *The Effect of the Welfare System on Nonmarital Childbearing*. Hyattsville, MD: U.S. Department of Health and Human Services, Public Health Service, Centers for Disease Control and Prevention, National Center for Health Statistics.

The Monee Project. 1999. "Women, Families and Policies." *Women in Transition*, UNICEF. Report (No. 6): 41–57.

National Center for Health Statistics. 2001. "Data for 1996 Welfare Reform Law Bonus to Reward Declines in Nonmarital Births: Change in Nonmarital Birth Ratios by State, 1996-97 to 1998-99. State Ranking Table." Hyattsville, MD: U.S. Department of Health and Human Services, Center for Disease Control. Accessed online (12/01): http://www.cdc.gov/nchs/about/otheract/welfare/owbonus01f.pdf.

———. 2000. *State Ranking, Department of Health and Human Services, Administration for Children and Families: 2000*.

———. 1999. *State Ranking, Department of Health and Human Services, Administration for Children and Families: 1999*.

Noble, H.B. 1998. "Incentive Program Raises Immunization Rates." *New York Times* (Oct. 7): 14.

North American Agreement on Labor Cooperation. Accessed November 2001. *The Employment Of Women In North America: The Female Labor Force and Female Employment in North America*. Washington, DC: North American Agreement on Labor Cooperation. Accessed online: http://www.naacl.org/english/publications/ewna_part1.htm.

Quah, S.R. 1998. *Family in Singapore: Sociological Perspectives*. Singapore: Times Academic Press.

Roberts, D.E. 1997. *Killing the Black Body: Race, Reproduction, and the Meaning of Liberty*. New York: Pantheon Books.

Stark S., and Jodie Levin-Epstein. 1999. *Excluded Children: Family Cap in a New Era*. Washington, DC: Center for Law and Social Policy.

State Policy Documentation Project. 1999. *Family Cap: Other Provisions*. Report by the Center for Law and Social Policy at the Center on Budget and Policy Priorities. Available online: www.spdp.org/famcap/famcapother.htm.

Turturro, C., B. Benda, and H. Turney. 1997. *Arkansas Welfare Waiver Demonstration Project: Final Report (7/94–6/97)*. Little Rock: University of Arkansas, School of Social Work.

U.S. Department of Health and Human Services. 2001. "HHS Awards $75 Million in Bonuses to States Achieving Largest Reductions in Out-of Wedlock Births." HHS News September 21. Accessed online (12/01): http://www.hhs.gov/news/press/2001pres/20010921.html.

Urban Institute. 1997. *Trends In The Well-Being of America's Children & Youth*. Report by Office of the Assistant Secretary for Planning and Evaluation, Department of Health and Human Services. Washington, DC.

Ventura, S., and Christine Bachrach. 2000. *Nonmarital Childbearing in the United States, 1940–99*. National Vital Statistics Reports, Volume 48, No. 16.

Whitehead, B.D, and D. Popenoe. 2001. "Who Wants To Marry A Soul Mate? New Survey Findings on Young Adults' Attitudes about Love and Marriage." *The State of Our Unions: The Social Health of Marriage in America, 2001*. Piscataway, NJ: National Marriage Project.

Wilcox, B.L., S.P. Limber, H. O'Bierne, and C.L. Bartels. 1996. *Federally Funded Adolescent Abstinence Promotion: An Evaluation of Evaluations*. Paper presented at the Biennial Meeting of the Society for Research on Adolescence, Boston.

Work Life Research Centre. 2001. "Childcare and Family Statistics: Sweden." Accessed online (October 12): http://www.workliferesearch.org/fw_stats_sw.asp.

## Notes

[1] This paper is a modification of a presentation given at a conference at the University of Oregon. An earlier version of this paper was published in the *Georgetown Journal on Poverty Law and Policy*, Summer 2000.

[2] Wendy Chavkin, MD, MPH, is professor of clinical public health at the Mailman School of Public Health and of Obstetrics & Gynecology at the College of Physicians & Surgeons, both at Columbia University. She is the co-principal investigator of the Finding Common Ground Project at the Mailman School, which investigates maternal and child health conflicts associated with various health policies. Dr. Chavkin's research has focused on policies related to pregnancy, drug abuse, and HIV; abortion; and maternal and reproductive health.

[3] Diana Romero, MA, MPhil, is project director for the Finding Common Ground Project at the Mailman School of Public Health at Columbia University. Most recently, the project has focused on the impact of welfare reform policies on women's and children's health. Ms. Romero is a doctoral candidate in sociomedical sciences at Columbia University, with an emphasis on women's and reproductive health issues, particularly among Hispanic and African-American populations.

[4] Co-principal investigator of the Finding Common Ground Project, Paul Wise, MD, MPH, is based in the Department of Pediatrics, Boston University School of Medicine, the academic link for child health at Boston Medical Center. At BMC, he is director of social and health policy research and professor of pediatrics.

[5] Penalty structures for noncompliance vary by state and may include a flat penalty or a progressive penalty for each subsequent month of noncompliance.

[6] Figures for 1999 represent the percent change in out-of-wedlock births from 1994–1995 to 1996–1997; figures for 2000 represent the percent change from 1995–1996 to 1997–1998; figures for 2001 represent the percent change from 1996–1997 to 1998–1999. Data from National Center for Health Statistics. State Rankings, 1999, 2000, and 2001.

[7] Birth statistics on race prior to 1980 are based on the race of the child; after 1980 statistics based on race of the mother.

[8] Figures from *Welfare, the Family and Reproductive Health*, National Academy Press, 1998.

[9] Figures from *Report to Congress on Out-of-Wedlock Childbearing*, U.S. Department of Health and Human Services, September 1995.

[10] Data from *Trends in the Well-Being of America's Children and Youth*, 1997 edition, Office of the Assistant Secretary for Planning and Evaluation, Department of Health and Human Services.

[11] Data for all but United States, Chesnais (1996); Data for the United States, US Dept. of Health and Human Services (1997).

[12] 100 percent of wage for sixteen weeks.

## PART III

# Work and Wages

Jared Bernstein

Lisa Morris

Laura Connolly

Peggy Kahn

Valerie Polakow

# Welfare Reform and the Low-Wage Labor Market

## *Jared Bernstein*[1]

The low-wage labor market is the laboratory where the Welfare-to-Work experiment is taking place. In this chapter I will attempt to sum up what I think we've learned about the impact of welfare reform on the lives of poor, mother-only families, with primary focus on their employment and earnings. How many welfare leavers have found work and what are they likely to earn? What kinds of labor market opportunities face other low-wage workers who may not have made it on the welfare rolls? Another key question is job mobility—the extent to which low-wage workers are either stuck in low-wage jobs or just at the bottom of an escalator.

I have some caveats. Despite much research, there are two good reasons why our knowledge of the impacts of welfare reform is limited. First, though the law is fully phased in, this is still a policy in transition. In particular, we've yet to see the full impact of time limits. Nor have we seen the impact of a recession. Unfortunately, as of this writing, we may learn about these two effects simultaneously. Second, by far the best way to learn about the impact of a new policy or program is to change one aspect of the program for one group of participants and see how their situation changes relative to a control group that is similar to the program's participants in every way except that they are unaffected by the policy change. But the changes wrought by welfare reform are so highly devolved to the state and even county levels, it is challenging, to say the least, to untangle their effects.

That said, many smart and devoted people have spent a lot of time trying to advance our understanding. Here are some impressions about what they've found.

### Things We Know So Far About Welfare Reform

Caseloads have fallen.

Between 1994 and 2001, welfare caseloads fell by about half. As far as I know, that is the fastest decline in caseloads in the history of the program, which should tell us something. The question is, of course, what is it telling us? What does this mean in terms of the wellbeing of former recipients and their families?

We know that this precipitous decline is not an adequate benchmark for the success of reform. Although the law does not legislate lower poverty rates as a policy goal, the framers of the policy were actually quite explicit about this; the goal was to lift the welfare poor out of poverty, not just to lower the rolls.

So there are two interesting questions about this trend in caseloads. First, what factors are most responsible? What portion of the decline can be explained by the new rules, the labor market, increased hassle factors, and whatever else drives caseloads? There is some debate on this point, summarized in the first section of a new volume edited by Danziger (1999). It is fairly straightforward to measure the strength of the economy, but the hard part is in 1) measuring sanctions, waivers, and a possible increase in the hassle factor by caseload administrators under pressure to keep caseloads down; and 2) untangling their effects from those of the improved labor market. My sense (based on my judgement of the literature in the Danziger volume) is that the increase in the demand for low-wage labor by itself probably explains about 80% of the decline in caseloads. The rest probably has something to do with reform.

Second, what's happened to those who've left the rolls? That takes me to the next thing we know, namely:

Many, certainly more than half, are working.

Now, as work by the Institute for Women's Policy Research (1995) has shown, as many as three-quarters had some connection to the labor market before welfare reform; in some cases, the labor force attachment — the extent to which recipients were either working or seeking work — was quite marginal, and many cycled in and out of the labor market. But, as shown in Figure 7.1, there is no question that the employment rates of poor single moms are higher than ever. Of course, these rates tell you nothing about how much they are working (i.e., how many hours) or how much, on average, they are earning. But this fact is certainly important, and, much more than falling caseloads, can be pointed to as a sign of success by welfare reformers.

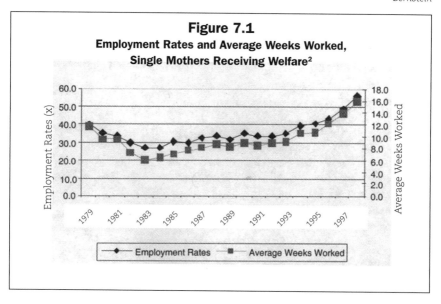

**Figure 7.1**
**Employment Rates and Average Weeks Worked,**
**Single Mothers Receiving Welfare[2]**

Let us take a moment to consider this question: Should we take the evidence in Figure 7.1 as a sign of success? If we are simply turning the welfare poor into the working poor, then the answer is "no." But it's a little more complicated.

During the debate over reform, the proponents of the new policy cited evidence, mostly from polls, that welfare — AFDC — was not only unpopular with the electorate, it was just as disliked by the recipients of welfare benefits themselves, who wanted very much to work their way out of poverty. These poll results are not surprising. I used to be a social worker in New York City, and at one time my beat was among the poor in East Harlem. My clients did not like the welfare system. I suspect that these polls were essentially answering the question, "Would you rather be permanently stuck in abject poverty or earn your way out of it?"

Anyway, the fact that more former welfare recipients are working more hours in the paid labor market seems to me to be a good thing. Ours is a society that values work more than ever, and looks suspiciously upon able-bodied nonworkers. Of course, there are many good counter arguments: poor single moms have always worked both inside and outside the home. But it's very difficult for such persons not to internalize the negative messages about so-called welfare dependence. Basically, to work is to be in the mainstream in our society, and I would argue that it's harder than ever existing outside that mainstream in today's America. In such a social/political environment, assuming their children are reliably cared for (I'll return to this below), people may feel better about themselves if they are earning their paycheck.

**117**

But there's work and there's work. How are society's goals advanced by forcing people to move from the welfare rolls into dead-end jobs that, given the loss of welfare benefits, leave them no better off on net? So, of course, the key question is: how are folks faring in the low-wage labor market?

Due to the increased demand for low-wage work, the reform-induced increased supply of low-wage labor has not led to lower wages.

When Welfare-to-Work was first introduced, a number of us made the uncontroversial prediction that unless labor demand expanded significantly, the increased supply of low-wage workers in the low end of the labor market threatened to lead to further deterioration of wages in a sector where wages had been falling for years. This possibility threatened to lower the earnings of both those already in the low-wage sector and those leaving the welfare rolls for work.

Instead, as Figure 7.2 shows, the inflation-adjusted wages of low-wage female workers have been rising lately. There are two reasons. The most important is that the demand for low-wage workers has increased by more than enough to offset the reform-induced increase in supply shown in the earlier figure. Though the overall unemployment rate fell by about two percentage points between 1994 and 1999 (from 6.1 percent to 4.2 percent), that of female workers with low-earning characteristics, such as young, African-American women with a high-school diploma, has fallen much further, by about eight percentage points, from 24.3 percent to 16.4 percent. Note, however, that though the trends have been especially favorable to low-wage workers, the level of their unemployment rate remained about four times that of the overall rate.

The other reason is the $0.90 increase in the minimum wage, which was phased in over the 1996–97 period. Though the forces who opposed

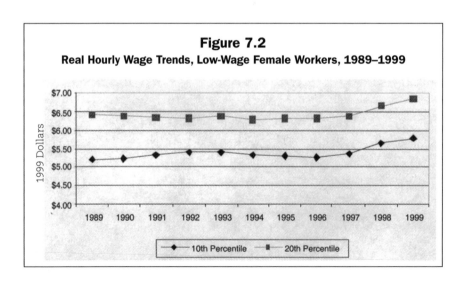

**Figure 7.2**
**Real Hourly Wage Trends, Low-Wage Female Workers, 1989–1999**

118

that increase argued that it would hurt the employment and earnings prospects of low-wage workers by pricing them out of the low-wage labor market, the figures and statistics reported thus far belie that claim.

Clearly, demand for low-wage work has increased significantly. But the more important question at hand is what does this increase in demand mean for those leaving welfare for work? What do we know about the earnings and hours of work by former recipients?

The average earnings and hours worked by former recipients are unlikely to be high enough to lift them out of poverty. We would expect former welfare recipients to be earning wages in the range shown in Figure 7.2, i.e., in the bottom 20 percent, and this appears to be the case. Loprest's recent study (1999) found that former recipients median hourly wage was $6.61 in 1997. Sharon Parrot's (1998) survey of various studies found that hourly wages ranged from $6 to $8.

Though much has been made of this important finding, it is perhaps not very elucidating to point out that low-wage workers make low wages. It is, however, useful to put the level of these low wages in a historical context. Even with recent growth rates, earnings in the low-wage labor market are no higher than they were in earlier periods. The female tenth-percentile wage remains 10 percent below its 1979 level in real terms, and the twentieth-percentile wage finally caught up to that earlier level last year.

Thus, though low wages have not progressed very far in a historical sense, they have gone up in real terms. At the same time, employment opportunities for low-wage workers expanded considerably. In this sense, the outcome of Welfare-to-Work so far has been better than many predicted, myself included.

That said, even with full-time work, these wage levels won't get a mother with two children very far past the poverty line. Though both of the above studies record substantial work effort, full-time, full-year work schedules do not appear to be the norm among former recipients (yet no less so than among most low-wage workers). About 70 percent of former recipients worked full-time weekly schedules in Loprest's study, and Parrot's review revealed similar findings. However, it is well known that rates of job tenure are lower and job turnover is higher in the low-wage sector, due in part to the less secure nature of jobs there. Thus, while I have seen no estimates of annual hours of work among former recipients, it is unlikely that they are in the 2,000-hours range.

So are most former recipients better off? Given the caveats I began with, no one knows — one can find anecdotal examples from both sides. There are good reasons, however, to be skeptical. Wendell Primus at the Center for Budget and Policy Priorities developed some convincing evidence that, as of 1998, the real income of the poorest single mother families, those in the bottom fifth of the income scale, was 4 percent lower than it had been in 1995, although their annual earnings were up significantly. For those in the second fifth, income went up only 3 percent between 1995 and 1998. For many of these families, the loss in welfare benefits was not outweighed by a gain in earnings. Primus and others have also pointed out that the receipt of noncash benefits, such as Food Stamps and Medicaid, have fallen faster than would be predicted given the income changes of the poor, suggesting that many are not getting benefits to which they are still entitled.

Even if a former welfare recipient is earning enough to make up for the loss of benefits, she now has various new expenses associated with work outside the home, of which childcare is the most significant. In a recent study of how much income a working single-parent family (with two children) needs to get by, we found that reliable, center-based childcare comprised the largest share of the budget after housing (Bernstein et al. 2000). While costs vary by location, decent childcare can cost more than $5,000 annually.

Of course, many low-wage workers are not purchasing this level of quality childcare, but this is probably one expenditure on which they should not have to skimp. Transportation costs are also significant. So even if her gross income is the same, her net disposable income is lower, and she's much busier. A welfare reformer would argue — correctly, in my view—that all this has to be weighed against the intangible psychological benefits of working. But my contention is that working poverty is no better —and in some ways it's worse (less family time, more stress, nervousness about substandard childcare)—than welfare poverty. So, my answer to the question posed a few paragraphs back (are most former recipients better off?) is: I doubt it.

But what does the future hold? Remember, this is a program in transition, and no one knows what the economic conditions of former welfare recipients will look like ten years hence. The best hope for wage and income mobility is that the low-wage workers of today are not stuck in deadend jobs but simply are on the bottom steps of an upward escalator. Unfortunately, this hope is not well supported by the mobility literature.

Although the evidence is sparse, there does not appear to be much upward mobility out of the low-wage labor market. Back in the 1970s, a number of insightful researchers described the labor market as "segmented." This work, associated with Harrison and Sum (1979), Gordon (1972), and others, and continued today by Howell (1997) argues that jobs are "organized into two institutionally and technologically disparate segments, with the property that labor mobility tends to be greater within than between segments" (Harrison and Sum 1979). Core jobs, those in the primary segment, pay higher wages and are more likely to provide fringe benefits, such as health insurance and paid vacations. Jobs in this segment also have ladders upward (often within the firm, called "internal labor

**120**

markets"), whereby workers can improve their earnings and living standards over time.

Conversely, jobs in the secondary segment, they claimed, tend to lack upward mobility. They pay lower wages, offer fewer benefits, tend to be non-union, and generally offer worse working conditions than primary-sector jobs. They are also less stable than core jobs, leading to higher levels of job turnover and churning in this sector. Race and gender–based discrimination are more common here than in the primary segment.

Recent examinations of the mobility of low-wage workers suggest that what the segmented labor market theorists described still exists. A recent study of low-wage labor markets by the US Department of Health and Human Services (1999, ix) concludes:

> Low-wage workers leaving welfare for work in the wake of welfare reform are likely to experience little wage growth. Although some studies suggest wage growth of about 4.5% over a year (which translates into only about $400 per year for a low-wage worker), other studies yield lower estimates. Even these may be on the high side, since they are based mainly on the experience of women who have left welfare voluntarily and found jobs.

Gottschalk's paper in that volume reviews the Welfare-to-Work experiments undertaken by various states over the 1980s. These programs looked something like the type of Welfare-to-Work efforts states are engaging in today; some focused exclusively on job search and placement; others offered more skills enhancements. All told, the impact of these programs was to lift participants earnings relative to those of nonpartici-pants. But Gottschalk points out that the annual gains were small in the sense that they were "not large enough to lead to self-sufficiency." Also the income gains generally came from working more hours, not from higher wages. And, importantly from the perspective of labor-market mobility, the benefits of these programs faded after about five years, thus failing to lead to a "lasting increase in wages or hours."

Another review of the mobility research by Newman (1999) reports that while there is evidence of some mobility, "there does seem to be agreement on the larger point at hand: low-wage jobs do not seem to be a stepping stone to better paying jobs." She cites numerous studies that track the wages progress of low-wage workers over time. If the segmenta-tion theory still holds, there should be empirical evidence that a signifi-cant share of these workers saw little wage growth over time. In fact, research of longitudinal data cited by Newman provides such evidence. Burtless (1995), for example, finds little wage growth—about 1 percent per year over the 1980s among women who received welfare in 1979 but who worked over the next ten years.

There are two important messages that come out of this mobility literature. First, low-wage workers can expect some measure of wage growth due to experience, but for those who stay in the secondary segment, these gains are unlikely to enable them to meet their basic needs. Second, much of the evidence on the earnings mobilityof low-wage workers should be considered an upper bound when we are trying to forecast the experience awaiting those leaving the welfare rolls. Remember, welfare recipients who found jobs before welfare reform (like those just mentioned in the Burtless study) did not face the same pressures to do so as they would today. In this regard, they may well represent those with a higher earnings capacity than others who did not leave the welfare rolls. In the current context, this means that many of those who already left welfare for the labor-market are probably generating higher levels of labor market success than we can reasonably expect from those still on the rolls.

### Thus, at this point, I think it is fair to conclude that...

The jobs available to most former welfare recipients are unlikely to enable such families to meet their basic needs, much less invest in raising their earnings capacity. Thus, a set of work supports in the form of subsidies will be necessary complement to welfare reform.

A stacked bars in Figure 7.3 show the situation for a low-wage worker earning $7 per hour. In each case, she pays payroll taxes and receives Food Stamps, which I take as equivalent to cash, and the EITC. Note that in the first bar, which assumes full-time, full-year work, her earnings and these benefits lift her well above the poverty line for a family of three with one parent and two children. But as noted earlier, there are two unrealistic assumptions in this picture. First, she is unlikely to work full-time, and if she does her children probably will need some childcare, depending on their ages. As noted above, this could account for as much as 20 percent of her income.

The second bar assumes three-quarter-time work, which according to my calculations of the March CPS data is close to the annual hours worked by single moms with low wages. These families also end up a few thousand dollars above the poverty line, thanks to the EITC and Food Stamps. The final bar shows the outcome for a single mom working half-year (1,040 hours). Here, even with the supplements, her income falls below the poverty line. Note, however, that under this scenario she doesn't need full-time childcare.

At any rate, the point, which should not be too much of a stretch for anyone who has tried to raise children, is that you can't get very far with a $7 per hour job. You can, thanks to the supplements included above, get up to and even above the poverty line. But the poverty line provides much too low a benchmark for working families who must pay for housing, childcare, health care, transportation, and other work-related expenditures.

**122**

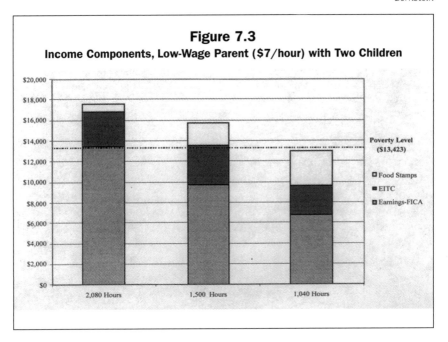

**Figure 7.3**

**Income Components, Low-Wage Parent ($7/hour) with Two Children**

Poverty Level ($13,423)

□ Food Stamps
■ EITC
▣ Earnings-FICA

2,080 Hours · 1,500 Hours · 1,040 Hours

There are a number of things that can help:

**Low Unemployment**

The lesson from the last few years of the 1990s recovery is that full-employment can be counted on to lift the wages of the lowest-paid workers. It was only when the labor market become tighter than it had been for three decades that the wages of workers in the bottom fifth of the wage distribution began to rise faster than inflation. Our Federal Reserve is charged with using monetary policy to balance the level of unemployment with the rate of inflation. Too often, this institution has favored the inflation side of the trade-off at the expense of the unemployment rate, which is kept unnecessarily above full-employment, placing downward pressure on the lowest-wage workers.

As of March of 2001, welfare reform faced recession for the first time. By October 2001, the overall unemployment rate had increased by 1.5 percentage points, while the rates for less-advantaged workers increased faster: 2.3 points for African-Americans and 2.2 for Hispanics. As labor demand has weakened, the positive trends in Figure 7.1 have already begun to reverse course. Thus, low unemployment is already ceasing to bolster the Welfare-to-Work thrust of welfare reform. In this sense, we will soon find out the extent to which the program is a "fair-weather ship," able to navigate effectively only in untroubled economic waters.

**Higher Minimum Wages**

As noted above, moderate increases in the minimum wage have been found to have their intended effect of lifting the earnings of low-wage workers in low-income families without pricing them out of the labor market. Setting the minimum wage to a reasonable level, and then indexing it to some measure of productivity, prices, or overall earnings, would help to shore up the floor on the low-wage labor market.

**Education and Training**

In the spirit of bridging the labor market segments discussed above, and thus generating more mobility, worker training is needed to lift the skills and productivity of low-wage workers. But given the amount of turnover in this sector, it is highly unlikely that firms will make such investments. Thus, the government has an obvious role to play in addressing this problem and should invest in training low-wage workers.

But generalized training by itself won't bridge the segments. We need to develop ways to help low-wage workers (and not just former welfare recipients) move from the low-mobility segment to the higher-mobility segment. Part of this solution may mean dealing with mismatch issues, both geographical (spatial mismatch, as in making sure job seekers can get to areas where primary-tier jobs exist) and skill-based (making sure training is finely targeted toward the skill demands of first-tier employers). Thinking about other ways to bridge the segments is a rich area of research that could make a real difference in the lives of low-wage workers and their families.

**Increased work supports through refundable credits**

Research on what it takes to make ends meet has shown that, even in a relatively low-cost part of the country, a family with kids cannot meet their basic needs on a $7 an hour job (Bernstein et al. 2000). The other factors mentioned above may, down the road, help to raise this wage level, but at the risk of sounding pessimistic, the low productivity levels of many jobs in the low-wage sector may mean that they are unlikely to ever pay the wages necessary to working families in that sector with enough income to meet their basic needs.

This presents a rationale for subsidizing these jobs. The message of welfare reform stressed that good faith efforts to work would lead the way out of poverty; but many, if not most, low-wage jobs are unlikely to do so —especially if we define poverty not as the out-dated federal threshold but as what it takes for a working family to meet its basic needs, including childcare, health care, transportation, housing, and food. There is little doubt that one of the stumbling blocks facing those trying to move from welfare to work is the difficulty of meeting these needs with their low-wage paychecks. For workers in higher quality jobs, problems such as unreliable childcare and car breakdowns are unlikely to cause major disruption in their work lives. But in the low-wage sector, these problems can more easily throw well-intentioned people off track.

Interestingly, subsidy programs exist for all of the above, not to mention the Earned Income Tax Credit, which suggests that perhaps the political system is more responsive to this gap between wages and need than is commonly thought to be the case. But these programs are generally fragmented and often not far-reaching enough in terms of coverage and level. For example, housing policy targeted at low-income families is almost exclusively based on small expansions of subsidies (e.g., rental vouchers), which fail to create much needed new housing stock. Similarly, the childcare and health-care systems desperately need a much more universal approach if we want to generate a stream of reliable quality services in these important areas.

## Conclusion

As we make the transition to work-based welfare, we have created a culture where work is widely considered more dignified than the receipt of welfare benefits. With welfare reform, those attitudes are embodied in a set of rules to enforce that culture among the poor. But there is no dignity in working poverty. In fact, one might argue that the new Democrats—like former President Clinton and HHS Secretary Shalala, who supported the policy, not to mention poverty scholar David Ellwood, who helped craft the original version — forged an implicit contract with mothers on welfare. Under this contract, the former recipients would enter the labor market and the policymakers would make sure they could earn their way out of poverty. Many of the moms have gone to work. It's time to implement the other side of the contract.

## References

Bernstein, Jared, Chauna Brocht, and Maggie Aguilar. 2000. *How Much is Enough: Basic Family Budgets for Working Families.* Forthcoming. Washington, DC: Economic Policy Institute.

Blank, Rebecca, David Card, and Philip Robins. 1998. "Financial Incentives for Increasing Work and Income among Low-income Families." Draft paper prepared for Joint Center for Poverty Research conference, "Labor Markets and Less-Skilled Workers" (November 5-6).

Burtless, Gary. 1995. "Welfare Recipients' Job Skills and Employment Prospects." In *The Work Alternative: Welfare Reform and the Realities of the Job Market.* Washington, DC: Urban Institute Press.

Danziger, Sheldon H., ed. 1999. *Economic Conditions and Welfare Reform.* Kalamazoo, MI: W.E. Upjohn Institute for Employment Research.

Gordon, David M. 1972. *Theories of Poverty and Unemployment.* Lexington, KY. Heath and Company.

Gottschalk, Peter. 1999. "Work as a Stepping Stone for Welfare Recipients: What is the Evidence?" In *The Low-Wage Labor Market: Challenges and Opportunities for Economic Self-Sufficiency.* Washington, DC: US Department of Health and Human Services, Office of the Secretary for Planning and Evaluation.

Harrison, Bennett, and Andrew Sum. 1979. "The Theory of 'Dual' or Segmented Labor Markets." *Journal of Economic Issues* 13 (3): 687–706.

Howell, David R. 1997. Institutional failure and the American worker: The collapse of low-skill wages. The Jerome Levy Economics Institute of Bard College, Public Policy Brief No. 29. Annandale-on-Hudson, NY: Bard Publications Office.

Institute for Women's Policy Research. 1995. *Welfare that Works: The Working Lives of AFDC Recipients.* Washington, DC: IWPR.

Loprest, Pamela. 1999. *How Families That Left Welfare Are Doing: A National Picture.* Urban Institute, Series B, No. B-1.

Newman, Katherine. 1999. "In the Long Run: Career Patterns and Cultural Values on the Low Wage Labor Force." Paper presented at the Inequality Summer Institute.

Parrott, Sharon. 1998. *Welfare Recipients Who Find Jobs: What Do We Know About Their Employment and Earnings?* Washington, DC: Center for Budget and Policy Priorities.

U.S. Department of Health and Human Services. 1999. *The Low-Wage Labor Market: Challenges and Opportunities for Economic Self-Sufficiency.* Washington, DC: US Dept. of HHS, Office of the Secretary for Planning and Evaluation.

## Notes

[1] Jared Bernstein is an economist at the Economic Policy Institute in Washington DC.

[2] Source: Blank et al (1998).

[3] Full-time, full-year work = 52 weeks x 40 hours per week, or 2,080 annual hours.

[4] Including the EITC, cash transfers, and Food Stamps.

[5] From unpublished tables provided by Wendell Primus. The statistics are derived from March Current Population Survey data.

[6] Piore (1975) argued that there exists upper and lower tiers within primary jobs. Upper tier jobs, available to those with the highest levels of education, are less routinized and involve more independent work. Lower tier jobs in the primary sector tend to be blue-collar, relatively high paying, and unionized.

[7] I used the Outgoing Rotation Groups from the March 1999 data to identify single mothers with hourly wages between $5.15 and $7.00. I then calculated these women's average annual hours of work in the previous year (1,555). Note that their average income in 1998 was about $13,800.

[8] See www.epinet.org/webfeatures/snapshots/archive/2001/1010/snapshots1010.html for evidence of this point.

[9] I would argue for about $6.70 in today's dollars, the level it stood at in 1979, before plunging in real terms over the 1980s.

# Job Types, Wage Mobility and Post-Exit Earnings of Welfare Recipients in North Carolina 1995–1999

*Lisa A. Morris*[1]

The objective of welfare reform is to make welfare receipt unattractive (and eventually unavailable), so that recipients will prefer (or will be forced) to accept even low-wage jobs. The implicit assumption underlying welfare reform with its work requirements and time limits is that while recipients will work at low-wage jobs when they first exit welfare, experience and on-the-job skill development will eventually enable them to qualify for jobs at higher wages. In an effort to begin to gauge the likelihood of success of welfare reform and inform upcoming reauthorization of reform policies, this chapter examines the types of jobs AFDC/TANF recipients in North Carolina are obtaining, the range of wages paid to these jobs, and the postexit earnings trajectories for recipients who remain off the rolls.

### Background

Earlier studies examining the earnings of former welfare recipients provide some insight into the feasibility of entry-level lower-skilled employment as a strategy for maintaining independence from welfare. For instance, a study conducted by Gary Burtless (1995) using an AFDC sample from the National Longitudinal Survey of Youth (NLSY) found that AFDC recipients who exited between 1979 and 1981 and obtained employment earned an average of $7 per hour.[2] Harris (1996), using an AFDC sample from the Panel Study of Income Dynamics (PSID) found that women who exited welfare between 1983 and 1988 and obtained employment earned an average of $8 per hour. This means that if a woman worked full-time (forty hours per week) year-round (fifty-one weeks per year), she would earn between $14,280 and $16,320, which is higher than the 1996 official poverty line of $12,600 for a mother and two children.

Setting aside the issue of whether the poverty line reflects economic well-being, this indicates that the family has at least the potential to earn incomes greater than both the maximum welfare benefit and the poverty line.[3]

The actual incomes for many former welfare recipients are, however, considerably lower, indicating that most are working neither full-time nor year-round. For example, Burtless (1995) found the average annual earnings in 1990, among an AFDC sample that exited between 1979 and 1981, were $11,575. A more recent study by Cancian et al. (1998) examined postexit earnings and employment among welfare recipients who left AFDC in Wisconsin during 1995–1996 and found the average annual earnings during the first year after exit were $8,460.[4] A study conducted by Mathematica Policy Research (Fraker et al. 1997) found that former welfare recipients in Iowa were earning an average of $170 per week. (A job paying $5.15 per hour for thirty-three hours per week grosses $170 per week and, if the individual works fifty-one weeks, $8,670 per year.)

Although earnings following exits are low, there is some evidence of earnings mobility. For instance, Burtless (1995) found that average earnings in 1980 were $4,538, but by 1990 — almost ten years after exiting — average earnings were $11,575. Cancian et al. (1998) found that for those who remain off the rolls continuously, average quarterly earnings were $2,628 during the first quarter after exit, increasing to $2,959 in the fifth quarter after exit.[5] However, these increases in earnings appear to arise from increases in hours worked, not from increases in wage rates. For example, two studies examining wage growth over time for AFDC recipients (Burtless 1995; Harris 1996) found that hourly earnings did not increase in real terms over time, but remained at about $6 to $8 per hour.[6]

The slow growth in wages may result, in part, from the welfare-eligible population's high rate of return to the welfare rolls (Pavetti 1993; Bane and Ellwood 1994; Blank and Ruggles 1994; Harris 1996). A number of longitudinal studies document these high rates of recidivism. Using an AFDC sample from the PSID, Harris (1996) found that 27 percent return within one year, 42 percent within two years, and 52 percent within four years. Using a sample of younger AFDC recipients from the NLSY, Pavetti (1993) found that 45 percent return within one year, 58 percent within two years, and 77 percent within seven years. Morris (1999) found that while welfare reform is reducing the rate of recidivism, 38 percent of those who exited returned within the forty-eight-month study period. Because of the easier ability to cycle between work and welfare under AFDC, many poor, single mothers did not generate continuous stable work experience histories. This may have reduced their ability to qualify for higher wages.

Because the work requirements and time limits under PRWORA restrict the ability to cycle between work and welfare, recipients may remain in jobs longer. As Meyer and Cancian (1996) point out, this may cause wage rates to increase over time more than is suggested by earlier studies. The extent to which more time in a job will help welfare recipients qualify for higher wages depends, however, on the types of jobs they are obtaining. If welfare recipients become trapped in "dead-end" low-wage jobs, the possibility of achieving financial self-sufficiency and security through work may not be feasible. Low-wage jobs with little potential for either wage growth or skills development promise only to shift AFDC/ TANF recipients from welfare dependency to working poverty.

Direct evidence on the types of jobs and wage experiences available to welfare recipients is limited. Holzer (1996) found the majority of jobs were in the service, retail, or manufacturing/industrial sectors.[7] Based on a survey of 900 firms, Holzer (1998) found the highest demand for welfare recipients in the retail trade, and the lowest demand in the manufacturing sector. When he asked the occupational categories for which employers would be willing to hire welfare recipients, Holzer (1998) found 67 percent were in "Production, Operating, and Material Handling" or "Service" occupations; 20 percent were in "Clerical and Administrative Support" occupations; 8 percent were in "Sales"; and the remainder (about 5 percent) were in other occupation categories. He found the occupations mentioned by employers were cashiers, receptionists, and general office clerks; restaurant workers; nurses' aides; maids/janitors; assemblers and fabricators; and freight and stock movers and handlers.

In an effort to add to the knowledge of the job and wage experiences of welfare recipients, I present findings from an ongoing study of experiences of AFDC/TANF recipients in North Carolina in the postreform labor market. Specifically, I present data on the types of jobs AFDC/TANF recipients are obtaining, the range of hourly wage rates paid to both newly hired and experienced workers in each occupational category, and the postexit earnings of former AFDC/TANF recipients. To perform this analysis, I extracted data from a number of state administrative computer systems in North Carolina.[8]

### Data, Sample and Methodology

Data were extracted from a number of state administrative computer systems in North Carolina including: (1) the AFDC/TANF system (monthly information on welfare receipt as well as demographic information); (2) the Unemployment Insurance (UI) system (quarterly earnings and industry code for each job held); (3) the North Carolina Employment Securities Commission (ESC) Jobs Listings system (monthly job vacancy information including applicant requirements, wage rate, industry code, hours, and whether job is permanent or temporary); and (4) the Labor Market Information Division, NC ESC survey, "Wage Rates in Selected Occupations, 1996–1997" (entry and average wages and number of employees).

The sample of individuals used in this study comes from AFDC/TANF files in twenty-five North Carolina counties.[9] A subsample of single women with children who began receiving AFDC payments in February 1995 was extracted creating a sample of 2,234 cases. The observation period extends from February 1995 through April 1999, providing up to fifty-two months of data on employment and earnings.

The analyses of job type and the potential for wage mobility were conducted by systematically analyzing the UI and ESC data. The UI files provide quarterly information on earnings for all individuals working in covered employment and include a four-digit Standard Industrial Code (SIC) for each job held. The UI files do not, however, provide information on occupational type or hourly wage rates. To get around this limitation in the data, two other sources of information on the local labor markets in North Carolina were utilized: *Wage Rates in Selected Occupations, 1996–1997*, a survey published by the Labor Market Information Division of the ESC of North Carolina, and the North Carolina ESC's Jobs Listing files. By matching and overlapping information from these three data sources, I was able to determine the most likely occupational and wage experiences of welfare recipients in North Carolina.

First, the UI files are used to determine in which industrial sectors welfare recipients are actually obtaining jobs. In order to determine the most likely occupation (e.g., clerical, service, sales, or product handling) and hourly wage rates of welfare recipients in these industrial sectors, the SIC information in the individual UI files is matched with the SIC information in the ESC's survey on wages in selected occupations. The survey is based on data obtained from more than 16,000 employers in North Carolina and covers forty-two industrial classifications. In addition to providing the number of employees in each occupation (enabling the determination of the types of jobs most likely to be available), it also provides hourly wage rates for both new employees and experienced employees. Finally, in order to limit the analysis to those jobs for which the typical welfare recipient is most likely to be competitive (those requiring a high school degree, GED, or less), a systematic examination of the job vacancy information contained in the ESC Jobs Listing files was conducted.[10]

After analyzing the occupation and wage prospects of welfare recipients, the actual earnings of recipients after they exit the rolls were examined. Earnings information is obtained from the individual UI files.[11] In the interest of space, this analysis will be limited to the earnings of those who did not return to the rolls (at least within the observation period).

## Findings

### Industries

AFDC/TANF participants in North Carolina[12] are most often employed in service, retail, or manufacturing industries. Table 8.1 shows that nearly 90 percent of all jobs obtained by AFDC/TANF recipients were in three major industrial groupings: 46.1 percent of all jobs obtained were in the service industries, followed by 32.2 percent in retail, and 10.5 percent in manufacturing.

### Table 8.1
#### Major Industry Groupings

| Industry[13] | % Employed |
|---|---|
| Agriculture, Forestry, and Fishing | 0.4 |
| Mining | 0 |
| Construction | 2.1 |
| Manufacturing | 10.5 |
| Transportation, Communications, Utilities, and Sanitation | 1.5 |
| Wholesale Trade | 2.2 |
| Retail | 32.3 |
| Finance, Insurance, and Real Estate | 1.9 |
| Service | 46.1 |
| Public Administration | 0.5 |

These findings are consistent with the firm-based research conducted by Holzer (1996) in Michigan described above. Most of the service-industry jobs fall within the "business service" industrial category — 23 percent of all jobs and more than 50 percent of all service-sector jobs are in business-service industries. This is important because this industrial subgrouping includes temporary-help agencies and establishments that provide services to businesses on a contract or fee basis, including advertising, credit reporting, collection of claims, mailing, reproduction, stenography, photo-copying, data entry, and janitorial services. Temporary-help agencies have their own SIC as a subcategory within the business-service sector, and it was determined that 17.8 percent of all jobs obtained by AFDC/TANF recipients in North Carolina are temporary-help positions, though this is probably an underestimate.[14] That so many welfare recipients are employed as temporary workers may, in part, explain the higher job turnover among these workers (Holzer 1996; Harris 1997; Edin and Lein 1997; Morris 1999).

### Occupations and Wage Mobility Prospects — All Jobs

Based on an analysis of North Carolina's ESC Jobs Listing database, most entry-level, lower-skilled positions (those requiring a high school diploma, GED, or less) fall under *nonprofessional* or *nontechnical* occupational classifications. These jobs are classified under the standard occupational categories of *sales, clerical and administrative support, service,* and *production, operating or material handling.* These jobs pay less and require less education and experience than do the occupational classifications *managerial and professional, professional, paraprofessional,* and *technical.*[15]

The most numerous entry-level, lower-skilled jobs within the service industry are service occupations,[16] including nurses' aid, housekeeper, janitor, security guard, food preparation worker, hotel desk clerk, and cafeteria cook. Lower-skilled clerical and administrative positions are also quite numerous and include receptionist, general office clerk, secretary, file clerk, mail machine operator, and typist. Some production, operating, and materials handling positions also tend to be numerous, such as hand-packer, freight and stock mover (hand), and stockroom/warehouse clerk. The most numerous lower-skilled jobs within the restaurant, food, and general trade–retail trade industries are service occupations, including cashier, waiter, food preparation worker, fast-food cook, counter and dining-room attendants, and sales jobs, including stock clerks and sales persons. The most numerous jobs in the manufacturing industries are production, operating, and materials handling occupations, including textile machine operator, sewing machine operator, hand packer and meat/poultry/fish cutter, trimmer, and packer, assembler, and fabricator.

Table 8.2 displays the wage rates for the most common occupations (based on number of employees) within service, retail, and manufacturing. The entry wage is the median rate paid to newly hired employees. The experienced wage reflects the median rate paid to the majority of experienced, or fully trained, workers in that occupation. Generally, such workers have held their position for two years.

Table 8.2 shows that clerical and administrative occupations and production, operating, and materials handling positions pay better than service and sales occupations. The wage rates paid to service and sales occupations in the retail trade sector are among the lowest. The wage growth—the difference between the entry and experienced wage—is generally greater in the manufacturing sector.[17]

The most numerous lower-skilled jobs are in the service and retail industrial sectors and are service and sales positions—nurses' aide, housekeeper, janitor, food preparation worker, cashier, security guard, and cook—and their wage rates and growth potential are among the lowest. For example, the starting wage for a certified nurses' aide (CNA)—by far the most numerous job opportunity based on employment figures reported by the ESC occupational wage survey—is $6.15 per hour. Thus, a newly hired CNA working forty hours a week, fifty-one weeks per year (assuming one week unpaid vacation) would earn about $12,546, while an experienced CNA would earn about $14,504 annually ($7.11 per hour). Though this is better than what an experienced housekeeper, restaurant worker, or cashier would earn,[18] CNA positions generally require more experience, training, and certification.

Although clerical and administrative support occupations generally require some previous related work experience, these positions are numerous and offer relatively higher wages. The most numerous positions

### Table 8.2
**Wage Prospects for Entry-level Jobs, North Carolina**
**(1996 wage rates)**

| Occupation | Entry wage | Experienced wage |
|---|---|---|
| Nurses' aid/orderly/attendant | | |
| —Service | $6.15 | $7.11 |
| Housekeeper—Service | $5.08 | $6.09 |
| Restaurant food worker | | |
| —Retail | $5.15 | $5.56 |
| Cashier—Retail | $4.87 | $5.72 |
| Hotel desk clerk—Service | $5.63 | $6.32 |
| Security guard—Service | $5.25 | $6.31 |
| Cook (institutional) | | |
| — Service | $6.08 | $7.26 |
| Receptionist—Service | $7.05 | $8.43 |
| Hand packer—Service | $5.96 | $7.22 |
| Stock Clerk—Retail | $4.69 | $5.80 |
| Freight/stock mover (hand) | | |
| —Manufacturing | $6.78 | $8.63 |
| Salesperson—Retail | $5.19 | $6.56 |
| Secretary—Service | $7.88 | $9.72 |
| General office clerk—Retail | $6.09 | $7.89 |
| General office clerk—Service | $6.97 | $8.18 |
| Hand packer | | |
| —Manufacturing | $6.70 | $8.29 |
| Textile machine operator | | |
| —Manufacturing | $6.66 | $8.70 |
| Shipping/Receiving Clerk | | |
| —Manufacturing | $7.50 | $9.47 |
| Sewing machine operator | | |
| —Manufacturing | $5.50 | $7.60 |
| Meat/poultry cutter/trimmer | | |
| —Manufacturing | $6.00 | $6.82 |
| Shipping /Receiving Clerk | | |
| —Service | $6.74 | $7.73 |
| Production Inspector | | |
| —Manufacturing | $7.31 | $9.59 |

are receptionists and general office clerks. A receptionist in the service sector can earn $7.05 per hour ($14,843 per year) her first year, and an average of $8.43 per hour ($17,197 per year) after she becomes experienced. A general office clerk in the service sector would earn an average of $6.97 per hour ($14,218 per year) starting out, and $8.18 per hour ($16,686 per year) after a couple of years. In addition to somewhat higher wages than sales and service occupations, these jobs offer a greater potential for on-the-job skill development, including basic computer use, composition and communications, and record keeping. It should be noted, however, that some welfare recipients do not have the literacy and numerical skills necessary to be competitive for these types of jobs.

On the other hand, certain production, operating, and materials handling occupations are relatively numerous and may require less literacy and numerical skill, as well as provide somewhat higher wages, than service and sales positions do. A newly hired hand packer in a manufacturing firm can earn $13,668 ($6.70 per hour) and once experienced, as much as $16,911 ($8.29 per hour). A freight and stock mover (hand) in manufacturing industries starts at $6.78 per hour ($13,831 per year) and once experienced, earns an average of $8.63 per hour ($17,605 per year). And while textile machine operator occupations offer relatively low wages, they eventually lead to textile machine setter positions, which are higher paying.[19]

Though they are less numerous and generally require more skills or previous work experience, shipping and receiving clerks and secretaries can earn higher wages and develop skills. A secretary in a service industry firm starts at $7.88 per hour ($16,075 per year) and can earn on average $19,828 per year once she becomes experienced. A shipping and receiving clerk can start at between $6.74 (service) and $7.50 (manufacturing) per hour and earn between $15,769 and $19,381 per year after becoming experienced.

**Welfare Recipients' Earnings**

The actual earnings of welfare recipients as reported in the individual UI files in each of the three major industrial sectors—service, retail, and manufacturing—reflect the occupational wage data examined above. Table 8.3 displays the mean quarterly earnings of welfare recipients, by industrial sector, after they have exited the rolls. It also includes the mean earnings of recipients working through a temporary-help agency.

It's clear from Table 8.3 that former recipients working through temporary-help agencies earn the lowest incomes. This probably reflects both the low wages paid to these positions and the intermittent nature of such work. Former recipients also have low earnings in both the service and retail industries, perhaps again reflecting the low earnings, the part-time and/or temporary nature of the work, as well as the tenuous labor force attachment on the part of former recipients. Though only 10 percent

**Table 8.3**
**Mean Postexit Earnings of Welfare Recipients**
**by Industrial Sector**

| Industrial Sector | Mean quarterly earnings |
|---|---|
| Retail | $1,431 |
| Service | $1,827 |
| Manufacturing | $2,838 |
| Temporary Agency | $1,045 |

of the jobs obtained by recipients are in the manufacturing sector, average wages within this sector are considerably higher, indicating that such jobs are more likely to be full-time and permanent.[20]

**Earnings Over Time for Former Recipients**

The final set of information used to estimate the ability of former welfare recipients to achieve financial security through market wages is the postexit earnings of recipients who have not returned to the rolls (at least within the fifty-two-month study period). The analysis is conducted on nonreturners in order to approximate the earnings potential once time limits are met. Table 8.4 shows the median and mean earnings for two years after exiting, as well as the percentage with nonzero earnings.

The first thing to note from Table 8.4 is that there is a wide range of earnings: The standard deviations are large, and the medians are lower than the means, indicating that many former recipients have zero earnings. An individual working forty hours per week at $5 per hour would

**Table 8.4**
**Postexit Earnings for Nonreturners (includes zero earnings)**

| Quarters since exit | Median | Mean | Standard deviation | % with nonzero earnings |
|---|---|---|---|---|
| 1 | $1,173 | $1,601 | 1,701 | 63.8 |
| 2 | $1,189 | $1,664 | 1,794 | 61.5 |
| 3 | $1,257 | $1,763 | 1,927 | 61.2 |
| 4 | $1,114 | $1,728 | 1,864 | 58.8 |
| 5 | $1,289 | $1,824 | 2,011 | 57.3 |
| 6 | $1,282 | $1,911 | 2,146 | 54.6 |
| 7 | $1,337 | $1,938 | 2,157 | 53.1 |
| 8 | $1,151 | $1,970 | 2,193 | 51.6 |

earn $2,400 per quarter. That the quarterly incomes displayed in Table 8.4 are all well below this figure indicates considerable intermittent and part-time employment. Indeed, only 33 percent of the nonreturning women have earnings of $2,400 or above during the eight postexit quarters. This indicates that 67 percent of the women are working less than full-time.

### Table 8.5
**Postexit Earnings Trajectories**

| Consecutive quarters postexit over which earnings were maintained or increased | Frequency | % |
|---|---|---|
| 0 | 1,495 (out of 2,299) | 65.0 |
| 1–2 | 840 (out of 2,275) | 36.9 |
| 1–3 | 329 (out of 2,252) | 14.6 |
| 1–4 | 127 (out of 2,212) | 5.7 |
| 1–5 | 47 (out of 2,183) | 2.1 |

Table 8.5 reports the number and percentage of former recipients who were able to increase or maintain their earnings over time. As indicated, only a small percentage of former welfare recipients were able to maintain their initial level of earnings. Only 36.9 percent of former recipients who had nonzero earnings in the first quarter after exiting were able to maintain or increase their earnings level through the second quarter. By the fourth quarter (one year postexit), only 5.7 percent were able to maintain their earnings level from the first quarter. This indicates little upward wage mobility among former welfare recipients.

### Table 8.6
**Postexit Earnings Trajectories**

| Consecutive quarters postexit over whichearnings were at least $1000 per quarter | Frequency | % |
|---|---|---|
| 1-2 | 952 (out of 2,275) | 41.8 |
| 1-3 | 807 (out of 2,252) | 35.8 |
| 1-4 | 684 (out of 2,212) | 30.9 |
| 1-5 | 605 (out of 2,183) | 27.7 |
| 1-6 | 540 (out of 2,140) | 25.2 |
| 1-7 | 490 (out of 2,091) | 23.4 |
| 1-8 | 441 (out of 2,026) | 21.8 |

Table 8.6 displays the number and percentage of individuals who were able to maintain quarterly earnings of at least $1,000 for consecutive quarters after exiting. Despite this less-than-optimistic measure ($1,000 per quarter is equivalent to sixteen hours per week at $5 per hour), only 30.9 percent of the former recipients were able to maintain it for four quarters. Only 21.8 percent were able to maintain earnings of at least $1,000 per quarter two years after exiting. Thus, not only is there considerable part-time work among former recipients, but also there is a high rate of participation in the intermittent labor force.

**Table 8.7**
**Total Earnings for First and Second Years after Welfare**

| Year | Mean | Median | Standard deviation |
|------|------|--------|--------------------|
| 1 | $6,748 | $5,527 | 6,624 |
| 2 | $7,747 | $5,963 | 7,903 |

Table 8.7 provides additional evidence that most former recipients are working part-time and have intermittent attachment to the workforce. A tabulation of the total earnings for the first and second years after exit shows the majority of former recipients are earning incomes below the poverty level.[21] Median earnings for the first year off welfare are $5,527, rising to $5,963 for the second year. Even if we calculate annual postexit earnings for only those with some earnings, the median earnings are $9,231 for year one and $10,159 for year two.

Even with wage supplements via EITC, food stamps, and health insurance, many of these women and their families will remain dangerously close to the poverty line. Unless unreported work and financial assistance from family and fathers of children is substantial—and according to research by Edin and Lein (1997) it is not[22]—these women and their children are experiencing considerable financial hardship.

### Implications

The analysis of job types indicates that most of the positions that welfare recipients are obtaining are low-paying "dead-end" jobs offering few prospects for wage mobility. Nearly 80 percent of all jobs obtained are within the service and retail industries where wages are low and wage growth is limited. In addition, many of these jobs are likely to be part-time and temporary. Indeed, almost 18 percent of all jobs obtained by welfare recipients are obtained through temporary-help agencies, and even this is likely to be an underestimate of the temporary jobs held by former welfare recipients. Only 10.5 percent of the jobs obtained are within the manufacturing industry, where the wages are higher, wage growth greater, and the positions more likely to be full-time and permanent. Moreover, analysis of actual postexit earnings indicate that labor-force attachment of the majority of former recipients is tenuous, and consistent upward income mobility is limited to a handful of individuals. This, in turn, means that while welfare reform may have reduced welfare-dependent poverty, working poverty remains.

If complete financial independence is the ultimate goal, attention must be paid to the fact that most of the jobs to which recipients are moving are low-wage and have limited potential for significant wage growth. Moreover, because working-poor parents, especially working-poor single parents, must struggle to balance the responsibilities of their provider and parenting roles, the problem of tenuous attachment to the workforce is not going to be easily or inexpensively solved.

At the very least, job search and placement services should focus on helping welfare recipients obtain jobs with more on-the-job skills development and wage mobility potential. Job support services should focus on enabling job retention and reducing turnover. Employers should be encouraged to raise wages (either through new minimum-wage legislation or through tax incentives) and to provide flexible schedules and time-share positions for working parents.

In order to enable recipients to compete for better jobs and attain significant upward wage mobility, human capital development should be reintroduced into the welfare-to-work strategy. Community college and adult learning centers should be used to develop targeted, short-term courses for the very-low-skilled and inexperienced welfare recipients to help them compete for better jobs at higher wages. Work requirements should be altered and subsidies provided to allow recipients to attend community colleges and universities. Reliable and quality daycare services and transportation assistance should be expanded.

Finally, it should also be noted that the employment and earnings data reported here occurred during strong labor market conditions. If these are the job prospects for the lower skilled in a period of sustained economic growth, supplemental assistance programs (e.g., EITC, food stamps, public health benefits) must be continued and even expanded in order to augment low earnings.

## References

Bane, Mary Jo, and David T. Ellwood. 1994. *Welfare Realities: From Rhetoric to Reform.* Boston: Harvard University Press.

Blank, Rebecca, and Patricia Ruggles. 1996. "When Do Women Use AFDC and Food Stamps? The dynamics of eligibility versus participation." *Journal of Human Resources* 31 (1): 57–89.

Burtless, Gary. 1995. "Employment Prospects of Welfare Recipients." In *The Work Alternative: Welfare Reforms and the Realities of the Job Market*, ed. Demetra Smith Nightingale and Robert H. Haveman. Washington, DC: The Urban Institute Press.

Cancian, Maria, Robert Haveman, Thomas Kaplan, and Barbara Wolfe. 1998. Postexit Earnings and Benefit Receipt among Those Who Left AFDC in Wisconsin. Report prepared for the Assistant Secretary of Planning and Evaluation (ASPE) of the U.S. Department of Health and Human Services, Washington DC.

Edin, Kathryn, and Laura Lein. 1997. *Making Ends Meet: How Single Mothers Survive Welfare and Low-Wage Work.* New York: Russel Sage Foundation.

Fraker, Thomas, Lucia Nixon, Jan Losby, Carol Prindle, and John Else. 1997. *Iowa's Limited Benefit Plan.* Washington, DC: Mathematica Policy Research, Inc.

Harris, Kathleen Mullan. 1996. "Life after Welfare: Women, Work and Repeat Dependency." *American Sociological Review* 61 (3): 407–426.

Holzer, Harry. 1996. *What Employers Want: Job Prospects for Less-Educated Workers.* New York, NY: Russel Sage Foundation.

———. 1998. "Will Employers Hire Welfare Recipients? Recent survey evidence from Michigan." Discussion Paper, no. 1177-98, Institute for Research on Poverty, University of Wisconsin-Madison.

Meyer, Daniel R., and Maria Cancian. 1996. "Life After Welfare: The economic well-being of women and children following an exit from AFDC." Report prepared for the Assistant Secretary of Planning and Evaluation (ASPE) of the US Department of Health and Human Services, Washington DC. Discussion Paper, no. 1101-96, Institute for Research on Poverty, University of Wisconsin-Madison.

Morris, Lisa A. 1999. Exits, Employment, Earnings, and Recidivism among Welfare Recipients in North Carolina, 1995 to 1998. Ph.D. diss., University of North Carolina, Chapel Hill.

Pavetti, LaDonna Ann. 1993. The Dynamics of Welfare and Work: Exploring the process by which women work their way off welfare. Ph.D. diss., John F. Kennedy School of Government, Harvard University. Malcolm Wiener Center for Social Policy Working Papers: Dissertation Series.

## Notes

[1] Lisa A. Morris is assistant professor at Washington University in St. Louis in the George Warren Brown School of Social Work. Her doctorate is in public policy analysis from the University of North Carolina, Chapel Hill, and she has a Master's degree in urban planning and public policy from Rutgers University, as well as a Master's in social welfare, also from Rutgers. She currently is working on a study funded by the U.S. Department of Health and Human Services, Office of the Assistant Secretary for Evaluation and Planning, examining welfare reform outcomes by race.

[2] Note that earnings data are for workers with earnings (i.e., averages do not include zeros for non-earners) and are reported in 1996 dollars.

[3] The fact that earnings from employment can exceed the welfare stipend and the poverty line does not automatically guarantee that work will be considered more attractive, because time, transportation, childcare, and other costs also are involved in the work/welfare decision. For example, Edin and Lein (1997) document both economic costs (e.g., increased childcare costs, medical care, transportation, housing, and appropriate work clothing) and non-economic costs (whether fulltime work interfered with

competent parenting and whether work would interfere with supervision and monitoring of children in order to ensure their wellbeing and safety) that single mothers considered when going to work.

[4] They go on to report that 76 percent of former AFDC/TANF recipients with two children earned incomes below the poverty line; 95 percent below 150 percent of the poverty line; and 44 percent below the state's maximum welfare benefit.

[5] Cancian et al. (1998) also report an average annualized change in quarterly earnings of $254, an average growth rate of 2.5 for median quarterly earnings, and an average annual growth rate of quarterly earnings of 10.4.

[6] Harris (1996) found no upward mobility in average hourly wage rates earned: $8 per hour right after exit, $7.78 after twelve months, $7.74 after twenty-four months, and $8 after thirty-six months.

[7] Based on a survey of 3,200 employers in four metropolitan areas on entry-level jobs available to workers without a college degree.

[8] Sources include: (1) the AFDC/TANF system (monthly information on receipts as well as demographic information); (2) the Unemployment Insurance system (quarterly earnings and industry codes for each job held); (3) the North Carolina Employment Securities Commission Jobs Listings system; and (4) the Labor Market Information Division, NC ESC survey, "Wage Rates in Selected Occupations, 1996–1997."A detailed explanation of the data and methodology is available upon request from the author.

[9] While the twenty-five counties were not randomly selected, they were chosen to represent geographical, urban-rural, and industrial variation as well as variation in timing and intensity of TANF implementation. In addition, they represent nearly 55 percent of the state's caseload.

[10] A more thorough and detailed explanation of the data and the methodology is available from the author upon request.

[11] Unemployment Insurance data do not include data on earnings from unreported or uncovered work. To the extent that former recipients are engaged in unreported work or uncovered employment, this analysis will underestimate their incomes.

[12] Based on actual job information from individual Unemployment Insurance files.

[13] A more detailed examination of industrial breakdowns of jobs held by AFDC/TANF recipients in North Carolina is available from the author.

[14] The business-service category also includes establishments that provide services to other firms on a temporary contract basis, in addition to firms that advertise for their own temporary help, rather than going through a temporary-help agency. These would not be included in the 17.8 percent estimate.

[15] Occupational classifications are based on the 1995 *Occupational Employment Statistics (OES) Program Dictionary*.

[16] According to standard classification systems, there is both a "service" industry and a "service" occupation. Similarly, there is an industrial sector called "retail trades" and an occupational category called "sales."

[17] Note that certain occupations pay more in one industrial sector compared to others. For example, cooks in the service sector (institutional cafeterias) earn more than those in the retail sector (restaurants); hand packers in manufacturing industries earn more than those in service industries.

[18] $12,423 ($6.09 per hour), $11,342 ($5.56 per hour), and $11,668 ($5.72 per hour), respectively.

[19] For example, a textile machine setter starts at $8.40 per hour ($17,136 per year) and eventually earns an average of $10.53 per hour ($21,481 per year).

[20] Note that because the UI data do not include hourly wages or number of hours worked, they cannot reliably determine whether low quarterly wages reflect part-time and temporary positions or higher job turnover and intermittent labor force participation on the part of individuals.

[21] For reference, an individual earning $5 per hour, working forty hours per week, fifty-one weeks per year (assuming one week unpaid vacation) earns $10,200. An individual earning $7 per hour working forty hours per week, fifty-one weeks per year earns $14,280.

[22] Based on an ethnographic study of single mothers on public assistance in poor neighborhoods in four different cities, they found that while virtually all the women supplemented their income in various ways, few made more than $20 to $90 per month in unreported work, and another $30 to $50 in unreported income from other sources (e.g., assistance from children's father, boyfriends, family, and friends).

# The Effect of Welfare Reform on the Incomes and Earnings of Low-Income Families

## Evidence from the Current Population Survey

*Laura S. Connolly[1]*

Many advocates of welfare reform have pointed to the dramatic drop in caseloads as evidence of the success of the newly designed programs.[2] However, the discussion has recently turned to the more difficult question of how former recipients are faring in the wake of welfare reform. This paper examines the effect of state-level welfare reform policies (which took place prior to the passage of PRWORA) on the incomes and earnings of those who were recipients of Aid to Families with Dependent Children (AFDC) and other cash benefits when the reforms were enacted. The work requirements enacted under PRWORA are very similar to those enacted by many states, so the findings presented in this paper are relevant for the upcoming decision on whether or not to renew the current law.

My methodology uses data from the Current Population Survey (CPS) to predict the change in family incomes and earnings over time, applying statistical analysis to determine the effect of welfare reform and economic conditions on these changes. If proponents of welfare reform are correct in their assumption that work is the key to self-sufficiency, then families living in states that enacted reforms with strict work requirements or increased work incentives should have higher income and earnings growth than their counterparts in states without such reforms, holding other relevant variables constant. On the other hand, if welfare reform makes it more difficult for families to make ends meet, then the opposite should occur.

## Model

The state-level policies enacted before PRWORA's passage were allowed under waivers from the federal rules regulating AFDC; thus, they are frequently referred to simply as "waivers." The requirements and conditions imposed by these waivers varied substantially across states and have been categorized in many ways (U.S. Council of Economic Advisers 1997; Crouse 1999; Ziliak et al. 1997; 2000). In this paper, I group them into three categories: those that require work (or participation in a job-training or job-search program) as a condition of eligibility; those that increase the incentives of current recipients to work (by increasing the earnings one can receive without losing AFDC benefits); and all other provisions. Because I am interested in the effect of waivers on earnings and incomes, I use this broad categorization to focus on the effect of the work-related waivers, i.e., work requirements and work incentives. For comparison, I also examine the effect of all types of waivers combined.

Economic theory yields ambiguous predictions regarding the expected effect of work requirements on the earnings and income of welfare recipients.[3] Some work-requirement waivers took the form of "workfare," meaning that recipients work at public jobs and are "paid" welfare benefits in lieu of wages. Because such benefits are not counted as earned income, earnings would not change in the short run in such cases. Similarly, there is no immediate effect for those who must participate in job-search or job-training activities instead of working at a publicly provided job. However, the assumption underlying many of the work requirements is that once welfare recipients gain work experience or training, they will move into higher paying, more stable jobs (and off the welfare rolls). Once this occurs, the earnings of these individuals would be expected to rise.

Work incentives, which may be combined with work requirements, also have ambiguous effects. These waivers allow a recipient to keep at least a portion of her benefit in addition to her wages, rather than decreasing benefits dollar for dollar, as was often the rule prior to the waivers.[4] Although this generally would be expected to increase work efforts among recipients, it will only do so if the additional income outweighs the extra costs of working. These costs, which include childcare, transportation, clothing, and, in many cases, health insurance, can be substantial and are not often covered by the increased benefits (Edin and Lein 1997).

While it is important to determine the effect on earnings, it is perhaps even more critical to understand what happens to incomes. After all, income from *all* sources—both earnings and welfare support—contribute to a family's wellbeing. Due to the decrease in welfare benefits resulting from increased earnings, incomes do not necessarily rise with work effort.[5] In addition, many waivers imposed sanctions for certain types of behaviors. When recipients were unable to comply with these provisions, their benefits were reduced, thereby reducing their incomes.

To empirically examine the question of whether earnings and incomes rise or fall as a result of work-related waivers, it is first necessary to isolate the effect of waivers from other factors that affect earnings and incomes. To do this, I used a two–step approach. First, I compared earnings or income growth in states with waivers compared to states with similar economic conditions, but no waivers. This isolated the effect of waivers from the effect of unobservable factors present in both types of states. However, the effect of waivers may still be confounded with other unobservable factors that differ across states. Therefore, a second step is necessary: to compare the measured waiver effects for AFDC recipients with those of two alternative control groups, all nonrecipient families and families headed by nonrecipient single females. Though the latter group may appear to be better for comparison because of its similarities with the group of recipients, it is not ideal because welfare reform may affect the behavior of single females who were not recipients at the time of the reform. For example, some of these women may find welfare a more attractive option after a work-incentive waiver is introduced. This would imply that their labor supply, and therefore their earnings, may *decrease* as a result. Similarly, a work-requirement waiver that subsidizes job training may induce some nonrecipients to apply for AFDC if they believe that this training would lead to a better job than they currently hold.[6]

One problem with using the CPS for this type of analysis is that it follows a given household for only one year, so it cannot be used directly to observe long-term changes in family incomes or earnings. Because it is important to follow those families who were receiving cash assistance *before* welfare reform policies took effect, it is not sufficient to examine the incomes and earnings of the set of families who are observed in the CPS in the years following the reforms. Instead, we need a data set that follows the same families over time (a "longitudinal" data set). To overcome this constraint, I used methodology developed by Connolly and Segal (2000) to construct a longitudinal data set "synthetically."[7]

## Data

### Earnings, income, and demographics

Data on family earnings, incomes, and demographics are taken from various years of the March surveys of the CPS. The CPS is valuable for this type of study because it includes information on participation in a wide variety of public assistance programs, as well as detailed data on demographic characteristics and sources of income and earnings for a large, representative sample of U.S. households. Indeed, Moffitt (1999) recently argued for the use of the CPS microdata for studying the effects of welfare reform on a variety of outcomes, including those examined here (earnings and incomes).[8]

**147**

Another important advantage of the CPS is that it provides information on family, not just individual, incomes and earnings. Welfare reform impacts entire families, not just individuals, so it is important to determine how family-level resources are affected.

## Measures of welfare reform

Many states received waivers from federal regulations governing public assistance programs (especially AFDC) during the mid-1990s, allowing them to experiment with work requirements, time limits, and a number of other policies. The variables used here to measure welfare reform are based on information available from the U.S. Department of Health and Human Services (Crouse 1999). I create a variable that equals the fraction of the year for which a given state had a waiver in effect. For example, if a state implemented a waiver in October 1993, this variable would equal 0 before 1993, 0.25 in 1993, and 1.0 thereafter for that state. There were many waivers that covered only small portions of the caseload, e.g., a single county, but I used only waivers that applied statewide, because these are likely to have the greatest impact.[9] I estimated the model using four different definitions of the waiver variable: (1) any work-related waiver (combines all waivers that contain work requirements or provide additional incentives for work); (2) work-requirement waivers only; (3) work-incentive waivers only; and (4) any waiver (combines waivers of any type, whether work-related or not).[10]

## Results

## Comparison with all nonrecipients

Table 9.1 shows the difference in the estimated effect for recipients compared with all nonrecipients, regardless of the gender and marital status of the householder. The effect of all four categories of waivers is shown for three time periods. The 1993–94 and 1993–95 time periods capture the one- and two-year effects of waivers that were implemented before or during 1993, respectively. The 1994–95 period indicates the one-year effect of all waivers implemented by the end of 1994.

The variable combining all work-related waivers had no statistically significant effect on the earnings growth of recipients compared with all nonrecipients in any of the three time periods. As discussed earlier, this is consistent with the fact that both work-requirement and work-incentive waivers have ambiguous theoretical effects on earnings. However, this combination variable had a *negative* and statistically significant effect on the income growth of recipients compared with nonrecipients in all three periods. For example, the estimated effect of this variable in the 1993–94 time period indicates that the family income of welfare recipients grew 0.068 percentage points more slowly than that of a nonrecipient family

### Table 9.1
**The Effect of Welfare Waivers on Earnings and Income Growth by Time Period**
**(AFDC recipients compared with all nonrecipients)[11]**

| Time period | Type of waiver | Change in predicted earnings | | Change in predicted income | |
|---|---|---|---|---|---|
| | | Estimated difference | p–value | Estimated difference | p–value |
| 1993–94[12] | Any work–related | –0.081 | 0.23 | –0.068*** | 0.00 |
| | Work requirement | –0.233** | 0.05 | –0.017 | 0.55 |
| | Work incentive | 0.020 | 0.82 | –0.066*** | 0.00 |
| | Any waiver | –0.043 | 0.48 | –0.041*** | 0.01 |
| | | | | | |
| 1993–95 | Any work–related | –0.104 | 0.15 | –0.074*** | 0.00 |
| | Work requirement | –0.251** | 0.04 | –0.027 | 0.39 |
| | Work incentive | 0.013 | 0.88 | –0.071*** | 0.00 |
| | Any waiver | –0.045 | 0.48 | –0.039** | 0.02 |
| 1994–95[13] | Any work–related | 0.093 | 0.18 | –0.063*** | 0.00 |
| | Work requirement | –0.016 | 0.90 | –0.032 | 0.34 |
| | Work incentive | 0.242** | 0.02 | –0.059** | 0.04 |
| | Any waiver | 0.067 | 0.27 | –0.037** | 0.03 |

*indicates significance at the .10 level;
**indicates significance at the .05 level;
***indicates significance at the .01 level.

living in the *same* state over that period. Though it may be disturbing to note a negative effect, it also should be noted that the magnitude is quite small. In summary, work-related waivers as a group did not lead to increased earnings of welfare recipients in the full sample; but did result in slightly lower income growth for these families, probably as a result of sanctions and other penalties.

The lack of effect of the combined work-related waivers could have been caused potentially by a confounding of the influences of work-requirement and work-incentive waivers, so I also examined the effect of each of these separately. Interestingly, the work-requirement waiver had a negative and significant effect on recipients' earnings growth only when waivers implemented by the end of 1993 were considered (the 1993–94 and 1993–95 results). The order of magnitude, while still small, was much greater than the effects discussed earlier. The estimates imply that work-requirement waivers caused family earnings of welfare recipients to grow approximately 0.25 percentage points more slowly than those of nonrecipients in the same state.

There are two possible explanations for this negative effect. First, some recipients may have worked at unreported jobs while receiving benefits.[14] When a workfare type of waiver is implemented, these recipients must report their work, so may no longer have time to work surreptitiously. This would result in an overall decrease in earnings.[15] The second explanation draws on the fact that many work-requirement waivers allowed participation in a state-sponsored job-training program in lieu of working. It may have been beneficial for some recipients who were originally working (whether reported or not) to participate in the job training program instead. The second explanation is consistent with another interesting finding shown by Table 9.1: The work-requirement waiver had no significant effect on recipients' incomes. This implies that lower earnings growth was offset by increased growth in unearned income.

Turning to the work-incentive waivers, we see another interesting pattern. The work-incentive waivers did have a positive and significant effect on recipients' earnings growth in the 1994–95 period, but simultaneously had a significant (but much smaller) negative effect on income. This pattern would be expected if the work-incentive waivers helped recipients find paying jobs, but the increased wages triggered a large decrease in benefits. Although work-incentive waivers were those that increased the earnings disregard, recipients still faced a steep phase-out period once their earnings exceeded the disregard.

Finally, I examined the effect of any type of waiver, work-related or not. These results are very similar to those of the variable that combines all work-related waivers. There is no significant impact on earnings and a statistically significant, but quite small, negative effect on incomes. Again, sanctions and penalties are the logical explanation for this drop. Note that the measure of the income growth rate allows for recipients to leave the caseload during the period in question for all reasons, not just because of increased earnings. The decrease in income growth also reflects the fact that many waivers were designed to reduce caseload without necessarily increasing earnings.

**Comparison with single-female householders only**

One criticism of the foregoing analysis is that it compares AFDC recipients with all nonrecipients, which may not be the most appropriate control group. Table 9.2 presents the results of restricting the sample (of both recipients and nonrecipients) to single-female heads of households only.[16]

Compared with the full sample, there are no differences in the pattern resulting from the variable that combines all work-related waivers, and only one difference in the estimated effect of all waivers combined (the negative effect on income growth in the 1993–95 period is no longer significant). There are some interesting differences in the effects of each type of work-related waiver when examined separately, however.

The effect of the work-requirement variable on earnings growth is now significant (at the .10 level) for the 1994–95 period in addition to the other two periods. The magnitude of that effect is also similar to that of the other two periods. This indicates that the effect of the later work requirement waivers was obscured when the sample was not restricted.

There are two major changes in the estimated effect of the work-incentive variable. First, the positive effect on earnings growth in the 1994–95 period is about the same magnitude, but is not significant in the restricted sample. Thus, when we focus only on families headed by single females, the apparent earnings benefit of the work-incentive waivers disappears. This suggests that the benefits accrue mainly to families with single-male heads and/or two parents.

## Table 9.2
### The Effect of Welfare Waivers on Earnings and Income Growth by Time Period (AFDC recipients compared with single-female householders only)[17]

| Time period | Type of waiver | Change in predicted earnings | | Change in predicted income | |
|---|---|---|---|---|---|
| | | Estimated difference | p–value | Estimated difference | p–value |
| 1993–94[18] | Any work–related | –0.044 | 0.56 | –0.057** | 0.02 |
| | Work requirement | –0.240* | 0.06 | –0.013 | 0.76 |
| | Work incentive | 0.059 | 0.53 | –0.056 | 0.93 |
| | Any waiver | 0.007 | 0.92 | –0.037* | 0.09 |
| 1993–95 | Any work–related | –0.032 | 0.67 | –0.055** | 0.02 |
| | Work requirement | –0.309** | 0.02 | 0.023 | 0.57 |
| | Work incentive | 0.124* | 0.09 | –0.069 | 0.64 |
| | Any waiver | 0.033 | 0.63 | –0.031 | 0.14 |
| 1994–95[19] | Any work–related | 0.064 | 0.40 | –0.057** | 0.02 |
| | Work requirement | –0.223* | 0.10 | –0.055 | 0.21 |
| | Work incentive | 0.299 | 0.53 | –0.031 | 0.67 |
| | Any waiver | 0.014 | 0.83 | –0.044** | 0.04 |

*indicates significance at the .10 level;
**indicates significance at the .05 level;
***indicates significance at the .01 level

The second difference in the effect of the work-incentive waiver is that the significant negative effect on income growth disappears. It appears that families headed by single females were less likely to have earnings growth high enough to incur benefit reductions.

In summary, this analysis suggests that early welfare waivers had little effect on the earnings and a slight negative impact on the incomes of welfare recipients.

## Conclusion

Designers of welfare-reform policies frequently argue that these policies will increase recipients' self-sufficiency. If so, then the policies should lead to higher earnings and income growth for former recipients. In this study, I estimated the effect of pre–PRWORA, state-level welfare waivers on the earnings and income growth of recipients compared with nonrecipients over three time periods, using two different CPS samples. Neither work-related waivers nor other types of waivers had any significant effect on earnings growth, regardless of the time period and sample used. Both types showed a negative and statistically significant (but small) effect on the income growth of welfare recipients.

I also separated the work–related waiver variable into two components: work requirements and work incentives. The effect of the work-requirement waiver on earnings growth was negative, though in one case it was insignificant. The negative effect may result from the fact that recipients who were previously working quit their jobs in order to participate in job-training programs or to work at an approved job. The former explanation is consistent with the finding that work-requirement waivers did not have a significant effect on income growth, because this implies that lost earnings were offset by some other source of income — perhaps the additional welfare benefits that participation in job-training programs would provide.

The significance of work incentive waivers on earnings growth varies, but the effect is always positive. However, the effect on income growth is negative (but small) in every case. The latter estimates are significant only for the model that compares welfare recipients with all recipients, regardless of gender and marital status.

Although the results presented here cover only the effects of waivers approved by the end of 1993 and 1994, they are suggestive of the impacts that may have occurred in later years as well. Most of the later waivers, as well as PRWORA, have similar provisions as those studied here. One purpose of welfare reform legislation was to reduce the number of recipients. While it may have succeeded in that respect, it is important to understand what has happened economically to those who relied on welfare at the time of the new policies, whether or not they continued to receive benefits. This analysis suggests that those families are generally no better off, and are potentially worse off, as a result of welfare reform.

## References

Blank, Rebecca M. 1997. *It Takes a Nation: A New Agenda for Fighting Poverty*. Princeton, NJ: Princeton University Press.

Connolly, Laura S., and Lewis M. Segal. 2000. Minimum Wage Legislation and the Working Poor. Unpublished paper. University of Northern Colorado, Greeley.

Crouse, Gil. 1999. State Implementation of Major Changes to Welfare Policies, 1992–1998. U.S. Department of Health and Human Services, Assistant Secretary for Planning and Evaluation, Office of Human Services Policy. Available online: http://aspe.hhs.gov/.

Edin, Kathryn, and Laura Lein. 1997. *Making Ends Meet: How Single Mothers Survive Welfare and Low–Wage Work*. New York: Russell Sage Foundation.

Ehrenberg, Ronald G., and Robert S. Smith. 1994. *Modern Labor Economics: Theory and Public Policy*. Fifth Edition. New York: HarperCollins.

Moffitt, Robert. 1996. "The Effect of Employment and Training Programs on Entry and Exit from the Welfare Caseload." *Journal of Policy Analysis and Management* 15, no. 1 (Winter): 32–50.

———. 1999. The Effect of Pre–PRWORA Waivers on AFDC Caseloads and Female Earnings, Income, and Labor Force Behavior. Joint Center on Poverty Research Working Paper No. 89.

Schiller, Bradley R. 1999. "State Welfare–Reform Impacts: Content and Enforcement Effects." *Contemporary Economic Policy* 17, no. 2 (April): 210–22.

Tapogna, John, and Tara Witt. 1998. *Making the Transition to Self–Sufficiency in Oregon*. Report prepared for the Oregon Coalition of Community Non–Profits Under Subcontract to Children First for Oregon. Portland OR: ECONorthwest. (A version appears as Chapter 16 in this volume.)

U.S. Council of Economic Advisers. 1997. Explaining the Decline in Welfare Receipt, 1993–1996. Technical Report.

Ziliak, James P., David N. Figlio, Elizabeth E. Davis, and Laura S. Connolly. 1997. *Accounting for the Decline in AFDC Caseloads: Welfare Reform or Economic Growth?* Institute for Research on Poverty Discussion Paper 1151–97. Madison: University of Wisconsin.

———. 2000. "Accounting for the Decline in AFDC Caseloads: Welfare Reform or the Economy?" *Journal of Human Resources* 35, no. 3 (Summer): 570–86.

## Notes

[1] Laura S. Connolly is assistant professor of economics at the University of Northern Colorado in Greeley, Colorado. Her research interests include public policy, the economics of poverty, and the economics of nonprofit organizations. She has published articles in the *Journal of Human Resources*, *Public Finance Review*, and the *Journal of Public Economics*.

[2] Empirical evidence shows that the drop in caseloads mostly resulted from a strong economy rather than from welfare reform policies. For examples, see Ziliak et al. (2000) and U.S. Council of Economic Advisers (1997).

[3] Simple models of the labor-supply effect of work requirements and certain types of work incentives can be found in Ehrenberg and Smith (1994).

[4] Under the original AFDC program, the "30 and 1/3 rule" allowed the recipient to keep the first $30 plus 33 percent of any wages earned during the first four months on AFDC. After that, benefits were reduced by one dollar for each dollar of earnings.

[5] Noncash assistance is also reduced, but this is not counted as income, so I do not address it here. For fascinating examples of ways in which the interactions among public assistance programs affect incomes at varying levels of work effort, see Blank (1997, ch. 3) and, especially, Tapogna and Witt (Chapter 16 of this volume).

[6] See Moffitt (1996) for a discussion of the incentive effects of these programs.

[7] Methodological details are available from the author upon request: University of Northern Colorado, Department of Economics, Campus Box 101, Greeley CO 80639; email: lsconno@unco.edu.

[8] There is some evidence that the amount of public assistance received is underreported in the CPS. This will cause measurement error in the income variable, but will not affect the dependent variable used here (the *change* in log incomes), unless underreporting is systematically different across years. It is also necessary that interviewees honestly report family participation in assistance programs. I have no evidence to suggest that participation levels are underreported in the CPS.

[9] Schiller (1999) makes a compelling case that local discretion in county welfare offices can lead to wide variation in the degree to which particular provisions are implemented within a given state. This means that statewide waiver data may not provide accurate information about the ways in which welfare reforms actually affect recipients. Unfortunately, no data measuring implementation at the county level, especially in terms of the behavior of case workers, are currently available.

[10] Work-requirement waivers include those that change the JOBS work-exemption requirements, those that affect JOBS sanctions, and those that impose work requirements after some time limit is reached. Work-incentive waivers are those that increase the amount of earned income a recipient can receive without losing a portion of her welfare payment.

[11] Control variables in all models: change in Gross State Product and change in state unemployment rate. Demographics and state-level dummies are controlled for in the first stage prediction of earnings and income.

[12] Estimates of the effects of waivers implemented by the end of 1993 are based on a sample of 3,065 recipient families and 57,440 nonrecipient families.

[13] Estimates of the effects of waivers implemented by the end of 1994 are based on a sample of 2,774 recipient families and 57,434 nonrecipient families.

[14] Edin and Lein (1997) report that this is relatively common.

[15] Working recipients have an incentive to hide earnings from unreported jobs, so it is possible that earnings for this group of families is underreported in the CPS. If so, this would strengthen the argument: Because fewer recipients are likely to be working against AFDC rules after the work requirement is imposed, reported earnings in the second period are probably more accurate than first period earnings in waiver states. In this case, predicted earnings growth in waiver states would be overstated relative to that of nonwaiver states. Thus, the actual effect of the waiver on earnings would be at least as large (in magnitude) as my estimates indicate.

[16] This results in a very small change in the sample of recipients because most recipient households are headed by single females. The control group is much smaller than before however.

[17] Control variables in all models: change in Gross State Product and change in state unemployment rate. Demographics and state-level dummies are controlled for in the first stage prediction of earnings and income.

[18] Estimates of the effects of waivers implemented by the end of 1993 are based on a sample of 2,107 recipient families and 16,735 nonrecipient families.

[19] Estimates of the effects of waivers implemented by the end of 1994 are based on a sample of 1,928 recipient families and 16,539 nonrecipient families.

[20] Recipients are identified by answering "yes" to the question, "At any time during [year], even for one month, did anyone in this household receive any public assistance or welfare payments from the State or local welfare office?" Thus, the sample includes AFDC–UP families and families receiving cash benefits from programs other than AFDC as well.

# Struggling to Live and to Learn
## Single Mothers, Welfare Policy and Post-Secondary Education in Michigan[1]

*Peggy Kahn*[2] *and Valerie Polakow*[3]

**Y**ou can take anything from a person, but you can't take away their education. Having an education means I'll be able to educate my child and others … It's what you need to get a good job in order not to be on assistance and take this type of harassment from social workers that think it's their money they are giving out … I have a son that really motivates me to go to school … He'll be saying his mother worked hard and struggled for it, and I want to be a role model for him… [But] they sent me letters saying I would have to immediately go to Work First, and work study doesn't count … [The caseworker] actually told me, 'We don't care about you going to school; Governor Engler wants ladies to work.'

—Sandra, a twenty-two-year-old African-American mother of a three-year-old boy, trying to complete a B.A.

To the day when the twins turned three months, I get a phone call, and the next day I get a letter saying I have to report to Work First.… And my goal was to finish school. I tried to enroll in school, but the lady told me I couldn't because I wasn't working yet. I said I have a work-study job and I took as many hours as they would give me. [Then, the caseworker] tells me, you're not eligible for daycare because you haven't done anything about child support.... They didn't refund the $1,000 I spent on childcare.... I go to school for fifteen hours, I work twenty-five hours, and I have no time for the babies. I have to take a lot of classes. I need to go ahead and get out. I don't sleep all night.... I was breastfeeding but I can't in the middle of the night anymore. I'm like the walking dead. My goal was to have the twins and finish my last year of college and ... make a better life for them, to try to provide for them and be a good mother. I never anticipated taking care of two infants, trying to go to school, and then trying to work these outrageous hours ... not being able to rest, not being able to sleep.

—Nicole, a twenty-three-year-old mother of infant twins, completing her last year of a B.A.

Single mothers struggling to stay in school describe how their commitment to postsecondary education is threatened by the rigid work-first welfare regime in Michigan. They understand their educational pursuits to be critical to their own development and ability to provide for their family's long-term economic independence, as well as their children's social and academic growth. The Welfare-to-Work (WtW) regime, however, requires that they conform to the exclusive priority of immediate entry into low-wage work and exit from welfare. The formidable obstacles to their educational achievements include not only formal work requirements in an unreformed labor market unfriendly to women with children, but also restrictive, punitive, and inconsistent implementation of a range of welfare provisions. Such policies and frontline delivery practices compromise student mothers' parenting, disrupt their educational progress, and disregard their work histories and aspirations, forcing independently minded low-income parents either to give up on college degrees or make painful short-term sacrifices in the hope that they will make long-term gains.

### Why Education Matters

Student mothers and other welfare clients who aspire to two- and four-year degrees perceive postsecondary education as their path out of poverty to self-sufficiency. Without postsecondary education they remain vulnerable and dependent upon public assistance. Public assistance consigns their families not only to financial shortage and privation but also to social powerlessness and degradation. Recognizing their own developmental potential where public policy denies it, single mothers pursue education to permanently transform themselves and their families. Pursuing education is an exercise of autonomy, yet public policy denies them autonomy while demanding that they become "independent" low-wage workers.

Studies of welfare recipients who have completed two- and four-year degrees show that postsecondary education has enormous benefits for women and children on assistance. Such women work more steadily, find jobs related to their fields of study, earn higher wages, receive more postemployment training, and report higher levels of family well-being after graduation (Alexander and Clendenning 1999; Boldt 2000; Gittell, Schehl, and Fareri 1990; Gittell, Gross, and Holdaway 1993; Gittell et al. 1996; Karier 1998; Reeves 1999).

Job search training, basic skills training, and short-term vocational training do not have the same impact as two- and four-year degrees on the employment and earnings potential of welfare recipients (Eberts 1995; Handler 1995). The importance of postsecondary education for single mothers is underlined by the fact that women's earnings and income increase dramatically when they have college degrees (Blau 1998; McCall 2000; Mishel, Bernstein, and Schmitt 1997). Women need more education to earn what men earn with a high school degree (IWPR n.d.), and completing four years of college sharply reduces women's chances of being poor, from 16.7 percent to 1.6 percent when compared to those with only a high school degree (Dept. of Labor 2000; Gittell et al. 1996).

Without a postsecondary education, recipients and those leaving the welfare rolls are employed in jobs that pay on average $6.61 per hour, do not raise families above even the artificially depressed official poverty line, and do not provide health insurance (Brauner and Loprest 1999; Parrott 1999). In the absence of postsecondary education, wages of women leaving welfare traditionally have risen excruciatingly slowly, failing to lift families even above the poverty line during children's critical developmental years (Burtless 1997; Cancian et al. 1999; Corcoran and Loeb 1999; Hershey and Pavetti 1997).

Postsecondary education for low-income mothers not only increases family income, but also increases parental expectations of children's achievement and children's own educational aspirations (Gittell, Gross, and Holdaway 1993; Gittell et al. 1996). Higher levels of parental education lead to early development of language and literacy skills and increase the likelihood that children will be successful in school (FIFCFS 1997).

### Federal and State Policy

PRWORA embodies and reinforces the idea that any entry-level low-wage job is good enough for welfare recipients, and that any non–labor market activity, including education, is merely work avoidance. By failing to treat postsecondary education as a work activity that counts toward work participation, PRWORA discourages state support for postsecondary education. Under PRWORA, clients face escalating work requirements.[4]

In fact, despite such requirements, states have both the flexibility and the funding to establish state-level postsecondary options. Precipitous caseload reductions have reduced states' required participation rates, so states can afford not to count those in fulltime training or education without jeopardizing federal funding. States could develop definitions of client work activities that include postsecondary education, and they could use funds from TANF programs or elsewhere to cover the costs of parents going to college. However, only a few states have permitted client access to postsecondary education degrees.

Maine, Illinois, Kentucky, California, and Wyoming are often cited as the five states that permit some form of postsecondary education, but most of the twenty-one states that have made limited provisions for education fall short of removing the work requirements that are formidable obstacles to degree completion (Greenberg, Strawn, and Plimpton 2000).

Though it is difficult to separate the impact of declining welfare caseloads from declining recipient enrollment, it is clear that changes in welfare policy have ejected many low-income parents from postsecondary institutions. Federal student-financial-aid data show the number of cash recipients applying for student aid falling 47.6 percent between 1994 and 1998; the U.S. General Accounting Office (GAO) found marked declines in participation in education and training between 1994 and 1997; and state reports on client activity under TANF show a drop from 3.9 percent of the caseload participating in postsecondary education in 1996 to 1.8 percent in 1998 (Greenberg, Strawn, and Plimpton 1999). Meanwhile, community colleges, colleges, and universities report precipitous declines in enrollment of public assistance recipients (IWPR 1998; Carter and Kirk 1997).

The state of Michigan has strongly endorsed a work-first approach that generally excludes postsecondary education, focusing only upon the reduction of the welfare caseload. Benefits are contingent upon immediate attendance and enrollment in job search programs. Lack of compliance brings rapid sanctions. Only a very restricted set of clients is exempted from attendance,[5] and clients must accept job offers of up to forty hours per week, regardless of work schedules. Despite these draconian work requirements, there has been no adequate provision of childcare, resulting in an acute crisis for low-income students with young children. Welfare-reliant student mothers frequently face a shortage of affordable, high-quality licensed care for infants and toddlers or cannot locate childcare during the nonstandard hours they work and study. The state's long delays in making childcare payments also result in children losing places in daycare programs.

In addition, Michigan uses a dualistic, partly deregulated, privatized structure for policy implementation. The social services department, renamed the Family Independence Agency (FIA), determines client eligibility for benefits,[6] delivering the message that welfare will be short-term and transitional. However, the Department of Career Development oversees the county-level MichiganWorks! Agencies, which hire subcontractors to administer the Work First program.

### Severely Restricted Postsecondary Education Options in Michigan

In its 1996 TANF plan, Michigan made no specific provision for postsecondary education. It did not take advantage of a provision in federal legislation allowing states to count up to a year of vocational training as meeting work requirements, for up to 20 percent of the caseload. On paper, however, the state had a largely unpublicized set of rules, called Post Employment Training (PET), that allowed clients working twenty hours per week to engage in job-related training for five hours per week, for up to one year. Such clients could decline offers of more than twenty hours if they interfered with an approved education program. In 1998, after intense lobbying efforts by various postsecondary and advocacy coalitions, state legislators and agencies enacted policies that permitted clients to use college-mandated fulltime educational internships, lasting six months or less, to fulfill work requirements.

In summer 1999, under further pressure from state advocates—and with more TANF money per case than expected, rapidly falling welfare rolls, and a state push for short-term technical training as a solution to certain labor shortages—state legislators and agency personnel crafted a new set of education and training provisions. These primarily were oriented toward short-term training, rather than postsecondary degrees. The new policy, administered primarily by Work First rather than FIA, allowed clients to use hours spent in certain types of education and training to meet some or all of their work requirements for limited periods of time, under restrictive conditions. Single parents could use an approved, fulltime vocational program (of less than six months) to meet requirements. Fulltime internships, practicums, or clinical assignments required by a school to complete a degree or for professional certification could also meet the thirty-hour requirement. In addition, programs requiring twelve months or less to complete, or the last year of two- or four-year degree programs designed to lead to an immediate job, could count toward work requirements. A client in the final year of a degree program was required to work only ten hours per week and could count up to ten hours per week of classroom time and up to one hour of study for each hour of class time towards her thirty-hour requirement.[7]

Approved educational programs qualified clients for tuition assistance, childcare subsidies for class but not study time, and transportation assistance. Though students completing their last year of approved programs could take advantage of these new provisions, other students lost the ability to count five hours of education toward work requirements.

### Organizational Practices and Policy Implementation

Despite the fact that formal policy marginally increased access to postsecondary education, agencies single-mindedly continued to stress the Work First message of mandatory employment and quick exit from welfare. Mandatory FIA/WF orientations emphasize that "self-sufficiency begins with a job" and "entry level jobs lead to career options." Recently, orientation presenters combined mechanical reading of new education provisions with the warning, "Education is not for everyone, your first responsibility is to work." They also gave incorrect responses to questions about education provisions.[8] The FIA's occupational culture of suspicion and control of clients, and the burdensome workloads of frontline workers, combine with the nearly exclusive Work First messages, marginalizing, misrepresenting, and denigrating educational options.

Overwhelmed by complex and changing rules in multiple programs, and by new demands to make home visits, caseworkers in Michigan appear to simplify their routines by neither learning nor using the education rules. In the minds of many agency staff, these provisions are irrelevant to the capacities and interests of the majority of their clients. However, research using data from the early 1990s has shown that one-third to one-half of all welfare clients have been capable of pursing higher education (Carnevale and Desrochers 1999; Kates 1991), and it is clear that many clients over the last five years have persisted in trying to continue or initiate postsecondary education despite the obstacles.

Michigan's Work First contractors, which number over one hundred and include nonprofits, for-profits, and school-based centers, have a particularly important role in administering the education policy: They approve educational hours as counting toward work requirements. In Michigan's dualistic welfare system, however, there is little regulation of the Work First subcontractors. The state office provides little direction and oversight, declining to standardize policies in favor of county-level autonomy. Contracts are awarded on the basis of few specifications, and contract selection automatically rewards the lowest bidder. Staffs face large workloads and have low levels of education, experience, or training in current policy. Contractors maximize scarce resources by focusing on job placement and retention for what they understand to be the "typical client."

Many contracts contain a specification stating that costs for mistakenly approved services will be deducted from the subcontractor's payments. Such stipulations institutionalize frontline worker caution in authorizing supportive services and resistance to approving educational programs. Until recently, contractors were discouraged from placing clients in postsecondary education because such placements were not counted positively in performance measures, while longer-hour job placements and job retention were (Kahn, forthcoming).

## Themes in the Lives of Student Mothers in Michigan

Student mothers' determined commitment to postsecondary education often comes into conflict with restrictive and punitive policies of social service institutions. Between October 1997 and February 2000, we followed ten single mothers on assistance and in postsecondary education and conducted open-ended interviews. Their voices testify to their resilience, tenacity, and capacity to overcome multiple obstacles and endure harrowing odds.

### Low-wage Work First, Education Last

Like other clients, student mothers in postsecondary education have been pressured, under threat of sanctions, to immediately enter the labor market, maximize their hours, and exit the welfare rolls. The pressure on students to maximize their hours of low-wage work endangers their psychological and physical well-being, undermines their academic success, subjects their educational priorities to ridicule and dismissal, and compromises their mothering.

In 1997 Lakeisha, a twenty-six-year-old African American mother of two children with intensive needs, was pursing a demanding computer science degree fulltime and working on her university campus.

> Well, the twenty-hour mandatory work requirement, it has caused me to leave my children in the care of daycare providers for the majority of the day. Like I go to school fulltime and have to work an additional twenty hours during the week, so my day here will begin at 9:00 in the morning and end at 6:00 in the evening.... There's no time for quality time with my children, and on the weekend I'm trying to play catch-up with homework ... I couldn't complete throughout the week because I was so tired when they got off to bed. It's really taken a toll on me.... I actually withdrew from the university because my grades were falling. I took two weeks off work to try to bring up my grades, but when I went back to work my grades started falling again. And my kids ... I don't know what kind of damage I'm doing in the long run, whether it can be repaired or not.

Julie, a white mother of a two-year-old son, encountered pressure to leave school and work forty hours per week at a minimum-wage job, though federal policy requires only twenty hours.

> I had work study at the College, and they're only allowed to give you twenty-five hours at most … (so) I said to my worker, "You're telling me that I should get a McDonald's job working forty hours a week and still be on welfare instead of being on welfare now, better myself, get my degree so I hopefully never have to be on welfare again?" And she said, "Yep, they want you to work forty hours a week."

Sandra's caseworker erroneously told her that her work-study job was not a real job, could not count toward meeting work requirements, and would not make her eligible for a childcare subsidy for her three-year-old.

> They sent me letters saying that I would have to immediately go to Work First and work study doesn't count … especially when I was trying to get childcare. She said, "No, that doesn't count. You have to have a Work First job, and you have to come to Work First on this day, and if you do not come, you are going to be terminated from the system." I went to Work First one time, and I didn't go back, and I just had to deal with finding a babysitter. The Work First job required me to actually quit going to school because it was like 6:00 a.m. to 2:00 p.m. an hour away, and it was only making $6.00 an hour. They said they could provide the way in and daycare, and whatever…. The caseworker actually told me, "We don't care about you going to school, that is not what we want. Governor Engler wants ladies to work."

But then Sandra faced another battle. Though she was already combining a work-study job at a writing center for twelve hours per week with a temporary job at a recreation center for fifteen-to-twenty hours, her caseworker called both employers to see if she could be working additional hours. The recreation center said that up to forty hours were available.

> Then he suspended my grant for another month because he said I was available, I could have worked forty hours a week at one of my jobs, and I refused it, and one of the rules is that you cannot refuse, reduce, or stop working. If

**164**

you're offered forty hours you have to work that forty hours. And I said, "Well, if I work forty hours, where would my school come in?" He said, "That's your personal goal. I don't have anything to do with that."

Carol, a thirty-two-year-old white mother of a fourteen-year-old daughter with hyperactivity and attention-deficit disorder, was instructed to report to Work First orientation in the middle of her final examination period.

I had to go in.... And basically all they do is they set you up for some kind of service industry job that's like never actually going to pay a living wage. I sat through the orientation. I didn't get any of my questions answered because every time I tried to ask them about what they did for schooling, they didn't want to have anything to do with that. They wanted to talk about how you can become an assistant manager at Walgreen's.

## Childcare: A Continuing Crisis

A critical problem confronting student mothers involves access to quality and affordable childcare. Children of welfare-reliant parents, including student mothers, frequently face cheap and poor quality care, as mothers can rarely pay the high costs of quality care, which far exceed FIA subsidy rates. Student mothers encounter many obstacles in using childcare subsidies: outright denials, inexplicable reductions or cut-offs, slow start-ups, withheld information about expedited approval processes, late payments, and under-calculation of subsidies. All these problems contribute to a tenuous and unstable family situation. Many mothers feel powerless, stressed, and deprived of the resources they need to be the parents they want to be.

FIA did not promptly authorize childcare subsidies when Lakeisha made a transition from her paid summer internship to the regular academic year and a low-wage work-study job.

I had been leaving messages for my caseworker, her back-up and their supervisor for three weeks, and no one called back. I was responsible for paying, and I just couldn't do it. I had to enroll him in a different daycare than where I wanted him to go. Although he's unhappy there, it's convenient for me, (because) they pick him up from school. I have enrolled my daughter there as well ... so she can keep an eye on him and see what's going on and what's making him unhappy.

At the same time that Lakeisha lost her subsidy for her young son, her best friend and informal caregiver to her children died prematurely of asthma at age twenty-seven, and Lakeisha helped to look after her friend's three children and mother, all while trying to maintain her academic commitments.

Tanya, an African-American mother of three, struggled with childcare throughout her community college and university years.

> Childcare payments were never reliable; I've never know them to be like something that's a guaranteed payment.... For one reason or another, they'll stop it mid-semester.... Sometimes I would owe my childcare provider, and I'm asking them, well would you keep them on next week, and they hadn't been paid for the last two weeks. So I would constantly wear out my welcome.... A couple of nights I didn't have childcare. I had to say, "Honey, now, kids, stay in bed 'til mommy gets home." I was just trying to get them all the snacks they wanted to eat and just say, "Okay, I have to go to this class, and if you could just watch your sister for me until I come home." ... I felt very bad, very guilty. I still feel very guilty today that I did that.

Tina, a twenty-five-year-old African-American mother with children eight and four, described a year-long ordeal that began when she lost her job for bringing her daughter to work, because her worker would not authorize childcare subsidies. Later when she began a job on campus and enrolled her daughter in the campus center, it took the combined efforts of the center director, a legal advocate, and threats of hearings before her subsidy was approved — four months after her initial application. All this time she was in compliance with work requirements and was attending school fulltime.

> ...[My] worker said I missed days at work and I said, "If you check the roster it was the days I was in this welfare office waiting to talk to you." And then the FIA paid some of it—but the lawyer said even if it goes back I'm still entitled to it because it's their fault and stuff, and I asked did she want to talk to the lawyer about it, and then they added more units to my childcare.... There are so many obstacles you got to go through just to get $2.50 an hour, which don't cover near the whole daycare cost!

When her school-age son needed care over the summer, Tina again experienced delays, was declared ineligible, had a difficult confrontation with the agency, and fell into debt.

**166**

**Concealed and Incorrect Information and Harassment**

FIA and Work First workers fail to disclose information that would support student mothers in their efforts to obtain postsecondary education. Workers did not inform student mothers about the possibility of using required internships to meet work requirements, the 10/10/10 program, eligibility for cash assistance, their children's eligibility for Medicaid, or domestic violence provisions. Not only was information withheld, but caseworkers also gave student mothers incorrect information that disadvantaged them and intensified surveillance and punishment, apparently because they were pursuing postsecondary education. Eight of the ten student mothers we interviewed over three years were given incorrect information that inflated the number of hours they were required to work, a serious problem for those trying to combine education, work and parenting, and none was voluntarily informed of the new 10/10/10 provisions when they were enacted.

Sarah, a white mother of a four-year-old biracial daughter, was consistently misinformed by FIA.

> The first letter said you had to work twenty-five hours.... I had gotten one of those that said they were going up to forty hours a week.... Then she came on a home visit and I was just filling out some forms and she told me I had to work twenty-five hours a week ... during fall of last year ... she had been talking to some other caseworkers and they told her that work study counts as income.... I had to go and look it up in the books in the library and the PEM [Program Eligibility Manual].... I looked it up in the manual and she still didn't believe me.... I'm like, "Look at it right here, and it's in black and white." She was looking at the Food Stamp section only, and she still didn't believe me. Then I finally explained to her that Work Study was Title IV Financial Aid, and I had to go over to the director of Financial Aid. She typed me a letter, and then I had to bring it to my worker.

Julie, still recovering from the shock of her husband's abandonment, faced with threats of violence, and responsible for a new baby, was not informed by her worker that she can get a cash allowance. She struggled for a year with only a food stamp allowance and had difficulties obtaining a childcare subsidy, but managed to go to school part time. Though she had a baby, she was told she would need to start working forty hours per week to qualify for benefits, and when she received high grades and tried to transfer to a four-year institution, her caseworker made bizarre threats and gave her patently false information.

**167**

Tanya, the African-American mother of three, and another successful community college graduate, was also misinformed about her work requirement.

> My caseworker seems more furious and harsh than ever.
> I have been cut off a few times since being enrolled
> here.... My workers ... seem to think that just because
> I attend a university, I don't deserve their assistance....
> It just got to be so tense with her because she started
> calling me a lot and calling my jobs a lot. "Is she on time
> every day?" "Could she be working more hours?" — asking
> things like that. She would call my boss every month, and
> if my immediate supervisor wasn't there she would just
> talk to anybody in the office.... It was so embarrassing,
> I just didn't even want to work in the office anymore.

## Conclusion

The multiple barriers to women's pursuit of postsecondary education pose two striking paradoxes. First, current Work First policies and practices have created severe pressures on low-income women to find jobs—jobs that are typically unstable, pay low-wages, and require nonstandard hours with little flexibility. These policies and practices threaten access to postsecondary education, which could insure long-term, meaningful economic self-sufficiency for women and their families. Secondly, the political rhetoric of welfare laments recipients' lack of a work ethic and their inability to make informed decisions. But self-initiated postsecondary education represents a rational, autonomous decision. Attending college builds women's human capital and is a self-conscious investment in their children. Yet this exercise of autonomy is rendered nearly impossible and devalued.

Clearly, national and state policies should guarantee welfare recipients access to postsecondary education. Welfare reauthorization should include provisions that encourage states to grant access to two- and four-year degrees. States need to develop plans that provide access to postsecondary education, allowing fulltime postsecondary education requirements to meet work requirements. Welfare agencies need to be redirected to support postsecondary education and see education as conducive to economic independence, rather than as work avoidance. All workers should receive appropriate training, and performance monitoring of staff and organizations should recognize and reward placements in education and client completion of postsecondary education programs.

Clearly, for student mothers, and welfare clients in general, the acute childcare crisis must be addressed. Promptly paid subsidies raised to reflect the actual costs of high-quality care should be available for hours of class work and study time, as well as for hours of paid employment.

Mothers who have persisted in postsecondary education since 1997 narrate harrowing experiences, as they resiliently continue to fight for the limited rights still available to them under existing law. But what of the other mothers—those who have given up and dropped out of colleges, those who aspire to postsecondary education but cannot find their way over the multiple obstacles erected in their path, those who have not succeeded in their self-advocacy and resistance to the welfare bureaucracy? Are their lives and struggles for education under the Welfare-to-Work regime also discounted and rendered invisible? For if Lakeisha, Julie, Sandra, Carole, Tina, Tanya, and Sarah continue to remain so vulnerable, what do their experiences tell us about other mothers who aspire to postsecondary education as the path out of poverty and powerlessness?

## References

Alexander, Michelle, and Dodie Clendenning. 1999. *The State of Maine's Parents as Scholars Program: Executive summary of early findings.* Orono, Maine: Center for Community Inclusion, University of Maine.

Blau, Francine. 1998. "Trends in the Well-being of American Women, 1970–1995." *Journal of Economic Literature* 36 (March): 112–65.

Boldt, Nancy. 2000. From welfare to college to work: Support factors to help students persist and succeed and the economic and social outcomes of college degree attainment. Ph.D. diss., University of Vermont.

Burtless, Gary. 1997. "Welfare recipients' job skills and employment prospects." *The Future of Children* 7 (1): 39–51.

Brauner, Sarah, and Pamela Loprest. 1999. *Where Are They Now? What States' Studies of People Who Left Welfare Tell Us.* Washington, D.C.: Urban Institute.

Cancian, Maria, Robert Haveman, Thomas, Daniel Meyer, and Barbara Wolfe 1999. *Work, Earnings and Well-being after Welfare: What Do We Know?* Madison, WI: Institute for Research on Poverty.

Carnevale, Anthony, and Donna Desroches. 1999. *Getting Down to Business: Matching Welfare Recipients' Skills to Jobs that Train.* Princeton, NJ: Educational Testing Services.

Carter, Sandra, and Arthur Kirk. 1997. Effects of Welfare Reform on Community College Students in Michigan. Report prepared for the State Board of Public Community Colleges.

Corcoran, Mary, and Susanna Loeb. 1999. "Will Wages Grow with Experience for Welfare Mothers?" *Focus* 20 (2): 20–21.

Eberts, R.W. 1995. *Welfare to Work: Local Observations on a National Issue.* Kalamazoo, MI: W.E. Upjohn Institute for Employment Research.

Federal Interagency Forum on Child and Family Statistics (FIFCFS). 1997. *America's Children: Key National Indicators of Well-being*. Washington, D.C.: FIFC&FS.

Gittell, Marilyn, Margaret Schehl, and Camille Fareri. 1990. *From Welfare to Independence: The College Option. Report to the Ford Foundation*. New York: Howard Samuels State Management and Policy Center.

Gittell, Marilyn, Jill Gross, and Jennifer Holdaway. 1993. *Building Human Capital: The Impact of Post-Secondary Education on AFDC Recipients in Five States. A Report to the Ford Foundation*. New York: Howard Samuels State Management and Policy Center.

Gittell, Marilyn, Kirk Vandersall, Jennifer Holdaway, and Katherine Newman. 1996. *Creating Social Capital at CUNY: A Comparison of Higher Education Programs for AFDC Recipients*. New York: Howard Samuels State Management and Policy Center.

Greenberg, Mark, Julie Strawn, and Lisa Plimpton. 2000. *State Opportunities to Provide Access to Post-secondary Education under TANF*. Washington, D.C.: Center for Law and Social Policy.

Handler, Joel. 1995. *The Poverty of Welfare Reform*. New Haven, CT: Yale University Press.

Hershey, Alan M., and LaDonna A. Pavetti. 1997. "Turning Job Finders into Job Keepers." *The Future of Children* 7 (1): 74–86.

Institute for Women's Policy Research (IWPR) n.d. *The Wage Gap: Men's and Women's Earnings*. Washington, D.C.: IWPR.

———. 1998. "Welfare Reform and Post-secondary Education: Research and Policy Update." *Welfare Reform Network News* 2 (April): 2.

Kahn, Peggy. 2001. "'Governor Engler wants ladies to work:' Single mothers, work-first welfare policy and post-secondary education in Michigan." *Journal of Poverty*. Forthcoming.

Karier, Thomas. 1998. *Welfare Graduates: College and Financial Independence*. The Jerome Levy Economics Institute. Available http://www.levy.org/docs/pn98-1.html.

Kates, Erika. 1991. "Transforming Rhetoric into Choice: Access to higher education for low-income women." In *Women, Work and School: Occupational Segregation and the Role of Education*. Leslie R. Wolfe, ed. Boulder, CO: Westview.

McCall, Leslie. 2000. "Gender and the New Inequality: Explaining the College/Noncollege Wage Gap." *American Sociological Review* 65 (April): 234–55.

Mishel, Lawrence, Jared Bernstein, and John Schmitt. 1997. *The State of Working America 1996–7*. Armonk, NY: M.E. Sharpe.

Parrott, Sharon. 1999. *Welfare Recipients Who Find Jobs: What Do We Know About Their Employment and Earnings?* Washington, D.C.: Center on Budget and Policy Priorities.

Reeves, Angela. 1999. *An Analysis of Economic Achievement Experienced by Graduates of a Perkins-funded Single Parent and Displaced Homemakers Program*. Flint, MI: Mott Community College.

U.S. Department of Labor. 2000. *A Profile of the Working Poor, 1998*. Washington, D.C.: United States Government Printing Office.

U.S. General Accounting Office (GAO). 1998. *Welfare Reform: States are Restructuring Programs to Reduce Welfare Dependence.* Washington, D.C.: Department of Health and Human Services.

## Notes

[1] This chapter is a modified version of our longer report, "Struggling to Stay in School: Obstacles to Post-Secondary Education Under the Welfare-to-Work Regime in Michigan," prepared for the Center for the Education of Women, University of Michigan, and available at www.umich.edu/~cew/pubs.html. The report is based upon research conducted between October 1997 and February 2000. We followed ten single mothers on assistance and in postsecondary education at the beginning of the study through cumulative open-ended interviews. We have also worked with public benefit advocates and educators in CFITE, the Coalition for Independence through Education. The research was funded by State of Michigan Research Excellence Funds through the Project on Urban and Regional Affairs at the University of Michigan-Flint and the Jean Campbell Fellowship through the Center for the Education of Women.

[2] Peggy Kahn is professor of political science and member of the women's and gender studies faculty at the University of Michigan–Flint. Since 1997 she has, together with Valerie Polakow, been monitoring the impact of new welfare policies on single-mother families and working as an advocate to increase the access of low-income single mothers to post-secondary education. Her current research interests are in women in the low-wage labor market: their work-family dilemmas, the dynamics of their workplaces, and their access to training and education. She is co-author of *Contesting the Market: Pay Equity and the Politics of Economic Restructuring* (Wayne State University Press 1997) and co-editor of *Equal Value/Comparable Work in the US and UK* (Macmillan/St. Martin's Press, 1992).

[3] Valerie Polakow is a professor of education at Eastern Michigan University. She was a Fulbright Scholar in Denmark in 1995–1996 and has written extensively about single mothers and children in poverty, homeless children, and cross-national welfare and childcare policies. She is the author of several books, including *Lives on the Edge: Single Mothers and their Children in the Other America* (University of Chicago Press, 1993), which won the Kappa Delta Pi Book of the Year Award in 1994. Her most recent works are *The Public Assault on America's Children: Poverty, violence, and Juvenile Injustice* (Teachers College Press, 2000) and *Diminished Rights: Vulnerable Lone Mothers and their Children in Denmark* (with Therese Halskov and Per Schultz Jørgensen, Policy Press, forthcoming).

[4] Current PRWORA work requirements are thirty hours per week for a single parent with children six and over, and twenty hours for a parent with a child under six.

[5] The exemption for single parents of newborn infants is only twelve weeks.

[6] Cash benefits in the Family Independence Program, childcare subsidies, Food Stamps, Medicaid, and others.

[7] Thus, the program is referred to as 10/10/10.

[8] As part of our research and advocacy work, we observed three joint FIA-WF orientations conducted between October 1997 and February 2000 in two counties in southeast Michigan.

## PART IV

# Welfare Reform as Social Control

Gordon Lafer

John Horton

Linda L. Shaw

Chariti Gent

Renee Monson

# Job Training for Welfare Recipients

## A Hand Up or a Slap Down?

*Gordon Lafer*[1]

**R**emember: 'WORK IS IN. WELFARE IS OUT.'
—Los Angeles County CalWORKS office flyer.

For more than thirty years, job training has been an integral part of federal welfare policy. Beginning in the War on Poverty, elected officials and policy analysts alike believed that a substantial share of the poverty population was poor because they lacked adequate job skills. Education and training would enable poor people to land decently paying jobs, and thus work their way out of poverty and off the welfare rolls.

For supporters of the Temporary Assistance for Needy Families (TANF) program, training remains a central concept. "Reformed" welfare policies focus above all on the transition from welfare to work. Thus, equipping welfare recipients to get work, and to succeed in the labor market, is a central goal of both federal and state policies developed since 1996. However, job training under TANF differs fundamentally from the training policies of the previous three decades. Rather than focusing on equipping poor people with marketable skills, the new programs focus primarily on shaping participants' *attitudes*. Above all, Welfare-to-Work programs seek to turn out diligent and disciplined workers who will enthusiastically embrace positions with low-wage employers.

In this way, the fundamental logic of job training has metamorphosed. Rather than serving as a vehicle for upward mobility, it now serves as a disciplinary mechanism designed to keep people committed to a fixed station at the bottom of the labor market.

### Job Training Under TANF: Work First

The Welfare-to-Work programs operated under TANF represent the triumph of the Work First model of employment policy. In a dramatic shift from previous welfare training efforts, these programs largely eschew education and training, focusing instead on placing participants as quickly as possible into the first available job.

The state Welfare-to-Work programs that have served as the primary models for national reform are, in fact, "training" programs in name only, since they offer very little instruction in either occupational skills or remedial education. One review of state Welfare-to-Work programs found that on average, only 6.3 percent of program participants were enrolled in training for specific jobs (McDonnell and Zellman 1993, Table 4.1). In Los Angeles' Jobs-First program, touted as a national model and imitated by cities and states across the country, only 8.5 percent of welfare recipients received any education or training whatsoever (Freedman et al. 2000) Where previous programs focused either on occupational skills or on basic English and math training, work-first programs focus on helping people find jobs they are already qualified for, rather than enabling them to obtain better-paying jobs than those they held prior to going on welfare.

Work First marks a fundamental break with the tenets of training policy from the 1960s through the mid-1990s. For previous training programs, simply placing people into the first available job was not considered a mark of success. On the contrary, the goal of training programs was to equip people to get *better* jobs than they previously had, by giving them the education or technical skills that would let them compete for higher-wage positions. In this sense, Work First also differs from previous training programs in its implicit assumption that program participants have never worked before. According to Congressional Republicans, the point of welfare reform is to "reintroduce...families to the dignity of work."[2] The truth is, however, that for the most part, no introduction is needed. The vast majority of welfare recipients already have extensive work histories, and most move in and out of the paid labor market or work at least part time while receiving welfare.[3] Welfare recipients don't need help landing jobs at the bottom of the labor market. Indeed, these are all too often the very jobs that paved the way to public assistance in the first place. For this reason, three decades of policy research and program evaluations concluded that effective training programs must offer intensive English, math, or technical skills training; anything less left people stuck in the same low-wage, high-turnover labor market that had already failed to provide for their families.

The lessons of policy research were embodied most clearly in the 1992 reformation of the Job Training Partnership Act (JTPA), the primary federal job training program.[4] JTPA was frequently criticized for wasting money by allowing programs to provide superficial services that had little impact on improving participants' employability. After repeated admonishment by both the U.S. General Accounting Office and the Department of Labor's own Inspector General, Congress amended the JTPA legislation. Among the key changes adopted in the 1992 amendments were requirements that participants receive real skills training rather than superficial job referral services. Most importantly, the new law banned programs from providing job-search assistance or job-search training (such as resume writing or interview skills) without also providing substantive education or occupational skills training. Program results showed that welfare recipients who enrolled in real education or skills training earned higher wages than those who were simply helped with referrals; thus, job-search assistance as a stand-alone service was widely condemned as undermining JTPA's mission of enabling low-income workers to reach higher levels of the labor market.[5]

In this sense, the current axioms of Welfare-to-Work training stand in direct contradiction to the lessons of three decades of program evaluation. Under the 1996 PRWORA, state after state has adopted exactly the model that Congress banned in 1992—short-term, superficial job-search assistance that may place participants into jobs but cannot equip them to get *better* jobs than they might previously have landed. In this sense, TANF marks the large-scale abandonment of job training as a strategy for alleviating poverty.

In some states, the switch to Work First was driven largely by budgetary concerns. Several states started out with ambitious programs in times of economic expansion, including education, job training, drug treatment, and childcare services. When the early 1990s brought a combination of recession and budget retrenchment, virtually all of these were eliminated, replaced with low-cost work-first policies (Handler and Hasenfeld 1997, 62–63, 77). California's Greater Avenues for Independence (GAIN) program, which provided the single most important model for TANF, began as a service-intensive program. However, initial assessments showed a very high share of recipients in need of basic literacy, effectively transforming GAIN into a large-scale remedial education program. The state had not budgeted for such an effort, however. Los Angeles County, for instance, was never funded to provide services to more than 8 percent of its welfare population. Instead of increasing funding to educate illiterate recipients, California abandoned the legislators' original goals—adopting a 180-degree shift in program objectives in order to accommodate budgetary concerns. Rather than assess the type of skills recipients would need to get good jobs and then provide the requisite training, the program legislation was amended to focus on putting to work as many people as possible as quickly as possible—in whatever job might be available. "Let the marketplace, not caseworkers, determine who is employable," insisted Governor Deukmejian (Handler and Hasenfeld 1997, 64).

Thus, in shifting to a work-first policy, state programs abandoned the original intent of job training: to improve the wages and job prospects of participants above what they could otherwise attain. Of course, there are jobs that welfare recipients can get without training; but they are overwhelmingly unstable, low-wage, no-benefit positions. To determine that recipients are "employable" in these jobs is meaningless in terms of the aim of self-sufficiency. And to declare this type of employability as the goal of Welfare-to-Work programs is to mark the end of any significant effort at education or training for the nation's poorest citizens. As more and more states have followed California's example, training has been largely abandoned as a strategy for welfare recipients.

The rejection of education as a strategy for upward mobility is seen most clearly in PRWORA's insistence that states may not count math or literacy training as "work activities" for the purpose of satisfying federal Workfare requirements.[6] Individual states have established similar policies. Massachusetts Governor Celucci fired his entire board of welfare advisors when they suggested that hours spent in the classroom should be counted toward satisfying recipients' Workfare requirements.[7] In Milwaukee, the mayor's office denounced proposals that recipients enrolled in school might be excused from Workfare as "a step back to the old welfare system ... a terrible mistake."[8] And New York Mayor Giuliani forced thousands of city residents to drop out of college in order to work off their grants raking leaves or alphabetizing files.[9] Instead of education, the primary emphasis of TANF is on simple work: paying jobs, on-the-job training, community service, or "unpaid work experience" (GAO 1999, 5). Under this rubric, the General Accounting Office reports that "training focuses more on job readiness than on acquiring new vocational skills, in some cases using unpaid work experience or community service work to teach job-readiness skills" (GAO 1999, 2–3).[10]

Similarly, the Department of Labor's Welfare-to-Work initiative, established in 1997 to fund programs for TANF recipients who need special help moving off the rolls, follows a work-first philosophy. While the Welfare-to-Work program allows states to offer education and training, it does not require these services; in an era of fiscal restraint, making costly programs optional is often tantamount to abolishing them altogether. Moreover, while the new initiative funds job placement services, "job readiness" classes, and unpaid work experience, states are statutorily barred from using funds for education or skills training except for recipients who have already been placed into jobs (U.S. Department of Labor 1999). The policy priority here is to put all welfare recipients to work; only after they are working are states even permitted to provide real training — if they have enough funds left over to devote to this effort.

Thus, in the new welfare regime, enabling recipients to further their education is not considered a policy-worthy goal, while forcing them to toil at unpaid, menial labor is treated as critical. This may reflect social aims unrelated to the labor market—for instance, the conviction that one should "give something back" in return for public assistance. But this is merely another way of saying that education and training have effectively disappeared from welfare policy.

### If Not Education, What?

Instead of genuine education or skills training, welfare "training" is increasingly defined by a combination of harsh discipline and hokey motivational seminars. In the early 1990s, the federal government designated "low self-esteem" one of the "barriers to employment" that keep welfare recipients from securing gainful employment—thus enshrining in federal policy guidelines the conviction that it is the attitudes of poor Americans that are substantially to blame for their poverty (GAO 1994, 10). In keeping with this assumption, state programs have placed self-help rhetoric at the heart of their Welfare-to-Work efforts. The very names of programs indicate the centrality of motivational discourse to welfare reform strategies. A partial review of state Welfare-to-Work initiatives lists programs titled GAIN, GOALS, REACH, REACH UP, JET, MOST, PATHS, NEW JOBS, JOINT JOBS, KANWORK, Project First Step, Project Independence, and in two different states, Project Success (McDonnell and Zellman 1993, Table 5.1).[11]

The primary training service provided in these programs is "job search assistance," described by the Manpower Demonstration Research Corporation as "sessions designed to build self-confidence and job-seeking skills" (Gueron 1990, 89). But what is the real content of this training? One participant-observer provides a partial answer to this question in the following account of Wisconsin's Gateway to Opportunity, Advancement, and Lasting Success program (GOALS), one of the "motivational seminars" that have become mandatory under welfare reform regulations:

> During the first week of GOALS, about a dozen women and two men sit around a conference table at the Dane County job center. The instructor, who introduces herself as Kelly, shows flashcards. One flashcard says, You'll never amount to anything.
> "Has anybody ever heard this in your life?" she asks.
> No response.
> "Good! Because it's not true!"

She holds up another flashcard: You can do anything you set your mind to. "How about this one? How often do we hear this?"

No one says anything.

This is day three of the two-week GOALS session. The topic: communication. From Kelly's point of view, things aren't going so well. "People aren't talking a lot," she says. Several participants are clearly trying, though. Kelly holds up a flashcard that says, I'm so proud of you. "How do we feel when someone says this to us?" she asks.

"Good?" one participant offers.

"Yeah!" says Kelly. She hands out pieces of paper and asks everyone to write down the names of two people who have had a positive influence in their lives.

"It's the person who believes in you," she says.

She writes 'belives' in magic market on a flip chart, then crosses it out and writes 'beleives.'

"Don't tell her," the woman in front of me whispers.

"What?" Kelly asks. "don't tell me what?"

"You still spelled 'believes' wrong," someone says.

Kelly stares at the flip chart.

"It's I before E except after C," another participant explains.

"That's okay," the woman in front of me says. "That's a hard one."

After a short break, Kelly lists some more rules for good communication.

"Here are two of the hardest things to say in the English language," she says, and writes "Thank you" and "I'm sorry" on the flip charts.

I interview some participants after class. "I don't want to knock the program or anything – maybe someone is getting their self-esteem raised," says one participant. "But … they've given me an ultimatum: You either go to this class or it's your check." (Conniff 1994)

Across the country, Americans who are unfortunate enough to need public assistance are being forced to undergo "training" programs such as that mandated by GOALS — programs that have virtually no content apart from "can do" hype. Under TANF, however, the goofiness of self-esteem training is backed by the ever-present threat of sanctions and the specter of time limits. The nation's largest Welfare-to-Work program, Los Angeles' Jobs First GAIN, exemplifies this two-pronged approach, combining a "strong Work First message" with regular financial penalties for those who don't participate in job search activities. Fully 70 percent of recipients are threatened with sanctions in a typical program year, and 23 percent have had their grants cut as punishment for non-participation — more than double the rate of punitive sanctions issued before TANF (Freedman et al. 2000, 5–6, 10).

The content of GAIN's motivation seminars varies between cloyingly pollyannaish and eerily Orwellian. In the six-hour orientation meetings, "the message [is] … upbeat, stressing how work can lift self-esteem and that a low-paying first job can lead to a better one in the future" (Freedman et al. 2000, 6). In one sense, the rhetorical hype serves to legitimize very low standards of program success. The program promises neither improved skills nor a living wage; expectations of the actual jobs that recipients are to be placed into are kept low, and justified on the unlikely assumption of upward mobility. "Even an entry-level job will benefit the family," GAIN's literature explains, "and will provide experience which will assist a parent in securing a better job later."[12] Indeed, the GAIN "message" rings with brutal cheerfulness, relentlessly hawking the idea that work is its own reward:

> By working, you demonstrate the self-growth and independence which provide the positive role model that your children need to become successful, productive adults. Participants are encouraged to work full or part-time even if they want to pursue education or training. A job is an education too.[13]

But the program provides stick as well as carrot. A flyer from the Los Angeles GAIN office captures the sense of impending doom that awaits those who resist this smiley-faced vision of the low-wage labor market:

> Everyone will be expected to work … Work experience is the best training. Remember: "WORK IS IN, WELFARE IS OUT" (Freedman et al. 2000, 5).

The motto of GAIN is, "A job, Another Job, A Career"—suggesting that any job is a first step up the ladder toward a middle-class standard of living. However, the reality is that, with few exceptions, most welfare recipients are unable to find decently paying jobs and therefore are condemned either to remain in long-term Workfare positions or to cycle through an unending litany of low-wage, no-benefit, dead-end jobs. It is for this reason that so many recipients were cynical or dismissive of JOBS and other earlier Welfare-to-Work initiatives. The type of jobs that welfare recipients are pushed toward are exactly the jobs they have held previously and found incapable of supporting their families.[14] As a Milwaukee welfare administrator explains, "People are placed in low-income and temporary jobs that they work a few days here and there for a few hours.

There's no chance for stability at a job with a livable wage that will allow them to lead a wholesome life" (Freeman 1997, 3).

In this context, the hype surrounding "Job Club" or "Job Search" activities becomes not merely useless, but offensive. As one recipient recalls:

> It was disgusting. Here were these women getting jobs at a fast-food restaurant for minimum wage, and people were clapping and cheering. And then they would find out that they couldn't make it on that amount, so they would just come right back on welfare a month or so later. And that was the best they seemed to do. They didn't offer any real good jobs to anyone (Edin and Lein 1997, 74).

If "job readiness training" is not preparing participants for living-wage jobs, then what is its function? In program after program, it appears that Welfare-to-Work "training" serves primarily as a disciplinary mechanism, aimed at breaking participants of the notion that they can refuse, resist, or even complain about the type of jobs they are offered. Simply put, the goal of welfare training is to get poor people to embrace hard work at low wages with little chance for advancement, and to suffer this fate quietly.

"Work First" training starts with the assumption that welfare recipients must be made into attractive candidates for private employers; however, employers may define their needs. In fact, employer surveys consistently find that the most important hiring criteria for entry-level jobs are attitudinal.[15] Rather than looking for good English, math, or technical skills, employers who are considering hiring recent welfare recipients report that the most important qualities they look for are "positive attitude," "reliable," and "a strong work ethic" (Regenstein and Meyer 1998).

When we consider that these jobs are usually unstable, with low wages, no benefits, and little prospect for upward mobility, the call for discipline and diligence seems offensive. These are the worst jobs in the labor market: the lowest paying, the dirtiest, the least secure, often with the most petty and personal supervision, or the most degrading demands to provide service with a smile while working for a pittance. For most healthy adults, it is appropriate to view such jobs with distaste and resentment. Indeed, if there is a chance of improving working conditions in such jobs, it lies partly in the ability of low-wage workers to participate in collective rebellion against the employers who prosper on the backs of such conditions. The goal of Welfare-to-Work programs, however, is to break the will of would-be rebels, to replace resentment with gratitude and rebellion with quiescence.

In a study commissioned by the U.S. Department of Labor, the American Society for Training and Development declared "self-esteem" one of the "basic skills" required by employers. But what exactly does this "skill" entail? "A good self-image," the authors explain, "means the employee takes pride in his or her work" (American Society for Training and Development 1988). While this definition makes arguable sense for artisans or academics, it makes no sense for low-wage workers. To insist that people pour their hearts into the work of sweeping floors, bussing tables, or making change—no matter how low the wage or how unreliable the hours—is to crush rather than raise their aspirations.

It is only an Orwellian logic that can declare the attitudes TANF seeks to inculcate "self-esteem." A commonsense definition of self-esteem would hold that a self-respecting person would resist or rebel against low-wage dead-end jobs. The goal of Welfare-to-Work programs is not to encourage *this* sort of self-esteem, but its opposite. In this vein, *HR Magazine* notes ominously that for private employers looking to hire welfare recipients, the primary need is for "training in workplace expectations." One of the programs approvingly cited by HR professionals is Project LIFE (Learning Independence From Employment),[16] which offers a four-week course "to teach former welfare recipients what it takes to maintain a job and what is expected of them in the workplace" (Leonard 1998).

Training programs under TANF are often explicit in the goal of eliminating workers' ability to rebel. One program lauded by the *Wall Street Journal*, Project STRIVE, aims explicitly at curbing "the self-defeating postures of passivity, racial blaming, or the strut of 'attitude.'" Instructors explain that harsh, tough-love treatment is needed for participants such as

> Gloria [who] … leans back with her arms crossed over her chest—just the kind of subtle gesture of defiance bound to irritate a supervisor on the job. Other participants will be challenged to recognize their own resistance to authority, displayed in their bored facial expressions, smirks, slouching, and unconscious clucks of disgust.[17]

Thus, the mission of "training" programs has been fundamentally transformed—no longer to provide the skills or education that might, in fact, enable participants to gain greater leverage in the labor market, but now aimed at lowering the sights and crushing the aspirations of participants, in the hopes of producing a docile class of low-wage workers. Back to work, you. And wipe that smirk off your face!

### The World of Workfare

Apart from "job readiness" seminars, the primary form of "job training" for many welfare recipients is Workfare. While this is often described as "training," it generally has no training content whatsoever.

Across the country, tens of thousands of Americans have been set to work at menial jobs that can be learned in hours. Furthermore, since many Workfare programs screen participants not for the skills they need but for those they already possess, thousands of impoverished workers are performing jobs that they have already done for years, with the caveat that they now do the work without pay. In both cases, there are no new skills being imparted, and there is generally no path that leads from Workfare assignments to decently paid jobs.

Conservative pundits nevertheless insist that Workfare is, in fact, training. The corporate-funded American Enterprise Institute, for instance, stresses

> Any entry-level job teaches the important skills of showing up to work, regularly and on time, suitably clothed and prepared to cooperate with other workers and to attempt to please customers (Stelzer 1997).

But the reality of what goes on in Workfare programs is quite different. New York City has the largest Workfare program in the country, with more than 40,000 workers sweeping streets, cleaning parks, changing bedpans, and filing records in dozens of public agencies. City officials acknowledge that their records show no more than 10 percent of Workfare workers getting regular jobs. Instead, the city's Work Experience Program has been used to facilitate the elimination of tens of thousands of regular civil service jobs. All told, the Giuliani administration cut 20,000 city positions at the same time as expanding the Workfare program (Greenhouse 1998). In the Parks Department, virtually the entire regular workforce has been replaced with Workfare — with the inevitable corollary that there are few regular Parks jobs that Workfare participants might aspire to graduate into (Gonzalez 1997). In 1997, the city's Parks Department gave full-time jobs to only 10 out of its 7,000 Workfare workers (Albanese 1997). As one Parks Department worker describes the problem:

> We were told that we would be on the WEP assignment for three months. It's supposed to be a training program. When you first hear this you say, 'Hey, maybe there's some hope after all.' It's a lie. You never get any training. The extent of your training is basically being given a broom and a dustpan. You can't go into the private sector submitting an application to be a computer technician when your training actually has been cutting branches and leaves and picking up dog feces.... You're in the WEP program and you're being trained to use Park equipment. But you are not going to get that job. The government says

it is downsizing. So why are they going to hire you when they just got rid of somebody?[18]

On the other end of the spectrum, skilled positions are not used as training slots, but are generally filled by those already familiar with the work. One WEP participant, for example, had twenty-five years' experience as a painting contractor before falling on hard times and finding himself serving as a Workfare painter.

> When I went to my first orientation, I was told that if I worked hard and I did my job well I might get a job with the City. My first WEP assignment was at a senior citizen's center. I painted walls, plastered ceilings, and 'tapped and floated' newly erected plasterboard walls ... my WEP supervisor also regularly asked me to order paint and materials from the same purveyors that I had built up a working relationship with over the past twenty years as a general contractor. On June 7, 1996, I received an award for my work at the senior citizen's center that was signed by Mayor Rudolph Giuliani.... At the conclusion of the award ceremony, my council member complimented me on my work and asked me if there was anything he could do for me. I told him that what I really wanted was a full-time job with the City.... Although he told me that he would see what he could do, he never contacted me.... The City is not going to pay me a real wage when it can get the same work by dividing my benefits by the minimum wage per hour.[19]

Partly in response to these conditions, 20,000 New York Workfare workers voted to unionize by a 98 percent margin. The city government, however, has refused to recognize the results of the election. "Welfare is supposed to be temporary," explained Deputy Mayor Randy Levine. "People are supposed to move off welfare to work" (Holloway 1997). Because Workfare is not a real job, the people doing it do not share the rights to collective bargaining afforded real workers. The city government may have multiple reasons for resisting unionization; but its treatment of Workfare participants makes it clear that, whatever Workfare is, it is providing neither skills nor career paths for its participants.

In this sense, it is instructive to compare Workfare under TANF with public service employment under the Comprehensive Employment and Training Act (CETA). Some of the same critics who derided CETA for enrolling participants in "make-work" projects that imparted no marketable skills now champion Workfare under TANF. Yet many of the jobs now being done by Workfare workers are identical to those performed under

CETA.[20] The only difference, it seems, is that CETA workers were paid regular wages, while Workfare participants are not. CETA positions were not only paid, but were paid decently.[21] The business lobbies attacked Public Service Employment precisely because CETA offered an alternative to the lowest-wage jobs in the private sector (Morgen and Weigt 1998, 25). It is understandable that employers might want to school poor people in the practice of low-wage discipline, or to guarantee that they have no right of refusal for even the worst of job offers. But this cannot be the goal of public policy.

### How Effective Are Welfare Training Programs?

It is unsurprising that the results of welfare training programs are modest at best. The heyday of welfare training programs ran from the early 1980s through the mid-1990s, a period during which the federal government encouraged states to experiment with programs to train public assistance recipients for jobs in the private sector. The most comprehensive review of AFDC training programs is that done by Gueron (1990), who summarized the findings in seven state demonstration programs. The programs, which provided a combination of work experience, job-search assistance, basic education, and occupational training, represent a cross-section of state innovations designed to enable public assistance recipients to work their way out of poverty. Unfortunately, this goal proved unattainable. Though participants in some of the programs realized substantial gains compared to control group earnings, none of them came close to earning above-poverty wages. The single highest-earning group of participants earned only 42.3 percent of the official poverty line after completing the training program; the single most effective program raised participants' earnings by only 7.5 percent of the poverty line. As with nearly every other form of training program, to the extent that Welfare-to-Work programs have increased participants' earnings, they have done so primarily by increasing employment rather than hourly wages (Porter 1990). This suggests that the programs have simply served to get a higher percentage of participants into the same type of jobs they would have gotten otherwise, rather than equipping them to compete for higher-paying jobs.

Even the most successful welfare training programs have showed only modest effects. In the early 1990s, California's GAIN program was touted as a national model of effective welfare reform. However, while GAIN participants earned 16.6 percent more than control group members, this increase lifted them only 2.6 percentage points closer to the poverty line, raising their earnings from 15.7 percent to 18.3 percent of poverty. Even in the state's single most successful county, the income of program graduates amounted to only 23.7 percent of the poverty line (Riccio and Friedlander 1992).[22]

Similarly, Massachusetts's celebrated "ET Choices" program, which provided the widest and most comprehensive range of training and support services for welfare recipients, produced an annual earnings increase equivalent to less than 10 percent of the poverty line (Nightingale et al 1991).

For the most part, however, it is simply impossible to evaluate welfare training programs. When discipline is defined as a "skill" and menial labor substitutes for "training," the notion of evaluating training programs becomes nonsensical. Rather than measuring the impact of education or skills training, most Welfare-to-Work programs now simply assume that participants will benefit, in unspecified and unmeasured ways, from simply being required to show up on time and perform whatever tasks they are assigned. The flip side of a definition of training unrelated to skills is a definition of success unrelated to income. The great majority of Workfare or welfare training programs have avoided stablishing criteria against which their success or failure can be measured. Rather than demanding concrete improvements in employment or earnings, for instance, Workfare advocates increasingly insist that work is its own reward—that there is no need for program justification beyond the enhanced self-esteem Workfare participants are presumed to enjoy and the improved role models they are imagined to offer their children. In this way, the success of Workfare is declared by ideological fiat rather than measured by empirical testing.

### Education vs. Discipline: Back to Work, You

On close inspection, then, what are sometimes termed "training" programs for welfare recipients are often not training programs at all. They are, rather, a simple mechanism for disciplining poor people to work hard at low wages. This shift in program content from education to discipline does, in fact, accurately represent the demands of private employers. Though pundits and policymakers often stress the centrality of education to employment policy, employers themselves do not agree. When employers are asked what skills they seek in new employees, virtually every survey reports the same finding: There is little concern with occupation-specific skills or even with basic English and math competencies. Rather, employers are overwhelmingly concerned with employees' attitude—respect for authority, willingness to follow rules, dedication, punctuality, loyalty, and "flexibility."

This is not a well-kept secret. For thirty years, employers have been quite open about the primacy of attitude as a desirable criterion for new hires. At the same time, the national business lobbies have regularly pursued a legislative agenda aimed at limiting the ability of workers to opt out of low-wage jobs and, above all, seeking to ensure that no combination of public assistance should be more attractive than the worst entry-level job. Thus, business lobbies have sought to cut food stamps, unemployment insurance, workers' compensation, and other social-insurance benefits, leaving increasing numbers of workers with no out but to accept whatever job they are offered, at whatever wage employers choose to pay.[23]

TANF now plays a significant role in both ends of the agenda for promoting labor-market discipline. On the one hand, Welfare-to-Work "training" serves employers' agenda by socializing would-be workers to low-wage discipline. On the other hand, by making it much harder for workers to refuse even the worst job, TANF's sanctions policy forces discipline even on those who might not learn it through self-esteem seminars. Thus, TANF has come to serve a sometimes chilling role in enforcing market discipline on the poorest of citizens.

Long before work requirements became part of the welfare system, the majority of welfare recipients sought opportunities to leave the rolls for paid employment. For TANF to insist that work is preferable to welfare, then, is not saying anything new. What is new, however, is the insistence that welfare recipients must take any job, at any wage, no matter what strains it may put on their or their family's well-being. Historically, the central problem encountered by public assistance recipients trying to get off welfare was the fact that most available jobs paid no more than welfare and offered few if any benefits. As long as welfare was an entitlement, prudent mothers might choose to remain on relief rather than subject their families to such conditions. It is this calculation that TANF now aims to break.

Under the new regime, the choice to resist the worst jobs has become increasingly untenable. In this sense, TANF provides a boon to the very worst sort of employers. For these firms—whether marginal or malevolent —TANF is a welcome source of market discipline that leaves them freer to impose extreme conditions on employees, knowing that the precariousness of welfare will make women think twice before missing a day, even at these least-desirable jobs.

Similarly, state programs that provide transitional health insurance for working welfare recipients end up not only subsidizing low-wage employers, but forcing workers into a position of utter dependence. In the low-wage labor market, very few jobs provide benefits. In one survey, welfare recipients who found work reported that less than half their jobs provided paid vacation, only one-third allowed any sick days at all, and virtually none offered health insurance (Albelda 1999). For this reason, even when welfare benefits amount to less than what one would make at even a minimum-wage job, welfare remains valuable because it provides health insurance. Under "Work First" policies, however, these benefits are contingent on working. This means that TANF recipients may be forced into low-wage jobs, and then threatened with the loss of their only source of health insurance if they quit or complain. In this way, TANF serves to

**188**

drive down the level of both wages and compensation that low-end businesses must offer.

Perhaps the most dramatic instance of this equation is Missouri's Direct Job Placement program, a joint venture between the state's welfare office and the poultry processing industry. The work in the chicken plants is exhausting and dangerous. For $6.75 per hour, workers hang forty to fifty chickens per minute on metal hooks, for shifts of four to six hours without a break. In 1995, one-third of the employees in this industry suffered work-related injuries, and the companies suffer from chronic high turnover. Rather than face the prospect of having to raise wages or improve conditions in order to attract a more stable workforce, agricultural giants such as Tyson Foods and ConAgra have entered into agreements with the Department of Family Services, in which people applying for welfare are instead told to apply for jobs at one of the poultry plants. Since the jobs are, in the company's own words, "repetitive-motion, unskilled labor," nearly everyone is offered a job. And anyone who turns down such an offer is classified as having refused to work and denied welfare on that basis.[24] In a small way at least, the ability of the state's most desperate workers to refuse such jobs and still receive AFDC increased the pressure for such employers to improve conditions. The elimination of that entitlement now forces the most marginal workers into a brutal choice between health and health insurance.

To the extent that Welfare-to-Work policies remove the incentive for low-end employers to raise wages, they restrict rather than expand the supply of good jobs. TANF operates on the assumption that decently paying jobs are available, and that the poor are best helped by establishing a work history in entry-level employment. However, if the key barrier to success of welfare policies is not recipients' willingness to work but the quality of jobs available, these programs will backfire. It is still possible, of course, that individual welfare recipients will find their way to family-wage jobs with the help of TANF programs. As a broad policy, however, the strategy of forced work is likely to worsen conditions in the low end of the labor market, and therefore worsen rather than improve conditions for the majority of the very poor.

### Discipline as Public Policy and The Politics of Training Curricula

The substitution of discipline for skills in welfare training programs is not a mistake, not illogical, and not ineffective. It represents a coherent approach to the low-wage labor market and accurately reflects the desires of private employers. It is not surprising that business advocates might promote this version of welfare reform. However, this does not make it sound policy for the federal government.

In both the public and private sectors, the rhetoric of "self-esteem" and taking charge of one's life serves to mask the reality that "world of work" programs primarily train workers to be submissive—to follow orders, to accept the superiority of the boss' judgment, to effect personalities that are pleasing to those in power, and above all to not challenge the prerogatives of management. The impact of this approach may be seen when we consider what an alternative curriculum might look like. Educator Ira Shor (1998) suggests a humanistic program of world-of-work training that aims at "empowering" its participants in a less Orwellian sense. Here, the work world is defined not by what management wants workers to think, but by what information is truly useful to workers. When approaching a specific occupation, Shor suggests that students be sent out to interview workers currently employed in the field. Among the questions he recommends for this survey are:

> Was there a union at the workplace? Does the union make a difference? Is this a place that treats women and minorities equally? Is health and safety taken seriously here? What do people like about this work? What do they complain about? ... What exactly do you do at work? What are your hours, your pay? What do you have to do to get promoted? Do you know how your work fits together into the larger operations of your company? ... How does your company fit into the larger economy? ... If you don't like something at work, can you change it?

This approach to the "world of work" includes a range of information which is critical for workers but often ignored or suppressed in management-sponsored programs.[25] The notion that workers should know something about how their job fits into the economy seems eccentric in a business-oriented training program, but it is integral for a public program that treats students as political citizens rather than merely as production inputs. The form as well as the content of Shor's curriculum aims at a more radical type of "self-esteem" than that allowed in existing job training. Each topic addressed in the course begins by drawing on the knowledge students already have from their own work experience. "By asking students to examine their lives and their knowledge," Shor explains, "I would hope to desocialize them from subordinate mentalities [so that they] feel dignified in taking on the world of work." (Shor 1988, 113).

When contrasted with Shor's curriculum, it is clear just how hard business-oriented training programs are working to suppress workers' self-esteem and to encourage a deracinated view of citizens as production inputs. The skills-as-discipline curricula of training programs is a predictable result of a business-dominated employment system. To the extent that this project is successful, training becomes an ideological tool for preventing the very type of poor people's protest or political mobilization

**190**

that alone promises the possibility of moving economic policy in a more progressive direction.

The shortage of decently paying jobs has made it impossible for even well-trained welfare recipients to work their way out of poverty. Thus, traditional training programs, focusing on English, math, and technical skills, have been correctly attacked as largely impotent wastes of money. In its latest incarnation as a molder of workplace attitudes, however, job training has become something worse than useless; it has become reactionary.

## References

Albanese, Sal. 1997. "How I'd Make Workfare Work." *New York Daily News* (July 9).

Albelda, Randy. 1999. "What Welfare Reform Has Wrought." *Dollars and Sense* (No. 221, January-February).

American Society for Training and Development. 1988. *Workplace Basics: The Skills Employers Want.* Washington, D.C.: U.S. Department of Labor, Employment and Training Administration.

Bader, Eleanor. 1997. "Unfair Workfare." *Dollars & Sense*. No. 213 (September-October).

Burkhalter, Stephanie. 1996. *The poor are not like the rest of us: The social construction of welfare mothers in congressional policy discourse.* M.S. Thesis, Department of Political Science, University of Oregon. Unpublished.

Conniff, Ruth. 1994. "Big Bad Welfare: Welfare Reform Politics and Children." *The Progressive* 58 (No. 8, August): 18–21.

Cook, Christopher. 1998. "Plucking Workers: Tyson Foods looks to the welfare rolls for a captive labor force." *The Progressive*. (August 1998): 28–31.

DeParle, Jason. 1998. "Committee to a Moral Motive for Work: The Designer of Wisconsin's Welfare System Comes to New York." *New York Times* (January 20): C11.

Edin, Kathryn, and Laura Lein. 1997. *Making Ends Meet: How Single Mothers Survive Welfare and Low-Wage Work*. New York: Russell Sage.

Freedman, Stephen, Jean Tansey Knab, Lisa Gennetian, and David Navarro. 2000. *The Los Angeles Jobs-First GAIN Evaluation: Final Report on a Work First Program in a Major Urban Center*. New York: Manpower Demonstration Research Corporation.

Freeman, Kimberly. 1997. *Welfare Reform As We Know It: First-Hand Accounts From the Frontlines*. Washington, D.C.: Jobs With Justice.

Gonzalez, Juan. 1997. "Read These Ballots and WEP." *New York Daily News* (October 21): 12.

Greenhouse, Steven. 1998. "Many Participants in Workfare Take the Place of City Workers." *New York Times* (April 13): A1.

Gueron, Judith. 1990. "Work and Welfare: Lessons on Employment Programs." *Journal of Economic Perspectives* 4 (No. 1): 79–98.

Handler, Joel, and Yeheskel Hasenfeld. 1997. *We the Poor People: Work, Poverty and Welfare.* New Haven, CT: Yale University Press, New Haven.

Holloway, Lynette. 1997. "Plurality of Workfare Recipients Said to Vote in Favor of a Union." *New York Times.* (October 24): B1.

Huston, Margo. 1998. "W-2 Work or Else: W-2 Cash for Training Called a 'Step Back'." *Milwaukee Journal Sentinel* (September 17): 1.

Hymowitz, Kay S. 1997. "Job Training That Works." *Wall Street Journal.* (February 13).

Leonard, Bill. 1998. "Welfare to work: filling a tall order." *HR Magazine* 43 (No. 6, May): 78–86.

McDonnell, Lorraine, and Gail Zellman. 1993. *Education and Training for Work in the Fifty States: A Compendium of State Policies.* Santa Monica: Rand Corporation.

Morgen, Sandra, and Jill Weigt. 1998. Poor women, fair work, and Welfare-to-Work that works. Unpublished manuscript

Nathan, Richard, Robert Cook, and V. Lane Rawlins. 1981. *Public Service Employment: A Field Evaluation.* Washington, D.C.: Brookings Institution.

National Center on the Educational Quality of the Workforce. 1995. *First Findings from the EQW National Employer Survey.* University of Pennsylvania.

Nightingale, Demestra S., Douglas A. Wissoker, Lynn C. Burbridge, D. Lee Bawden, and Neal Jeffries. 1990. *Evaluation of the Massachusetts Employment and Training (ET) Choices Program.* Washington, D.C.: The Urban Institute Press.

Office of the Inspector General. 1998. *Profiling JTPA's AFDC Participants.* Report No. 06-98-002-03-340. U.S. Department of Labor (May 7).

Porter, Kathryn. 1990. *Making JOBS Work: What the Research Says About Effective Programs for AFDC Recipients.* Washington, D.C.: Center on Budget and Policy Priorities.

Regenstein, Marsha, and Jack Meyer. 1998. *Job Prospects for Welfare Recipients: Employers Speak Out.* Washington, D.C.: Urban Institute.

Riccio, James, and Daniel Friedlander. 1992. "GAIN and the Prospect of JOBS's Success: MDRC Reports Short-term Positive Trends in California." *Public Welfare* 50 (3): 24.

Roditi, Hannah. 1992. "Youth Apprenticeship: High Schools for Docile Workers." *The Nation* 254 (No. 10, March 16): 340–343.

Schein, Virginia. 1995. *Working from the Margins: Voices of Mothers in Poverty.* Ithaca: Cornell University Press.

Shor, Ira. 1988. "Working Hands and Critical Minds: A Paulo Freire Model for Job Training." *Journal of Education* 170 (No. 2).

Stelzer, Irwin. 1997. *Lessons of the U.S. Job Machine*. Washington, D.C.: American Enterprise Institute.

U.S. General Accounting Office (GAO). 1994. *Welfare to Work: Current AFDC Program Not Sufficiently Focused on Employment*. Washington, DC: U.S. General Accounting Office.

———. 1999. *Welfare Reform: States' Experiences in Providing Employment Assistance to TANF Clients*. GAO/HEHS-99-22. Washington, DC: U.S. General Accounting Office.

U.S. Department of Labor, Employment and Training Administration. 1999. Fact Sheet: Welfare-to-Work Grants. Available at www.doleta.gov.

U.S. Secretary of Labor. 1997. *Report to Congress: Implementation of the 1992 Job Training Partnership Act (JTPA) Amendments*. Washington, DC: U.S. Department of Labor.

## *Notes*

[1] Gordon Lafer is an assistant professor at the University of Oregon's Labor Education and Research Center, and author of the forthcoming *Let Them Eat Training: The False Promise of Federal Employment Policy Since 1980* (Cornell, 2002). He has written about employment policy and labor organizing for *Politics and Society*, *Urban Affairs Quarterly*, *International Journal of Manpower*, *The American Prospect*, and *Dissent* Magazine.

[2] Congressman English, *Congressional Record* 1995, H3362, cited in Burkhalter (1996, 124).

[3] Edin and Lein (1997) report that welfare recipients in their sample had an average of 5.6 years' work experience before enrolling in AFDC. They cite a 1993 finding by the U.S. House of Representatives that 60 percent of AFDC recipients had worked in the previous two years. Similarly, the U.S. Department of Labor found that 59 percent of AFDC recipients enrolled in JTPA programs had worked within the past three years. (Office of Inspector General, *Profiling JTPA's AFDC Participants*.) On this point see also Morgen and Weigt (1998) and Schein (1995).

[4] The Department of Labor explained that one of the "basic goals" of the 1992 amendments was "to focus JTPA on providing more training and less stand-alone job placement." Quote is from the preamble to the amendment's Final Rule. *Federal Register, 20 CFR Part 626, et. al.: The Job Training Partnership Act: Final Rule*, Vol. 59, No. 170, September 2, 1994, p. 45805. The 1992 amendments mandated that 65 percent of JTPA Title II — a participant must face one or more "barriers to employment" — such as deficient literacy skills — in addition to meeting the program's income eligibility criteria (U.S. Secretary of Labor 1997, 1–4).

[5] For the employment and earnings of welfare recipients receiving various types of JTPA services, see Office of the Inspector General (1998).

[6] For a useful summary of the TANF work provisions, see GAO (1999).

[7] "Celucci Ousts Advisers," *Boston Globe*. August 14, 1994.

[8] David Riemer, quoted in Huston (1998).

[9] In 1996 alone, 8,000 New York City welfare recipients were forced to leave the City University system in order to perform Workfare assignments (Bader 1997, 31). As Bader explains, "The government thought it was more important for them to sweep the streets than to learn English or get a high school equivalency diploma or degree."

**193**

[10] The same report (GAO 1999, 13) cites the example of Ohio's program, where the share of clients receiving either job skills or education fell from one-third in the pre-TANF era to one-tenth under the current regime.

[11] Somewhat less misleading is Illinois' Project Chance. Nevertheless, this is still quite a ways from a truly honest welfare program, which I assume would have to be named Project Not Very Likely.

[12] "Why is LA GAIN So Successful?," Los Angeles County GAIN Web page (http://dpss.co.la.ca.us/gain).

[13] From the Los Angeles County GAIN Web page. An even more romantic view is that of Jason Turner, the chief architect of Welfare-to-Work programs in both Wisconsin and New York City. Explaining the importance of Workfare, Turner insists, "Work is one's gift to others, and when you sever that relationship with your fellow man, you're doing more than just harm to yourself economically. You're doing spiritual harm" (DeParle 1998).

[14] Edin and Lein (1997, 73) report that overwhelmingly, "Women who had been through [Welfare-to-Work programs] believed the jobs that the caseworkers recommended were not a realistic alternative to welfare."

[15] See for example, National Center on the Educational Quality of the Workforce (1995).

[16] The program's acronym is one more in the seemingly endless litany of Orwellian terms that assault welfare recipients daily. It is impossible to learn independence from employment. Employment, of course, is an experience of dependence and insecurity. Independence is winning the lottery or living on trust funds. What can be learned from employment is simply another form of dependence—dependence on the whim of private employers rather than the security of a government check.

[17] This and preceding quote are from Hymowitz (1997).

[18] "Pierre," quoted in Freeman (1997, 7).

[19] "Robert," quoted in Freeman (1997, 2).

[20] Public works, park maintenance, protective services and health services were among the most common occupations of CETA workers (Nathan, Cook, and Rawlins 1981).

[21] Until 1978, CETA legislation required that workers be paid the prevailing wage for their occupations.

[22] Poverty thresholds are for 1990, family of three. Much has been made of the success of the GAIN program in Riverside County, the single most successful program site, where participants earned $2,468 in the program's first year, compared to $1,499 for controls. The Riverside program was notable for adopting a Work First policy. Participants were given very few services, were required to take any job at any wage, and were more heavily sanctioned than in any other county. Riccio and Friedlander (1992) suggest, however, that the program's results may be significantly due to the fact that the economy of Riverside county was expanding more rapidly than that of any other county in the study, and that the increased earnings appear to represent short-term gains which diminish after six months. Programs for unemployed fathers in two-parent families on welfare have been even less successful. Porter (1990, xii) reports, "The research does not demonstrate that either low-cost services such as job search or more intensive services have been effective in increasing employment or earnings among AFDC recipients in two-parent families."

[23] See Web sites of U.S. Chamber of Commerce (www.uschamber.org), Business Roundtable (www.brt.org), and National Federation of Independent Businesses (www.nfib.org).

[24] Quote is from Tyson Foods spokeswoman Jennifer Cave, quoted in Cook (1998).

[25] On managers' influence over the curricula of school-to-work transition programs, see Roditi (1992).

# Opportunity, Control and Resistance
## Living Welfare Reform in Los Angeles County

*John Horton*[1] *and Linda Shaw*[2]

### Regulating the Poor under Welfare Reform

In their classic work of 1971, *Regulating the Poor: The Functions of Public Welfare*, Frances Fox Piven and Richard A. Cloward argue that the character of welfare is determined by a shifting constellation of political forces. In times of social unrest, the state, responding to an increase in progressive political pressure, tends to regulate and discipline the poor by increasing their welfare benefits and entitlements. In times of class peace and relative economic prosperity, the state, responding to an increase in conservative pressure, tends to regulate the poor by cutting their welfare benefits and entitlements and pushing them into the labor market. This second strategy certainly characterizes welfare reform in the United States today. Here we discuss how Los Angeles County is implementing this strategy among welfare parents.

Specifically, we ask: What programs and methods of regulation does the county use to motivate welfare parents to comply with its work requirements? What assumptions underlie them? How do parents experience them—positively, as services needed to achieve self-sufficiency; negatively, as control over their lives; or some combination of both? Do they comply, and does compliance open up opportunities for their economic independence? Do they resist, and does their resistance suggest grounds for challenging and transforming the current assumptions and practices of welfare reform?

## Documenting the Voices of Paricipants in Welfare Reform

We base our answers on data gathered from thirty focus groups conducted from December 1998 to June 2000 with participants in LA GAIN (Greater Avenues for INdependence), the county's mandatory program for welfare parents with a work requirement.[3] Under contract with the county, we conducted our research as part of a team that used a variety of methods (including survey research, focus groups, and administrative records) to collect and analyze data for an evaluation of its implementation of the provisions of California's welfare reform act.[4]

One hundred and thirty-one parents attended our focus groups, each of which lasted approximately two hours. They were enrolled in GAIN's eighteen- or twenty-four-month Welfare-to-Work program and selected from different stages in the program, such as attending Orientation, Job Club, looking for work, and looking for a better job. The majority came from the two largest racial/ethnic groups in the county's welfare population—Hispanics (immigrant and U.S.-born) and African Americans. Reflecting the larger population of welfare parents, more than 90 percent of our participants were women, the majority of these single parents (LA DPSS 2000). All were still on some form of aid.

Although we recruited participants who reflected a range of experiences with Welfare-to-Work programs, they were, of course, not representative, in a statistical sense, of the caseload average of 99,000 participants during the research period.[5] For example, we did not interview the small population of participants who had successfully moved from Welfare-to-Work without aid or the large population who, for whatever reason, had voluntarily failed to register or had left the Welfare-to-Work program.[6] Our purpose was to acquire an in-depth understanding of the meaning and success of Welfare-to-Work and the effectiveness of organizational practices from the lived experiences of the people involved in the GAIN program. Our qualitative methods reveal important data obscured by most statistical assessments, a concrete sense of how things were experienced, and the unexamined link between individual actions and the broad patterns or trends revealed in quantitative data. The members of our focus groups told us what they experienced in their own words, something that surveys with predetermined categories cannot reveal.

## Pressures for a Strongly Enforced Work First Program

A configuration of new federal, state, and local welfare reform policies have overturned the old system of entitlements, required work as a condition of time-limited aid, and dramatically increased the pressure to change and regulate the lives of welfare recipients. The primary pressure to move participants from Welfare-to-Work comes from the federal government to the county through the state. California, like other states, stood to lose large sums of federal dollars if it did not meet federal job quotas requiring that 25 percent of its entire CalWORKs caseload be engaged in work or work-related activities by 1997, and another 5 percent annually thereafter until achieving a 50 percent work-participation rate by 2002 (Moreno et al. 1999). The pressure to meet quotas has been especially urgent in Los Angeles County given the size of its welfare population and the enormity of the task of moving welfare parents into work. With some 573,000 parents and children on cash aid, the county has the largest number of welfare recipients after the states of California and New York (Rivera 2000).

In responding to this pressure, Los Angeles County adopted a strongly enforced Work First, as opposed to the training-first, program of welfare reform that has been favored by some counties (Freedman, Friedlander et al. 2000). In practice, this means that priority is given to getting any job, no matter how humble, before getting education and preparation for a better job or a career that promises economic independence. Vocational assessment takes place, if at all, only after a participant has failed to get a job. Moreover, "post-employment" activities are voluntary and do not count toward the requirement of thirty-two hours of GAIN activities. As for "responsibility to kids," the program is first and foremost oriented to getting their parents to work.[7]

With the help of a booming economy, LA County succeeded in reducing welfare rolls by 28 percent during the last three years (Rivera 2000). According to officials, "The county has surpassed its work participation rate and, in fact, has received enhanced funding through performance incentives."[8] However, the meaning of this success is in the eye of the beholder: A report by the Manpower Demonstration Research Corporation praises the country for moving participants to work with modest wage gains (Freedman, Knab et al. 2000). However, the Economic Roundtable (Flaming et al. 2000; Flaming et al. 2001), a nonprofit public research organization, points out that current gains in income will not move the majority of former welfare recipients out of poverty without greater job training. Whether "success" is defined as any work or as economic self-sufficiency, the results of county policy are partly attributable to its methods of implementing the mandatory work requirement.

### Forms of Regulation and Control

The Work First philosophy of LA GAIN is summed up by an oft-repeated slogan: "A job, a better job, and a career." GAIN employs an interrelated set of "controls" to move participants along this path. We have identified four interrelated types of control: the carrots of opportunity, the sticks of discipline, the restructuring of everyday life, and moral control. These controls were implemented by GAIN service workers in conjunction with LACOE, the semi-public Los Angeles County Office of Education, that was under contract to provide the required orientation to GAIN and Job Club.[9]

## The Carrots of Opportunity

From the viewpoint of participants, important incentives for compliance to the work requirement are the carrots of economic independence and freedom from the demands of the welfare bureaucracy. To lessen the familial and financial barriers to work, GAIN offers other crucial material incentives such as childcare and transportation support, employment services, and personal counseling.

Even without these incentives, few of those in our focus groups needed to be convinced about the goals of the program—like others in society, welfare parents want a better life for their families. As one participant said, "I was happy when I got the notice [to come to the Orientation] because now I'm able to take care of my son the way that I want to." And everyone looked forward to the day when they would be working, off of the "county," and free from its bureaucratic requirements and the stigma of welfare:

> Lucy: I got to land on my feet. I'm just, uh, I don't really like answering to anybody.... I do not like answering, I just don't want to fill out the paperwork. I don't like this recertification.
> Lily: Once you get a job ... we don't have the county telling us, "You have to be here today, you have to fill out this paper and send it in today."

But along with their disdain for bureaucratic practice and their desire for work, most participants in our groups who lacked skills wanted assessment and job training opportunities. They were doubtful that the program's Work First philosophy alone would provide sufficient opportunity to move from dependence on welfare to a job that paid a living wage. Alejandro, a member of one of our Spanish speaking focus groups, is representative of the skepticism expressed by many in our focus groups:

> What I was looking for from GAIN was a resource that could motivate us. Well, it does motivate us, improve our self-esteem to go forward, but we have the handcuffs on. The talk is beautiful, but what we need is to study.

Given the frequently expressed opinion that welfare reform would not lead to meaningful work, how does GAIN get welfare recipients to participate in a program that many believe is based on a mismatch between their goals for finding work and means for achieving them? Part of the answer lies in their fear of time limits for finding work and, more immediately, strict discipline and threats of sanctions. (However, unlike some states, California does not cut off aid to dependent children of needy families.) Another part of the answer lies in two less visible, but more invasive, types of control: the restructuring of the rhythm of time and daily life, and the reinforcement of a morality that stresses the financial and psychological value of work and individual responsibility. The shift from welfare-as-an-entitlement to temporary-assistance-that-must-be-earned-through-work was made possible by defining welfare dependency in terms of moral character. From the point of view of the county, if welfare dependency is a problem of character, the path from Welfare-to-Work is paved with rules designed to stimulate motivation and instill the discipline necessary to take advantage of opportunities the program offers.

**The Sticks of Discipline**

Compliance with the Welfare-to-Work program begins with a letter of "congratulations" requiring participants to attend a GAIN Orientation session (often in the next day or two) followed by Job Club, a three week job search program designed to teach basic skills required to get a job. At Orientation and Job Club, participants learn about and are persuaded to accept the new program designed to move them from Welfare-to-Work and the rewards and opportunities for doing so—childcare and supportive services and the promise of eventual economic independence. They also learn about time limits on receipt of cash aid and sanctions that would take away the adult portion of cash aid for failure to adhere to program requirements. And they receive a motivational lesson about how they can turn their lives around with effort and a "can do" attitude. GAIN casework-ers ask them to sign a Welfare-to-Work plan, and unless they have a child under one year, have been referred to special services for help in overcom-ing barriers to work (i.e., domestic violence, alcohol or drug abuse, or mental health), or are exempted for medical reasons, the time clock for receipt of cash aid begins (LA DPSS 1999).

Participants experienced Job Club as a kind of "boot camp" designed to instill the work ethic and discipline necessary for success in the world of work. They must follow strict rules of attendance and wear work-ready attire at all times. During the last two weeks of job search, participants are required to make fifty calls and submit five job applications per day (LA DPSS 1999). To prepare for work, participants learned proper grooming and comportment that included lessons in hygiene (they were to bathe, brush their teeth, wear deodorant, cover their tattoos) and how to dress (dresses, nylons, and heels, no open toes, for women; white shirts, ties, dress pants, and shoes for men).[10]

Despite the uncertainties that many faced in getting to Job Club and potential employers located far from home, particularly when depending on public transportation, those who were late or failed to meet their quota of five job applications per day were required to start Job Club all over again. Others suffered public humiliation. One participant tells what happened when a woman attending her Job Club failed to adhere to the dress code:

> Mona: One lady came in [to Job Club]. She had on open-toed shoes. Well, uh, they just kind of blew her out the front of the class and told her, uh, she should be ashamed. That if she came in like that again, they'd put her out of the program.
> Facilitator: They said this in front of the class?
> Mona: Yeah, they told her she could go over to the clothing closet [free clothes provided by Job Club] and get something out of there to wear for the day. And, uh, it was totally demeaning. They look at you everyday when you come in and assess how you were dressed. And like I told 'em, you know, I've worked in a professional atmosphere, environment. I don't need anyone half my age telling me how to dress. I know what's appropriate. And they would write everything like you don't have common sense. And, uh, it was really just—really demeaning.

Of the participants in our focus groups who found work, most did so outside of Job Club, using their own networks and job-search strategies. They would do almost anything to escape Job Club's strict regimen, particularly when they felt it provided little meaningful help in finding a job.[11] One middle-aged man with a sixth-grade education clearly expressed his many reasons for seeking a job on his own:

> Eduardo: I participated in the GAIN program, and I don't like the way they treat people because they force you, if you don't want to look for a job, for example, to go to the [temp] agencies, and I didn't want a job from the agencies … Apart from that, they didn't show me how to fill out the applications, they would push me towards the agencies…. But, I told them, "You know what, I want to work. I want to work but not with the agencies." They told me, "You have to go, you have to go, because it's not voluntary."

Eduardo resisted the discipline of Job Club by dropping out of the program and losing his aid.

External rewards and punishments are ever present in the GAIN program. We have described some of the overt ways in which GAIN enforces the work requirement. But embedded in the Work First philosophy are more indirect and invisible structural controls—the discipline of work and bureaucratic accountability—that begin to structure and control the rhythms and time of participants' everyday lives.

**Structuring Discipline into Everyday Life**

Whether attempting to fill their job-search quotas of five applications a day or holding down a job, focus group participants repeatedly told us stories of rising before dawn to get themselves ready for work and their children off to school. Some, particularly those dependent on public transportation, often spent up to two to three hours each way traveling to work and transporting their children to childcare, only to return home to a round of "homework"—cooking, cleaning, preparing meals, and helping kids with schoolwork.

To this exhausting list of tasks necessary to fulfill the work and job search requirements, time must also be found somehow to attend special services or to meet with caseworkers who checked for compliance with the work requirement and other conditions for receipt of aid. Maria talks about the extra stress of program requirements:

> So it does get stressful, and like I said, especially like when they have you going in and out of the programs because you not only have to take care of the household, take care of the kids, take care of your personal business, and you got to make sure that you get to the program on time, that everything goes the way it's supposed to with the program.

Together, the overt controls contained in the rules and regulations, and the endless round of tasks that filled participants' time, left little energy for school or job training that would prepare them for a better future – just those activities that lead to achieving the goals of Welfare-to-Work.[12] Mona expressed her frustration at days filled with time-consuming job search requirements that lessened, rather than enhanced, her opportunities for finding work:

> I went everywhere. Some places it would take me almost four hours to get to on the bus. And I would explain to them, "I have an appointment. I'm putting in my application, they're gonna give me an interview afterwards." It didn't make any difference. I had to make my quota. And I told them – I asked my worker, "Well, what are you more interested in? Me putting in my quota or getting a job?" I said, "My goal is to try and get a job, get out of the system." They told me it didn't matter. I had to make my quota of applications or I'd be kicked out, and I'd have to start again. They spoke to us like we didn't have any common sense, no decency.

**203**

**Moral Control**

While the carrots of opportunity and sanctions visibly motivate participants to work, the restructuring of everyday life painfully, but less visibly, makes paid employment an organizing principle of family life. Also invisible are the stigmas of welfare and low self-esteem of many participants, factors that help the county achieve compliance to the work requirement. Negative attitudes toward welfare recipients are part of the dominant ideological climate: Good people work for a living and have high self-esteem. Bad people live off the dole and have low self-esteem.

In countries with strong labor movements that defend hard-won gains for the poor, welfare recipients would riot in the streets against any threat to their entitlements. By contrast, welfare recipients in the United States have faced the demands of reform with few ideological and political weapons of collective resistance. It would be unthinkable for many to defend welfare entitlements and protest the work requirement on moral and political grounds because they have internalized the societal image of themselves as stigmatized and inferior to good people who work. Participants complied with the goals of the program because it was the only way to get support but also because they often undervalued themselves as welfare recipients, had low self-esteem, and were socialized to value work and self-reliance as a basis of self-esteem.

Welfare reform relies on participants' moral and ideological acquiescence to the work requirement and the end of entitlements. In fact, GAIN encourages and reinforces this compliant mindset. Its motivational messages are designed to counter the presumed psychological barriers to working—low self-esteem, the habit of dependency, and the avoidance of responsibility for one's sad situation. They are expressed in the Orientation to GAIN, the three-week Job Club, and even in the posters on office walls, one showing a victorious and confident climber reaching the summit of a high mountain.

At their Orientation to GAIN, all participants receive a glossy, New Age motivational book by Jack Canfield (Canfield et al. 1998), based on his popular self-help series, *Chicken Soup for the Soul* (1993). The messages are meant to evoke self-esteem and a positive, individualistic, you-can-make-it attitude. The recipe for Chicken Soup, powerfully sold to the middle classes, is: accentuate the positive, set goals, visualize success, persevere, and reap the awards. Motivators and slick videos also tell participants that, while they can expect help and support, they must realize that they alone—and not society—are responsible for their situation, the choices they have made, and the choices they will make in the future.

However, positive thinking and embracing the work ethic does not help everyone to move ahead but can do them harm and lower their self-esteem if they fail to move ahead. Having the "right" attitude is not enough, as we can see in comparing the experiences of Alicia and Latania, two participants in GAIN. Both embraced the work ethic and complied

**204**

with the program but with different results. Alicia got a job and began moving off of welfare. Latania kept getting recycled through the program without landing a job. Her case shows the limits of psychological motivation and an individualistic attitude in the absence of skills and support to develop them. The two cases give a feeling for the way different people experience and are affected by the motivational messages of GAIN, as well as a sense of what can be learned by listening to welfare recipients struggling to meet the new work requirements.

Alicia is an example of a GAIN success story. An immigrant from Latin America and a single parent in her mid-thirties with three children, she entered the program with distinct advantages that were recognized and nurtured by her caseworkers: white, bilingual in Spanish and in English, a high school degree plus vocational training, a work history, middle-class social skills, and very depressed about being on welfare. She described how she moved quickly through GAIN, got a better job, then an even better position in a county office that will eventually help her to get off welfare altogether. Her story is also one of moving from low self-esteem, "feeling down all the time," to feeling proud:

> It took me only a few months. And I think it's that we're determined, and we have a positive attitude, and since the beginning, since the first day, I knew what I wanted to do. I knew that I wanted to improve my life and be a good role model for my children. And, so, that's what motivated me.... For me, it's good because I didn't want to rely on welfare all my life. And I didn't want to go to the grocery store and pay for food in stamps. For me it was like I was feeling down all the time. So now that I'm able to pay with my money and that I'm able to buy clothes for my kids and pay my rent without expecting a check through the mail, that makes me feel really proud. And my children, they know that.

In the focus group, Alicia used every opportunity to sing the praises of GAIN, counter the negative attitudes, and tell participants that the program will work for them:

> I feel happy now.... I would like to say thank you to the program because it motivates a lot of people and we, we receive all this support from all of you guys ...And I keep on telling all my participants, you know, we can make it.

Latania, like Alicia, had internalized the stigma of welfare and wanted to work, but she has gone through Job Club three times and is still without a job. An African-American diabetic woman in her mid-thirties with four children and few work skills, she was not likely to capture the special attention of a caseworker. In the following quote, she blames herself entirely for being on welfare, even though she makes an allusion to a situation that limited her choices:

> My problem was I was too young and too dumb to stop havin' babies. …At the time, my mother—she was there, but she wasn't there to tell me, "Look, don't sit here and have all these kids where you're going to have to go on welfare, and they're going to have to help you take care of these kids." You know, I wasn't listening to that. But now that I'm older, and I see how it's hard to struggle with these four kids, I wish I can turn it back…. I'm glad I have my kids, but in my mind, I been saying all this time, "Dang, you stupid to sit down and have all these babies!" … I put myself in this predicament, you know; it's nobody's fault but my own.

Believing that her circumstance as a welfare mother was her fault, she complied with the work requirement, followed the rules, made no demands, and ended up without a job and with a feeling of frustration and depression:

> I put in the application with you guys. I passed your test. I did it all. I meet all your requirements. Why you all ain't hired me yet?… You tellin' me to get off of assistance and stuff. I'm waiting for you to hire me. So it's a no-win situation.

Latania's life was shaped by a complex set of circumstances. She had made choices to be sure, but not under conditions of her own making. Having babies gave meaning to her life under the difficult circumstances of her adolescence.[13] Now she was suffering the social consequences, being punished, and feeling badly about her choices. The regulation of Latania and others like her is successful not simply because they think badly about themselves and therefore submit. The program inadvertently relies on internalized negative stereotypes of welfare recipients such as Latania as a way to reinforce images of recipients individually responsible for their plight.[14] In the absence of an alternative understanding (one that empowers them as parents rather than degrades them as dependent welfare recipients), it is a short step from accepting personal responsibility for one's plight to accepting the work requirement, attacks on entitlements, and the regulation used to implement them.

## Welfare Reform as a Site of Opportunity, Control and Resistance

We have discussed several methods that LA County uses to achieve compliance with the work requirements of welfare reform. How did our focus group participants experience these methods of regulation? A few, like Alicia, who entered with education and skills and moved toward self-sufficiency, saw the program and its regulations in a positive light. However, the majority of our participants, like Latania, were ambivalent to negative. They looked to the program to provide opportunities for self-sufficiency but experienced it as a complicated set of external controls driving them into the ranks of the working poor, without the safety net of welfare entitlements.

However, there is more to the story. Welfare reform in LA is also a site of resistance that suggests grounds for challenging and transforming its current assumptions, goals, and practices. We found that LA GAIN was a site of resistance at the points where control broke down. The motivational message to think positively and take self-responsibility rings false when participants play by the rules but remain unemployed or poorly and insecurely employed. The sticks of discipline—stiff sanctions for not complying and humiliation—cause complaint and resistance.

The total restructuring of the day toward work activities increases stress and cuts into parental roles and quality time with kids. Mistrust and cynicism follow the recognition that a serious mismatch exists between what the program offers and what is needed to achieve the goal of economic independence.

Much of the resistance we observed was individualistic. In some instances, such as when participants opted out of GAIN, resistance actually helped reduce the welfare rolls. But there were also opportunities for collective responses. By bringing together otherwise isolated parents, Welfare-to-Work programs create solidarity, criticism, and opposition. Parents who attend the same Orientation and Job Clubs become friends and share information about what is good and bad about welfare reform. They also cooperate with each other to make their lives more tolerable, for example, by giving rides to parents unlucky enough to depend on LA's often inadequate transportation system. Many parents are thus a resource for collective cooperation, organization, and resistance.

Focus groups also resulted in a form of consciousness raising because we asked participants their opinions about what did and did not work in the program, and what could be done to improve their situations. They had clear answers and wanted them to be heard by policy makers. Basically, they wanted to have a say about what was happening to their lives. Invariably, in the more heated sessions, some potential leader emerged to speak out for participant power and received nods of agreement. At the conclusion of one session, an angry parent had this to say:

> I think they (the policy makers) need to pick the lowest person on the shelf, you know, somebody who really doesn't have any family to help them, who has actually survived, you know, get some people who really know what it's like to start like this, and let them help make those decisions.

> I see people that work, you know, they work in DPSS, and they say [mimics an officious voice], "Oh, yeah, I understand, I understand it." They really don't. You know? I see the car they drive and the clothes they wear, and you can tell by looking at them, they have never had to live like this, ever.

What we found in our focus groups were the methods of control and the seeds of resistance. Control is not monolithic. Rather, it is a complex site of accommodation, contestation, and individual resistance that holds the potential for collective resistance and social change.

### Acknowledgments

We wish to thank the staff of DPSS, Urban Research, and LA GAIN, and Job Club/LACOE (Los Angeles County Office of Education) for their cooperation and assistance in helping us to carry out our research. In particular, we would like to thank the project director of our research at LA County for his ongoing support of our work. We also wish to express our appreciation to Amy Denissen and especially to Shelley Feldman for their thoughtful critique and contributions to our analysis; to Manuel Moreno for his ongoing support of our work; to Margarita Gonzalez-Kojima for her invaluable help in conducting and transcribing Spanish-speaking focus groups; and to Julie Peggar for her invaluable assistance in transcribing, organizing, and analyzing data. Not least of all, we wish to thank the parents who participated in our focus groups. They were eager to tell us about their lives, and we feel obliged to bring their voices to the ongoing debate about the course of welfare reform.

## References

Canfield, Jack et al. *Motivation Program: A Guidebook to Personal Success, More than a Job, a Foothold for life.* 1998. Culver City, CA: The Foundation for Self-Esteem.

Canfield, Jack, and Mark Victor Hansen, eds. 1993. *Chicken Soup for the Soul: 101 Stories to Open the Heart & Rekindle the Spirit.* Deerfield Beach, FL: Health Communications.

Fleming, Daniel, Mark Drayse, and Peter Force. 2000. *The Cage of Poverty.* Los Angeles: The Economic Roundtable.

Fleming, Daniel, Mark Drayse, Peter Force, and Frederic Deng. 2001. Los Angeles Labor Market Action Plan. Los Angeles: The Economic Roundtable.

Freedman, Stephen, Daniel Friedlander, Gayle Hamilton, JoAnn Rock, Marisa Mitchell, Jodi Nudelman, Amanda Schweder, and Laura Storto. 2000. *National Evaluation of Welfare-to-Work Strategies Evaluating Alternative Welfare-to-Work Approaches: Two-Year Impacts for Eleven Programs.* New York: Manpower Demonstration Research Corporation.

Freedman, Stephen, Jean Tansey Knab, Lisa A. Gennetian, and David Navarro. 2000. *The Los Angeles Jobs-First GAIN Evaluation: Final Report on a Work First Program in a Major Urban Center.* New York: Manpower Demonstration Research Corporation.

Horowitz, Ruth. 1995. *Teen Mothers: Citizens or Dependents?* Chicago: University of Chicago Press.

Human Services Alliance of LA. 2001. *In the Loop: Welfare Reform in LA County.* Newsletter.

Kaplan, Elaine Bell. 1997. *Not Our Kind of Girl: Unraveling the Myths of Black Teenage Motherhood.* Berkeley and Los Angeles: University of California Press.

Los Angeles County Department of Public Social Service (LA DPSS). 1999. *CalWORKs. L.A. GAIN Program Handbook.* Sections 210.1-4: 310, 330; Section 712.1.

————. 2000. Caseload Characteristics. Available at http://dpss.co.la.ca.us/r_and_s/99_june/caseload_characteristics_selection.cfm.

Moreno, Manuel, John Hedderson, Michael Lichter, Elizabeth González, and Jeff Henderson. 1999. *From Welfare-to-Work and Economic Self-Sufficiency: A Baseline Evaluation of the Los Angeles County CalWORKs Program.* Los Angeles County Urban Research Division, Chief Administrative Office.

Piven, Frances Fox, and Richard A. Cloward. 1971. *Regulating the Poor: The Functions of Public Welfare.* New York: Random House.

Rivera, Carla. 2000. "Beyond Welfare-to-Work: A Job Is Only the Start When It Doesn't Provide Self-Sufficiency." *Los Angeles Times* (October 16).

Schorr, Lisabeth B. 1989. *Within Our Reach: Breaking the Cycle of Disadvantage.* New York: Doubleday.

## Notes

[1] John Horton is professor emeritus of sociology at the University of California, Los Angeles. Favoring critical and qualitative approaches to issues of inequality and social justice, he is an author of many articles and a book, *The Politics of Diversity: Immigration, Resistance, and Change in Monterey Park, California* (1995).

[2] Linda Shaw is associate professor of sociology at California State University, San Marcos. She has authored articles in the area of community care for chronic mental patients and qualitative research methods, and is co-author of the book *Writing Ethnographic Fieldnotes* (1995).

[3] GAIN is the name of the county's version of CalWORKs (California Work Opportunity and Responsibility to Kids), the state's response to the federal Personal Responsibility and Work Opportunity Reconciliation Act of 1996. Los Angeles County implemented CalWORKs on April 1, 1998.

[4] Our work was conducted under contract with the Urban Research Division, Chief Office of Administration, of Los Angeles County for the Los Angeles Department of Public Services (LA DPSS) as part of their evaluation of CalWORKs. The views expressed here are our own based on the data we collected and not necessarily those of county officials or employees. In fact, delegated DPSS readers of our original draft (a prepublication review was a condition of our contract) disagreed with some of our findings and interpretations. We have noted their disagreements in our endnotes.

[5] Source: DPSS reviewers of our draft article.

[6] L.A. County has by far the highest percentage of CalWORKs applicants who withdraw from the program in the state. In March 2000, 42 percent of the 9,075 parents who applied for CalWORKs withdrew their application. The average withdrawal rate for all California counties was only 10 percent, according to Professor Robert Buck of San Diego State University. (Human Services Alliances of L.A. 2001).

[7] A DPSS reviewer notes: "Prior to welfare reform, GAIN had a training-first approach, which did not have as much success in moving people into self-sufficiency as the work-first approach. Furthermore, California law mandates a work-first approach for all counties. At the same time, the county is preparing to implement a revised Welfare-to-Work strategy, which will emphasize the combination of paid work with education training.... Besides these services, the Department now has a comprehensive Long-Term Family Self-Sufficiency Plan, which promises to address a vast number of issues and provide the much needed assistance to the working poor." The researchers note the voluntary character of LA GAIN's previous training-first programs and their implementation during times of economic downturn when jobs were scarce. We see the county's planned changes as positive steps to address some of the problems participants identified with its strongly enforced work-first approach — in particular, the lack of needed training and education necessary to move out of poverty.

[8] Source: DPSS reviewers of our draft article.

[9] DPSS reviewers objected to the negativity of the word *control* as applied to incentives to complete the mandatory work requirement and sanctions for failure to participate in the program. They see these measures as integral to successful welfare reform: "However, we

**210**

believe that without any incentives to complete the mandatory work requirement or without the possibility of having the sanction imposed for failure to participate in the program, there would be no reasons for the CalWORKs participant to get off aid. We do not see the two procedures as a form of controlling, but of one providing service and assistance." From a sociological perspective, the researchers see these aspects of the program as social controls designed to achieve the state's goal of moving welfare participants into the labor market. Moreover, *control* best describes how many parents in our focus groups experienced DPSS's methods of achieving compliance, that is, as an external force not necessarily operating in their interests.

[10] DPSS reviewer comment: "It is important to emphasize that the skills taught to our participants are designed to assist them with skills that are to be used not only when looking for work, but also for everyday survival. The skills taught are the same used and required of any individual in the labor force and are by no means intended to demean or belittle participants…" The researchers agree that participants must be prepared for the requirements of the workplace. However, they came from diverse backgrounds, some with work histories and job skills but felt they were treated as though they lacked both the discipline and skills needed to succeed at work. For some, this was indeed the case. But participants often felt that the program failed to recognize or assess their past experience and treated them all according to the lowest common denominator — as people who lacked both the skills and willingness to work.

[11] DPSS reviewer comment: "We believe that participants entering Job Club should adhere to the same requirements and demands made from an employed individual. Participants must comply with the goals, discipline, and expectations of the employer, which, in turn, prepares them for the rigid and sometimes difficult real world." Data from our study show that most participants shared the goals of the program — to get off of welfare and into the workforce — but objected to the inflexible, coercive, and ineffective way it was implemented that resulted in resistance to the program rather than a productive learning experience. These findings are consistent with previous research that shows that behavioral change may be more effectively achieved through supportive rather than coercive means (see Horowitz 1995; Schorr 1989).

[12] DPSS reviewer comment: "Although these changes … are difficult for participants to become accustomed to, it should be noted that these changes represent the reality of modern work life. We seek to help participants become contributing members of society by instilling in them the sacrifices and rewards of working." The findings reported in this study are intended to highlight the particular burdens that poor parents bear in fulfilling this obligation. Our data show that the program requires sacrifices that may exceed those found in the workplace. It is possible, for example, to find work close to schools and childcare or to negotiate working hours that enable parents to get children off to school or to be home at the end of the school day. But GAIN participants have no choice about attending Job Clubs located far from home or adhering to strict requirements that conflict with school schedules, childcare arrangements, or the time they have to spend with their children. Finally, we are concerned about the perspective that the regulations imposed by Welfare-to-Work programs are necessary to help parents to become contributing members of society by instilling the sacrifices and rewards of working. In talking to poor parents, we came to appreciate the largely unrecognized and unpaid work necessary to care for their children and other family members.

[13] For a vivid portrait of how teenage mothers view their decisions and lives, see Kaplan (1997).

[14] Our DPSS reviewers objected strongly to our interpretation: "We agree that the types of moral control stated in this section are real, and participants face discrimination and societal pressures on a daily basis. However, we *do not* use the 'internalized negative stereotypes' of welfare recipients as a resource to reinforce and reproduce images of recipients individually responsible for their plight. Our methodology is directed toward the advancement of the poor, the financial stabilization of the family, and its continued moral support." To this we respond: We do not want to suggest that those involved in implementing the Welfare-to-Work program consciously employ negative stereotypes about welfare recipients. We believe that most sincerely want to do whatever they can to encourage participants to get off of welfare and become self-sufficient. However, an examination of the methodology used to reach this goal reveals that the program draws upon commonly held beliefs that anyone can get ahead through individual effort and hard work. As a society we believe that the poor and welfare recipients are a drain on society and simply lack the initiative to become contributing members. An extension of this ideology is that any poor person can pull herself out of poverty if she just tries hard enough. We do not take issue with attempts to motivate welfare parents and help them to improve their self-esteem. But we are concerned about the ideological message that the causes of poverty are matters of individual, moral character. The implicit message is that if they are poor, it is their fault. It is in this sense that we argue that, while not consciously intending to do so, the Welfare-to-Work program implicitly draws upon "internalized negative stereotypes" of welfare recipients as a methodology for motivating welfare parents to participate in the program.

# Talking Across the Welfare Divide

*Chariti Gent*[1]

In order to gauge how changes in welfare laws affect recipients and communities, it is important to gain a thorough understanding of the context in which these new rules and regulations are being implemented. The ways in which assorted participants in any local welfare reform context view reform can differently impact the success of implementation and the overall wellbeing of the community. The question for communities and concerned citizens becomes: How do various welfare reform participants at the local level — officials from the Department of Social Services, recipients, nonprofits, welfare rights advocates, businesses, etc.—view the problems and solutions of welfare and welfare reform? In essence, what's the context? Without a more complete understanding of the context, policies aimed at alleviating and/or solving the problems encountered by reform are likely to fail.

In this paper, I argue that in order to find workable alternatives that will successfully provide for and protect the health, welfare, and dignity of the local community, as well as meet federal reform guidelines, local participants within the welfare debate first must recognize and understand the context in which they are operating. Although this may seem a simple and obvious point, it is nonetheless overlooked in various policy analyses. In this paper I show that the different ways in which various participants socially and politically construct the meaning behind the various aspects of welfare and welfare reform in Boulder County, Colorado—that is, the way they think about, talk about, and discuss reform—are important to our overall understanding of the local reform context there.

## Understanding the Need for Context-Sensitive Analyses

Policy scholars have long argued the need for context sensitivity when conducting public policy analyses. According to Lasswell, individuals are predisposed to act *on their own perspectives* in a way that will leave them "better off" than if they had acted differently (Lasswell and Kaplan 1950; Brunner 1996; 1998). As such, human behavior and actions are highly dependent upon their perspectives of the context of which they are a part—and the context is highly variable and always subject to change (Lasswell et al. 1952; Cronbach 1975; Brunner 1991). The justification for an emphasis on context sensitivity in any policy inquiry is best summed up by Cronbach (1975):

> Generalizations decay. At one time a conclusion describes the existing situation well, at a later time it accounts for rather little variance, and ultimately it is valid only as history.

Similar conclusions are drawn from specialists in the fields of policy management and decision. Ralph Sui (1978) notes that the context of practice in the policy arena is characterized in the following manner:

> Everything is continually changing—not only the events themselves, but also the very rules of governing those events. This kind of arena is alien to the scientific tradition of fixed boundary conditions, clearly defined variables, nonsubjective assessments, and rational consistency within a closed system. In the ball game of competitive actualities, everything is in flux, and all systems are open.

More recently, scholars of public policy within political science have reiterated the need for contextually based research. Scholarship by Schneider and Ingram (1994) suggests that context sensitivity is a "must" in conducting any line of policy inquiry. In addition, Rochefort and Cobb (1994), in their book on problem definition, utilize context-sensitive case studies to make their argument that the way individuals and groups define and/or think about problems is often a result of the unique circumstances in which they are operating.[2]

## Using Qualitative Software Packages to Guide Inquiry

### Word Freq—A Quick Look at the Context

Word Freq software, available widely as shareware on the Internet, provides the mechanism by which researchers conduct basic content analysis. Through generation of an alphabetical list of words by frequency that are found in the text, Word Freq software can direct and guide the researcher to a richer understanding of where the "focus of attention" lay with regard to a particular policy issue. That is, by analyzing which words are used in the text, and how often they are used, Word Freq software provides a detailed yet snapshot-like account of the kind of dialogue surrounding a particular policy debate or issue. By illuminating where the focus of attention of various participants lay, the Word Freq software can aid in constructing a more thorough understanding of the context from which individual perceptions are gleaned and consequent actions carried out.

### Nudist and Concordance Generation

Once frequency counts of words within text are generated, and the most commonly used words are identified, concordances (i.e., indices of words in a text that show every context in which the words occur) are generated using software packages such as QSR Nudist. Essentially, concordances are word strings of varied length that expose for the researcher the context in which a particular word or group of words is used. The systematic generation of concordances is useful for recognizing differences and changes in manifest meanings of particular words across spatial, temporal, or other contexts.

## Results from the Qualitative Analysis

### Why Boulder County?

A case study of Boulder County, Colorado, was conducted in order to investigate the ways in which the various participants within the welfare reform debate think about, and discuss the problems, issues, and potential solutions regarding reform in that locale. Boulder County was chosen for several reasons. First, I wanted to combine scholarship with activism and, in the case of Boulder County, I was in a position to do just that. As a member of a local welfare-rights group, I am able to share my scholarly research results with other welfare activists and interested parties in hopes of generating a more thorough understanding of the context in which the activist community and others are operating with regard to welfare reform.[3] I believe that doing so provides all members of the welfare community with a better base from which to develop workable, sustainable public policies.

Second, I chose Boulder County because of its proximity to the University of Colorado, which is situated there. Being able to access documents and data regarding welfare reform with relative ease and speed facilitated the rate at which this research on Boulder County welfare reform could be conducted. Given the need for timely solutions to the problems being encountered by welfare officials and recipients, as peoples' lives are "on the line," I felt it appropriate to conduct the study "close to home."

Finally, preliminary research on the "success" of Boulder County welfare reform programs suggested that local social service officials are beginning to encounter a "recycling" of individuals back to the welfare rolls. Given the potential problems that such a situation creates for all members of the community, I decided it would be worthwhile to investigate the ways in which various participants within the welfare debate view the problems of reform as well as what solutions they discuss in order to remedy those problems. Doing so illuminates the broader context in which welfare reform in Boulder County is unfolding and, hopefully, sheds some light on previously misunderstood and/or misconstrued aspects of reform at the local level, allowing for more workable, sustainable policy alternatives to be developed.

## The Data Source

In order to conduct a content analysis of participant views and discussion surrounding welfare reform in Boulder County, I utilized meeting minutes from an ad hoc community governing board that was formed to oversee the implementation of welfare reform there. Boulder County Department of Social Services officials formed the Welfare Reform Review Committee (WRRC) in 1997. The purpose of this committee was to bring together the "major players" in welfare reform in Boulder County, including county officials, bureaucrats, local activists, welfare recipients, and other concerned parties, in order to gather information about the effects of local welfare policy changes on the local welfare population and find ways to "improve" the system. As such, this was an appropriate group for study. The WRRC met twice monthly for a period of one year, after which the group was disbanded.[4] During the monthly WRRC meetings, detailed minutes were recorded by a welfare rights activist and approved by all committee members before being added to the formal record.

## Content Analysis: Word Freq Procedures and Results

In order to determine the focus of attention of the various participants in the welfare reform process and to illuminate the context in which the various actors are operating, I conducted a word frequency on WRRC meeting minutes from August 1997 to June 1998.[5] Overall frequency counts of words found in WRRC meeting minute texts are listed in Table 13.1.[6]

## Table 13.1
### Word Frequency Results for All Text

Words used most often in the text of the WRRC meeting minutes
(in descending order of usage)

Work
County
TANF
Paula
Recipients
Program
Welfare
Toya
Committee
Services
Childcare
Reform
Boulder
Staff
Training
Child
Families
Information
Care
State
Clients
Programs
Need
Time
Assistance
Support
Money
Mentors
Parenting
Providers
Review
Center
Children
People
Women
Data
Impact
Issues
Mothers
Parents
Problem
Project
Commissioners
Family
Low

According to this word frequency distribution, aspects of welfare reform garnering the most attention from welfare reform participants in Boulder County include but are not limited to: work and training, children and families, and welfare and services. These findings are hardly surprising. What is surprising to note, however, is what's not being focused on in this dialogue. For example, *education, community, employment, health, economy, immigrants, poor, poverty, responsibility, opportunity,* and *father(s)* are just a few of the words that lack emphasis in this discussion.[7]

In order to determine the focus of attention *of each of the various participants* in the welfare reform debate in Boulder County, the dialogue of the WRRC meeting minutes was separated according to participant type, and a Word Freq was performed on each. The results of those analyses are listed in Table 13.2.

## Table 13.2
### Word Frequency Results for Each Participant
Words used most often in the text of the WRRC meeting minutes *by the separate participants*
(in descending order of usage)

| Social Service Officials | Business Officials | Recipients | Agencies and Advocates |
|---|---|---|---|
| Work* | Studies | Recipients* | Work* |
| Recipient(s)* | Work* | Work* | Program |
| Childcare* | Area | Information | TANF |
| County | Group | Children* | County |
| Boulder | Mentors* | Mentor* | Families* |
| TANF | Training* | Parents | Recipients* |
| WRRC | Workplace | Workplace | Childcare* |
| Services | | Family* | Welfare |
| Child* | | Childcare* | Welfare Reform |
| Program | | Training* | Services |
| State | | | |
| Family* | | | |
| Training* | | | |
| Mentor* | | | |
| Mother | | | |
| Education | | | |
| Client | | | |

* indicates words that appear on at least three of the four participant lists

What's interesting to note from these various analyses is that, for each participant, the word *work* was used frequently, if not the most, suggesting that at the focus of every participant's attention is the *work* aspect of welfare reform. Also noteworthy is the emphasis placed on *children* and/or *childcare* by Social Service officials, agencies and advocates, and recipients; clearly, these participants are concerned for the children that are affected by welfare reform. Also worthy of mention, because they appear on at least three of the four participant lists, are *recipients, family,* and *job training and mentoring.* Interestingly, recipients are the only category of participants to use the word *information* frequently, just as Social Service officials are the only participants using the words *education, mother,* and *client.* Likewise, local business officials are the only participants concerned with *studies* of welfare reform and various agencies and officials are the only participants that frequently and explicitly use the term *welfare reform.*

### Understanding Words In Context: Nudist Analyses

Once the decreasing frequency counts were tabulated, I context-analyzed key words (i.e. those words that were most frequent and "in common" in the text counts for each of the participants), including *work, recipient, child, family,* and *job training and mentoring* (see asterisked terms).[8] Using Nudist, I identify the context in which each of these words is used, further illuminating the symbols and focus of attention surrounding the local welfare reform dialogue for each of the participants.

### Work

Concordances generated from the dialogue of **Social Service officials** during the WRRC meetings reveal the following about the term *work.* First, the term refers to programmatic work requirements of new TANF regulations. Social Service officials are concerned with TANF requirements and responsibilities, how to insure participation in work, how to handle exemptions from work for good cause, etc. Second, *work* was used in terms of *work skills* that welfare recipients have and/or will need to succeed in the workplace. Social Service officials are concerned that a portion of the recipient population simply may not be "employable" without further education or training. Finally, *work* was discussed in terms of barriers to work, like mental illness, domestic violence, etc., as well as opportunities of and availability for work for recipients.

Concordances generated from the dialogue of **recipients** during the WRRC meetings reveal that, in terms of *work,* recipients are most concerned with their ability to "fit in" and succeed in the workplace. Unlike Social Service officials, *work* is not something that is thought of by recipients in terms of program goals or implementation. In addition, recipients do not formally recognize the various obstacles to working that some people face or the solutions for overcoming them.

**219**

Concordances generated from the dialogue of **business officials** during the WRRC meetings reveal that they are concerned primarily with *work* in terms of *workplace* training and mentoring. Unlike Social Service providers and recipients, business officials are most concerned with the ability and skills that recipients have and can bring to the *workplace* and in helping them to succeed once they are there (hence the need for *work* mentors).

Concordances generated from the dialogue of **agencies and advocates** during the WRRC meetings reveal that, like Social Services, the term *work* is used to discuss difficulties that recipients have with barriers to *work* (e.g. mental illness, drug use, etc.). There also exists a perception on the part of agencies and advocates that some recipients are finding it difficult to meet TANF *work* requirements because of problems associated with transportation, childcare, etc. In addition, like Social Service and business officials, advocates and agencies believe that a *workplace* mentorship requirement is a necessary program for all TANF recipients.

### Recipient(s)

Concordances generated from the dialogue of **Social Service officials** during the WRRC meetings reveal that Social Service officials used the word *recipient* primarily as a reference term for the clients whom they serve. The term *recipient* was also discussed in terms of TANF program requirements for *recipients,* the costs of keeping *recipients* in the programs, and how to elicit and include *recipient* feedback with regard to basic TANF program implementation. Also mentioned by Social Service officials were personal difficulties *recipients* were experiencing with the new TANF system, as well as the need to move *recipients* into jobs and/or a self-sufficient position without making them feel isolated or alone.

Concordances generated from the dialogue of **advocates and agencies** during the WRRC meetings reveal that the use of the word *recipient* by advocates and agencies is in regard to determining the needs of *recipients* and the impact that changes in the welfare laws are having on *recipients'* families. There is also concern about the need for job support and mentorship for TANF *recipients,* as well as job availability. In addition, information flows to *recipients* regarding TANF rules, regulations, changes, etc., are mentioned as a primary concern.

Concordances generated from the dialogue of **TANF recipients** during the WRRC meetings reveal that *recipient* is used to refer to TANF program participants and usually concerns how such individuals are faring under the new programmatic requirements. Like advocates and agencies, *recipients* are concerned with the impact that TANF changes are having on individuals, particularly with regard to job availability and opportunity, information flows, and mentoring requirements.

### Child/Children/Childcare

Concordances generated from the dialogue of **Social Service officials** during the WRRC meetings reveal that the term *child* is used mainly by Social Service officials in reference to *child*care costs, *child*care worker pay rates, funding for *child*care, and access and quality of *child*care. Social Services seemed especially concerned with the ability of TANF recipients to meet program work requirements when *child* needs impact these abilities negatively (e.g. a sick *child* means a parent cannot make it to work).

Concordances generated from the dialogue of **agencies and advocates** during the WRRC meetings reveal that, like Social Service officials, reference to *child*care regarded the impact of reform on *child*care delivery, accessibility, cost, availability, and funding. Discussion also revolved around training TANF recipients as *child*care workers in the local "Neighbor to Neighbor" childcare job opportunities program.

Concordances generated from the dialogue of **recipients** reveal that the term *child*ren is used by recipients in terms of the concern they have for the welfare and care of *child*ren whose parents participate in TANF programs. Specifically, TANF recipients are concerned that the changes in welfare policy may force families into situations where the stability of the household is eroded, causing adverse psychological and behavioral effects in *child*ren. The TANF recipients that took part in the WRRC discussions believe that making sure that the impacts of reform are mitigated for children is of utmost importance.

### Family

Concordances generated from the dialogue of **Social Service officials** during the WRRC meetings reveal that the term *family/families* is discussed in terms of the services that are provided to TANF *families*, how to meet the needs of "hard-to-reach" *families* (i.e. those without phones, cars, etc.), and how to handle those *families* that are being sanctioned and feel threatened by changes in welfare laws that they (the recipients) do not understand. In addition, *families* were discussed in statistical terms (i.e. caseload numbers, the number collecting Medicaid, food stamps, etc.).

Concordances generated from the dialogue of **advocates and agencies** during the WRRC meetings reveal that most advocates and agencies are primarily concerned with the impact of welfare reform on TANF *families* with regard to childcare, quality of life issues, understanding and compliance with rules and regulations, etc. Advocates mentioned concern about the ability of *families* to really achieve self sufficiency, that is, to find suitable employment that will help them permanently transition off of welfare and into work, as dictated by welfare reform guidelines. Advocates also show concern regarding the number of *families* turning to the nonprofit sector for assistance when they no longer are eligible to receive aid from the government. Like Social Service officials, advocates and agencies are especially concerned with at-risk families, e.g. those without a phone or car, those without the ability to function "normally" on a daily basis, etc.

Concordances generated from the dialogue of **recipients** during the WRRC meetings reveal that recipients are concerned that particular *family* living conditions/situations facilitated by changes in welfare regulations might be detrimental to all families and their members, particularly children and young teenage mothers. For the recipients involved in this dialogue, like agencies and advocates, *families* are usually discussed in terms of *families* in crisis.

### Training and Mentoring

Concordances generated from the dialogue of **Social Service officials** during the WRRC meetings reveal that the word *training* was discussed by Social Service officials in terms of the types of *training* available to recipients (e.g. literacy *training*, job readiness *training*, etc.) Costs and funding for these *trainings* was also an issue for the service providers, as was *training* for the *mentors* of these various programs. Social Service officials also reveal concern with recipient demand for and satisfaction with the family and *job mentor* programs currently available. In addition, *mentor* availability and the flexibility of the current *mentor* programs to adapt to future changes and demands is also an issue.

Like Social Service officials, **business officials** seem to be convinced that one of the keys to workplace success for recipients is to have a *mentor* in place that can guide and teach the recipient as she begins her new employment. Unlike Social Services, however, business officials seem less concerned with making certain that recipients receive the skills or workplace *training* necessary to succeed in the workplace. This is peculiar given the earlier emphasis that business leaders place on recipient workplace success in their discussions of the term "work."

Concordances generated from the dialogue of **recipients** during the WRRC meetings reveal the following about the term *training*. Recipients think of *training* as *training* for *job mentors*, not *job* or *skills training* for themselves. Recipients are concerned that not enough *mentor training* is occurring, especially *mentor training* that teaches *mentors* how to be sensitive to the special needs and expectations of transitioning Welfare-to-Work participants. Unlike Social Service officials, recipients do not hold family or *job mentor* programs in high regard; however, recipients are aware that *mentorships* can be useful to transitioning mothers if the programs are structured and conducted with a degree of sensitivity and care.

### Discussion of the Analysis: Room for Improvement

Overall, the ways in which the various participants think about and discuss issues like work, family, and training, etc. is very telling. Social

Service officials, for the most part, concern themselves with programmatic aspects of welfare reform, particularly the overall administration of the new TANF rules and regulations, and the measures that need to be taken to insure the overall "success" of welfare reform.

Advocates and agencies, like Social Service officials, are also concerned about TANF rules and regulations, but they are more interested in the overall impact that these new rules and regulations are having on TANF recipients and families, as well as local nonprofit organizations that assist the poor. For advocates and agencies, services and support programs that aid recipients in overcoming barriers to work and transitioning off of welfare are necessary and crucial if the harsh impacts of welfare reform are to be lessened for recipients and their children.

Business officials, while definitely concerned with the impact of welfare reform, are less concerned about the impact on families and more with how to "absorb" the influx of new, often unskilled, workers that are entering the workplace as a result of reform. Insuring the success and survival of these women in the workforce is not only critical for the recipient's success but is crucial for overall business success, as well.

Recipients, while taking issue with such things as work and training, are nonetheless more concerned that the overall dignity and pride of the recipient is maintained as she transitions off of welfare. There seems to be an overriding belief on the part of recipients that sensitivity training is necessary for workplace mentors, family mentors, and others in dealing with them (recipients) and their children. Furthermore, recipients, like the advocates and agency officials, are also concerned with the impact that welfare reform is having on families and, especially, children. Finally, it is worth noting that recipients also place a heavy emphasis on information. While not included in the analysis here, recipients do mention that a basic lack of information is one of the most troubling aspects of welfare reform for them.[9]

While the scope of this study was limited to Boulder County, content-focused case studies of this kind that aim to illuminate the overall welfare context at the local level are appropriate for any community or researcher that wishes to better understand the whole context. Context sensitive studies are crucial if communities are to begin to effectively counter the problems of welfare reform. Without a complete understanding of the big picture in which these actors are functioning, solutions that truly work are impossible to fashion. In addition, illuminating the local context surrounding reform is useful because it highlights previously misunderstood, misconstrued, and/or overlooked aspects of reform, all of which contribute to poor public policymaking.

## References

Brunner, Ronald D. 1991. "The Policy Movement as a Policy Problem." *Policy Sciences* 24: 65–98.

——. 1996. Central Theory Seminar. Paper read at Yale School of Forestry and Environmental Studies Conference, February 13-14.

——. 1998. "Making Connections: A Policy Sciences Primer." Chapter 2 in *Political Science*.

Cobb, R.W., and M.H. Ross. 1997. *Cultural Strategies of Agenda Denial: Avoidance, Attack, and Redefinition*. Lawrence: University Press of Kansas.

Cronbach, L.J. 1975. "Beyond the Two Disciplines of Scientific Psychology." *American Psychologist* 30: 116–127.

Edelman, Murray. 1964. *The Symbolic Uses of Politics*. Urbana: University of Illinois Press.

Kingdon, John. 1984. *Agendas, Alternatives, and Public Policies*. New York: Harper Collins.

Lasswell, Harold, D. Lerner, and I deS. Pool. 1952. *The Comparative Study of Political Symbols: An Introduction*. Stanford: Stanford University Press.

Lasswell, Harold, and Abraham Kaplan. 1950. *Power and Society*. New Haven: Yale University Press.

Rochefort, D., and Roger Cobb. 1994. *The Politics of Problem Definition*. Lawrence: University of Kansas Press.

Schneider, Anne, and Helen Ingram. 1994. "Social Constructions of Target Populations: Implications for Politics and Policy." *American Political Science Review* 87: 334-347.

Sui, Ralph G.H. 1978. "Management and the Art of Chinese Baseball." *Sloan Management Review* 19: 83–89.

## Notes

[1] Chariti Gent is a former research associate with the University of Colorado and currently works as a policy analyst for the State of Wisconsin's Department of Transportation. Her primary research interests include the politics of poverty and work, HIV/AIDS politics, and the problems and solutions of modern urban governance. Gent has published articles most recently in the journals *Legislative Studies Quarterly* and *The Policy Sciences*.

[2] For further elaboration on the need for context sensitivity, see Edelman (1964); Kingdon (1984); and Cobb and Ross (1997).

[3] While I understand and appreciate the general tendency of most social science researchers to criticize my lack of "objectivity," I nonetheless believe that such a state of objectivity is nearly impossible to achieve when studying policy issues within a particular context; whether researchers, practitioners, scholars, activists, etc., we all carry certain biases to our research. As such, I try to maintain an awareness of my particular biases as

an activist and a scholar, taking them into account as I conduct my research, so as to minimize their effect on my study results.

[4] While I have no definitive statements as to why this group no longer meets, I was informed by a welfare rights activist that the group was disbanded because it was not serving its intended purpose. According to this activist, the meetings were dominated by local county officials, with welfare recipients and other participants given little chance to interact or be heard. However, local county social service officials report that the group no longer meets because it has fulfilled its mission of overseeing welfare implementation.

[5] Upon request for copies of all WRRC meeting minutes from Social Services, this is what was sent to me. I assume that this is the universe of formally recorded meeting minutes.

[6] Not all frequency counts are listed, as articles, pronouns, etc. are not considered significant enough to be listed here and are therefore omitted. In addition, in order to highlight those words that are found most often in the text, I list only those words that received twenty or more "hits," as this seemed to be a natural breakpoint in the word frequency lists that were generated.

[7] This is not to say that these words are not present in the Word Freq counts. Rather, they are mentioned so few times that it is not accurate to include them in the list of emphasized words.

[8] By "in common," I mean those words that were used most frequently by three or four of the participant groups in the debate.

[9] "Information" was not included in the original analysis because it is only mentioned frequently by one of the participants, recipients.

# Ties That Bind
## Child Support Enforcement and Welfare Reform in Wisconsin

*Renee A. Monson*[1]

Policies regarding child support enforcement and paternity establishment receive far less academic and media attention than work requirements and time limits, the other cornerstones of PRWORA. This was not always the case. Child support enforcement and "deadbeat dads" were important issues in the 1992 presidential campaign. But as President Clinton and a Republican-led Congress ended "welfare as we knew it" in 1996, most supporters, as well as critics, of this legislation highlighted the Welfare-to-Work provisions. Child support enforcement and paternity establishment have become noncontroversial and understudied components of welfare reform, even though these policies are intended to serve the same purpose as work requirements: shifting the provision of social welfare from the state to the labor market and individual families. In this paper, I build on feminist analyses of the effects of work requirements and time limits on poor, single mothers and their children to construct a parallel analysis of the effects of child support enforcement and mandatory paternity establishment.

The feminist critique of Welfare-to-Work policies rests on two arguments about single mothers' interests. Work requirements are criticized first as contrary to single mothers' economic interests, and second as contrary to single mothers' interests as primary or sole caregivers. Welfare reform's work requirements and time limits have not resulted in economic security for most single mothers and their children, and these policies ignore (or selectively construct) what constitutes good mothering. (See Part II).

The critique is not premised on the argument that women should be mothers and not workers. Many poor, single mothers want to get and keep paid jobs. Many say they are better off working than receiving public assistance. And supporting and encouraging women's access to paid work has been central to first- and second-wave feminist politics. The argument, therefore, is not that paid work itself is contrary to all single mothers' interests. It is the *mandatory character* of these policies that is contrary to many single mothers' interests, given that the quality of jobs and childcare available to them varies, as does their assessment of the sort of caregiving their children need.

In this paper, I build on and extend this critique in my analysis of mandatory paternity establishment and child support enforcement policies in Wisconsin. Although many poor, unmarried mothers want paternity established and child support enforced, these policies also can conflict with these women's interests economically and as mothers. In addition, cooperating with these policies places some mothers at risk of fathers' violence.

### Child Support Enforcement and Paternity Establishment Policies

Unmarried mothers are more likely than divorced or widowed mothers to be poor, to receive public assistance, and to receive public assistance for longer spells. This is partly because they have lower earnings and partly because they are less likely to receive child support (Ellwood 1988; McLanahan and Sandefur 1994; U.S. Bureau of the Census 1995).

In the latter half of the twentieth century, federal welfare reform efforts increasingly have included legislation designed to strengthen and routinize paternity establishment[2] and child support enforcement, as well as Welfare-to-Work programs. PRWORA continued this trend by increasing pressure on states and individual mothers to identify biological fathers of nonmarital children. First, it required states to establish paternity for 90 percent of cases.[3] This reflected a gradual escalation of performance standards since 1967, when states were only required to initiate, not successfully complete, paternity actions for all nonmarital children receiving welfare.

Second, it increased the financial pressure on unmarried mothers to cooperate with the states' efforts to establish paternity. Mothers of nonmarital children seeking TANF benefits were required to cooperate with the state's efforts to establish paternity and enforce child support before they could qualify for assistance (not, as under AFDC rules, as a condition of continuing to receive public assistance). If mothers didn't cooperate with the state's efforts, states could opt to cut the entire family's TANF benefit (not, as under AFDC rules, just the mother's portion of the grant). Finally, the federally funded $50 pass-through payment was discontinued; states could opt to pass all, some, or none of the child support collected to the custodial parent receiving welfare. As of 1999, fewer than half of the states elected to pass through some or all of the child support collected (Roberts 1999).

Wisconsin's reform of welfare and child support enforcement predated many of the provisions in the 1996 federal legislation. In 1979, a welfare reform committee recommended a set of reforms to the state legislature that included a plan for reforming child support enforcement. Adopted in 1983, this plan largely anticipated many of the federal reforms in the 1984 CSEA and the 1988 FSA, such as percentage standards for child support awards and automatic wage withholding. In 1987, Wisconsin passed legislation that required the state to initiate proceedings to establish the legal paternity of *all* children born to unmarried mothers within six months of the birth. This legislation prefigured PRWORA's emphasis on increasing the percentage of nonmarital children with legal paternity (Corbett 1992).

Thus, prior to 1996, Wisconsin frequently was cited as a model state for its child support enforcement as well as Welfare-to-Work programs. In 1994, it ranked second in the nation for child support collections. In 1995, the state's paternity-establishment rate ranked first in the nation. And Wisconsin's total AFDC caseload dropped by nearly one-fourth between 1986 and 1994 (U.S. Bureau of the Census 1995; Wiseman 1996). Thus, an analysis of Wisconsin's policies and their effects on unmarried mothers can shed light on the implications of the strengthened child-support-enforcement and paternity-establishment policies under PRWORA.

### The Responses of Poor, Unmarried Mothers

Between 1994 and 1996, I conducted ethnographic research on paternity establishment and child support enforcement policy implementation in four Wisconsin counties. These data include observations of and interviews with dozens of child support workers and unmarried mothers. My analysis of these data suggest that a variety of factors shape poor, unmarried mothers' willingness to cooperate with mandatory paternity-establishment and child-support-enforcement policies: economic interests; their desire for fathers' legal ties to children; and the risk of violence by fathers. Given the complex effects of these policies on economic, social, and legal ties between mothers, fathers, and children—as well as the state's use of sanctions to force mothers' cooperation—unmarried mothers sometimes make risky or misinformed tradeoffs as they respond to mandatory paternity and child support enforcement policies.

## Unmarried Mothers' Economic Interests

Mothers of nonmarital children who seek public assistance must assign their rights to child support to the state as a condition of eligibility for welfare benefits. After PRWORA, most states opted to discontinue the $50 pass-through, while a handful chose to continue it. Thus, most poor, single mothers receive little, if any, of the child support collected from their children's fathers while they receive public assistance, as was the case in Wisconsin between 1994 and 1996.

In my study, most of the poor, unmarried mothers who viewed child support enforcement to be in their economic interests received public assistance only for brief periods, or not at all, or had just one child to support. Martha, a twenty-eight-year-old mother, sought to establish paternity and child support when her son was four months old, after investing a fair amount of time gathering information about the father's employment. At the 1995 adjudication, Martha was employed full-time as a clerical worker at $8.50 per hour. She had never received AFDC, and her private health insurance had paid for birth expenses. The father was employed full-time as a community organizer at $12 per hour. She told me that her main reason for establishing paternity was to get a formal child support order:

> He said that he didn't want to fight, and we could work things out without going through the court system. But knowing him, I knew that it wouldn't have been consistent. So that's why I went ahead into court. I mean, it would probably be like $50 here, $30 here, and I know he could have done better.

The court's child support order granted Martha $340 per month, a 30 percent increase in her monthly household income. Other mothers who did not benefit as much as Martha from the enforcement of child support nevertheless were willing to cooperate on general "fairness" principles, or in the hope that the state could force the father to find steadier or better-paying employment. Seventeen-year-old Josie had received just $20 in child support in the year since her child's father was adjudicated, but she was strongly in favor of enforcing child support. "He's got to take responsibility, too," she said. "I need some help, and that's his daughter, too. Why should I be the only one paying for it?"

More often, however, child support enforcement was not in poor, unmarried mothers' economic interests, precisely because few fathers of nonmarital children made enough money or had sufficiently stable employment to make child support enforcement a reliable route out of poverty or off welfare for the mothers of their children. These fathers generally face the same labor market (low wages, minimal benefits, little chance for advancement) as do the mothers of their children. Thus, these mothers often count on a combination of informal support from the father (and other kin), welfare benefits, and unreported paid work to make ends meet (Edin and Lein 1997). As a result, child support enforcement could actually reduce a mother's economic wellbeing if the informal (covert) support she had been receiving was more than the $50 pass-through she later received from the state's collection of formal child support.

Serena was living with the father of her child and didn't want paternity established and child support enforced for economic reasons. Though she would have received an additional $50 per month from the state if he were identified as the legal father and began paying child support, this would have left them worse off financially because the remainder of his monthly payment would have gone to the state to reimburse her welfare benefits. She told me,

> I thought, the money that they're gonna take from Larry we can use on other things. I had a car, he had a car, we had bills … and we couldn't afford it. He already had two kids [for whom he was paying child support], and you know, it was hard, hard already.

## Unmarried Fathers' Rights of Custody and Visitation

At the moment of paternity adjudication, legal fathers acquire rights of custody and visitation, as well as obligations of financial support. Unmarried mothers varied in their view of this result of establishing paternity. Many mothers wanted to have the father's name placed on the birth certificate to assure that he had legal rights to the children he was helping to raise and support. Jeannie lived with the father of her two nonmarital children and explained, "My main concern was to get his name on the birth certificate. They're his kids. I mean, his name should be there right along with mine." Danielle, who had been on and off welfare for five years and was in a stable, three-year relationship with the father of her two youngest children, willingly cooperated with paternity establishment for these children. She had lost placement of all her children while in a drug rehabilitation program, and asked the child support worker if legal paternity would have allowed her boyfriend, rather than her parents, to have gotten placement of their daughter.

But paternity establishment frequently is not in the interests of unmarried mothers who are primary or sole caregivers. They may not trust biological fathers' involvement in childrearing, particularly if the sexual or romantic relationship was brief, or has ended; and they may prefer that a current partner function as father to their children. Despite her willing cooperation with paternity establishment for her two youngest children, Danielle refused to divulge to the child support worker any information about her oldest daughter's father, other than his first name.

The worker tried to persuade her that "the visitation thing could be a separate issue, and that you could get help on that [in court], and there may not even be any [visitation]—especially if social workers get involved and decide this is not good for the child." Despite the worker's assurances, Danielle insisted that she didn't want the father around.

> I don't want to have anything to do with him. He's alcoholic, a drug abuser, he's flighty, and schizo, never really held any responsibility in his life—I don't know what I ever saw in him. He had another son who he was supposed to be taking responsibility for, and he would make appointments to go see the little boy when I was dating him and he would never show up because he would be hung over. And he has a terrible temper ... like I say, when she gets older, if she wants to meet him then I'll make an attempt to find him; but ... there's been so many terrible things going on in my life right now that I'm just not [going to cooperate].

### The Risk of Fathers' Violence

Once paternity is established, mothers are required to participate in the state's ongoing surveillance of nonresident fathers and efforts to enforce child support obligations.[4] Some workers suggested information-gathering tactics to mothers, including trading on whatever romantic feelings the father still had for them, asking friends or relatives for information about his whereabouts or current employment, and sending pictures of the child to the father or his family at Christmas or on birthdays and encouraging them to contact her or the child. One woman, who said she had become pregnant after having been raped at a college party, was told to ask her friends to help her find out more about him, including his last name and address. In practice then, so long as women assign their rights to child support to the state, they were expected to maintain some level of contact with the fathers of their children. These policies limit mothers' ability to choose whom they will associate with, and sometimes increase the risk of violence from fathers.

Some fathers threaten or deliver violence in retaliation for women's cooperation with state efforts to enforce child support or establish paternity (Brandwein 1999). Marilyn was thirty years old, unemployed, divorced, and the sole supporter of four children, ages fourteen to infancy (three from her marriage and one nonmarital). She received Medicaid and disability benefits for herself, welfare and Medicaid for her children, and no child support. At the time of her paternity statement, Marilyn was six months pregnant with her fifth child. She told the worker that the father lived out of state and she didn't know his address, date of birth, or phone number. A week after the child support office notified her that she would be sanctioned for non-cooperation if she did not supply additional information about the father, she wrote to the child support office and gave them the father's name, address, and his mother's address. She also explained:

> ...I'm sorry that I lied to you all about my baby father....The reason why I lied is because I was being threating [threatened] by him. He is a gang member and he threating to make me loose my baby. He tried once when he hitted me in my back and I was rush to [the hospital] every week until they just kept me because I kept himmitching [hemmoraghing]. I all most lost my baby that why she was eight week earlie. And he came up to the hospital threating me about putting her in his name [identifying him to the child support office]. The nurses even wrote things on my chart about how he was threating me. They had to give me medication to help me rest. I'm still taking the medication.

The child support file included a printout from the criminal justice computer database, which listed various charges and convictions for this man, including battery, disorderly conduct, and second-degree sexual assault of his stepdaughter, lending additional credence to her letter.

Mothers may apply for a good-cause exemption from cooperating with the state's efforts to establish paternity and enforce child support if they fear that doing so could harm themselves or their child. Nationwide prior to PRWORA, claims of good cause were filed in fewer than 0.5 percent of all welfare child support cases; fewer than two-thirds of these claims were successful (Brandwein 1999; Josephson 1997).[5] Under PRWORA, we can expect the number of these claims to remain very low. Although states now have greater discretion in how they define and dispose of good-cause claims, most have elected to retain the pre-1996 federal definition of good cause (Raphael and Haennicke 1999).

**Unmarried Mothers' Tradeoffs: Misinformation and Risk**

Because the law links unmarried fathers' support obligations and rights of custody and visitation with proof of their biological paternity—and because the state makes eligibility for welfare benefits contingent on cooperation with paternity establishment and child support enforcement—some mothers are forced to weigh economic well-being against personal safety, as in Marilyn's case, or against the desire to retain decision-making control over how to raise their children. Some mothers make these tradeoffs based on misinformation or risky assumptions.

Monya, a twenty-seven-year-old mother, was receiving AFDC for her seven-month-old son when she came into the child support office of her own accord, without having received an appointment letter. She brought Brian, the father, to get the paternity establishment process started more quickly. At that time, they had been dating for several years, and he was employed full-time (although his work history included periods of unemployment that had lasted several weeks). While Monya was on AFDC, she and her son lived at home with her parents and she took courses in office management at a local technical college. In an interview, Monya told me that she wanted a formal child support order even if she only received the first $50 collected:

> I wouldn't have had big, major problems getting things from him [without an order], but this way I know every month no matter what, unless he isn't working, that I would get this certain amount.... He [might have preferred] to say, "We can do it by ourselves," and I would have tried it at first, and then I would have said, "See it's not working, you only contributed $25 this month when you supposed to give me $50."

Monya planned to go back to work within a month or two and was counting on the full $188 Brian was paying in child support to help with daycare costs once she left AFDC. However, she had some concerns about custody. Although Monya was considering marrying Brian, she asked the child-support worker whether by forgoing a support order or not giving her son Brian's last name she could prevent him from "getting full rights to him [their son]," thus ensuring that her mother, not Brian, would gain custody if she died. During an interview, while Brian fed and played with their son in the next room, Monya told me that she had reservations about his ability to provide a secure home life, "because of him not keeping steady employment and, you know, the little things ... the cigarettes and the beer." In contrast, if her mother raised him, she said, "I *know* 100 percent that he's going to be taken care of and not in no way neglected." In the end, Monya decided to pursue paternity establishment because she believed (incorrectly) that she could ensure that her mother would raise her son, so long as she specified in her will that this was her wish. In actuality, as the legal father, Brian would be their child's closest legal kin in the event of Monya's death; Monya could not "will" custody of her son to her mother.

Elsa, a twenty-six-year-old mother of four nonmarital children, came in to the child support office for a paternity statement only after she had been sanctioned for non-cooperation. Elsa and Ruben, the twenty-two-year-old father of her youngest child, were willing to cooperate with paternity establishment but not child support enforcement, because

Ruben earned about $35,000 per year, and only $50 of his $500-per-month support payment would go to Elsa's household. They felt that the state was penalizing Ruben and their son for the other fathers' failure to pay support for Elsa's older children. Because AFDC rules required that each child in the household for whom the adult recipient has placement (physical custody) be listed on the AFDC grant, so long as Elsa had placement of their son and was receiving AFDC she had to assign her rights to child support to the state. Ruben and Elsa went to court and agreed to a number of stipulations: Ruben would have placement for their son and waive his rights to child support from Elsa (as the nonresident parent); the baby would actually live in Elsa's household; and Ruben would buy everything the baby needed—diapers, formula, clothes, medical care. Elsa then would not have to declare his contributions as income and could remain eligible for AFDC. Thus, Elsa agreed to give up her legal right to placement of her son in order to increase her household income, despite her girlfriends' warnings that she was taking a big risk. In her view, the risk was low given her stable relationship with Ruben (they were considering marriage) and her confidence in the courts' preference for mothers in custody disputes.

> I knew that if I gave Ruben physical placement of my son, he wasn't gonna use it against me. Some fathers would.... But if Ruben and me got broken up and Ruben said, "I'm gonna come and pick up Keanu and you'll never get him back"—take Keanu! I know that on Monday morning I will be in court and I will be getting placement of my son again. And I know that no judge would say, "Well Elsa, we can't do that for you." I know that they'll say, "You're right, he's your kid, he needs to be with you. Thank you [to the father] for taking care of him and thank you for helping her out, but now she's got a good job, she's stable, give her her kid." And the father can do visitations.

Both Monya and Elsa took risks in permitting the fathers of their nonmarital children to acquire particular rights of custody and visitation. If their trust in the fathers of their children proved misplaced, or if the fathers proved unworthy of these rights, both women gambled that the state ultimately would settle any disputes in their favor, because as mothers they were the best judges of their children's needs and/or the ones best equipped to care for their children.

As with the feminist critique of work requirements, the argument here is not that child support enforcement or paternity establishment itself is contrary to unmarried mothers' interests. A plethora of studies have demonstrated the negative economic effects of divorce and nonresident fatherhood on mothers and children, due in part to inadequate child support orders and weak child support enforcement. Many single mothers want and desperately need child support payments from the fathers of their children. Many women want the fathers of their nonmarital children to be involved in their children's lives. It is the *mandatory character* of these policies that is contrary to many unmarried mothers' interests, given that unmarried fathers vary in their ability to be a caregiver, likelihood of holding steady jobs, and propensity to violence. Although many unmarried fathers are good providers, many are not. Although many are good "dads," some are not. Although many do not threaten or commit violence, some do. Moreover, this variation in fathers' characteristics arguably is more difficult to redress than the variation in the quality of paid jobs and childcare available to poor, single mothers.

## Directions for Future Policy

Since PRWORA, there have been a number of policy responses to various criticisms of the role of child support enforcement in welfare reform. Responsible fatherhood initiatives aim to increase nonresident fathers' earnings, encourage their involvement in their children's lives, and improve their access to their children through stronger enforcement of visitation orders. These programs respond to charges that a strong child support enforcement system, within larger welfare reform efforts, has impoverished many poor and near-poor fathers, devalued fathers as "just a support check," and ignored children's need for fathers' active involvement in their lives (Blankenhorn 1995; Popenoe 1996; Roy 1999; Waller 1997). A few states (including Wisconsin, Iowa, Connecticut, and Vermont) have experimented with disregarding and/or passing through all of the child support collected to custodial parents who are receiving welfare. These experiments respond to the criticism that small or nonexistent pass-throughs are a disincentive for both mothers and fathers to cooperate with formal child support enforcement.

These efforts at improving child support enforcement will fall short of real reform insofar as they are not undertaken from the point of view of improving the lives of custodial parents, who are most often single mothers. What is needed is a more coherent plan for rethinking mandatory paternity establishment and child support enforcement policies from the perspective of poor, unmarried mothers, informed by the evidence from Wisconsin that the current system is inconsistent with many of these mothers' interests. I argue for a system that is strong but not mandatory, which eliminates the disincentives to mothers for cooperating with paternity and child support policies as well as the link between cooperation with these policies and welfare eligibility.

***Eliminate disincentives to mothers for cooperating with paternity and child support policy.***

First, all child support collected should be passed through to the custodial parent. This would eliminate the complicated calculations some mothers make concerning whether to rely on informal rather than state-enforced child support, as well as some of the bases for stereotypes of unmarried mothers as cheating the welfare system. Moreover, preliminary data from Wisconsin suggests that the loss of state funds due to passing through all child support collected to custodial parents would be offset by savings in other programs (Meyer and Cancian 1999).

Second, although the biological fact of paternity should be the basis for unmarried fathers' obligations to provide material support to nonmarital children, it should not be the basis for unmarried fathers' rights to custody and visitation in the minority of cases when mothers object to the establishment of these rights. In such instances, unmarried fathers' rights to custody and visitation should be based on whether they have provided care to their nonmarital child,[6] as well as whether his acquiring these rights would pose a threat to the child or the custodial mother. This is a modified application of the "primary caretaker" rule used in some states in custody disputes in divorce cases, where custody is awarded to the parent who has done the majority of the daily caregiving, such as feeding, bathing, dressing, caring for the child during illness, arranging for the child's doctor and dental visits, and interacting with the child's friends and teachers. Under such a policy, the recent responsible fatherhood initiatives would take on new meaning: instead of (forcibly) "encouraging" previously "irresponsible" unmarried fathers to "take responsibility" for their children, such programs might be seen as providing men with important skills that they can use to earn the reward of rights to visitation and custody of their child.

***Eliminate link between cooperating with paternity and child support policy and welfare eligibility.***

Either the mother or father, but not the state, should be permitted to initiate paternity and child support cases, whether or not the custodial parent receives public assistance. Most unmarried custodial mothers likely would establish paternity, and many would cooperate with child support enforcement voluntarily, as they do under the current system. Even more would do so if the disincentives for cooperation were eliminated as I have proposed above. Many of the remaining cases are those that would have been difficult or impossible to adjudicate successfully under the old system. Making cooperation voluntary likely would not entail any overall loss of state revenue, because the child-support-enforcement program ceased to generate overall program savings as of 1989, when federal and state expenditures first outstripped child support collections in AFDC

**237**

cases (Josephson 1997). It is the hard-to-adjudicate and hard-to-enforce cases that consume the most administrative dollars.

Each of these policy options would be enhanced by a more effective system of public assistance than is currently available under TANF—one with adequate income supports, support for education and job training, flexible expectations for paid work by single custodial parents of young children, subsidized childcare, and subsidized health benefits for parents who work at low-wage jobs without employer-provided health benefits.

## References

Blankenhorn, David. 1995. *Fatherless America: Confronting Our Most Urgent Social Problem.* New York, NY: Basic Books.

Brandwein, Ruth, ed. 1999. *Battered Women, Children, and Welfare Reform: The Ties That Bind.* Thousand Oaks, CA: Sage.

Corbett, Thomas. 1992. "The Wisconsin Child Support Assurance System: From Plausible Proposals to Improbable Prospects." In *Child Support Assurance: Design Issues, Expected Impacts, and Social and Political Barriers as Seen from Wisconsin,* Irwin Garfinkel, Sara S. McLanahan, and Philip K. Robins, eds. Washington, DC: The Urban Institute Press.

Edin, Kathryn, and Laura Lein. 1996. "Work, Welfare, and Single Mothers' Economic Survival Strategies." *American Sociological Review* 61: 253-266.

———. 1997. *Making Ends Meet: How Single Mothers Survive Welfare and Low-Wage Work.* New York: Russell Sage Foundation.

Ellwood, David T. 1988. *Poor Support: Poverty in the American Family.* New York: Basic Books, Inc.

Horowitz, Ruth. 1995. *Teen Mothers: Citizens or Dependents?* Chicago: University of Chicago Press.

Josephson, Jyl J. 1997. *Gender, Families, and State: Child Support Policy in the United States.* Lanham, MD: Rowman and Littlefield.

Kaplan, Elaine Bell. 1997. *Not Our Kind of Girl: Unraveling the Myths of Black Teenage Motherhood.* Berkeley, CA: University of California Press.

Little, Deborah L. 1999. "Independent Workers, Dependable Mothers: Discourse, Resistance, and AFDC Workfare Programs." *Social Politics* 6 (2): 161–202.

McLanahan, Sara, and Gary Sandefur. 1994. *Growing Up with a Single Parent: What Hurts, What Helps.* Cambridge, MA: Harvard University Press.

Melli, Marygold S. 1992. "A Brief History of the Legal Structure for Paternity Establishment in the United States." In *Paternity Establishment: A Public Policy Conference, vol. 1, Overview, History, and Current Practice.* Madison, WI: Institute for Research on Poverty.

Meyer, Daniel R., and Maria Cancian. 1999. "Initial Findings from the W-2 Child Support Demonstration Evaluation." Report prepared for the Wisconsin Department of Workforce Development.

Mink, Gwendolyn. 1998. *Welfare's End.* Ithaca, NY: Cornell University Press.

Oliker, Stacy J. 1995. "The Proximate Contexts of Workfare and Work: A Framework for Studying Poor Women's Economic Choices." *The Sociological Quarterly* 36 (2): 251–272.

Popenoe, David. 1996. *Life Without Father.* New York, NY: The Free Press.

Raphael, Jody, and Sheila Haennicke. 1999. Keeping Battered Women Safe Through the Welfare-To-Work Journey: How Are We Doing? Report to the Taylor Institute.

Roberts, Paula. 1999. *State Policy Re: Pass-Through and Disregard of Current Month's Child Support Collected for Families Receiving TANF-Funded Cash Assistance.* Center for Law and Social Policy.

Roy, Kevin. 1999. "Low-Income Single Fathers in an African American Community and the Requirements of Welfare Reform." *Journal of Family Issues* 20 (4): 432-457.

Spalter-Roth, Roberta, and Heidi I. Hartmann. 1994. "AFDC Recipients as Care-givers and Workers: A Feminist Approach to Income Security Policy for American Women." *Social Politics* 1 (2): 190–210.

U.S. Bureau of the Census. 1995. *Child Support for Custodial Mothers and Fathers: 1991.* Current Population Reports, Series P-60, No. 187. Washington, D.C.: U.S. Government Printing Office.

Waller, Maureen R. 1997. "Paternity Establishment, Child Support, and Paternity Responsibility: Reconciling Formal and Informal Systems of Support in Low-Income Communities." Paper presented at the Annual Meetings of the American Sociological Association, Toronto.

Wisconsin Bureau of Child Support. 1994. *Wisconsin's Child Support Program.* PES-812. Madison, WI: Department of Health and Social Services, Division of Economic Support.

Wiseman, Michael. 1996. "State Strategies for Welfare Reform: The Wisconsin Story." *Journal of Policy Analysis and Management* 15 (4): 515–546.

## Notes

[1] Renee A. Monson is an assistant professor of sociology at Hobart and William Smith Colleges in Geneva, New York. Her research focuses on welfare state restructuring and gender relations, particularly how men's and women's gendered interests and identities as parents are at stake as the United States shifts the provision of social welfare from the state to families and markets. Her previous work has been published in *Gender & Society.* She would like to thank the unmarried mothers and child support workers, administrators, and attorneys who generously agreed to be a part of this study. For helpful comments, she thanks Philip Gleason, Pamela Oliver, and Ann Orloff.

[2] Children who are born to unmarried mothers have no legal father and thus no rights to financial support from a father. Therefore, the first step in enforcing child support for nonmarital children is establishing legal paternity (see Josephson 1997; Melli 1992; Mink 1998).

[3] Cases could be defined either as all nonmarital child support cases receiving public assistance or as all nonmarital children born in the preceding year.

[4] Pamphlets distributed to mothers in child support offices emphasize their responsibilities for supplying the office with information: "You are responsible for telling the county child support agency any information necessary to establish paternity and an order for child support.... Be prepared to give any information you may have about the other parent, including full name, place of birth, a current address, employment or other income information, and a Social Security number.... Stay in touch with the agency and report any new information about the other parent that may help enforcement" (Wisconsin Bureau of Child Support 1994).

[5] In my observations of more than fifty paternity case starts in child support offices, I only saw one case of a good-cause claim that had been filed and approved. In that instance, the father of the woman's child was serving a prison sentence for her attempted murder.

[6] In the Netherlands, courts adjudicate paternity over the objections of the mother only when the father can show that he has established a parent-child relationship.

## PART V

# The Impact of Welfare Reform on Family Wellbeing

Joan Acker

Sandra Morgen

John Tapogna

Tara Witt

Doris Ng

Karen Seccombe

Phil Gleason

Carole Trippe

Scott Cody

# The Impact of Welfare Restructuring on Economic and Family Wellbeing[1]

### Joan Acker[2] and Sandra Morgen[3]

**D**ramatic declines in the numbers of welfare recipients have occurred across the United States since the passage of the Personal Responsibility and Work Opportunity Reconciliation Act of 1996. While many politicians claim that these declines show that the "reform" has been a success, advocates for the poor, policy makers, researchers and others point out that a drop in the numbers of recipients could mean that an increasing number of families are enduring extreme hardship. Moreover, declines in the numbers receiving cash assistance result from a number of processes: Some people who received assistance have left the program, others applied but did not become clients, still others did not apply although their economic need might have made them eligible. Differences may exist between these groups in their experiences of economic hardship. Researchers in every state have been looking at the consequences of restructuring for "leavers," those who have left the system (Devere 2001).

In this chapter we look at the consequences of welfare restructuring in one state, Oregon, where welfare roles dropped by 45 percent between 1996 and 1999. The data are from our study of the economic and family wellbeing of Oregon families who left or were diverted from TANF in the first quarter of 1998. Our sample also includes families who left the Food Stamp program, providing us with a comparison group of others with low incomes.

What has happened to the families who left the roles, or who applied but left the agency before receiving cash assistance—the diverted? How are the clients who leave or are diverted from Oregon's TANF program, or who leave the Food Stamp program, faring economically? How are their families doing? Have these families achieved self-sufficiency?

This study spans the first two years after leaving public assistance programs. We used telephone survey interviews with a statewide random sample of program leavers at two points in time, along with in-depth, in-person interviews of a subsample.[4] Administrative data from the Oregon Department of Adult and Family Services (AFS) and the Oregon Department of Employment were also part of the study.

The people we interviewed differed from media representations of the "typical" welfare recipient in two ways: They were predominantly white (82 percent), and a sizeable minority (19–38 percent) lived in two-parent families. This racial distribution is consistent with that of Oregon. Although most families had a single parent, the minority of two-parent families reminds us that poverty afflicts men as well as women, although men often have access to income support programs not so available to women, such as workers' compensation or unemployment insurance. The presence of two-parent families probably contributed to the mean household size of 3.6 people.

Study respondents had an average age of 32.5 years. Most were women, although 13 percent were men. The gender of respondents varied somewhat by category of leavers. Ninety-three percent of TANF leavers were women, as were 79 percent of the TANF diverted and 86 percent of Food Stamp leavers. At the first contact, about 20 percent of the sample had less than a high school degree or GED, 40 percent had only a high school degree or GED, about 30 percent had some college, and less than 10 percent had an associate's or bachelor's degree or more.

The demographic characteristics of a sample of those who left or were diverted from TANF and Food Stamps may differ somewhat from the demographics of the AFS caseload. This is possibly due to the fact that those who have left the programs differ in some ways from those who have not. For example, there is a higher percentage of two-adult households in the leaver sample than the current caseload sample, because two-adult households may have the advantage of additional fulltime or part-time income. In addition, AFS's eligibility requirements for a two-parent family are more stringent than for a one-parent family, making it more difficult to get benefits, and often forcing an earlier exit from the program for two-parent families.

### Welfare Restructuring in Oregon

The motto of Oregon's Adult and Family Services during the study period (1999–2000) was "Work Is Always Better than Welfare." This work-attachment model requires new applicants to do an immediate job search for a period of thirty to forty-five days before a cash grant can begin. This is called the assessment period; during this time the client may receive money to cover basic needs so that she/he can engage in the job search. Those who already receive TANF must also look for a job or participate in activities to remove barriers to employment, such as substance dependencies. Each client must develop an Employment Development Plan (EDP) and follow it, or risk disqualification. Attending college or a training program of a length sufficient to qualify for a skilled job is not considered an allowable part of the EDP. New mothers are required to work or participate in a work search program when the baby is three months old. Clients are assigned to case managers who assist them in work-seeking activities and monitor their progress.

### Employment, Earnings and Economic Wellbeing

Our Oregon study shows what other "leaver" studies show—during this period of economic expansion, people get jobs, but they are not economically secure nor self-sufficient in the sense of earning enough to cover expenses and save a bit for financial crises. In Oregon, a substantial proportion of leavers were employed—66 percent at the first interview and 72 percent at the second interview. The proportion employed ranged from 60 percent of TANF diverted at the first interview to 75 percent of Food Stamp leavers at the second interview. The TANF-diverted group was less likely than other groups to be employed (see Table 15.1). Very low unemployment rates and plentiful jobs during the study period, we believe, were the primary causes of the high employment rate among study respondents.

Those in our study who are employed make a heavy commitment to work. They put in long hours—more than half work forty hours per week or more; three-fourths work thirty hours per week or more (see Table 15.2).

### Table 15.1
#### Employment Status of Respondents at AFS Case Closure, First Survey and Second Survey[5]

| | At case closure | | At first survey | | At second survey | | |
|---|---|---|---|---|---|---|---|
| | % employed | % not employed | % employed | % not employed | % employed | % not employed | % not answering |
| TANF leaver | 71 | 29 | 64 | 36 | 71 | 28 | 1 |
| TANF diverted | 55 | 45 | 60 | 40 | 66 | 33 | <1 |
| Food Stamp | 68 | 32 | 69 | 31 | 75 | 24 | <1 |
| Total | 66 | 34 | 66 | 34 | 72 | 27 | 1 |

### Table 15.2
#### Hours of Work per Week of Employed Respondents
#### (at First Survey and at Second Survey)

| Weekly work hours | % at first survey | % at second survey |
|---|---|---|
| 50 or more | 9.28 | 10.1 |
| 40–49 | 45.75 | 43.7 |
| 30–39 | 24.06 | 22.9 |
| 20–29 | 11.64 | 13.6 |
| 19 or less | 8.49 | 9.7 |
| Don't know | .79 | - |
| Total Employed | 100 | 100 |

Despite working full time, their earnings were low. The average monthly take-home pay was $990 at the first interview and $1,016 at the second interview. Over the six months between the two telephone surveys, the average monthly take-home pay rose by a modest $26. Median earnings were somewhat lower than mean earnings (see Tables 15.3 and 15.4).

### Table 15.3
#### Mean Take-home Earnings (net) of Employed Respondents

| At first survey | | At second survey | |
|---|---|---|---|
| % with earnings | Average monthly take-home pay | % with earnings | Average monthly take-home pay |
| 65 | $990.24 | 69 | $1,016.32 |

### Table 15.4
#### Median Take-Home Earnings (net) of Employed Respondents

| At first survey | | At second survey | |
|---|---|---|---|
| % with earnings | Median monthly take-home pay | % with earnings | Median monthly take-home pay |
| 65 | $957.50 | 69 | $1,000 |

To achieve a more detailed picture of earnings growth, we looked beyond aggregate earnings data to understand also the experiences of individual families over time. We used Oregon Department of Labor data on earnings over the seven calendar quarters after these families left the programs, and plotted earnings trend lines for the 756 respondents who participated in both surveys. We found that earnings increased for about half the respondents. For one-fourth of the sample, earnings actually decreased. Another one-fourth had earnings in too few quarters (0-2) to plot, meaning their incomes were unstable, or that they had too little income over time to plot.

We also learned, and were not surprised, that gender affects earnings among low-wage workers. Women earned $382 per month less than men. This is 72 percent of the mean take-home earnings of men, a wage gap about equal to the wage gap in the labor force as a whole (see Table 15.5).

### Table 15.5
**Usual Earnings per Month, Women and Men, at First and Second Surveys**

|  | First Survey: mean monthly earnings | Second Survey: mean monthly earnings |
|---|---|---|
| Women | $939 | $966 |
| Men | $1,325 | $1,348 |

What do these low incomes mean in terms of poverty? Using household income from all sources almost two years after leaving, 43 percent of TANF leavers, 52 percent of TANF diverted, and 54 percent of Food Stamp leavers had incomes above the federal poverty level for their family size. Thus, about half had incomes below the poverty level (see Table 15.6). It is important to recognize that the federal poverty level's unrealistically low standard means that many families who technically live above the poverty level still live in essential poverty. The Northwest Job Gap Study (Northwest Policy Center 2001) estimated that, in the year 2000, a living wage for a family of one adult and two children was $17.95 per hour, or $37,336 per year. This amount was about 200 percent of the federal poverty level and about 300 percent of the average annual earnings in the Oregon study sample.

### Table 15.6
**Respondents With Family Incomes Below Federal Poverty Guidelines[6]**

|  | % living *below* poverty level | % living *above* poverty level | % that don't know |
|---|---|---|---|
| TANF leavers | 55 | 43 | 2 |
| TANF diverted | 46 | 52 | 2 |
| Food Stamp leavers | 45 | 54 | 1 |
| **Total** | 48 | 50 | 2 |

About one-third of our sample were not employed. Most kept house (basically taking care of children) or dealt with chronic or acute health problems. Some had difficulty findings jobs (see Table 15.7).

## Table 15.7
### Work Status and Reasons for Not Working

| Status | % from first survey | % from second survey |
|---|---|---|
| Working | 66 | 72 |
| Not working | 34 | 28 |
| Keeping house | 12 | 9 |
| Going to school | 4 | 3 |
| Looking for work | 8 | 5 |
| Unable to work, disabled | 5 | 5 |
| Unable to work, not disabled | 2 | 1 |
| Retired | 0.3 | 0 |
| Unemployed, not looking | 0.5 | 2 |
| Temporary layoff | 1 | 0.4 |
| Volunteer | 0.5 | 0.7 |
| No answer | 0.3 | 0.7 |

Most study respondents had work experience, even if they were not working on the day they were interviewed. About two-thirds had last worked within the past twelve months. Almost one-third had last worked over thirteen months before. Only 3 percent had never worked. Many people with family responsibilities and/or low-wage, unstable work cycle in and out of the labor force, a pattern revealed by other studies of welfare recipients.

The "leavers" in this study experience barriers to achieving employment in good and stable jobs. The ability of former clients to move from welfare to work is most impeded by (1) the low pay and irregular hours of available jobs; (2) problems with childcare; (3) health problems of themselves or family members; and (4) lack of skills, education, and/or job experience. Both the employed and the unemployed identified these as barriers, but the unemployed faced them in higher proportions (see Table 15.8).

We further investigated the quality of jobs held by respondents by developing what we call the "good jobs measure." We defined a *good job* as one that is fulltime, stable, pays a wage that can support a family, and has good benefits. We operationalized *good job* as one that was thirty-five hours or more per week, with take-home earnings equal to or greater than $1,200 per month, and with predictable hours, sick leave, paid vacation, and health insurance. We also developed a second measure using take-home

### Table 15.8
**Barriers to Getting or Keeping a Job, by Employment**

| Barrier | | Percent with barrier | |
| --- | --- | --- | --- |
| | | **Of employed** | **Of not employed** |
| Childcare | Costs | 24 | 31 |
| | Still a problem? | 47 | 79 |
| | Transportation to & from | 8 | 19 |
| | Still a problem? | 47 | 83 |
| | Locating high-quality care | 26 | 32 |
| | Still a problem? | 38 | 76 |
| | Trouble with childcare | 18 | 17 |
| | Still a problem? | 45 | 67 |
| Job-related | Jobs have no benefits | 39 | 48 |
| | Jobs have low pay | 51 | 62 |
| | Jobs have irregular hours | 40 | 59 |
| | No jobs available | 20 | 42 |
| Health | Own health | 15 | 47 |
| | Still a problem? | 69 | 72 |
| | Pregnancy | 5 | 18 |
| | Still pregnant? | 0 | 36 |
| | Family member's health | 11 | 28 |
| | Still a problem? | 52 | 69 |
| | Permanent disability | 5 | 19 |
| | Not able to adjust | 27 | 44 |
| Family violence | | | |
| | Domestic violence | 3 | 8 |
| | Still a problem? | 0 | 50 |
| | Child abuse | 2 | 5 |
| | Still a problem? | 50 | 29 |
| Legal, transportation & housing | | | |
| | Legal problems | 10 | 18 |
| | Still a problem? | 36 | 87 |
| | Transportation | 21 | 32 |
| | Still a problem? | 44 | 79 |
| | Housing | 5 | 14 |
| | Still a problem? | 42 | 94 |
| Lack of training, skills, experience, or being in school | | | |
| | Lack of training, skills | 30 | 47 |
| | Still a problem? | 61 | 87 |
| | Being in school | 8 | 25 |
| | Still a problem? | 50 | 97 |
| Other problems | | 13 | 26 |

earnings of $1,500 per month. As Table 15.10 shows, almost two years after leaving assistance programs, only a tiny proportion of respondents had good jobs, even at the lower earnings level.

We then developed a less rigorous definition of a *good job* —one that only offered health insurance as a benefit, along with predictable hours and with the same income levels. Using these criteria, the proportions with good jobs increased somewhat. But even at the lower pay level and with the fewest criteria, fewer than 1 in 5 respondents obtained employment that qualified as a good job (see Tables 15.9 and 15.10).

Those who were diverted were less likely than the others to have a good job, consistent with our finding that those diverted were less likely than others to be employed at all (see Table 15.10).

### Table 15.9
**TANF Leavers, TANF Diverted, and Food Stamp Leavers with Good Jobs (based on six components)**

| | Greater than or equal to $1,200 per month | | Greater than or equal to $1,500 per month | |
|---|---|---|---|---|
| | % at first survey | % at second survey | % at first survey | % at second survey |
| TANF leavers | 11 | 13.8 | 6 | 6.7 |
| TANF diverted | 5.8 | 4.3 | 3.9 | 3 |
| Food Stamp leavers | 9.4 | 11.8 | 3.5 | 5.5 |

### Table 15.10
**Food Stamp Leavers, TANF Leavers and TANF Diverted with Good Jobs (based on three components)**

| | Greater than or equal to $1,200 per month | | Greater than or equal to $1,500 per month | |
|---|---|---|---|---|
| | % at first survey[7] | % at second survey | % at first survey | % at second survey |
| TANF leavers | 13.8 | 16.2 | 6.7 | 7.1 |
| TANF diverted | 10.1 | 11.6 | 5.8 | 7.9 |
| Food Stamp leavers | 13.8 | 18.1 | 4.8 | 7.9 |

Many of our respondents knew all too well the difference between any job and a good job—between a job that pays the bills and one that does not. For these reasons, getting a good job was a primary goal for many. Our respondents also recognized a connection between a good job and an education. Both surveys confirmed that education contributes to the likelihood of gaining employment (see Table 15.11).

### Table 15.11
**Education by Employment Status of TANF Leavers and TANF Diverted at First and Second Surveys[8]**

| Education | At first survey | | At second survey | |
|---|---|---|---|---|
| | % employed | % not employed | % employed | % not employed |
| Less than a high school diploma | 48 | 52 | 52 | 48 |
| High school diploma | 66 | 34 | 71 | 29 |
| Some college | 68 | 32 | 74 | 26 |
| Associate's degree | 82 | 18 | 71 | 29 |
| Bachelor's degree or more | 70 | 30 | 90 | 10 |

Those with more education also are more likely to have household incomes above the poverty level (see Table 15.12).

### Table 15.12
**Educational Attainment by Poverty Level of TANF Leavers and TANF Diverted (at first survey)**

| Education | % living **above** poverty level | % living **below** poverty level |
|---|---|---|
| Less than a high school diploma | 17 | 83 |
| High school diploma | 28 | 72 |
| Some college | 29 | 71 |
| Associate's degree | 53 | 47 |
| Bachelor's degree or higher | 40 | 60 |
| Totals | 28 | 72 |

Respondents wanted to improve their chances of getting out of poverty through preparing for better jobs—86 percent wanted more education or job training. However, few were able to get the education or training they believed they needed for job advancement. It is very difficult to increase education or secure hard-skills job training while working fulltime and caring for children, and very few respondents were able to do this in the two years after leaving the assistance programs in 1998 (see Table 15.13).

## Table 15.13
### Education Acquired After Leaving Assistance

| | % who acquired education during the six months between surveys |
|---|---|
| **TANF leavers** | |
| Less than high school diploma; high school diploma | 2 |
| Some specialized training | 5 |
| Job training other than on-the-job training | 9 |
| Some college | 4 |
| Associate's or Bachelor's degree | <1 |
| Graduate degree | No answer |
| **TANF diverted** | |
| Less than high school diploma; high school diploma | <1 |
| Some specialized training | 3 |
| Job training other than on-the-job training | 7 |
| Some college | 9 |
| Associate's, Bachelor's, or Graduate Degree | No answer |
| **Food Stamp leavers** | |
| Less than high school diploma; high school diploma | 1 |
| Some specialized training | 4 |
| Job training other than on-the-job training | 9 |
| Some college | 3 |
| Associate's degree | 1 |
| Bachelor's or Graduate Degree | No answer |

## Family Wellbeing

Our findings about employment, earnings, and the number of households with incomes below the poverty level tell part of the story about family wellbeing. The families we interviewed experienced extensive economic hardships after leaving assistance. At the one-year point in our tracking, 80 percent often had to pay their bills late; 50 percent had to depend on money or gifts from family or friends to get by; 47 percent had eaten at a food kitchen or received a food box; and 25 percent had skipped meals because of lack of money. At the second interview, these percentages dropped somewhat, but a substantial number still had to resort to these strategies to make ends meet. Though the proportion of the sample who used food banks and soup kitchens declined in year two, those who had to rely on food charities did so more heavily or more frequently.

Other indicators of economic hardship, such as evictions, telephone and utility cut-offs, and not getting needed medical care, were revealed in smaller percentages. Because of such hardships, the majority of respondents continued to need and use Food Stamps, the Oregon Health Plan (OHP), and Employment Related Day Care (ERDC). Table 15.14 shows usage of these programs during the nearly two years after initial exit.

### Table 15.14
**Usage of Safety Net or Transitional Programs by Former TANF Leavers and TANF Diverted[9]**

|  | OHP | ERDC | Food Stamps |
|---|---|---|---|
| Percent who never used benefits | 12 | 58 | 9 |
| Percent who used benefits | 87 | 42 | 91 |
| Number of months used | % | % | % |
| 1-3 | 14 | 8 | 14 |
| 4-6 | 11 | 9 | 11 |
| 7-9 | 12 | 4 | 10 |
| 10-12 | 9 | 4 | 9 |
| 13-15 | 13 | 6 | 10 |
| 16-18 | 9 | 5 | 7 |
| 19-21 | 19 | 6 | 30 |

Although safety-net program usage was high, we repeatedly heard that families were losing these benefits before their need had disappeared. Many families had earnings increases that put them just over income eligibility for Food Stamps, OHP, and ERDC. However, they did not have sufficient disposable income to provide food, insurance, rent payments, and childcare. Health insurance is an example: 38 percent relied on OHP even two years after exit; 32 percent had employer-provided health insurance; and 29 percent of respondents were not covered by health insurance at all. Respondents told us over and over that either their employers provided no coverage or they could not afford that coverage. They were doing without—and many had accumulated considerable debt as a result (see Table 15.15)

**Table 15.15**
**Type of Health Insurance Coverage at Second Survey**

|  | % receiving OHP | % receiving other health care | % receiving no health care | % who don't know |
|---|---|---|---|---|
| TANF leaver | 46 | 28 | 26 | - |
| TANF diverted | 42 | 30 | 27 | 1 |
| Food Stamp leaver | 34 | 34 | 31 | 1 |
| Total | 38 | 32 | 29 | 1 |

In addition to seeking medical coverage, childcare subsidies, and Food Stamps, a sizeable minority, 33 percent, of TANF leavers and diverted received TANF cash assistance in the two years after leaving. Again, the diverted seemed to be in the greatest need—46 percent received TANF during that period.

This need for services or resources no longer available to clients probably helps explain a troubling finding. At the first interview, 22 percent of respondents said they needed help from Adult and Family Services but did not get it. By the second interview, that percentage had increased to 27 percent (see Table 15.16).

**Table 15.16**
**TANF Leavers and Diverted Needing Help But Not Receiving It**

|  | % responding when asked if they needed help but did not receive it at first survey | % responding when asked if they needed help but did not receive it at second survey |
|---|---|---|
| Yes | 22 | 27 |
| No | 78 | 73 |

We examined the life situations of those who are doing better than their counterparts in this study to understand the conditions that contributed to less family and economic stress. We learned, especially from those in the in-depth sample, that the families doing better than others were more likely to be two-earner families. They were also families that could count on more support from families and friends; they very often had housing subsidies or were in programs to help them purchase a home; and they had higher-wage jobs, often after gaining job training or education.

Our study is only a first step at assessing family wellbeing. A better assessment would be more far-reaching, would include more focus on how children are doing, and would seek to learn what it means for former recipients to balance responsibilities to work, family, and themselves over the long haul. For the women and men we interviewed, paid work was something they wanted. But they were adamant that they need TANF and other supports at times, when their families need them at home or when they lose or cannot find a decent job. They talked often and eloquently about what it means for them not to have enough time with their children. This was especially true of mothers of very young children who admitted they would do just about anything if it meant they could stay home with infants.

## Client Assessments of AFS Services

A considerable number of ex-clients had serious criticisms of case management and agency services in general. Respondents clearly found the most value from the financial resources associated with the JOBS program. Clients expressed more lukewarm support for, and often downright criticism of, many of the classes and requirements of the JOBS program, including the assessment program. This did not seem to stem from disagreeing with the goal of helping people achieve self-sufficiency. That goal was supported. Rather it had more to do with finding the assessment process and JOBS classes unhelpful or demeaning, a series of "hoops" rather than help.

One of the strongest critiques had to do with a widespread perception that there is a climate of shaming and stigmatization associated with the agency and its workers. It is not a tiny minority that holds this view. AFS clients want to be treated with dignity and respect; they want more choice, more say about their lives. They yearn for respect, recoil from judgmental, punitive attitudes, and hope for a worker who will pay attention to their particular circumstances and *their own* goals. In principle, the agency values these things, too—principle-based decision-making, case management, and agency rules endorse respectful treatment of clients. But in practice, this does not always happen. Caseloads are unrealistically high for staff to effectively fulfill all agency mandates and give clients the help, time, and support they deserve.

## Conclusion

Those leaving TANF and Food Stamps had very diverse experiences. If the final measure of program success is how many leavers are employed, our study suggests that a considerable majority have attained this goal. A robust economy, a Welfare-to-Work program that supports employment seeking and making work pay, and the persistent efforts of clients to sustain their families have all contributed to a high rate of employment. If the measures of program success encompass family wellbeing and helping families really be self-sufficient, then there is more to do:

▶ help people get higher-paid jobs with real potential for advancement

▶ invest in education and job training

▶ ensure that families are not hungry and that they have health insurance and high-quality child care

▶ fill in the holes that exist in the safety net

▶ begin as a state to address the systemic causes of unacceptably high poverty rates.

It is expensive to help people escape poverty, but poverty is also costly to our society. It is expensive to invest in job training and higher education, but it is also expensive to have people stuck in low-wage jobs that keep them reliant on so-called "transitional benefits" that end up being longterm supplements to low-wage jobs. It is expensive to provide good case management, but that is essential to providing services in respectful and supportive ways.

## References

Devere, Christine. 2001. *Welfare Reform Research: What Do We Know About Those Who Leave Welfare?* Washington DC: Congressional Research Service Report for Congress.

Edin, Kathryn, and Laura Lein. 1997. Making Ends Meet. New York: Russell Sage Foundation.

Northwest Policy Center. 2001. *Northwest Job Gap Study: Searching for Work that Pays, 2001.* Seattle, WA: Northwest Policy Center.

# Notes

[1] This paper is a revision of one presented at the *Welfare and Work* Conference, when we only had preliminary data. This revision used data from the survey's final results and, thus, differs from what we presented at the conference. For more detailed information about data collection and methodology, contact the authors at csws@oregon.uoregon.edu.

[2] Joan Acker was a founder and the first director of the Center for the Study of Women in Society at the University of Oregon and has dedicated her scholarship to issues of social equity. A professor emeritus of sociology, she has authored books and articles on feminist sociology, gender and work, welfare reform, issues of class gender, and race politics in organizations, labor and workplace issues, and other topics.

[3] Sandra Morgen, an anthropologist, is director of the Center for the Study of Women in Society at the University of Oregon, where she also is a professor of sociology. Her book *Into Our Own Hands: The Women's Health Movement in the U.S. 1969–1990* will be published by Rutgers University Press in 2002

[4] Nine hundred and seventy respondents completed the first telephone survey. Seven hundred and fifty-six of this group completed the second telephone survey. A quota sample of 78 from the original 970 was drawn for in-depth interviews. The sample was chosen based on race, gender, geographic location, family structure, number and age of children, and age of respondents. Sixty-five of these respondents were located for a second in-depth interview.

[5] First column derived from Oregon Department of Employment wage data (n=756); second and third columns derived from authors' surveys of welfare and Food Stamp leavers and diverted (first survey, n=970; second survey, n=756).

[6] As measured by last month's 1999 earnings in second survey.

[7] Percentages based on total samples.

[8] These relationships — education by employment at first survey and education by employment at second survey — were significant ($p<.01$).

[9] Source: Administrative Record Data, Adult and Family Services, State of Oregon, February 1998–October 1999.

# Making the Transition to Self-Sufficiency in Oregon[1]

*John Tapogna[2] and Tara Witt[3]*

With the passage of PRWORA, Congress effectively authorized fifty-one state experiments to develop the best means to move families from welfare to self-sufficiency. State reformers have created a number of innovative program structures and training models to direct welfare recipients into the labor force. The ultimate success of these models depends heavily on the economic incentives presented to a family as they make the transition from welfare to work. In short, if work does not noticeably improve a typical family's economic wellbeing, reformers will have difficulty reducing their welfare rolls.

In the aftermath of these key policy changes, the Oregon Coalition of Community Non-Profits requested a reexamination of the transition from welfare to work from the perspective of low-income families across the state. Specifically, the sponsors were seeking answers to the following questions:

▶ How does the composition of a family's monthly income change as a worker moves from no work to fulltime employment, and from minimum wage to higher wage levels?

▶ What are the monthly expenses a family incurs to meet their basic needs? Do the expenses differ by county?

▶ How does a family's discretionary income change as earnings rise?

▶ How much better off—in economic terms—is a family with a worker than a family receiving cash assistance?

To help answer these questions, ECONorthwest constructed a two-part model that details the transition to self-sufficiency for a variety of family compositions. We used this model to illustrate the transition from welfare to work for a number of hypothetical families. Our major findings include the following:

▶ State and federal policies have created a strong incentive to move from welfare to work. If a single parent with two children works twenty hours per week for minimum wage, the family of three's spendable income rises by almost 50 percent. If the parent works forty hours per week, spendable income increases by more than 80 percent above the no-work scenario.

▶ A family of three whose single parent works forty hours per week for the minimum wage can afford the basic-needs budget defined in this chapter. However, the family has no discretionary income for leisure activities or savings.

▶ The economic rewards of moving from a minimum-wage job to a higher-paying job are weak. In fact, under some scenarios, a family's economic position actually worsens as the parent moves from a job paying $6 per hour to one paying $8 per hour. In many cases, the increase in the family's earnings is more than offset by decreases in Food Stamp benefits, childcare subsidies, and tax credits.

▶ The cost of childcare is a critical variable in a family's ability to meet their basic necessities. A family that pays the maximum rate reimbursable by the state will struggle to balance its basic-needs budget, regardless of whether they earn the minimum wage or $12 per hour. A family that reduces its childcare costs, by relying on unpaid care or selecting a lower-cost provider, will have more discretionary income and improved incentives to seek higher-paying jobs.

⟩ Families in areas of the state with lower housing and childcare costs will generally have an easier time meeting their basic necessities than families residing in high-cost, metropolitan areas. In fact, some rural families that are officially poor according to the poverty measures may have more discretionary income than some nonpoor, urban families.

## The Benefit and Tax Calculator

The model's benefit and tax calculator reports a family's eligibility for a number of government benefits, assuming differing levels of earned and child-support income. It additionally calculates federal and state tax credits net of payroll taxes and tax liabilities. We based all calculations on federal and state laws as of July 1, 1998. Here we provide brief summaries of the programs included in the model and illustrate how the programs interact as a family's earned income rises.

### Eligibility Criteria of the Modeled Programs

⟩ *Temporary Assistance for Needy Families (TANF)*
TANF provides cash assistance to low-income families with children. Adult recipients must actively seek employment or engage in job training services as a condition of eligibility. The maximum TANF grant for a family of three is $503 per month. The state reduces the TANF grant by $0.50 for each $1 of earned income.

⟩ *Food Stamp Program*
The Food Stamp Program supplements food budgets of low-income households with children, as well as the working-poor, elderly, and disabled individuals. The maximum benefit for a household of three is $321 per month, which is based on the US Department of Agriculture's thrifty-food plan. After certain deductions and allowances, a household's food stamp benefit declines by $0.30 for each $1 in earned or unearned income.

⟩ *Oregon Health Plan/Employer-Subsidized Health Insurance*
Families with monthly incomes below the federal poverty threshold are eligible for OHP coverage. In

addition, families that formerly received TANF may also be eligible for OHP—regardless of their poverty status—for up to twelve months after leaving TANF. We estimate the value of the OHP "subsidy" as the family's total medical expenses (see Section III) less the OHP premiums that range from $6 and $28 per family per month and other out-of-pocket expenses. We estimated out-of-pocket medical expenses using data from the National Medical Expenditures Survey, which details such expenses by age group for Medicaid participants.

For families with employer-provided insurance, the reported medical subsidy equals total health care expenditures minus the worker's shareof premiums and out-of-pocket medical expenses. To calculate premium costs, we assumed enrollment in the Blue Cross/Blue Shield Personal Blue Plan. Personal Blue is a federally-qualified HMO health plan, which requires a $10 to $20 co-payment for each visit to a preferred provider.

▶ *Federal Housing Assistance*
The U.S. Department of Housing and Urban Development (HUD) provides rent subsidies to about one in five cash-aid-recipient families. HUD subsidizes rents for only those families residing in units where gross rent (that is, rent plus utilities other than telephone) is less than or equal to the area's Fair Market Rent (FMR). The department sets the FMR at the fortieth percentile of the rent distribution of a county's standard-quality rental housing. A family with no earnings or other income is eligible for a housing subsidy equal to their total rent and utility expenses up to the FMR. After certain deductions and allowances, the subsidy declines by $0.30 for each $1 in earned or unearned income.

▶ *Employment-Related Day Care (ERDC)*
Oregon's ERDC program subsidizes work-related, childcare expenses for low-income families. The state pays a portion of the family's total childcare bill, which declines as the family's income rises. Moreover, the state subsidizes expenses only up to a maximum payment standard. The standard varies by number of children in the family, ages of children in care, type of care purchased, and place of residence.

▶ *Federal Taxes and the Earned Income Tax Credit (EITC)*
Federal tax rules can either add or subtract to the family's

net income depending on their financial circumstances. At lower earnings levels, families are eligible for the EITC, which typically more than offsets any tax liability. Families with two or more children are eligible for a refundable credit of up to $3,656 per year. Families receive the EITC even if they do not owe taxes. In addition, families can deduct out-of-pocket childcare expenses from their federal tax liability through the Child Care Tax Credit (CCTC). Unlike the EITC, the CCTC is not refundable.

To calculate a family's federal tax liability, we assume adults file as a head of household unless their combined TANF and Food Stamp payments exceed their earnings. Taxable income equals earnings less the standard deduction and the deduction for number of dependents. The family's tax liability equals 15 percent of taxable income.

▶ *State Taxes*
Oregon taxes 9 percent of taxable income in excess of $5,700 per year. The state tax liability is offset by up to four tax credits: the personal exemption, the state earned income tax credit, the childcare and dependent credit, and the working family credit. Unlike the federal EITC, however, state credits are not refundable, and therefore, provide no benefit once a family's tax liability is reduced to zero. Families can carry excess credit amounts to subsequent tax years.

### Program Interactions as Earnings Rise

As an individual moves into the labor force, their earnings directly affect the level of benefits available to their family in each of the programs described above. The figures below illustrate this transition and highlight a key tradeoff facing officials who design welfare programs. Namely, as a benefit package available to nonworking families becomes more generous, the incentive for the worker to increase her earnings weakens. That is because the more benefits a family has to begin with, the more benefits the government must take away as her earnings rise.

### Interactions of Earnings and Standard Low-Income Programs in the ERDC Program

Figure 16.1 illustrates the change in total income for a Multnomah County family of three as the worker moves from no work to fulltime work at $12 per hour.[4] The family participates in the TANF, Food Stamp, and OHP, and receives federal and state tax credits. In this example, the family

**263**

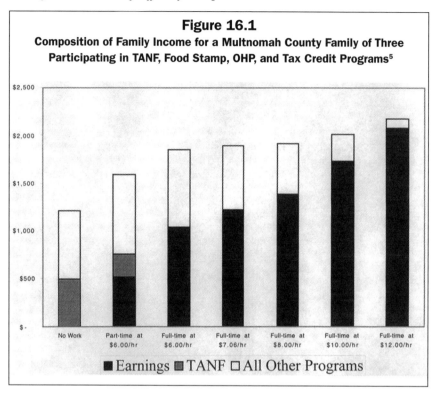

**Figure 16.1**
**Composition of Family Income for a Multnomah County Family of Three Participating in TANF, Food Stamp, OHP, and Tax Credit Programs[5]**

■ Earnings ■ TANF □ All Other Programs

relies on unpaid childcare with relatives and does not participate in the ERDC program.

When the adult is not working, the family is eligible for a total of $1,208 in government subsidies: $503 in TANF, $285 in Food Stamps, and $419 in health plan benefits.[6] Moving to part-time work at the minimum wage generates a $380 net increase in the family's total income. The increase in earnings plus tax credits (+$687) more than offset the decline in TANF (-$260) and Food Stamp benefits (-$46). The incentive to move to part-time work is created—in part—by the state's generous disregard of earnings in the TANF program. Under current law, TANF recipients keep 50 percent of their earnings while the remaining 50 percent reduces their TANF grant dollar for dollar.

The family also sees an increase in total income (+$260) by moving from part-time work at the minimum wage to fulltime work at the minimum wage. This terminates the family's participation in the TANF program and reduces their Food Stamp benefit. Additional earnings and an increase in the EITC compensate those losses.

The incentive to increase earnings declines considerably once the worker attains the fulltime, minimum-wage job. Making the transition from fulltime at minimum wage to fulltime at $8 per hour increases the family's total income by only $64. In other words, the worker keeps less than 20 percent of the additional income she earns by obtaining a better-paying job. In this example, reductions in the Food Stamp benefit (-$119) and federal/state tax credits (-$164) largely offset the family's additional monthly earnings (+$347).

The rewards of higher wages return to some degree as a worker moves beyond $10 per hour. At these levels, our family is not participating in the Food Stamp program and is ending participation in federal/state tax credit programs. With fewer benefits to deduct, the worker keeps about half of her additional earnings.

### The Effect of Participation in the ERDC Program

Figure 16.2 illustrates the same transition from welfare to work but assumes our Multnomah County family of three uses paid childcare and participates in the ERDC program. The family consists of an infant and a

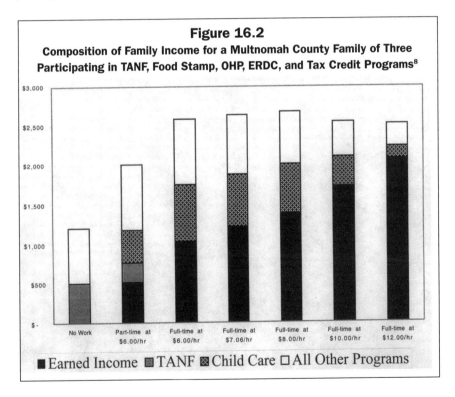

**Figure 16.2**
**Composition of Family Income for a Multnomah County Family of Three Participating in TANF, Food Stamp, OHP, ERDC, and Tax Credit Programs[8]**

■ Earned Income ■ TANF ▩ Child Care ☐ All Other Programs

preschooler. We assume the family places each child in a facility that charges the maximum rate reimbursable by the state.

As in the previous example, state and federal policies reward the initial decision to leave cash assistance with a noticeable increase in the family's total income. Moreover, workers earning the minimum wage—

whether part-time or fulltime— receive a childcare subsidy that almost equals the full cost of care of a provider who charges the maximum rate reimbursable by the state. For example, a fulltime worker earning $6 per hour would pay only $60, or about 8 percent of the $765 in childcare services they use. The difference ($705) is the value of the state subsidy, which is shown as part of the family's total income.

Like the other government benefits, the childcare subsidy decreases as earnings increase. Assuming childcare costs of $765 per month, even workers who earn $12 per hour are eligible for some state assistance. But ERDC availability at higher wage rates affects the incentive to see higher-paying jobs. In the previous example, moving from $8 per hour to $12 per hour generated a modest increase in the family's total income. In this case, the family's total income actually decreases as the child subsidy, Food Stamp benefit and tax credits phase out. A worker can mitigate this disincentive by choosing lower-cost or unpaid care, which many do.

### Table 16.1
**Effective Incremental Marginal Tax Rates on Earnings for a Family of Three as Work Effort and Wage Rate Increase**

|  | Standard Benefits: TANF, Food Stamps, OHP, Tax Credits | Standard Benefits plus ERDC | Standard Benefits plus ERDC and Housing Assistance |
|---|---|---|---|
| No work to part-time at $6 | 26.9% | -54.0% | -39.0% |
| Part-time at $6 to fulltime at $6 | 49.6% | -10.3% | 2.2% |
| Fulltime at $6 to fulltime at $7.06 | 74.9% | 70.6% | 92.9% |
| Fulltime at $7.06 to fulltime at $8 | 88.4% | 74.5% | 98.9% |
| Fulltime at $8 to fulltime at $10 | 72.2% | 140.1% | 147.9% |
| Fulltime at $10 to fulltime at $12 | 52.4% | 106.0% | 117.1% |

**Marginal Tax Rates**

Economists routinely evaluate Welfare-to-Work initiatives through an estimate of marginal tax rates. If, for example, a worker increases her earnings by $1 but in doing so loses $0.75 in benefits, economists say the marginal tax rate is equal to 75 percent. A lower tax rate generally increases the incentive to work additional hours or seek a better-paying job.

Table 16.1 reports the incremental tax rates for three sets of benefit packages. In all three cases, the rates are lowest between no work and work at the minimum wage. Families participating in only the standard welfare programs face the lowest rates. Nevertheless, these families keep less than 30 cents of each additional dollar earned as they move from fulltime at the minimum wage to fulltime at $10 per hour. Negative tax rates appear in the two columns that include the ERDC program, because the value of the ERDC subsidy produces a sharp increase in total income when the worker enters the labor force. This ERDC "income" is more than offset by the family's childcare expenses.

For participants in the ERDC and housing assistance programs, marginal tax rates peak at more than 140 percent for fulltime workers earning between $8 per hour and $10 per hour. In other words, the loss in benefits and tax credits over this range erases the worker's additional earnings and then some.

## Constructing the Basic-Needs Budget

With a family's earnings, subsidies, and net tax liabilities calculated, analysts often compare the resulting net income to the federal poverty threshold. Because the poverty threshold fails to account for childcare costs and geographic disparities in the cost of housing, the Oregon Coalition of Community Non-Profits requested an alternative measure of economic self-sufficiency for each of Oregon's counties.

The alternative presented in the paper—called the basic-needs budget—is based on a market-basket approach first conceived by Dr. Diana Pearce, former director of the Women and Poverty Project of Wider Opportunities for Women, Inc. (Pearce and Brooks 1997). The method draws on expenditure data from federal and state government sources for six essential categories of family spending: housing/utilities, food, childcare, transportation, medical care, and miscellaneous expenditures. Unlike the poverty threshold, which varies only by family size, the basic-needs budget illustrates that Oregonians face different expenses depending on where in the state they live and the age of their children. The budgeted amounts for housing, childcare, and transportation vary by county while the food, medical, and miscellaneous budgets do not.

## Data Sources for the Basic-Needs Budget

> *Housing and Utilities*
The basic-needs budget uses the Fair Market Rent (FMR) for housing and utility costs, which HUD calculates annually. The rates vary with the number of bedrooms and geographic location.

> *Food*
We based the food budget on the USDA's low-cost food plan. The low-cost plan is the second-least expensive of four USDA plans that specify food purchases that families might make to provide nutritious diets for their members. The least-expensive plan—the thrifty-food plan—is used as the basis of the Food Stamp program.

> *Medical*
The medical budget reports a family's total consumption of health services, which we estimated using a 1998 update of the National Medical Expenditure Survey (NMES). The NMES provides average annual expenditures for medical services based on an individual's age, sex, region of residence, and insurance status. A family's estimated budget varies by the number of members and their ages but not by place of residence.

> *Childcare*
The budget uses the state's ERDC-payment standards to determine the family's total childcare expenditures. The Oregon Department of Human Resources based the standards on a 1992 market survey of childcare providers and has since converted them to reflect approximately the seventy-fifth percentile of the rate distribution in 1994. The ERDC standards vary by age of child served, type of provider, and location of the provider. The budget assumes children less than three years of age receive fulltime care in licensed daycare homes and that preschoolers go to daycare centers fulltime. The budget also assumes school-age children receive part-time care in a group facility.

> *Transportation*
The transportation budget is limited to work-related travel only. Our estimates take into account county-by-county variation in travel times and modes based on data

from the 1990 Census. For each county, we calculated the percentage of commuters using public and private transportation and estimated separate budgets for each group.

▶ *Miscellaneous Items*
In addition to the major categories discussed above, the basic-needs budget allows for items such as clothing, shoes, diapers, and housekeeping supplies. Based on data from the 1995 Consumer Expenditure Survey, we assumed spending on these miscellaneous items equal to two-thirds of a family's food budget.

## Variations in the Basic-Needs Budget Across Counties

Figure 16.3 reports the model's calculated budgets for a family of three in six counties. Only housing and childcare costs vary significantly across counties. While our method allows for variations in transportation costs, the differences tend to be small.

As expected, the budgets are higher in metropolitan areas and lower in counties east of the Cascades. Multnomah County is the most expensive place to live, with a family of three needing $2,540 per month to balance its basic-needs budget. Union County and a number of less-populated

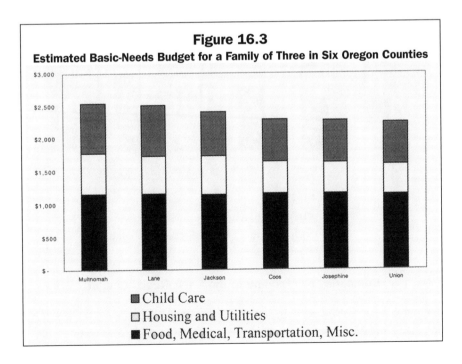

**Figure 16.3**
**Estimated Basic-Needs Budget for a Family of Three in Six Oregon Counties**

■ Child Care
□ Housing and Utilities
■ Food, Medical, Transportation, Misc.

counties are the least expensive. Higher housing and childcare costs explain roughly equal shares of the $297 difference between the Multnomah and Union County budgets

### Variations in the Basic-Needs Budget

The basic-needs budget—like the federal poverty threshold—varies by family size, but our budget additionally varies by family composition.

Figure 16.4 reports the basic-needs budgets for pairs of two-, three-, and four-person families. For example, the budget for an adult and infant equals $1,928, which is $153 more than the budget for an adult and school-age child. Lower childcare costs for the school-aged child explain this difference. Budget differences are larger between the two four-person families. The family with younger children incurs higher childcare expenses, while the family with older children spends more on food and miscellaneous items.

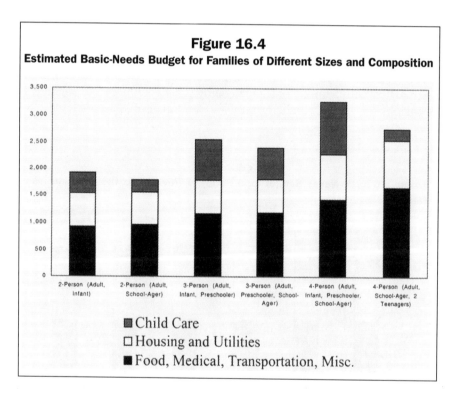

**Figure 16.4**

**Estimated Basic-Needs Budget for Families of Different Sizes and Composition**

■ Child Care
□ Housing and Utilities
■ Food, Medical, Transportation, Misc.

### Comparing Net Income to the Basic-Needs Budget

The chief objective of our study is to explore by how much a family's economic position improves by increasing its work effort and wage levels.

By combining outputs of the benefit/tax calculator and basic-needs budget, we can illustrate changes in the three major components of our family's finances: earnings/child support, benefits net of taxes, and expenses. Furthermore, by subtracting expenses (the basic-needs budget) from the two income components, we can estimate how much discretionary income the family has to spend on leisure activities or to save.

Below we report the incomes and expenses for several hypothetical families. The first figure reports the circumstances of a family of three living in Multnomah County. This "reference" family consists of one adult,

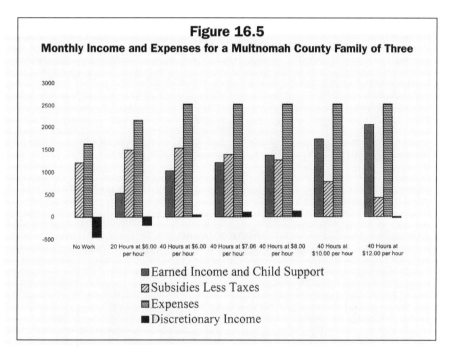

**Figure 16.5**
**Monthly Income and Expenses for a Multnomah County Family of Three**

one infant, and one preschool-aged child and uses a childcare provider who charges the maximum reimbursable rate. The reference family participates in all subsidy programs discussed in this report except federal housing assistance and does not receive child support. Subsequent sections will report how the economic outcomes vary as we change assumptions about place of residence and cost of services.

### The Transition to Work for a Multnomah County Family of Three

As expected, our Multnomah County family has a strong incentive to go to work (see Figure 16.5). Fulltime work—regardless of the wage level—provides the family with just enough income to meet the basic-needs budget. If the adult works less than fulltime, the basic-needs

**271**

budget is unrealistic, and the family must seek lower-cost housing, food, and childcare.

As discussed in the previous sections, the worker has very little incentive to seek higher-paying jobs. Working fulltime at the minimum wage allows the family to purchase its basic needs and do little else. About $40 in discretionary income remain for savings or leisure activities. Moving up the wage scale, discretionary income peaks at about $140, assuming the worker earns $8 per hour, and then falls to zero as the hourly wage continues to increase. The phasing-out of Food Stamp benefits, childcare subsidies, and tax credits explain the fall in discretionary income at the higher wage levels.

### The Effect of Changing the Place of Residence

If our family of three moves from Multnomah County to Union County, the lower cost of living translates directly into additional discretionary income (see Figure 16.6). (In this example, we use the model's standard assumptions for childcare and housing costs.) In Union County, a part-time worker/TANF recipient can balance her basic-needs budget. By working fulltime, the family can generate $150 to $250 in discretionary income. The phasing-out of childcare subsidies and tax credits creates a disincentive to move above the $8 per hour wage level.

Ironically, this analysis suggests a Union County family with a fulltime worker earning minimum wage actually may be better off than

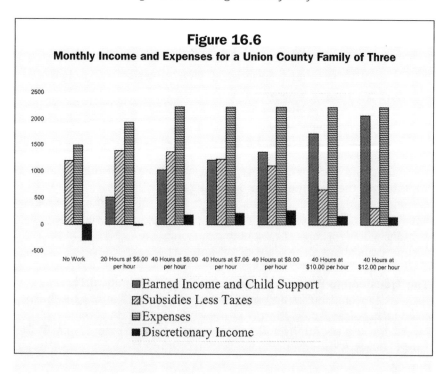

**Figure 16.6**
**Monthly Income and Expenses for a Union County Family of Three**

- Earned Income and Child Support
- Subsidies Less Taxes
- Expenses
- Discretionary Income

a Multnomah County family whose worker earns $12 per hour. The Union County family is officially poor but has almost $200 in discretionary income, while the Multnomah County family has escaped poverty but has no discretionary income. In other words, the availability of higher-paying jobs in Multnomah County may be of little benefit to welfare participants.

## Conclusion

Federal and state policy changes over the past decade have greatly enhanced the incentives to move from welfare to work. The expanded Earned Income Tax Credit boosts a worker's earnings if they accept a low- or moderate-paying job. The Oregon Health Plan and federal Medicaid rules ensure that most families do not have to go without health care when they leave the welfare rolls. Finally, DHR's more generous disregard of earnings in the TANF program and its expanded daycare subsidy have additionally made work more attractive for families with an able-bodied adult. There is little doubt that these policies are partly responsible for the decline in families receiving TANF since 1993.

However, once a single parent joins the workforce, the incentive to seek a higher-paying job is weak. Depending on which benefits the family receives and how much it pays for childcare, moving from a minimum-wage job to a higher-paying job can actually leave the family worse off. This disincentive may explain why Oregon's Food Stamp caseload has fallen much more slowly than the TANF caseload. In short, single parents find low-paying jobs and leave the TANF rolls. Once off TANF, however, they see little benefit to seeking a higher-paying job that would discontinue their Food Stamp participation and remove their family from poverty. Improving these incentives will require a restructuring of federal and state tax credit and childcare-subsidy programs.

## References

Agency for Health Care Policy and Research. 1997. *Data from the 1987 NMES Household Survey Projected to 1995-2005*. Rockville, MD: Center for Cost and Financing Studies.

Blank, Rebecca M. 1989. "The Effect of Medical Need and Medicaid on AFDC Participation." *Journal of Human Resources* 24: 54-87.

Murray, Michael P. 1994. "How Inefficient are Multiple In-Kind Transfers?" *Economic Inquiry* 32: 209-227.

Oregon Center for Public Policy. 1998. *Welfare and Work Assumptions: A Guide to Comparing Spendable Income*. Silverton, OR.

Pearce, Diana, and Jennifer Brooks. 1997. *The Self-Sufficiency Standard for Pennsylvania*. Washington, DC : Wider Opportunities for Women.

Smeeding, Timothy M. 1984. "Approaches to Measuring and Valuing In-Kind Subsidies and the Distribution of Their Benefits." In Marilyn Moon, ed., *Economic Transfers in the United States*. Chicago: University of Chicago Press.

Winkler, Anne E. 1991. "The Incentive Effects of Medicaid on Women's Labor Supply." *Journal of Human Resources* 26: 308-337.

## Notes

[1] This paper was originally published for the Oregon Coalition of Community Non-Profits for ECONorthwest, an Oregon-based economic consulting firm. ECONorthwest would like to thank Dr. James Ziliak, University of Oregon; Charles Skeketoff, Oregon Center for Public Policy; Norma Coe, The Urban Institute; and Dee Smith, Oregon Department of Human Resources for their comments and suggestions. ECONorthwest takes full responsibility for all errors.

[2] John Tapogna is a project manager with Eugene-based ECONorthwest. He analyzed welfare reform legislation for the US Congressional Budget Office during 1991–1995.

[3] Tara Witt, a former research assistant with ECONorthwest, currently works as a market analyst for Nike.

[4] Throughout this chapter, forty hours per week represents fulltime work and twenty hours per week represents part-time work.

[5] Calculated by ECONorthwest based on program rules as of July 1, 1998. Other programs include Food Stamps, OHP, and federal and state tax credits, less payroll taxes, and federal and state tax liabilities.

[6] Economists differ on how best to value medical benefits, with some using the full value of the medical services consumed by the family and others using a fraction of that amount (see Blank, 1989; Winkler, 1991; Murray, 1994; Smeeding, 1984). We report the full value of medical benefits consumed. However, the distinction is not critical because we've assumed our family would receive the same amount of medical benefits at all earnings levels (that is, they would receive OHP or transitional OHP). Consequently, switching between methods does not affect the analysis of work incentives.

274

[7] Under prior law, the state disregarded the first $120 in earnings plus one-third of the balance.

[8] Calculated by ECONorthwest based on program rules as of July 1, 1998. Other programs include Food Stamps, OHP, and federal and state tax credits, less payroll taxes, and federal and state tax liabilities. Calculations assume family consists of one adult, one infant, and one preschool-aged child and that the family selects a childcare provider who charges the maximum rate reimbursable by the state.

[9] Later in this paper, we consider the economic circumstances of a family that pays less than the maximum rate reimbursable by the state.

[10] See Agency for Health Care Policy and Research (1997).

[11] That is, in 1994, 75 percent of the rates in a given area were lower than standard, and 25 percent of the rates were higher than the standard.

[12] Source: ECONorthwest. Note that a family of three consists of one adult, one infant, and one preschool-aged child. Family chooses a childcare provider who charges the maximum rate reimbursable by the state.

[13] Source: ECONorthwest. Families reside in Multnomah County and chose a childcare provider who charges the maximum rate reimbursable by the state.

[14] Source: ECONorthwest. Family consists of one adult, one infant, and one pre-school-aged child. Family chooses a childcare provider that charges the maximum rate reimbursable by the state. Family participates in TANF, Food Stamps, OHP, ERDC, and federal and state tax credit programs. Estimated subsidies are net of payroll taxes and federal and state tax liabilities.

[15] Source: ECONorthwest. Family consists of one adult, one infant, and one pre-school-aged child. Family chooses a childcare provider that charges the maximum rate reimbursable by the state. Family participates in TANF, Food Stamps, OHP, ERDC, and federal and state tax credit programs. Estimated subsidies are net of payroll taxes and federal and state tax liabilities.

# From War on Poverty to War on Welfare

## The Impact of Welfare Reform on the Lives of Immigrant Women

*Doris Ng*[1]

The 1960s' declaration of "War on Poverty" evolved into the 1990s' promise to "end welfare as we know it." On August 11, 1997, California Governor Pete Wilson signed the California Work Opportunity and Responsibility to Kids (CalWORKS) law. As required under federal welfare laws, CalWORKS establishes a five-year lifetime limit for receipt of aid. The clock started ticking for all California welfare recipients on January 1, 1998. If an adult reaches her five-year limit, her portion of aid ends, but her children may continue to receive cash aid or vouchers (for rent, utilities, etc.).

When a recipient enrolls in CalWORKs, she generally attends an orientation, followed by an appraisal and job search. If she has not located a job after completing her job search, she receives an assessment of her barriers to self-sufficiency, signs a Welfare-to-Work plan, and begins her assigned work activities. Work activities can include ESL, GED, on-the-job training, or vocational training. Supportive services can include childcare and transportation. Under CalWORKs, adult recipients have approximately two years to find employment.

Like many other state welfare programs, CalWORKS adopts a "Work First" approach to moving people from welfare to work, which aims to minimize government spending by forcing welfare recipients to take the first job they can get. Unlike most other states, however, in California, immigrants make up a significant portion of the population, increasing from 21 percent in 1990 to 25 percent in 1996 (U.S. Bureau of the Census

Current Population Survey). In 2001 California became the first state in which whites are not in the majority.[2] Immigrants make up one-fifth (17 percent) of California's welfare recipients (California Department of Social Services 1996). Despite California's sizable immigrant population, CalWORKs does not address the needs of immigrant families.

To examine the impact of welfare reform on immigrant women, Equal Rights Advocates (ERA) conducted a study in Santa Clara County that documents immigrant women's experiences with CalWORKs and their struggles to make ends meet.

### ERA's Immigrant Women and Welfare Project, Santa Clara County

ERA conducted its study in Santa Clara County, which has one of the largest and most diverse immigrant populations. Immigrants comprise 25 percent of a total population of 1.6 million. Twenty percent of the county's residents are Asian; 23 percent are Latino; less than 53 percent are white.

Home to Silicon Valley and a burgeoning economy, Santa Clara County also stands out as one of the wealthiest counties in the nation. In 1995, the median income in the county was $53,490 (U.S. Census Bureau 1995), and the median monthly housing cost was $939 (Bay Area Social Services Consortium 1997). Yet wealth in Santa Clara County, as in the rest of California, is not distributed equally. The success of private employers has not benefited the community as a whole. An adult in Santa Clara County needs a wage of $14.24 per hour to make ends meet without

## Table 17.1

**Participant Demographics**

|  | Mexican | Vietnamese |
|---|---|---|
| Number of Survey Participants | 75 | 75 |
| Current Welfare Recipients | 76% | 95% |
| Members of Two Parent Families | 9% | 51% |
| Lived in US for Minimum of 10 Years | 72% | 10% |
| Have "Poor to No" English Proficiency | 48% | 87% |
| Average Number of Children | 3.6 | 3.0 |
| Average Age | 34.1 | 38.8 |
| Average Years of Schooling | 6.5 | 8.7 |

government assistance (Pearce 1996). Five of the ten fastest growing occupations in Silicon Valley, however, pay less than $10 per hour for entry-level positions (Brenner 1998).

In 1997, there were 63,618 people on welfare in Santa Clara County; approximately 21 percent were immigrants (Santa Clara Social Services Agency 1997). Because the largest number of immigrants who receive welfare benefits in Santa Clara County are of Mexican and Vietnamese origin, ERA chose to interview seventy-five Mexican-American and seventy-five Vietnamese-American women[3] (see Table 17.1).

The survey contained a combination of quantitative and qualitative questions on topics that fell into eight broad categories: (1) English Proficiency and Native Language Literacy; (2) Experience with CalWORKs; (3) Education and Training; (4) Employment Opportunities; (5) Childcare and Transportation; (6) Health, Hunger, and Housing; (7) Domestic Violence; and (8) Isolation.[4]

## Research Findings and Discussion

With the advent of welfare reform, the outlook for poor immigrant women has worsened. Indeed, our study shows that immigrant women face significant barriers to locating self-sufficient employment, something welfare reform largely ignores. Consequently, even after participating in CalWORKs, many immigrant women on welfare will reach their time limits but will not be better off.

### Immigrant Women Want to Work But Need Training and English Classes

The overwhelming majority of our survey participants wanted to work and preferred work to welfare. Indeed, our participants worked about as much as welfare recipients in other studies: 67 percent had been employed at some time in their lives. And among those who have worked, half (43 women) were currently working. The Vietnamese women were more likely never to have been employed than the Mexican women, with thirty-five Vietnamese women compared to fourteen Mexican women who had no work history.

Due to their limited English proficiency and few job skills, however, the women in our study had extremely limited employment opportunities, and almost no opportunities to move into stable, higher-wage jobs. They described many employment-related barriers to self-sufficiency, such as low wages, lack of benefits and job protection, and temporary or otherwise unstable jobs.

> ❯ Limited English proficiency, low levels of education, and lack of job training are major barriers to achieving self-sufficiency for immigrant women.

A striking percentage of our participants had limited or no English proficiency. More than 86 percent of the Vietnamese women indicated poor to no understanding of English, compared to 48 percent of the Mexican women. Only one of the Vietnamese women had an understanding of English that was "good."

Due to their lack of English skills, 53.3 percent of our participants used their children to translate for them. Most used their children for talking with teachers and filling out forms. More than half encountered problems, however, when using their children to translate. These problems included information that was too technical for the child and children responding to questions without first asking their parents.

Limited or no English proficiency affects many different aspects of immigrant women's lives, often leaving them vulnerable to discrimination and mistreatment. It affects their ability to access CalWORKs services and influences how caseworkers treat them. A Mexican woman with limited English and only two years of education said, "I feel that my caseworker discriminates against me and ignores me because I do not speak English."

Both Mexican and Vietnamese women said they had experienced difficulty getting other types of services or benefits because they do not speak English. One single Vietnamese woman who was in the United States for only two years described the kinds of problems caused by her lack of English skills: "I have had problems with CalWORKs because of language difficulties. Sometimes my child's school calls me, and I do not understand them. I want to go to the food bank but they do not understand me. I feel lost and afraid."

The immigrant women we surveyed lacked sufficient access to job training. Only sixteen of the Mexican and twenty-seven of the Vietnamese women in our study had ever received job skills training. If these women are to find and retain self-sufficient jobs, they need to receive English-language classes and job training.

The participants themselves identified lack of English and job skills as barriers to getting and keeping jobs. When asked about what they needed to avoid problems with work, thirty-two women total said they needed English classes, thirty said they needed secure jobs, twenty-seven said they needed childcare, and twenty-four said they needed skills training.

> ▶ Immigrant women are employed in low-wage jobs, at times earning less than minimum wage.

As the targets of multiple forms of discrimination, immigrant women on welfare are employed in jobs that offer low pay, few benefits, and limited opportunities for upward mobility. As welfare recipients, they are affected by societal discrimination, which results in earning between 40 percent and 88 percent of what all workers in the same occupation earn (Force et al. 1998). Immigrants earn lower wages compared to similarly situated natives (Lapham 1990). Pay inequities based on gender are widely publicized: Women earn 74 cents and women of color earn 64 cents for every dollar that a white male earns (Women's Bureau 1998). Women, immigrants, and welfare recipients are concentrated in low-wage positions that offer few benefits and limited opportunities for advancement.

The Vietnamese and Mexican immigrant women we spoke with illustrated the effects of these multiple forms of discrimination. The most common job held by the Vietnamese women was assembly work. Mexican women most commonly worked in food services, house cleaning, and childcare. Low pay is the norm for immigrant women on welfare. The wages our participants earned ranged from below minimum, in some cases, to the $9-per-hour range for three participants. The majority earned just above minimum wage.

A Vietnamese woman who worked part-time at night as a packager and earned $6.20 per hour, explained: "There is only one other Vietnamese speaker where I work. My limited language skills are a problem at work. I would need [someone to recommend me for a job] because my English is not good enough to pass an interview." Another woman told us, "Language is a problem for me at work because people get frustrated with me."

Several participants were not earning minimum wage. Two women said they had received job training for electronics assembly and found temporary jobs in that industry. They worked at home and were being paid by piece rate. Their pay added up to less than California's minimum wage. The electronics industry is not the only industry that sometimes pays participants less than minimum wage. A Vietnamese woman, who had been trained as a dressmaker in Vietnam, disclosed, "I work twelve hours per week for $2.75 per hour. I work as a cook's helper."

> ❯ Employed, but lacking employer-provided medical benefits or job protection, immigrant women will require additional supports.

Of the forty-three survey participants who were working, many reported working in temporary jobs. For example, one Mexican woman had a temporary job working nights as an assembler and earned only $6.50 per hour for herself and six children. Nevertheless, she wanted very much to stay in the job and hoped to become a permanent employee there.

The rise of the contingent workforce contributes to the decline in economic status for low-wage workers. Sixty percent of temporary workers are women who earn low wages and receive few employment benefits (Seavey 1996). Corporations that contract out functions previously performed by permanent employees have fueled the rise in temporary workers. In the Silicon Valley, a range of contract electronics assembly companies, which employ large numbers of immigrant women, handle much of the labor. Contracting out work helps corporations increase their production but leaves contract employees earning 30 percent less than those at the original equipment manufacturing companies (Brenner 1996).

Channeled into temporary jobs, only ten of our participants reported receiving health insurance from their employers. One Mexican woman with no formal education and no understanding of English had worked fulltime making tortillas for eighteen years earning $6.50 per hour with no health benefits.

In light of the limited employment opportunities available to immigrant women on welfare, one woman recommended, "They should continue aid if you only have a temporary job with no benefits and discontinue only after you have found a stable job with benefits."

Many participants also complained about the lack of workplace protections, such as employment discrimination or health and safety protections. For example, one woman, who worked as a packager earning $6.10 per hour, told ERA, "It is a very heavy job. I was in the emergency room once because of work, but my employer did not compensate me for my injury." A Mexican woman complained that her former employer gave better jobs to Anglos.

### Immigrant Women Receive Few Welfare Services

Our survey asked a series of questions to learn whether immigrant women have accurate information about the changes to the welfare system, what kinds of welfare services they have received or currently are receiving, and their experiences with those services. In each category, we found that welfare reform largely has failed to address immigrant women's needs.

> ▶ Immigrant women lack accurate information about the welfare reform law.

Seventy-six percent of the immigrant women we interviewed had received some information about the changes to the welfare laws, but there were many gaps in their information. Particularly alarming is the fact that only about 62 percent received information about the five-year time limit and the work requirements. In addition, only 30 percent received information about exemptions from having to work. Almost four times as many Mexican women as Vietnamese women received information on the family-cap and child-exclusion provisions.

Fifty percent of the Mexican and 65 percent of the Vietnamese women had attended welfare orientations since January 1, 1998. Most reported that the orientation was conducted in their native language. Of the eighty-seven respondents who had attended an orientation, only forty received information about the good-cause reasons for not complying (e.g., if appropriate childcare is not provided). Information about the domestic violence waiver also was extremely low.

**282**

Exacerbating the confusion about changes to the law and about work requirements was the fact that one out of four women received that information in English only.

▶ Immigrant women experience problems accessing services.

Many women described problems they experienced accessing and using services. Of the forty-three responses to this question, half said that they had experienced problems with CalWORKs services. The Vietnamese women indicated that childcare and transportation were major barriers to accessing and getting services. They also identified language barriers and a mismatch of services. The Mexican women said childcare was the biggest problem, followed by language barriers.

Only 38 percent of our participants received any CalWORKs services. Nearly one year into their five-year time limit, a majority of the women had not received any Welfare-to-Work services.

▶ Job Search fails to meet immigrant women's needs.

When asked if any of the CalWORKs services were helpful in finding a job, only 11 of the 150 women (7.3 percent) found them helpful. A Vietnamese woman with no English proficiency told ERA that many of the things Job Search instructed her to do made no sense: "I was supposed to read the [San Jose] *Mercury* to find a job, but I cannot read English."

A Mexican woman explained that job search was not for everyone: "I spent forty hours a week for two months in Job Search. I did not find a job. What I need is ESL."

The Work First approach forces women into job search when they really need other kinds of services. As a result, recipients either accept the first job they can get or, if they cannot find a job, feel rejected and waste months searching.

### Many Immigrant Women Lack Adequate Childcare

Ninety out of 150 respondents said they needed childcare in order to work. Recognizing this need, CalWORKs is supposed to pay for the cost of placing children in childcare centers, home-based providers, or care by relatives. Despite this promise, several participants reported that CalWORKs' supportive services were lacking. One woman explained that some of CalWORKs' rules are problematic:

> I work beginning at 3 a.m. My relatives take care of my three kids [ranging from four months to five-years-old] but the county won't pay them because they don't have Social Security numbers.

Finding childcare for sick children and providers that accept government payment was difficult for several participants. Moreover, one Mexican woman who was working as a temporary assembler earning $7.50 per hour told ERA that the welfare office stopped paying for her childcare as soon as she found a job. Given that the average cost of fulltime care for a child under two in the county exceeds $8,000, even when immigrant women find jobs, low pay and the unavailability of subsidized childcare force families to return to the welfare rolls.

**Immigrant Women Face Health Problems and Hunger**

Mexican and Vietnamese women reported very different levels of health problems. Three out of four Mexican women in our survey reported that their health is excellent or good, while almost the same number of Vietnamese women reported having fair or poor health. Only 10.7 percent of the Mexican women reported that their youngest child's health was fair or poor, but 35 percent of the Vietnamese women reported this. Many of those surveyed in two-parent families were disabled, or had spouses who were disabled. More Vietnamese women than Mexican women had disabilities or were caring for family members with disabilities.

Other differences between Vietnamese and Mexican women were revealed by questions dealing with hunger. About 50 percent of the Mexican women, compared to 26.6 percent of the Vietnamese women, indicated that they often or sometimes had insufficient food. Interestingly, several of the Vietnamese women who reported "never" experiencing insufficient food also described how they coped whenever they ran out of food. For example, one single Vietnamese woman with two children, who stated that she never has insufficient food, explained that she sometimes had to—figuratively speaking—"tie her stomach" because there was not enough food for all of them.

Our study found that the amount of Food Stamps that immigrant women receive was insufficient. One Mexican woman with two preschool children said she and her children sometimes go through days without food. Another woman with a diabetic child said she could not afford to buy the special food that her child needed. Others cope by eating less meat and no fruit, asking for help from the county welfare office, eating less nutritious food, or getting help from relatives. Many Mexican women said they manage to get by on feeding their children mostly tortillas and beans.

As a result of welfare reform, several participants no longer were eligible for Food Stamps. One Mexican woman, who had been cut off due to her "not being a citizen," reported that she and her children often had insufficient food and had to obtain free food from community organizations.

**284**

**Immigrant Women Spend Most of Their Cash Aid on Housing**

Nationwide in 1995, only about 10 percent of welfare recipients lived in public housing. The same percentage received Section 8 housing subsidies to live in private housing (Edin and Lein 1997). Similarly, only 10 percent of participants received housing subsidies.

Without housing subsidies, participants were forced to spend an enormous portion of their incomes on housing. During the time of our survey, rents in Santa Clara County had increased more than 16 percent since 1990. The average rent for a one-bedroom apartment was $1,100 per month (Brenner 1998). Despite doubling and tripling up, rent consumed the bulk of cash aid for many immigrant families in our study. One Vietnamese family of four paid $500 per month to live in a garage. A family of five paid $700 to share a bedroom. A Vietnamese family of ten rented a small mobile home for $1,000 per month.

The average monthly rent for participants was about $500, but the average cash aid was about $495. It therefore comes as no surprise that the exorbitant cost of housing in Santa Clara County causes immigrant women on welfare enormous stress. Several participants cried as they described the difficulties they faced paying rent.

**Many Immigrant Women Are Domestic Violence Survivors; Few Receive Information About Domestic Violence Waivers**

A total of forty-one participants experienced domestic violence, approximately 38.7 percent of the Mexican women and 16 percent of the Vietnamese women. CalWORKs, which adopted the Family Violence Option under TANF, provides applicants and recipients who identify themselves as domestic abuse victims with referrals to appropriate services, and waives requirements that make it more difficult for them to escape violence. However, only one in four women in our survey who experienced domestic violence had received information from the welfare office about domestic violence waivers.

**Many Immigrant Women Lack Any Connection to the Outside World Other than their Children**

Isolation was a significant problem for many participants, particularly for Vietnamese women. For some immigrants, arrival in the United States meant the loss of kin, friends and family living nearby, and the loss of their connection to the larger community. Several women told ERA they stay at home all day, take care of their children, and know no one else. A single Vietnamese woman stated: "My only connection to the outside world is my children."

Most participants had no connections to social or community groups. The only significant connection was to church. Of the Mexican-American participants, 40 percent belonged to a church, while half as many of the Vietnamese indicated the same.

Isolation affects an immigrant woman's life in a variety of ways. Our participants found jobs through friends and relatives more than any other method. Information about changes in the law or available resources often are passed by word of mouth. Studies of welfare recipients have documented their substantial reliance on social networks for financial and in-kind support to make ends meet. One study of single women on welfare found that most received financial or other support from boyfriends, family members, and neighbors (Edin and Lein 1997).

Low-income immigrant households rely heavily on social networks. In a recent Santa Ana study, researchers found "a strong and impressive tendency for members of the low-income immigrant community to share with other family members, with relatives, and with neighbors" (Freeman 1998). For the most part, the immigrant women in our survey did not have such supportive networks on which to rely.

### Recommendations

1. Amend state welfare laws to require counties to evaluate the participant's English proficiency and native language literacy before assigning them to certain activities. Provide limited English proficient participants with the option of going to job search or education and/or job training.
2. Explore innovative methods to provide immigrant women with opportunities to acquire the skills they need to secure self-sufficient jobs.
3. Allow recipients to choose a balanced mix of part-time work, school, and job training and ensure that they receive all necessary supportive services.
4. Provide accurate, culturally sensitive, and standardized training to all caseworkers, employment technicians, and other county welfare employees.
5. Combat discrimination against immigrant women.

## Long-term Recommendations

1. State policymakers should extend the time limit for welfare applicants and recipients who have significant language barriers. California's two-year time limit for locating employment is unrealistic for many immigrant women who have limited or no English and job skills. These women likely will need additional time for education and training. Similarly, California's five-year lifetime limit is insufficient time for many immigrant women to learn English, acquire job skills, and attain self-sufficient employment.

2. Amend TANF to eliminate the one-year time limit on vocational education and count participation in ESL toward work participation rates. This amendment would allow more recipients to matriculate in vocational education and ESL courses, which will provide them with the skills that they need most.

## Conclusion

If welfare reform continues to push immigrant women with limited or no English proficiency and no job skills to take any job, these jobs will likely be temporary, with limited employment protections, and few, if any, benefits. Even if these jobs are steady for several years, most will not lead to higher-wage jobs or pay close to what a family needs to live without government benefits (see Pearce 1996).

If states like California hope to help immigrant women and their families lift themselves out of poverty, they must establish policies that will ensure that monolingual and limited English speakers have access to English and job-skills classes that target higher-wage jobs.

## References

Bay Area Social Services Consortium. 1997. *Social Welfare at a Crossroad at 51.*

Brenner, C. 1996. *Shock Absorbers in the Flexible Economy: The Rise of Contingent Employment in Silicon Valley.* San Jose: Working Partnerships, USA.

Brenner, C. 1998. *Growing Together or Drifting Apart? Working Family and Business in the New Economy, A Status Report and Economic Well-being in Silicon Valley.* San Jose: Working Partnerships, USA and Economic Policy Institute.

California Department of Finance Demographic Research Unit. 1999a. *California Population Projection with Race/Ethnic Detail.* (Visited April 5.) Available on http://www.dof.ca.gov/html/Demographic/Proj-rac.htm.

California Department of Finance Demographic Research Unit. 1999b. *California Population Projection with Race/Ethnic Detail.* (Visited April 8.) Available on http://www.dof.ca.gov/html/Demographic/Proj-rac.htm.

California Department of Social Services. 1996. *1996 AFDC Characteristic Survey*, 14.

Edin, K., and L. Lein. 1997. *Making Ends Meet: How Single Mothers Survive Welfare and Low Wage Work*, New York: Russell Sage Foundation.

Force, P., D. Flaming, J.R. Henly, and M. Drayse. 1998. *By the Sweat of Their Brow: Welfare to Work in Los Angeles.* Los Angeles: Economic Roundtable.

Freeman, G. 1998. *Poverty and Welfare Among Immigrants in California: A Santa Ana Neighborhood Study*, 6. Tomas Rivera Policy Institute.

Lapham, S. 1990. *We the American Foreign Born*. Ethnic and Hispanic Statistics Branch, Population Division, U.S. Bureau of the Census.

Pearce, Diana. 1996. *California Self-Sufficiency Standard*. Washington, D.C.: Wider Opportunities for Women.

Santa Clara Social Services Agency. 1997. *Santa Clara County Status Report on Welfare Reform*. (October 7).

Seavey, Dorothy. 1996. *Back to the Basics: Women's Poverty and Welfare Reform*. Wellesley: Center for Research on Women.

U.S. Census Bureau. 1995. *Model-Based Income and Poverty Estimates for Santa Clara County, California in 1995*.

U.S. Bureau of the Census Current Population Survey. *Selected Characteristics of the Population by Citizenship for Selected States*.

Women's Bureau, U.S. Department of Labor. 1998. *Equal Pay: A Thirty-five Year Perspective*.

## Notes

[1] Doris Ng is a staff attorney with Equal Rights Advocates, a twenty-eight-year-old public interest law firm dedicated to ending discrimination against women and girls. The Immigrant Women and Welfare Project was made possible in part by The Emma Lazarus Fund of the Open Society Institute, The Women's Foundation, and the Rosenberg Foundation. To find out more about ERA's welfare reform work, contact the author at ERA, (415) 621-0672 or dng@equalrights.org.

[2] Whites represent 49 percent of the population; Latinos, 31 percent; Asians, 12 percent; and African Americans, 7 percent (California Department of Finance Demographic Research Unit 1999a; 1999b).

[3] To be eligible for the study, the participant had to be (1) either Mexican or Vietnamese; (2) a woman; (3) currently receiving welfare or a recipient within the past seven months; and (4) a noncitizen. By limiting the survey to noncitizens, we hoped to capture the particular concerns of individuals who have not yet naturalized, including fear of the Immigration and Naturalization Office and termination from Food Stamps or SSI. ERA conducted nearly all survey interviews in person, in Spanish or Vietnamese. The interviews began in September 1998 and were completed in December 1998, nearly one year after CalWORKs took effect.

[4] Rosina Becerra, Ph.D., an experienced researcher and professor at the UCLA School of Public Policy and Social Research, provided technical assistance in designing the survey instrument and analyzing the quantitative data.

# Integrating Meaningful Health and Welfare Reforms

## *Karen Seccombe*[1]

I've never had to use my Medicaid myself, but my daughter couldn't do without it. So Medicaid is the most important benefit to me. If I didn't have my Medicaid, I don't know what I'd do, at least for my daughter. There would be absolutely no way that I could pay for the medical care that she has received. It's a lifesaver.

—Stephanie, welfare recipient and mother of a seven-year-old girl born with a defective kidney (Seccombe 1999)

Despite a robust economy in the late 1990s, with inflation and unemployment at near-record lows, the United States made less headway in combating poverty than one might expect. Poverty rates in 2000 were only slightly below those reported in 1980. The percentage of our population—of families and of children—in poverty rose slightly in the early 1990s, leveling off around the middle of the decade and then dipping somewhat. The most recent data available indicate that in 2000, 11.3 percent of the total population, 9.6 percent of families, and 16.2 percent of children lived below the poverty line, defined as a single individual living below $8,794 and a family of four living below $17,603 per year (U.S. Bureau of the Census 2001). (See Table 18.1.)

### Table 18.1
**Percentage of Individuals, Families, and Children in Poverty, 1980, 1990, 2000[2]**

|             | 1980  | 1990  | 2000  |
|-------------|-------|-------|-------|
| Individuals | 13.0% | 13.5% | 11.3% |
| Families    | 11.5% | 12.0% | 9.6%  |
| Children    | 17.9% | 19.9% | 16.2% |

The poverty rate among children is particularly troublesome. Rank and Hirschl (1999), using data from the Panel Study of Income Dynamics (PSID), present the prevalence of poverty among children another way: Overall, 34 percent of children will spend at least one year in poverty during their lifetime; however, this increases to 69 percent among African-American children, 81 percent among children in single-parent households, and 63 percent among children whose heads of household have not completed twelve years of school. The cumulative effects are staggering. Ninety-nine percent of children who are African-American, who live in single-parent households, and who live with heads of household with less than twelve years of education have experienced poverty—in contrast to only 15 percent of children who are white, live in two-parent households, and live with heads who have completed at least twelve years of education.

This chapter addresses one of the most understudied aspects of welfare reform: the role that health insurance plays in reform efforts. Drawing upon national data, along with in-depth interviews with participants and focus groups, I suggest that adequate access to health insurance lies at the core of a sound social welfare program and is integral to any meaningful welfare reform.

My particular interests are:

▶ What happens to families when they leave welfare? Do they lose their health insurance?

▶ What are the consequences of being without insurance?

▶ Are welfare recipients and former welfare recipients concerned about this?

To better understand the views of welfare recipients themselves, I conducted, at the end of 1995, in-depth interviews with forty-seven women on welfare in several small and medium-sized communities in North Florida. They were a diverse group of women, ranging in age from nineteen to forty-two, with a mean age of thirty. Eighteen respondents were white and twenty-nine were African American. Although this overrepresents the overall proportion of African Americans on welfare in the United States, it reflects the race and ethnic background of welfare recipients in the interview region. Twenty-eight respondents had only one or two children; only two had five children or more.

I also conducted ten focus groups with women and men transitioning off welfare in both urban and rural regions of Oregon (n=45). Three of the focus groups were conducted in the city of Portland, the largest metropolitan area in Oregon, and seven groups were conducted in small towns sprinkled throughout the eastern and western portions of the state. The ages of participants ranged from seventeen to forty-seven years. Nearly one-third of residents outside the Portland metropolitan area were Hispanic, as I focused on communities and regions of the state that had higher than average rates of ethnic minority groups. Forty percent of respondents ranked their health as either poor or fair. I used these qualitative studies to elaborate on the national data.

### What Happens to Families When They Leave Welfare?

National data indicate that the drop in welfare caseloads was accompanied by a decrease in the number of people receiving Medicaid. During the first year of welfare reforms, it was estimated that 1.25 million people with incomes under 200 percent of the federal poverty line lost Medicaid coverage as a direct result. Despite the creation of the State Children's Health Insurance Program (S-CHIP), which is designed to extend health insurance coverage for children up to 200 percent of poverty, the majority of people who lost coverage were children under the age of nineteen. Minority children were particularly affected (Families USA 1999). The reasons for this drop in Medicaid coverage are not altogether clear, but it could be due in part to a lack of knowledge, confusion, or error on the part of either recipients or their caseworkers regarding eligibility (Greenberg 1998; Larkin 1999).

This decline in Medicaid coverage would be of little concern if we could assume that previous recipients and their families now receive health insurance from their new employers. Unfortunately, the low-wage jobs that most welfare recipients have to take usually do not provide health insurance as a fringe benefit. According to analyses from the National Medical Expenditure Survey (NMES), less than half of persons working for minimum or near minimum wage received health insurance from their employers in 1987, compared to 90 percent of persons with incomes twice that of the poverty line (Seccombe and Amey 1995). Moreover, comparing the years 1977 and 1987, I found that the erosion of health insurance benefits had occurred most dramatically among workers with the lowest wages (Seccombe 1996). Others have found this trend continuing into the 1990s (O'Brien and Feder 1998). Given that most former welfare recipients are employed in jobs that pay approximately

$6.50 per hour, according to data collected by the U.S. General Accounting Office (1999), it is unlikely that these families have the resources to purchase health insurance privately.

My interviews and focus groups revealed that "good jobs" were defined as those that paid more than $6.50 per hour, especially if the job included health insurance benefits. Most residents of North Florida or rural regions of Oregon did not expect to make more than $7 or $8 per hour. Unemployment in rural Oregon, where the focus groups were conducted, ranged from 5.2 percent to 9.1 percent higher than state or national averages. Wages were depressed. Most also did not expect their jobs to provide health insurance. "Only if you're lucky," I was told repeatedly. Dee, a mother of two children, revealed:

> I graduated and then applied all over this place. I went to XX (Temp Agency), and they got me a job for two months. I have a CNA and high school diploma and I competed with lots of women for the job. A "good job" is $12 an hour with benefits and thirty-seven hours a week. But I applied for over fifty jobs down to $7 to $8 an hour.

The welfare reform bill allows for twelve months of transitional Medicaid assistance for former welfare recipients and their families who would otherwise lose eligibility because of their earnings. But analyses from the Survey of Income and Program Participation (SIPP), based on a large nationally representative sample, reveal that one year was not long enough to find permanent coverage. Instead, former welfare recipients were prone to frequent changes in insurance status (Short and Freedman 1998). Changes in coverage have been found to affect access to health care. A recent study by Burstin et al. (1998/1999) reviewed the cases of 2,000 patients at five urban teaching hospital emergency departments, whose medical conditions ranged from stable to life-threatening. They report that patients who lost insurance coverage or changed coverage during the previous year were more likely to report having no primary care provider and experience a delay in getting needed care, and they were less likely to have the recommended follow-up care, compared to those who had no change in insurance coverage.

What happens to families as they leave welfare for work? There is no requirement that states conduct studies of what happens to former recipients, although many states and research organizations have elected to track them for a brief period of time. However, these studies are fraught with problems, such as very low contact rates because it is difficult to find former recipients. Response rates, once people are found, tend to be around 90 percent or even higher. Generally, these studies report that one-quarter to one-third of adults and at least 15 percent of children are completely uninsured after leaving welfare (Families USA 1999; GAO 1999; Larkin 1999; Loprest 1999).

Drawing upon data from the National Survey of American Families (NSAF), Loprest (1999) analyzed how more than 1,200 individuals leaving TANF between 1995 and 1997 have fared. She reports that 41 percent of former TANF recipients have no health insurance. About one-third of adults (34 percent) and nearly half of their children (47 percent) continue to receive Medicaid, with the remainder presumably obtaining insurance from some other source.

A statewide survey conducted in the state of Washington by the DSHS Economic Services Administration (1998) with nearly 600 single-parent families who left TANF is typical. More than one-third of former adult recipients and 16 percent of their children were completely uninsured. Two-thirds of respondents were employed at the time of the telephone survey, yet only 21 percent of these adults reported that they were currently covered by an employer-sponsored health plan. Uninsured families surveyed reported that they are worse off now with respect to health and wellbeing since leaving TANF, whereas families with health insurance did not report this.

It would appear that Welfare-to-Work training programs successfully assist recipients with finding employment of some sort, but they do little to secure health insurance coverage. Conversations with officials in several states reveal that it is not clear whether former welfare recipients and their children are getting the health care they need.

### Consequences of Being Uninsured

Having adequate health insurance can make a tremendous difference in the amount and type of health care that people receive. Both adults and children who are without this "passport" to health care use the health care system less often, are less likely to have a regular source of health care, are more likely to rely upon emergency rooms for their treatment, and often experience unnecessary pain, suffering, and even death (Brown et al. 2000; Kaiser Commission 1998; Seccombe 1996; Weigers et al. 1998).

Table 18.2 reports the results of the recent Kaiser/Commonwealth 1997 National Survey of Health Insurance (Kaiser Commission 1998), which reported that more than half of uninsured adults have no regular source of health care. Fifty-five percent of adults without insurance postponed getting medical care, compared with only 14 percent of adults with private insurance. Thirty percent of uninsured adults reported that they did not get needed medical care, compared to only 7 percent with insurance. Twenty-four percent reported that they did not fill a prescription, compared to 6 percent of adults with insurance.

Uninsured children are also disadvantaged. One in five uninsured children has no regular source of health care, and consequently they are 30 percent more likely to fall behind on well-child care and 80 percent more likely to never have had routine care. Moreover, uninsured children are 70 percent more likely than children with insurance to have failed to receive needed medical care for common but serious conditions such as asthma, which when left untreated may lead to even more serious health problems (Kaiser Commission 1998). Data reveal that having health insurance increases the responsible use of health services.

### Table 18.2
**Percentage of Adults Who Postponed or Did Not Obtain Needed Care, 1997[3]**

|  | % of uninsured | % of those with private insurance |
|---|---|---|
| Postponed medical care | 55 | 14 |
| Did not receive needed medical care | 30 | 7 |
| Did not fill prescriptions | 24 | 6 |

In the focus groups, respondents were asked if they had ever gone without insurance coverage as an adult. Most claimed that they had and reported that they or their children suffered severe consequences because of it, including going without needed medical or dental care or forgoing prescribed medicines. Kate summarizes the sentiment from the focus groups: "If I didn't have insurance, I didn't get help. They want their money upfront. You just suffer."

Another woman, Janice, explained that she was unable to receive necessary prenatal care: "When I was pregnant I didn't have insurance until two weeks before the baby was born. So I missed all the prenatal check-ups. It was terrible."

Many women spoke of the hardship that being uninsured causes for their children. One described the pain her daughter experienced because of a urinary tract infection. They postponed treatment until the pain was unbearable: "You just can't imagine the pain of hearing your daughter scream like that. Finally, I had to take her to the emergency room. It's taking three months to pay the bill. I even sold my ring." She lifted her hand to show the absence of her wedding ring.

A common theme throughout the focus groups was cost—most women who finally did seek treatment were unable to pay the bills and have bad credit as a result. They accumulated a large debt and are now followed by collection agencies. Some women made token payments, perhaps $20 per month. Others simply did not pay. As Jeannie told me: "I have thousands of dollars in medical bills. Thousands. When I had my son, there were problems. I had to have two epidurals and stuff. There's no way I'm paying. It's like $10,000. There's no way."

### Are Welfare Recipients Concerned about Health Insurance?

Being without insurance is extremely stressful to many poor families. Concerns about health and how to pay for health care emerged frequently in the in-depth interviews conducted in North Florida and the focus groups across Oregon. Many women expressed genuine fear that their future jobs may not offer health insurance. The stress associated with being uninsured often discouraged them from seeking employment (Seccombe 1999).

Many women interviewed in depth in North Florida admitted that they had stayed on welfare longer than they really wanted to because they needed the medical benefits and feared they would lose them by accepting work. "I'm a good mother. I'm all they got. I can't go being irresponsible," one woman said, in response to my question of why she turned down a job and instead remained on welfare.

When I asked my respondents in personal interviews to rank the importance of all the different types of aid they received, Medicaid was most often at the top of the list—more important than Food Stamps or the check itself (Seccombe 1999). They know that, without insurance, they may not be able to get the care that their children really need, and that their families could face serious health risks as a result. Rhonda, a woman on welfare, had a five-year-old son who suffered from lead-paint poisoning. She told me:

> He has lead-paint poisoning. And he's sick off and on, off and on. He got it from a place we rented. He was just a baby at the time, but ate some of the paint. When he's sick he just lies there. He don't play, he don't eat. The medical benefits—definitely it's the medical benefits that are the most important.

Even healthy women often ranked Medicaid above other welfare benefits. As one woman, Toni, revealed: "You can always get a place to stay by shacking up if you have to, and you can get food at a soup kitchen. But how am I supposed to pay for all those high price fancy doctor bills?"

Their concerns are not unfounded. Poor adults, particularly ethnic minorities and rural residents, are more likely to suffer a wide variety of chronic and acute ailments than their nonpoor counterparts (Loprest and Acs 1996). Many respondents in my interviews and focus groups suffered from poor health themselves or had children who were often ill or suffered from chronic conditions such as asthma. These health conditions reportedly interfered with their ability to look for or keep a job, and thus they continued to rely on welfare. These qualitative findings parallel and elaborate upon national trends. For example, welfare recipients are nearly three times as likely as other women to report poor or only fair health. Approximately 10 percent nationally report that they are limited to some degree in the type or amount of work that they can do because of a medical condition. Eight percent report that they need help to perform specific tasks of daily living, such as dressing, eating, bathing, or walking up stairs (Loprest and Acs 1996).

Their children are also significantly more likely to suffer a wide array of ailments, both chronic and acute, than are more affluent children (Children's Defense Fund 1998; Heymann and Earle 1999). Interviews and focus groups revealed high levels of asthma or other ailments among respondents' children. Using data from the National Longitudinal Survey of Youth, Heymann and Earle (1999) found that mothers who had been on welfare were significantly more likely than other mothers to have at least one child with serious asthma or another chronic condition. Other national data suggest that poor children are more likely to be iron deficient, to have frequent diarrhea or colitis, to have asthma and lead-paint poisoning, to suffer from partial or complete blindness or deafness, and to die during childhood (Children's Defense Fund 1998).

Yet my research in differing communities—from small and medium-sized communities in North Florida to the urban metropolitan area of Portland, Oregon, to rural communities throughout Oregon—suggests some divergent findings with respect to the concern over access to health care once transitional Medicaid expires. While interview respondents in North Florida expressed great fear and trepidation over losing Medicaid, focus group participants in metropolitan Portland revealed a higher degree of confidence that their health insurance would be automatically taken care of. Why this difference?

Oregon is the site of the well-known Oregon Health Plan, which has greatly expanded medical insurance for lower-income individuals. For those who earn too much to qualify for free medical care, they are allowed to pay small monthly premiums based on a sliding scale. The Oregon Health Plan has been credited with greatly reducing the number of Oregon residents who are without health insurance, down from 18 percent in 1990 to 11 percent in 1999. The decline among uninsured children is even more dramatic: from 20 percent to 8 percent (Office for Oregon Health Plan Policy Research 1998). All focus group participants in Portland were on the Oregon Health Plan. Very few expressed concern with losing their health insurance. Many presumed that they virtually would always be eligible for the Oregon Health Plan, or they felt confident that their employer would provide them with insurance. Others, enamored by a strong economy, mentioned the high salaries they were going to get in the metropolitan area, believing they could easily purchase the Oregon Health Plan monthly premiums, or purchase health insurance themselves privately if need be. As Francis, a Portland mother who was working on her GED told me, "Yeah, well at $12 or $14 an hour, I can just buy it myself if I need it. I looked in the newspaper, and I think I can get a job that pays that." These views of employment opportunities are quite optimistic, if not inflated, given the national average wage of $6.50 per hour for women coming off of welfare.

Respondents in rural areas of Oregon were considerably less optimistic about securing health care in the future. Like the women interviewed in North Florida, they believed that lack of health insurance is a serious social problem, and one they personally will experience. Facing a less certain economy with more restricted job opportunities, they did not assume high pay or benefits would be part of employment packages. And they worried whether they would be able to afford the monthly premiums needed to continue coverage from the Oregon Health Plan. Others spoke of ways in which employers tried to avoid offering health insurance, by offering only part-time or temporary work (in which they were laid off before health benefits kicked in). A woman in a focus group told me a common story: "No, I don't get benefits because I work 16 hours a week." Another woman immediately chimed in: "A lot of employers try to avoid 40 hours. They call 32-35 hours 'full-time.' But no benefits."

One common feature among all respondents was the silence surrounding health insurance in the Welfare-to-Work transition process. Virtually all respondents told me that neither their welfare caseworkers nor their Welfare-to-Work case managers ever talked seriously with them about the possibility that they could lose their insurance, how to plan for future coverage, or that their premiums for the Oregon Health Plan might rise dramatically. When asked in focus groups whether health insurance was discussed by staff at the welfare office, I was told repeatedly, "No. Their idea is to find a job. Get a job, and that's all there is to it."

Virtually all respondents replied that health insurance and planning for insurance is not a component of any Welfare-to-Work curriculum or part of any serious conversations. To many of the participants, I was the first one to raise these issues with them. Consequently, they had not planned for when their transitional Medicaid expires.

### Conclusion: Health Insurance is a Pressing Social Welfare Issue

Meaningful welfare reform and access to health care are critically linked to one another. We cannot truly reform our welfare system unless we attend to recipients' greater-than-average health care needs. Joining the ranks of the working poor, many adults and children will become uninsured, even with transitional Medicaid and S-CHIP programs in place. This likely will affect their access and use of health care services and interfere with their ability to use the health care system appropriately.

These issues are becoming increasing salient as states witness the expiration of the one-year transitional Medicaid benefits among the first cohort of Welfare-to-Work participants. There are other cohorts right behind them. It is ironic that we can consider the welfare system reformed simply because people are encouraged or forced to leave it for work, without systematically and thoughtfully examining the subsequent health and wellbeing of these families.

## References

Burstin, H.R., K. Swartz, A.C. O'Neil, E.J. Orav, and T.A. Brennan. 1998/99. "The Effects of Change of Health Insurance on Access to Care." *Inquiry* 35: 389-397.

Brown, E.R., R. Wyn, and S. Teleki. 2000. *Disparities in Health Insurance and Access to Care for Residents Across U.S. Cities*. The Commonwealth Fund and UCLA Center for Health Policy Research.

Children's Defense Fund. 1998. *The State of America's Children Yearbook*. 1998. Washington DC: Children's Defense Fund.

DSHS Economic Services Administration. 1998. *Washington's TANF Single Parent Families Shortly After Welfare: Survey of Families Which Exited TANF Between December 7 and March 1998*.

Families USA. 1999. *Losing Health Insurance: The Unintended Consequences of Welfare Reform*.

Greenberg, M. 1998. *Participation in Welfare and Medicaid Enrollment*. Issue Paper. Washington DC: Henry J. Kaiser Family Foundation.

Heymann, S.J., and Earle, A. 1999. "The Impact of Welfare Reform on Parents' Ability to Care for Their Children's Health." *American Journal of Public Health* 89: 502–505.

Kaiser Commission on Medicaid and the Uninsured. 1998. *The Uninsured and Their Access to Health Care*. Washington DC: Henry J. Kaiser Family Foundation.

Larkin, H. 1999. "Are More Uninsured an Unintended Consequence of Welfare Reform?" *Advances* 2. Princeton, NJ: Robert Wood Johnson Foundation.

Loprest, P. 1999. *Families Who Left Welfare: Who Are They and How Are They Doing?* Washington DC: The Urban Institute.

Loprest P., and G. Acs. 1996. *Profile Of Disability Among Families on AFDC*: Washington DC: The Urban Institute Report to the Henry J. Kaiser Family Foundation.

O'Brien, E., and J. Feder. 1998. *How Well Does the Employment-Based Health Insurance System Work for Low-Income Families?* Issue Paper. Washington DC: Henry J. Kaiser Family Foundation.

Office for Oregon Health Plan Policy Research. 1998. *The Uninsured in Oregon 1997*. Salem, OR: The Office for Oregon Health Plan Policy Research.

Rank, M.R., and T.A. Hirschl. 1999. "The Economic Risk of Childhood Poverty in America: Estimating the Probability of Poverty Across the Formative Years." *Journal of Marriage and the Family* 61: 1058–1067.

Seccombe, K. 1996. "Health Insurance Coverage Among the Working Poor: Changes from 1977 to 1987." *Research in the Sociology of Health Care.* Volume 13. Greenwich, CT: JAI Press.

Seccombe, K. 1999. *"So You Think I Drive a Cadillac?" Welfare Recipients' Perspectives on the System and Its Reform.* Needham Heights: Allyn & Bacon.

Seccombe, Karen, and C. Amey. 1995. "Playing by the Rules and Losing: Health Insurance and the Working Poor." *Journal of Health and Social Behavior* 36: 168-181.

Short, P.F., and V.A. Freedman. 1998. "Single Women and the Dynamics of Medicaid." *Health Services Research* 33: 1309–1336.

U.S. Bureau of the Census. 2001. "Poverty in the United States: 2000." Pp. 60–214 in *Current Population Report.* Washington, DC: U.S. Government Printing Office.

U.S. General Accounting Office. 1999. *Welfare Reform: Information on Former Recipients' Status.* GAO/HEHS-99-48. U.S. Government Printing Office.

Weigers, M.E., R.M. Weinick, and J.W. Cohen. 1998. "Children's Health Insurance, Access to Care, and Health Status: New Findings." *Health Affairs* 17: 127–136.

## Notes

[1] Karen Seccombe is a professor in the School of Community Health and Director of the Center for Public Health Studies at Portland State University. Her research interests include access to health care among low-income families. She is the author of *"So You Think I Drive a Cadillac?" Welfare Recipients' Perspectives on the System and Its Reform* (1999). She is currently researching the effects of welfare reform and access to health care throughout Oregon, a statewide quantitative and qualitative study funded by the Agency for Healthcare Research and Quality (AHRQ). She would like to thank Renato Carletti, Richard Lockwood, and Cheryl Richardson for their assistance in the focus groups, and Richard T. Meenan for his comments on this manuscript.

[2] Data are from the U.S. Bureau of the Census (2001).

[3] Data are from the Kaiser/Commonwealth 1997 Survey of Health Insurance (Kaiser Commission 1998).

# The Effects of Welfare Reform on the Characteristics of the Food Stamp Population

*Phil Gleason,*[1] *Carole Trippe*[2] *and Scott Cody*[3]

During the middle to late 1990s, the size and characteristics of the Food Stamp Program (FSP) caseload changed dramatically. The size of the caseload plummeted by 31 percent between 1994 and 1998, dropping from an average of 11.1 million cases each month in 1994 to 7.7 million cases in 1999. The caseload composition also changed during this time, with more long-term recipients, more employed recipients, and fewer recipients receiving welfare benefits. In particular:

- the number of long-term Food Stamp recipients increased by 14 percent

- the number of recipients with earnings increased by 25 percent

- the number of recipients receiving welfare benefits declined by 28 percent.

There are two, often competing, explanations for these changes in the Food Stamp caseload:

- Welfare reform changes, which were designed to promote work and self-sufficiency among cash welfare recipients, may also affect many Food Stamp recipients because of the overlap in participation between the two populations. Furthermore, the Food Stamp provisions of welfare reform restricted the eligibility of legal aliens and able-bodied adults without dependents (ABAWDs).[4] Welfare reform is defined here to include both policy changes implemented during the early 1990s through state waivers and the broad reform effort mandated by the Personal Responsibility and Work Opportunities Reconciliation Act (PRWORA) of 1996.

▶ Under the economic expansion of this period, declining unemployment, low inflation, rising productivity, and the creation of millions of new jobs caused many individuals to work instead of or in addition to receiving Food Stamps. Those who remained on the program were more likely to be long-term recipients.

Understanding the effects of these factors on the observed changes in the Food Stamp population is important for guiding future policy decisions. If the changes are due to particular welfare policy changes, then adjustments in these policies can alter future consequences for the Food Stamp caseloads. Alternatively, if changes were mostly due to the improving economy, then future policy changes will have little effect on the FSP caseload, and future declines in the economy will likely result in Food Stamp caseload increases and returns to former caseload compositions regardless of particular policies.

In this chapter, we assess the effects of specific welfare reform policies, as well as other factors, on the observed changes in the Food Stamp caseload between 1994 and 1998.[5] Specifically, we address the following three questions:

▶ How have different types of welfare reform policies affected the size and composition of the Food Stamp caseload? Are subgroups affected differently?

▶ How much have other factors, such as the economic expansion between 1994 and 1998, affected the Food Stamp caseload?

▶ What are the policy implications of our findings regarding the competing explanations for recent changes in the Food Stamp caseload?

We find that *specific* policies central to the welfare reform effort during the time of the study, such as work requirements and time limits, did not strongly influence the Food Stamp caseload and cannot explain the dramatic recent decline in the size of the caseload. Other factors, such as economic expansion and more general aspects of welfare reform—for example, the strong message that recipients were expected to find work and leave welfare—explained a much greater portion of the dramatic changes in the FSP caseload.

## Methodological Approach

Our study uses both a descriptive and a multivariate analysis. The descriptive analysis examines how average Food Stamp caseload characteristics changed as states moved from basic AFDC policies to low-, medium-, and high-intensity welfare reform policies under waivers and PRWORA. The multivariate analysis examines the effects of the welfare reform policies on mean caseload characteristics after accounting for differences in other factors, such as state unemployment rates, poverty rates, median wages, and time trends.

We used monthly data from the Food Stamp Program Quality Control (FSPQC) system to track changes in each state's caseload size and characteristics from fiscal year 1992 through 1999. FSPQC data are based on a national probability sample of between 50,000 and 60,000 Food Stamp households.[6] We obtained data on each state's individual welfare reform policies under waivers and PRWORA from existing compilations of state policies by organizations such as the Urban Institute, the National Governor's Association (NGA), and the Administration for Children and Families (ACF).[7] We collected information on state characteristics from 1992 through 1999 for the econometric analysis from sources such as the U.S. Bureau of Labor Statistics and the U.S. Census Bureau. The state characteristics include state unemployment rates, mean income, poverty rates, mean wages, population size, and Medicaid policies.

For the descriptive and multivariate analysis, we classified state welfare reform policies according to the intensity of three aspects of these policies: (1) work requirements, (2) work encouragement policies, and (3) time limits. We defined "intensity" according to the degree to which the policies promote work and/or discourage welfare receipt. For example, some states imposed "high intensity" work requirements, which required a large number of hours of work soon after program entry, exempted few recipients, and enforced severe consequences for failure to comply with these requirements. Other states imposed "low intensity" work requirements, which required fewer hours of work and gave recipients more time to find jobs, exempted larger numbers of recipients, and made the consequences of failure to comply with the requirements less serious. The tremendous variation in both the type

**303**

of requirements and in the intensity of a given requirement across states and over time provided an excellent opportunity to examine the effects of these different approaches on the FSP caseload. The state policies were classified as states implemented welfare reform at various times over the 1992 to 1999 period. Policies implemented under state waivers and policies implemented under PRWORA were treated similarly.

In the descriptive analysis, we estimated the change in average FSP caseload characteristics such as the size, percentage of long-term recipients, percentage with earnings, and the percentage on AFDC/TANF as states moved from basic AFDC policies to specific types and intensities of welfare reform policies. We also estimated these changes for key subgroups of the FSP caseload, such as AFDC/TANF recipients, single parents, aliens, and ABAWDs.

The changes in FSP characteristics estimated in the descriptive analysis could have come about not only because of the welfare reform policies but also because of any number of other factors, such as differences in the economic conditions of the states at the time that they implemented the welfare reform versus when basic AFDC rules were in effect. Therefore, we also estimated the effect of each type of welfare reform policy on the mean characteristics of the FSP population after accounting for factors such as the economic conditions, time period, population, and Medicaid policies unique to a given state.[8]

The multivariate models used to estimate the effects of specific welfare reform policies on caseload characteristics also yield estimates of the effects of the other factors on caseload characteristics. These estimates, along with data on how the average weighted values of the explanatory factors changed between 1994 and 1999, allowed us to determine the extent to which changes in the size and characteristics of the Food Stamp caseload were driven by various explanations. In particular, we measured the extent to which Food Stamp caseload changes could be explained by four different factors: (1) the implementation of work requirements; (2) factors associated with the implementation of PRWORA (not counting the effects of work requirements, time limits, and work encouragement policies); (3) economic expansion; and (4) other observed and unobserved factors.[9]

### Effects of Specific Welfare Reform Policies on the Size and Composition of the FSP Caseload

Various welfare reform policies, such as work requirements, work encouragement policies, and time limits, affected the size and composition of the FSP caseload. In this chapter, we focus mostly on the effects of work requirements, because they influenced the Food Stamp caseload over the 1994 to 1999 period to a greater extent than the other types of policy changes we examined.

## Work Requirement Policies

Tables 19.1a and 19.1b present two sets of findings concerning the relationship between work requirement policies and FSP caseload characteristics. The descriptive results in Table 19.1a show how average caseload characteristics differed when states were under basic AFDC policies versus when they were under low-, medium-, and high-intensity welfare reform work requirements. The regression-adjusted results in Table 19.1b show estimates of the effect of these work requirement policies on mean caseload characteristics after accounting for economic conditions, time trends, and other observed time-varying and unobserved time-invariant factors unique to a given state.

### Table 19.1a
#### Food Stamp Caseload Characteristics under Alternative Policy Regimes: Work Requirement Policies

**Descriptive Analysis**

| | Base AFDC policy (% of total FSP households) | Change from base AFDC policy (percentage point difference) | | |
|---|---|---|---|---|
| | | Low intensity work requirement | Medium intensity work requirement | High intensity work requirement |
| **Program Size and Tenure** | | | | |
| Caseload size (as % of 1991 caseload) | 122 | -16**[10] | -18** | -19** |
| % on Food Stamps for more than 1 Year | 43 | +6** | +6** | +6** |
| % at-risk of long-term dependency | 33 | +1 | +2** | +3** |
| **Income Type** | | | | |
| % with earnings | 23 | -1 | +4** | +5** |
| % with AFDC/TANF income | 40 | -7** | -5** | -10** |
| % with earnings among Those w/AFDC/TANF | 13 | +8** | +7** | +5** |

**Table 19.1b**
**Food Stamp Caseload Characteristics under Alternative Policy Regimes (Work Requirement Policies)**

Regression-adjusted Analysis

| | Base AFDC policy (% of total FSP households) | Change from base AFDC policy (percentage point difference) | | |
|---|---|---|---|---|
| | | Low intensity work requirement | Medium intensity work requirement | High intensity work requirement |
| **Program Size and Tenure** | | | | |
| Caseload size (as % of 1991 caseload) | 115 | 0 | 0 | -3**[11] |
| % on Food Stamps for more than 1 Year | 50 | -1 | -2* | -6** |
| % at-risk of long-term dependency | 35 | 0 | +1 | -4** |
| **Income Type** | | | | |
| % with earnings | 22 | 0 | +1* | +1* |
| % with AFDC/TANF income | 37 | +3** | +1* | -1 |
| % with earnings among Those w/AFDC/TANF | 12 | +5** | +3** | +2* |

**Descriptive Results**

The descriptive results show that, under work requirements, regardless of their intensity, state FSP caseload characteristics were very different than they were under basic AFDC rules over this time period. Most strikingly, the size of the caseload was substantially lower under work requirements. Whereas, under AFDC rules, the average state had a monthly caseload over the 1992 through 1999 period that was 122 percent of the 1991 caseload, the comparable figure for states with welfare reform work requirements was only about 104 percent. In addition, Food Stamp recipients in work requirement states were more likely to be long-term recipients, less likely to be on AFDC/TANF, and more likely to be working.

For the most part, differences between states with low-intensity work requirements and those with high-intensity work requirements were fairly small. However, while the percentage of the caseload with earnings was about the same in states under low-intensity work requirements as it was in states under basic AFDC rules (22–23 percent), it was significantly higher in states with high-intensity work requirements (28 percent).

### Regression-adjusted Results

Despite the large changes in the Food Stamp caseload as states moved to implement work requirements, these changes were largely brought about by factors other than work requirement policies themselves. The regression-adjusted estimates show that once these other factors are held constant, the effects of work requirements are much less dramatic. In addition, the estimated effects of low-intensity work requirements differ from the effects of high-intensity work requirements in several important respects.

High-intensity work requirements are estimated to decrease the size of the FSP caseload, but this effect is much smaller than suggested by the descriptive results (3 percentage points compared with 19 percentage points). Other characteristics, such as the percentage of Food Stamp households with earnings, the percentage with AFDC/TANF, and the percentage with AFDC/TANF and earnings, are estimated to be influenced by high-intensity work requirements in the same direction as suggested by the descriptive results, but by much smaller amounts.

The most striking difference between the descriptive and regression-adjusted results is that while the descriptive results indicate an increase in the percentage of long-term recipients under high-intensity work requirements, the regression-adjusted results indicate that high-intensity work requirements led to a decrease in the percentage of long-term recipients (all else held constant). Hence, while a number of factors conspired to increase the fraction of long-term Food Stamp recipients as states moved to high-intensity work requirements (for example, economic expansion or attitudinal changes), the work requirements were not one of them.

In general, the effects of high-intensity work requirements are similar across subgroups of the FSP caseload. However, the effect of the requirements on the size of the caseload is strongest among AFDC/TANF households rather than Food Stamp–only households. The individual high-intensity work requirement policy with the strongest effect on most FSP caseload characteristics is a state's sanction policy (Gleason et al. 2001).

Low-intensity work requirements do not significantly influence the size of the Food Stamp caseload, but do lead to an increase in the percentage of Food Stamp recipients who also receive AFDC/TANF. These requirements also lead to an increase in the percentage of AFDC/TANF recipients who are working.

### Work Encouragement Policies

High-intensity policies designed to encourage work *among* those still receiving AFDC/TANF (such as more generous earnings disregards) led to a significant increase in the size of the FSP caseload and the percentage with earnings among those receiving AFDC/TANF, but no significant change in the percentage of FSP recipients on AFDC/TANF (see Table 19.2a and 19.2b). The effects are strongest among single parents, but tend to be similar for most of the subgroups we examined. Policies designed to encourage work while at the same time keep households *off* the AFDC/TANF program (such as diversion payments) do not strongly affect the FSP caseload. High-intensity policies of this type have no significant effect on the size of the caseload and have only a small negative effect on the percentage of the caseload receiving AFDC/TANF benefits.

## Table 19.2a
**Food Stamp Caseload Characteristics under Alternative Policy Regimes: Policies to Encourage Work among those on AFDC/TANF**

### Descriptive Analysis

| | Base AFDC policy (% of total FSP households) | Change from base AFDC policy (percentage point difference) | | |
|---|---|---|---|---|
| | | Low intensity work encourage-ment | Medium intensity work encourage-ment | High intensity work encour-agement |
| **Program Size and Tenure** | | | | |
| Caseload size (as % of 1991 caseload) | 121 | -12**[12] | -18** | -12** |
| % on Food Stamps for more than 1 year | 42 | -5** | +9** | +13** |
| % at-risk of long-term dependency | 33 | -2* | +2** | +4** |
| **Income Type** | | | | |
| % with earnings | 23 | +5** | +2** | +2** |
| % with AFDC/TANF income | 36 | -12** | -4** | -4** |
| % with earnings among those w/AFDC/TANF | 13 | +3** | +5** | +8** |

## Table 19.2b
**Food Stamp Caseload Characteristics under Alternative Policy Regimes:
Policies to Encourage Work among those on AFDC/TANF**

Regression-adjusted Analysis

| | Base AFDC policy (% of total FSP households) | Change from base AFDC policy (percentage point difference) | | |
|---|---|---|---|---|
| | | Low intensity work encouragement | Medium intensity work encouragement | High intensity work encouragement |
| **Program Size and Tenure** | | | | |
| Caseload size (as % of 1991 caseload) | 116 | $+6^{**13}$ | $+2^*$ | $+3^{**}$ |
| % on Food Stamps for more than 1 year | 48 | $-7^{**}$ | -1 | $+3^{**}$ |
| % at-risk of long-term dependency | 35 | $-4^{**}$ | $-1^*$ | $+3^{**}$ |
| **Income Type** | | | | |
| % with earnings | 22 | 0 | 0 | $+1^*$ |
| % with AFDC/ TANF income | 37 | $-2^{**}$ | +1 | -1 |
| % with earnings among those w/AFDC/TANF | 12 | -2 | 0 | $+3^{**}$ |

### Time Limit Policies

Not surprisingly, we found that state time limit policies did not strongly influence Food Stamp caseload characteristics over the period covered by the data. Because most time limits were enacted in 1997, most recipients hadn't reached the time limit by the last month of our analysis (September 1999). Only a handful of recipients in states that had enacted short time limits under a waiver had reached the time limit. The true effects of the time limits should be addressed when additional years of data become available.

## How Welfare Reform has Affected Behavior

Because the FSPQC data used in this analysis do not follow individual Food Stamp recipients or Food Stamp–eligible individuals over time, they cannot be used to directly estimate how welfare reform policies have affected individuals' behavior. However, the patterns of results obtained in the analysis suggest several behavioral implications. Below, we make three inferences based on the findings of this study. The inferences should be seen as hypotheses that should be tested in further research using more appropriate data, such as longitudinal data that track Food Stamp recipients over time.

▶ Inference 1: High-intensity work requirements cause relatively disadvantaged Food Stamp recipients to leave the program.

> ▶ Although the overall percentage of long-term Food Stamp recipients increased under welfare reform policies, high-intensity work requirements had a negative effect on the percentage of long-term recipients. This suggests that this policy caused long-term recipients to leave Food Stamps or not enter the program.

> ▶ We examined the specific work requirement policies implemented by states and found that high-intensity sanctions were the policies with the largest negative effect on the size of the caseload (Gleason et al. 2001). This is consistent with Inference 1, since disadvantaged recipients not complying with high-intensity work requirements could be sanctioned, perhaps leading them to leave the welfare/Food Stamp system altogether rather than face these requirements.

> ▶ Recent studies of welfare leavers (Loprest 1999; Rangarajan and Wood 1999; and GAO 1999) show that a substantial proportion of leavers do not work after exiting the Food Stamp and welfare programs. Nearly all of these leavers who do not work and do not receive welfare are poor, and most are likely to have to struggle to make ends meet. It seems likely that some of these individuals would not have left welfare without work requirements enforced by the threat of sanctions. This is consistent with a proportion of leavers being the disadvantaged recipients who exit Food Stamps as a result of high-intensity work requirements.

▶ Inference 2: Low-intensity work requirements lead relatively advantaged Food Stamp and AFDC/TANF recipients to stay on AFDC/TANF longer and to work more.

> ▶ The estimated effects of low-intensity work require-
> ments are to increase the percentage of the Food Stamp
> caseload receiving AFDC/TANF and to increase the
> proportion of this joint Food Stamp/welfare population
> who are working.

> ▶ Since only 13 percent of the joint Food Stamp/welfare
> population is working, it is likely that an increase in the
> percentage working results from a change in behavior
> among those who are relatively advantaged and who have
> relatively few barriers to employment.

▶ Inference 3: Policies that encourage work among households on AFDC/ TANF lead to more work among these households and allow them to remain on Food Stamps longer.

> ▶ Work encouragement policies lead to a positive effect
> on the Food Stamp caseload size.

> ▶ High-intensity work encouragement policies lead to a
> positive effect on the percentage of joint Food Stamp/
> welfare recipients who are working.

### Explaining the Recent Changes in the Food Stamp Caseload: Economic Expansion or Welfare Reform?

Imposing stringent work requirements slightly reduced the size of the Food Stamp caseload, the percentage of long-term Food Stamp recipients, and the percentage of the caseload on AFDC/TANF. Work requirements also slightly increased the percentage of recipients with earnings. For the most part, however, the key policy changes associated with the passage of PRWORA—work requirements, work encouragement policies, and time limits—did not strongly influence the size or character- istics of the Food Stamp caseload. Thus, other factors must explain the dramatic changes in the caseload during the middle to late 1990s, including the sharp decline in the number of Food Stamp recipients and the change in caseload composition from fewer to more long-term and employed recipients, and from more to fewer households on AFDC/TANF.

**Caseload Decline**

The factor that played the biggest role in explaining the decline in the Food Stamp caseload between 1994 and 1999 was the economic expansion that occurred during this same period. In particular, the unemployment rate fell by 28 percent, mean state income increased by 6 percent, the poverty rate fell by 10 percent, and average wages in the manufacturing industry increased by 11 percent. The combined effect of these economic changes explains 47 percent of the caseload decline (See Figure 19.1). The size of this effect is consistent with Figlio et al. (2000) who found that "approximately 35 percent of the Food Stamp caseload reduction from 1994 to 1998 is due to state differences in macroeconomic conditions." Similarly, Wallace and Blank (1999) found that the decline in the unemployment rate could explain between 28 and 44 percent of the Food Stamp caseload decline over the same period.

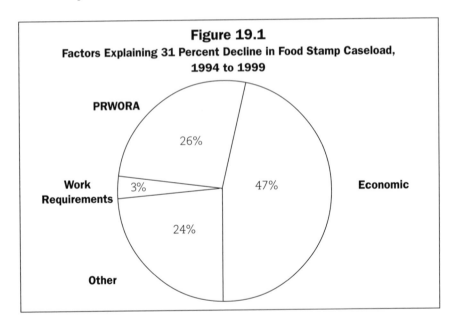

**Figure 19.1**
**Factors Explaining 31 Percent Decline in Food Stamp Caseload, 1994 to 1999**

Although work requirements explain almost none of the Food Stamp caseload decline (23 percent) and the effects of work encouragement policies and time limits are negligible, other aspects of PRWORA account for 26 percent of the decline. In other words, other aspects of PRWORA not captured by the model are estimated to reduce the Food Stamp caseload from 125 to 115 percent of its 1991 level (or from 11.1 to 10.2 million households), all else being equal.[14]

If work requirements, time limits, and work encouragement policies had little effect on the size of the caseload, what aspects of PRWORA could have led to this caseload decline? One possibility is the cutback in Food

Stamp eligibility for aliens and ABAWDs. We estimate that this explanation accounts for just under half of the overall effect of PRWORA on the Food Stamp caseload (Gleason et al. 2001).

Another possibility is that policy changes other than work requirements, time limits, and work encouragement policies that were brought about by PRWORA influenced the size of the Food Stamp caseload. For example, under PRWORA, states must require unmarried teenage parents to live with their parents and attend school until they receive a high school degree or the equivalent. Also under PRWORA, states are allowed to impose "family caps" and change their child support policies. We believe these other policy changes are unlikely to be the explanation for the other PRWORA effects for two reasons. First, since major policy changes like work requirements and time limits did not have large effects on the size of the caseload, it seems unlikely that these policies that affect smaller numbers of Food Stamp recipients would have large effects. Second, these policy changes would primarily influence Food Stamp households that also receive AFDC/TANF, but it turns out that the other aspects of PRWORA are as important for non-AFDC/TANF Food Stamp households as they are for AFDC/TANF Food Stamp households.

The two aspects of PRWORA (other than the cutback in eligibility for aliens and ABAWDs) most likely to have influenced the caseload decline are, in our view, the attitudes and perceptions of Food Stamp recipients and the specific way in which welfare workers actually implemented Food Stamp and TANF policies. PRWORA was a major policy initiative that radically changed the system for providing cash assistance in the United States. When PRWORA was passed and then implemented by states, it was accompanied by a great deal of publicity and rhetoric that stressed the requirement that welfare recipients work and that long-term welfare receipt is undesirable and would no longer be tolerated. The result of this message for many welfare recipients may have been for them to begin to look for ways to get off public assistance. For others, the message may have intensified the stigma of receiving welfare, and therefore they did not apply for benefits. Many Food Stamp households heard the same message and their attitude towards receiving Food Stamps was likely affected in the same way. In some cases, they may have incorrectly perceived that the work requirements and time limits applied to them. Any of these possibilities or a combination of them could have led to the observed effect of PRWORA on the Food Stamp caseload decline.

Finally, the practices of welfare caseworkers may have changed with the implementation of PRWORA. For example, some caseworkers may have tried to divert potential welfare applicants from going on the program in the first place by suggesting they attempt to find work first. Since the same workers handle Food Stamps and TANF in many states, their message to Food Stamp recipients probably mirrored their message to

TANF recipients. Thus, not only would the TANF rolls decline as a result of these actions, so would the Food Stamp rolls.

Aside from the effects of welfare reform and economic expansion, the remaining decline in the Food Stamp caseload was brought about by "other" factors, both observed and unobserved. These other factors, which account for 24 percent of the overall decline, include the time limits and work encouragement policies mentioned earlier, changes in state populations, a general time trend, and other unobserved factors. The time trend accounts for the largest portion of the "other" factors, and could reflect either policy or economic effects not captured in other aspects of the model.

### Changes in Other Food Stamp Caseload Characteristics

In addition to exploring how various factors affected the size of the Food Stamp caseload between 1994 and 1999, we also examined the extent to which these factors could explain other changes in the characteristics of the caseload:

▶ **Growth in long-term Food Stamp receipt.** Although the percentage of long-term Food Stamp households grew moderately from 1994 to 1999, work requirements had a *negative* effect on the percentage of long-term Food Stamp households. Therefore, PRWORA, economic factors, and "other" factors must account for the overall increase in the percentage of long-term households. However, most of the increase is explained by "other" factors.

▶ **Increase in employment among Food Stamp households.** Welfare reform changes explain about half of the increase in employment among Food Stamp households (17 percent from work requirements and 34 percent from other factors associated with PRWORA). This suggests that welfare reform policies led members of Food Stamp households to find jobs in increasing numbers, although the resulting earnings were not necessarily sufficient to enable them to leave the program.

▶ **Decline in the percentage of Food Stamp households with AFDC/TANF.** Economic factors have a large effect on the decline in the percentage of Food Stamp households that also receive AFDC/TANF, explaining 57 percent of this change. PRWORA explains only 5 percent of the decline among these households, supporting the point that the effects of PRWORA led to declines in Food Stamp participation both among AFDC/TANF participants and nonparticipants.

## Policy Implications of Findings

The findings presented in this paper suggest that welfare reform policy changes played an unexpected role in the recent decline and changes in the Food Stamp caseload. The specific policy changes most closely associated with welfare reform—work requirements, work encouragement policies, and time limits—explain very little of the caseload decline. The most striking effect of these policies has been that very stringent work requirements, which apply not to Food Stamp but to TANF recipients, seem to have led disadvantaged Food Stamp recipients to leave the program. On the other hand, factors associated with the passage and implementation of PRWORA (rather than its specific policies) have had a substantial negative effect on the caseload. In our view, the primary reasons for these effects are that PRWORA has changed the perceptions and attitudes of Food Stamp recipients and the way in which caseworkers administer welfare and Food Stamp policies. Although most of the policy changes were directed at those receiving AFDC/TANF, Food Stamp recipients seem to have been strongly influenced as well.

If the above interpretation is correct, then policymakers should be cautious in using the estimated effects of PRWORA to predict how future changes in welfare policy might influence the Food Stamp caseload. The interpretation suggests that it was not the easily replicable changes to welfare policies that led to the decline in Food Stamp caseload (and changes in other caseload characteristics), but the not-so-easily replicable (one-time) changes in perceptions, attitudes, and behavior brought about by PRWORA and its attendant publicity and rhetoric that were responsible. While many people surely believed that PRWORA really did "end welfare as we know it," it is unlikely that the same could be said for future legislative efforts to reform welfare policy.

Another major implication of the results is that economic growth during the middle to late 1990s explains a substantial part of the decline in the Food Stamp caseload. The question that follows is: When the economy takes a downturn and goes into recession, will the caseload increase? It is likely that the caseload will increase under a recession, although it may not reach previous levels (this would depend on what happens to other factors and the degree to which the unobserved effects of the model are related to the economy). Thus, the results suggest that the recent decline in the size of the Food Stamp caseload is probably not permanent.

## References

Administration for Children and Families (ACF). 1998. *Temporary Assistance for Needy Families (TANF) Program, First Annual Report to Congress.* Washington, DC: U.S. Department of Health and Human Services.

Figlio, David N., Craig Gunderson, and James P. Ziliak. 2000. "The Effects of the Macroeconomy and Welfare Reform on Food Stamp Caseloads." *American Journal of Agricultural Economics* 82 (3): 635–641.

Gallagher, L. Jerome, Meghan Gallagher, Kevin Perese, Susan Schreiber, and Keith Watson. 1998. *One Year After Federal Welfare Reform: A Description of State Temporary Assistance for Needy Families (TANF) Decisions as of October 1997.* Washington, DC: The Urban Institute.

Gleason, Philip, Carole Trippe, Scott Cody, and Jacquie Anderson. 2001. The Effects of Welfare Reform on the Characteristics of the Food Stamp Population. Draft report submitted to the U.S. Department of Agriculture, Economic Research Service. Washington, DC: Mathematica Policy Research, Inc.

Loprest, Pamela. 1999. "Families Who Left Welfare: Who Are They and How Are They Doing?" *Assessing the New Federalism.* Discussion Paper Number 2. Washington, DC: The Urban Institute.

National Governors' Association (NGA). 1999. *Round Two Summary of Selected Elements of State Programs for Temporary Assistance for Needy Families.* Washington, DC: National Governors' Association.

Office of the Assistant Secretary for Planning and Evaluation (Office of the ASPE). 1997. *Setting the Baseline: A Report on State Welfare Waivers.* Washington, DC: U.S. Department of Health and Human Services.

Rangarajan, Anu, and Robert G. Wood. 1999. *Work First New Jersey Evaluation: How WFNJ Clients Are Faring Under Welfare Reform: An Early Look.* Report submitted to the State of New Jersey, Department of Human Services. Princeton, NJ: Mathematica Policy Research, Inc.

U.S. General Accounting Office (GAO). 1999. *Welfare Reform: Information on Former Recipients' Status.* Washington, DC: GAO.

Wallace, Geoffrey, and Rebecca M. Blank. 1999. "What Goes Up Must Come Down? Explaining Recent Changes in Public Assistance Caseloads." In *Economic Conditions and Welfare Reform*, Sheldon Danziger, ed.. Kalamazoo, MI: Upjohn Institute.

## Notes

[1] Phil Gleason is a senior researcher at Mathematica Policy Research. His research areas include welfare, education, and food and nutrition policy, and he has recently published studies on the status of Food Stamp leavers in *Policy and Practice* and on children's diets in the *Journal of the American Dietetic Association.*

[2] Carole Trippe is a senior researcher at Mathematica Policy Research. Her research areas include Food Stamp and welfare policy analysis and microsimulation modeling. Her recent work includes studies of participation rates among the eligible Food Stamp population, the effects of multiple program participation among the low-income population, and the characteristics of Food Stamp recipients affected by welfare reform.

[3] Scott Cody is a researcher at Mathematica Policy Research. His research areas include Food Stamps and education policy. His recent research includes studies of the effects of welfare reform on participation in the Food Stamp Program and a study of efforts to increase participation in the Food Stamp Program among the elderly.

[4] Although PRWORA reduced eligibility for some Food Stamp aliens and able-bodied adults without dependents, these two groups represent a small proportion of the overall FSP population in FY 1994 (5 percent and 12 percent, respectively). The number of aliens and ABAWDS affected by the Food Stamp provisions is substantially smaller than this due to legislation in 1998 that restored eligibility to many aliens, and legislation that allowed states to waive or exempt many ABAWDs from the requirements.

[5] See Gleason et al. (2001) for a more detailed description of the methodological approach and results of this study.

[6] Annual state samples range from a minimum of 300 to 2,400 households, depending on the state's caseload.

[7] For example, see Gallagher 1998; ACF 1998; NGA 1999; and Office of the ASPE 1997.

[8] In this multivariate analysis, we estimated a fixed state effects model. Estimates of the effect of state welfare policies in this model are driven by what happens to a state's Food Stamp caseload characteristics when that state's welfare policies are changed (after controlling for other observable changes within the state). We also estimated several alternative specifications of the basic model in order to address possible weaknesses and additional research questions. Finally, we estimated the basic specification for the key subgroups examined in the descriptive analysis. More details on the estimation of these models can be found in Gleason et al. (2001).

[9] The effects of time limits and work encouragement policies tend to be quite small. We therefore combined the effects of these policies with the "other" group.

[10] A double asterix (**) indicates the difference from the base AFDC policy is statistically significant at the 5 percent level.

[11] A double asterix (**) indicates the difference from the base AFDC policy is statistically significant at the 5 percent level. A single asterix (*) indicates that the difference is statistically significant at the 1 percent level.

[12] A double asterix (**) indicates the difference from the base AFDC policy is statistically significant at the 5 percent level.

[13] A double asterix (**) indicates the difference from the base AFDC policy is statistically significant at the 5 percent level. A single asterix (*) indicates that the difference is statistically significant at the 1 percent level.

[14] The "other" PRWORA effects were measured in the model by adding a dummy variable for the month in which PRWORA was implemented in the state (and all months after that).

## PART VI

# The Structure of Welfare Reform

**Mary Ann E. Steger**
**Michael Reisch**
**Ursula Bischoff**

# Is Welfare Reform Working in Arizona and Oregon?

*Mary Ann E. Steger*[1]

I t is difficult to generalize about the success of welfare reform in Arizona and Oregon because many recipients face various combinations of issues related to their gender, race, class, and culture, and must deal with situations created by problems of physical and mental health, drug and alcohol abuse, and domestic violence. Yet, I believe that welfare reform is not working in these states if the measure of success is moving large numbers of welfare families out of real poverty; instead, welfare reform seems to be very successful in removing families from the caseload, with significant numbers of these families dropping out of sight or entering the ranks of the working poor (Parrott 1998; Welfare and Human Rights Monitoring Project 1998; DeParle 1999; Eisinger 1999; Wiseman 1999).

The way decision-making is structured in state welfare agencies and the manner in which programs are implemented help to explain whether a program has the potential to assist welfare families in taking some initial steps out of poverty. To demonstrate this argument, I compare agency decision-making structures and the operational definitions of self-sufficiency and work activities used in Arizona's and Oregon's welfare programs. Both programs are based on the Work First philosophy, but each state structures decision-making and program implementation in a unique way, so there are important comparisons to be made. My information comes from the transcripts of in-person interviews with welfare agency and service provider personnel, which I conducted during the years 1997 to 2000, and from numerous reports and documents that are relevant to these programs.

## Decision-Making in Oregon and Arizona

In Oregon, welfare services are provided by the Division of Adult and Family Services (AFS), a unit within the state's Department of Human Resources. AFS is responsible for administering Temporary Assistance for Needy Families (TANF), the Job Opportunities and Basic Skills (JOBS) program, and the Employment Related Day Care and TANF day care programs. AFS coordinates services related to welfare, including medical benefits, Food Stamps, and the provision of emergency and support services. When the *Family Support Act* was passed in 1988, AFS administrators were experienced in running a tightly structured program that required recipients to work, and they also had run a voluntary Welfare-to-Work program that stressed education and extensive training as a preparation for work. A new program was created through federal waivers in which welfare recipients were required to participate in the JOBS program, teen parents were required to stay in school, and those recipients with drug, alcohol, or mental health problems were expected to get treatment. The central AFS office developed an overall model of what they wanted the program to look like, and one administrator described what happened next:

> Then, the next big shift was made. And that was a shift that said we're going to move from being a central office-driven system to being a local office-driven system.... We're going to move from this being a program that is administered and operated by the welfare system, AFS, to one that is planned and operated and driven locally.

To accomplish this move to a decentralized system, the agency was reorganized, and about 50 percent of the management positions but no line staff positions were eliminated.

The new decentralized structure that was put into place and implemented in 1990 divided the state into fifteen districts that, in general, covered one or more counties. District and local operations managers were appointed, and prime contractors were selected in each district to coordinate the delivery of services. AFS offices handled case management services and support service dollars, but training, education, placement, and all other services came from community-based agencies that had this expertise. Besides encouraging a partnership relationship among AFS offices, prime contractors, and other community agencies, the district-based structure allowed local AFS personnel and their partners to decide how programs would be implemented in their geographic area. As one local AFS manager described:

> I feel as though I have a fair amount of autonomy. We certainly report to our district managers … and we all pretty much have the same opinions about operating the same way. But we … do have a budget that we need to work towards, some standard rules that we need to work with, and some expectations, but pretty much how we get there is up to us.

The reasoning that produced the reorganization was pragmatic. The central staff wanted to stop processing welfare recipients through the system and instead to focus on outcomes. The practice of the agency administration is to learn by doing, with planning being a supplement but not a precursor to implementation. The AFS staff that I interviewed seemed comfortable with this pragmatic approach and told me that changes continue to be made. In addition, communications within the agency appear open, with top administrators listening to what the field staff are saying about what is and is not working, and making changes when appropriate. One central office AFS staff member explained:

> [Our] role [is] to keep reflecting everything back to the community-driven model. I think that is really critical to our success. Because what works in Portland in one neighborhood may not even work in another Portland neighborhood. It certainly would not be the model we would put in place in a rural area.

Another change centers on how policy is treated by administrative staff and caseworkers. The focus has shifted from a narrow reading of agency policy (to insure that welfare recipients are in compliance) to what is referred to as "principle-based decision-making," which means that staff use common sense in making day-to-day benefit and service decisions. Because the agency goal is to achieve particular outcomes, staff are supported when they "bend" policies that do not produce these outcomes. Principle-based decision-making was described by one staff member in these words:

> You follow the policy as far as you can. If it doesn't make sense, then you need to find ways to bend the policy to get the outcomes we're looking for, and, if you need help, then go to your supervisor or call central office. We'll try and support you … [to] do the right thing.

There also was an active effort to eliminate policies. Formerly, agency policies were put in thick binders and distributed to all staff, one for each program and subprogram, with guides that gave examples of how the policies should be interpreted and how the computer technology should be used. To prevent staff from relying solely on these written manuals, some policies were eliminated and others were streamlined. Now, updated policies are distributed to branch offices, one copy per branch, and also are available online.

In the move to a welfare program that focused on measurable outcomes—that demonstrated how well the program was promoting the self-sufficiency goals of recipients—Oregon's welfare agency created a decentralized, partnership-based structure that promotes a culture of open, cooperative decision-making and a common sense approach to compliance. This culture, however, took time to develop. According to one staff member:

> It has been an evolving process.... I've been working for the state now for ten years. This is my fifth or sixth "new" JOBS, as they've introduced new aspects to it and they've developed some policy-based organization and case management for the organization.... I don't think that it was a big jump. There was a decision made at some point that we're going to move this giant human services state agency in this direction, and it slowly went along that way over that period of time, lurching and going along, but it has been a process.

In contrast, welfare reform in Arizona is centralized at the state level, and decision-making is structured hierarchically within three administrations located in two divisions of the Arizona Department of Economic Security (DES). The three administrations are: (1) the Family Assistance Administration, located in the Division of Benefits and Medical Eligibility, which is responsible for determining TANF and Food Stamp Program eligibility and TANF medical eligibility; (2) the Jobs Administration, located in the Division of Employment and Rehabilitative Services, which administers the Jobs Program; and (3) the Child Care Administration, also located in the Division of Employment and Rehabilitative Services, which administers the childcare programs for TANF recipients and other income-eligible families. Each of these units is structured as a vertical hierarchy with its own state, regional, and district administrators.

Within each of the three administrations—Family Assistance, Jobs, and Child Care—a management team approach is used to facilitate decision-making, and the teams include state-level program administrators, section managers, and local-level district managers. Issue papers are written and policy options are presented in management team sessions so that various options can be discussed and consensus reached on the best policy changes to make. Although input on decisions is solicited from local-level program managers and field staff, the management teams operate within their separate administrations, and program implementation at the local level appears fragmented. Policy is coordinated at the highest administrative level, but it is unlikely that caseworkers at the local level are aware of this coordination. Caseworkers only feel comfortable talking about the rules and practices that are relevant to the specific work of their administration.

In Arizona, welfare reform was initiated in November 1995 with the EMPOWER program (Employing and Moving People Off Welfare and Encouraging Responsibility), which fed into the new federal TANF program in August 1997. In fall 1997 and spring 1998 when I conducted my initial interviews with DES personnel, administrations primarily responsible for implementing TANF were still working on operating policies. One state-level staff person described the need to coordinate programs within one of these units, the Family Assistance Administration:

> The one thing that continues to be an absolute nightmare, though, is … the differences between the programs that are really kind of a package. To me, cash assistance, Food Stamps, and medical, they're a package… But yet their eligibility and how they correlate to each other, up until now, was practically nonexistent. At least with welfare reform there is some recognition that there needs to be a crossover.… It's still very difficult to align, simplify things for the clients' benefit. It takes time to re-program.

The staff member was referring to the difficulty in coordinating areas within one administration; yet, the problem of coordination across administrations that exist in separate divisions within DES is still an issue, especially at the local level.

In Arizona, coordination at the local level is complicated further by the maintenance of separate computerized data systems in the three administrations. For example, the Family Assistance and Jobs administrations share the computerized information entered for families receiving benefits, but staff in one administration cannot change the computerized files maintained by the other, so there is the possibility of time lags in updating recipients' files. Since decisions about whether recipients have reached their time limit or whether they must be sanctioned are based on the computerized information, these time lags lead to errors in the notices sent to families, which often cut or eliminate benefits.

Due to its size and hierarchically organized and fragmented structure, DES could be characterized, during the time of the study, as a centralized model of decision-making where the main emphasis was on creating the policies necessary to implement the changes brought about by welfare reform and ensuring that program rules were followed. The department has received considerable criticism from state legislators who say it is inefficient in implementing welfare reform.[2] I believe this is related to the difficulty any large bureaucracy would have in streamlining its operations. The criticism also is the result of the almost-libertarian beliefs of legislators who feel that privatization is the only way to bring about efficiency. For several years, the legislature wanted to turn welfare implementation over to a for-profit firm, and federal waivers were sought to privatize eligibility determinations for the Food Stamp and Medicaid programs as well. The waivers were not granted, but in April of 1999, the for-profit firm Maximus began administering the TANF program in one of the four welfare districts in Maricopa County, which includes areas in the cities of Phoenix, Tempe, and Mesa. A bill to hand over the entire state's welfare program to private contractors was defeated by the Senate in April 1999 (Davenport and Kelley 1999). One DES administrator expressed mixed feelings about the move to privatize welfare:

> DES believes in [privatization] where they've studied it,
> and it's the right thing to do. So, it's not that we're afraid
> of it. The other thing is … that when it comes to eking out
> a profit, which is what private companies do … with the
> programs that involve the most vulnerable of all people…,
> I can't handle it…. I believe there is a lot to learn from the
> private sector, and I certainly believe that we've got to do
> things better, but I think that when it comes to these
> kinds of programs there has to be a conscience. And that
> conscience I believe is … the government.

The strong feeling in Arizona that the private sector is more efficient than the public sector threatens the jobs of DES field staff at the local level. The situation is complicated by the fact that some local staff are not earning much more than welfare recipients are receiving in cash assistance and medical and childcare benefits. These DES workers may be categorized as the "working poor," or in danger of becoming the working poor. In Oregon, by contrast, local case workers have considerable discretion in making decisions on the package of services welfare recipients receive, and the emphasis is on producing favorable outcomes for recipients. Meanwhile, local staff in Arizona are under pressure to implement welfare reform efficiently by closely adhering to the rules in an atmosphere where both the staff and the clientele are under extreme scrutiny by those who have the power to significantly affect their circumstances.

The differences described above are summarized in Table 20.1, which compares the decision-making structures of Arizona's Department of Economic Security and Oregon's Division of Adult and Family Services under the following four characteristics: location of power; organization of the decision-making process; relationships with community-based organizations; and the extent to which case workers have decision-making discretion.

## Table 20.1
### Comparison of Decision-Making in Welfare Agencies of Arizona and Oregon

| CHARACTERISTIC | ARIZONA | OREGON |
|---|---|---|
| Location of power | Centralized at the state level within three administrations located in two divisions of the DES | State-level control of budget and policy in AFS; district-level control over implementation |
| Organization of decision-making | Fragmented within DES: three units organized as vertical hierarchies | Coordinated by AFS: local level decision-making shared with community partners |
| Relationships with community-based organizations | Limited to contracts for services— a contractual relationship | Involves contracts for services and input into program implementation— a partnership relationship |
| Extent to which case workers have decision-making discretion | Minimal discretion: must adhere to program rules and practices | Considerable discretion: principle-based decision-making |
| Conclusions about the culture of the welfare agency | A culture of limited and isolated decision-making in which rule enforcement is the major priority | A culture of open, cooperative decision-making and a common sense, outcome-driven approach to compliance |

My interpretation is that the decision-making power structure in Arizona reflects an organizational culture of limited and isolated decision-making, in which rule enforcement is the major priority. In contrast, the decision-making power structure in Oregon reinforces a culture of open, cooperative decision-making and a common-sense, outcome-driven approach to compliance. Welfare recipients in Arizona, therefore, are expected to follow program rules and practices closely or suffer sanctions, which lead to reductions in and possibly the elimination of the cash assistance grant. Moreover, recipients are subject to program rules and practices as local staff in separate administrations interpret them. This reinforces the coercive nature of welfare reform in Arizona.

In Oregon, where the emphasis is on outcomes, and caseworkers have some degree of decision-making flexibility, welfare recipients are more likely to get support for the individual problems they face as mothers who are poor, especially when case workers view these problems as barriers to recipients' self-sufficiency.

### Comparing Definitions of "Self-Sufficiency" and "Work Activities"

In addition to differences in decision-making structures, welfare agencies in Arizona and Oregon use different operational definitions of *self-sufficiency*—the overall goal of welfare reform—and the *work activities* that recipients are required to perform in order to qualify for benefits. These definitions affect the manner in which programs are implemented and, because of this, have an impact on each program's ability to assist poor families in their attempts to fight poverty. In addition, the differences in definitions exist, even though both states follow the Work First philosophy of welfare reform. Under the Work First philosophy, the focus is on creating a work-oriented, transitional assistance program that encourages recipients to find unsubsidized employment as quickly as possible. In both programs, work is viewed as the best means to attain the goal of self-sufficiency, and welfare recipients are required to participate in one or more specified work activities to continue to receive benefits.

Program administrators in Arizona define *self-sufficiency* as economic independence, which in practice means that the person has a job at an income level higher than the TANF cash assistance payment and is no longer eligible for cash assistance. The person is "off" welfare and not considered "dependent" on cash assistance. Those with jobs qualify for transitional medical benefits and childcare assistance until time or income limits are exceeded. Following the Work First philosophy that promotes unsubsidized employment as soon as possible, cash assistance recipients face a time limit of two years, unless they are temporarily deferred. Defining *self-sufficiency* in this way affects the length of time and the extent to which DES staff can work with welfare recipients. Under the current DES administration, this restricted definition is being re-thought, especially for recipients who face multiple barriers to employment. One top state-level administrator explained the conceptual change he thought was needed when working with recipients who are not able to succeed in a Work First environment:

> There's a whole other group of people who ... need a
> combination of post-secondary training or education
> longer than we have allowed them to have before, and we

need to start measuring family stability in terms of self-sufficiency as a measure that's beyond just not being on TANF anymore.... We might just strike a balance between quick short-term measures and ... helping families get to a point where they can improve their well-being and reach their potential.

In comparison, Oregon's definition of the goal of self-sufficiency is escaping poverty, which is a more ambitious goal than that found in Arizona. Work is the escape route, and the objective is to get welfare-reliant mothers into jobs that pay well and offer benefits so that families can get along without cash assistance and medical and childcare benefits. Staff realize that this may not happen with the first job, and AFS offers services that allow staff to continue working with families after they get that first job. This definition of self-sufficiency is summarized in the words of one agency staff person in Oregon:

We know that when we first started and we were moving clients from welfare to work, we were just starting them on that continuum. That actually, then, they needed to get that next job and a raise and a better job and a career, and at that point they would be leaving the programs and that would be self-sufficiency.

Oregon's definition of self-sufficiency requires an investment of state dollars to supplement the federal block grant money. An array of support services are offered in addition to cash assistance, medical coverage, and childcare assistance, and program administrators are convinced that they are using the money saved from caseload reductions and legislative appropriations wisely because their program is considered an "investment in the self-sufficiency of clients." A time limit exists, but it is enforced only when recipients fail to participate in any of the barrier-removing or work-related activities that are included on the list of work activities.

In summary, I believe that Arizona's program uses the rhetoric of self-sufficiency but, in the past, has not supported this rhetoric with actions that promote some degree of economic independence for people making the transition from welfare to work. This is changing, and DES issued contracts for a number of programs providing a range of services for welfare recipients, including a $9 million Employment Transition Program that provides support and intervention services for TANF families. At this time, it is too soon to know if these programs will be successful in promoting some measure of economic independence for recipients.

Oregon's program, on the other hand, does define *self-sufficiency* as escaping poverty, and an array of retention and support services are in place to assist recipients to take steps to find jobs with decent wages.

It should be noted, however, that neither state has significantly improved the lives of poor families through welfare reform, even though caseloads have dropped.

Another difference in the implementation of the Work First philosophy within the two states involves the way required *work activities* are defined. This difference has implications for the long-term success of recipients in their fight against poverty. In Arizona, welfare recipients are required to participate in a list of activities that include job readiness classes and job searches; unsubsidized work; subsidized work in a JOBSTART program; unpaid work experience; unpaid community service work; vocational training for up to one year; and for teen parents, high school or GED training, remedial education, and ESL programs. Although some welfare recipients are exempt from the requirements, and there is a community service category for mothers who are not employable, the emphasis is on spending the federal block grant money to move most recipients into work without providing them with the job-skills training needed for entry into well-paying jobs or supporting them while they pursue the post-secondary education that is required for professional-level jobs. As is the case with other states, Arizona follows the definition of *work activities* found in the federal legislation.

Requiring a set of work activities focused solely on getting most welfare recipients into the labor market as soon as possible is, at best, a short-term strategy. The strategy appears successful because the caseload has dropped significantly, but the record shows that not all reductions in the caseload are due to employment. DES administrative data, as reported in an exit study of the 10,647 cash assistance cases closed from January 1998 through March, lists the following reasons for case closures: failure to comply with procedures (37 percent); sanctioned (20 percent); employment (19 percent); increased nonemployment income (9 percent); voluntary withdrawal (7 percent); changes in circumstances (5 percent); and loss of contact (3 percent) (Westra and Routley 2000).

In contrast, Oregon's definition of *work activity* is quite broad and includes a range of activities that serve to address barriers to employment, including counseling or treatment for domestic violence, mental health problems, drug and alcohol abuse, teen and adult parenting training, life skills training, crisis intervention, self-initiated training, as well as working on situations such as child support collection, medical emergencies, school retention (for children), and Supplemental Security Income (SSI) applications or issues. Spending time on one or more of these barrier-removing activities fulfills the work requirement in the same way that participation in job searches, on-the-job training, voluntary work experience, sheltered/supported work (for those not able to hold a regular job), and subsidized or unsubsidized work fulfills the requirement.

As was the case in Arizona, Oregon's program provides neither extensive jobs-skills training nor adequate support for women who want to pursue post-secondary education, but Oregon's work participation requirements include barrier-removing activities that are considered crucial to the eventual success of participants in attaining the goal of self-sufficiency. The broad definition of work requirements indicates that addressing the problems that may be present in the life situation of the welfare mother is considered an integral part of the state's responsibility.

## Is Welfare Reform Working?

Welfare reform in Oregon is working to a greater degree than in Arizona because the measure of success is helping recipients take steps to overcome both the poverty associated with welfare *and* the poverty associated with low-wage work. In Oregon, the definitions given to *self-sufficiency* and *work activities* can potentially help poor mothers take initial steps out of poverty, and the district- and principle-based decision-making structure created by AFS facilitates this process.

Until quite recently, the definition of self-sufficiency used in Arizona's program was very narrow, and the same criticism can be applied to the list of Arizona's work activities. The definition of *self-sufficiency* appears to be changing, at least among the state's top administrators, and programs have been created to address some of the barriers that welfare families face as they attempt to fight poverty. But the hierarchical structure of decision-making within DES and the continued emphasis on rule enforcement hamper administrators' efforts to address poverty issues and reduce the program's capacity to assist recipients.

## References

Davenport, Paul, and Matt Kelley. 1999. "Senate Rejects Welfare Privatization Plan." *The Arizona Daily Sun* (April 28): 4.

DeParle, Jason. 1999. "Bold Effort Leaves Much Unchanged for the Poor." *New York Times* (December 30): A1.

Eisinger, Peter. 1999. "Food Pantries and Welfare Reform: Estimating the Effect." *Focus* 20 (Fall): 23-28.

Fischer, Howard. 1999. "Senate Kills DES Disband Plan." *The Arizona Daily Sun* (April 21): 1.

Parrott, Sharon. 1998. Welfare Recipients Who Find Jobs: What Do We Know about their Employment and Earnings? Online report: http://www.cbpp.org/11-16-98wel.htm. Center on Budget and Policy Priorities.

Welfare and Human Rights Monitoring Project. 1998. *Is It Reform: The 1998 Report of the Welfare and Human Rights Monitoring Project*. Cambridge, MA: Unitarian Universalist Service Committee.

Westra, Karen L., and John Routley. 1999. *Cash Assistance Exit Study, First Quarter 1998 Cohort, Interim Report.* Arizona Department of Economic Security, Office of Research and Evaluation.

Wiseman, Michael. 1999. "In the Midst of Reform: Wisconsin in 1997." *Focus* 20 (Fall): 15-22.

## Notes

[1] Mary Ann E. Steger is a professor of political science at Northern Arizona University. Her most recent publication is her contribution to the multi-authored book, *Political Culture and Public Policy in Canada and the United States: Only a Border Apart?* (John C. Pierce et al., Edwin Mellen Press, 2000), and her current work focuses on welfare reform. In Summer 2001, she worked with John Stuart Hall to complete a report on Medicaid expansion in Arizona, which was prepared for the Nelson A. Rockefeller Institute of Government as part of a twenty-one state study. She is now working as a field researcher in Arizona for the Rockefeller Institute's follow-up study of the TANF program.

[2] In both 1998 and 1999, bills were introduced into the Arizona Legislature that would abolish the Arizona Department of Economic Security, the state's welfare agency. The argument was that the agency had "grown too large to be useful" (Fischer 1999). These bills had support but were ultimately defeated.

# Welfare Reform Strategies and Community-based Organizations

## The Impact on Family Wellbeing in an Urban Neighborhood

*Michael Reisch*[1] *and Ursula Bischoff*[2]

The Personal Responsibility and Work Opportunity Reconciliation Act of 1996 significantly expanded the private sector's role in policy implementation. It made the supportive services provided by non-profit community-based organizations (CBOs), critical to the successful transition of welfare recipients into the labor force and the economic survival of low-income families, particularly in urban neighborhoods (Bloom 1997). Yet, to date, there has been little current research assessing how strategies of welfare reform implementation have affected these CBOs (Johnson 1998; Besharov et al. 1997; Hassett and Austin 1997).

This chapter reports on a study of the effects of welfare reform on CBOs' ability to respond to client and community needs in an urban neighborhood with a high incidence of poverty. Through in-depth interviews, surveys, and focus groups, executive directors assessed the impact of policy changes on client populations, agency staff, program objectives and outcomes, inter-organizational relationships, and their preparedness for the implementation of time limits on the receipt of cash assistance. The findings indicate substantial changes in client populations, program goals, and inter-organizational relationships.

### Review of the Literature

Few studies have examined nonprofits' role in implementing welfare reform or the impact of this policy change on the organizations themselves

(Briggs 1999; Raffel 1998; Perlmutter 1997; Riccio and Orenstein 1996). Yet, research on community wellbeing has established the relationship between poverty and organizational infrastructure at the neighborhood level (Figueira-McDonough 1995; Etzioni 1996; Fellin and Litwak 1968; Warren 1983). One recent study in Cuyahoga County, Ohio, examined how the survival strategies adopted by nonprofits in response to welfare reform have affected their role in maintaining civil society (Alexander et al. 1999). In a related article, Alexander (1999, 68) reported that, as a consequence of devolution, "nonprofits were under pressure to alter their traditional character."

Other research has revealed how changes in nonprofits' external environment, particularly those elements that determine access to resources and critical information, produce new patterns of intra-organizational behavior and inter-organizational relationships, including alternative resource development strategies and the creation or expansion of collaboratives and networks (Reitan 1998; Roberts-DeGenarro 1997). Little work has been done, however, on the nature of emerging collaborative activities among public and nonprofit providers at the community level (Johnson 1998; Hassett and Austin 1997).

### Welfare Reform in Pennsylvania

Pennsylvania is a typical state in terms of its welfare population and its PRWORA implementation plan (PCCY 1998; Commonwealth of Pennsylvania 1997). Pennsylvania adopted a "middle of the road" Work First plan with no extraordinary provisions or sanctions. The plan did not provide for job creation or guarantee childcare assistance. It made it more difficult for women to obtain education or training, failed to cover them by existing workplace laws, and imposed family sanctions after twenty-four months for failure to comply with mandatory work requirements (Commonwealth of Pennsylvania 1997).

The City of Philadelphia's Welfare-to-Work plan also emphasized job creation by the private and nonprofit sectors. It included, however, both pre- and post-placement services to provide job skills, basic literacy training, and a broad range of social supports. It authorized modest investments in childcare, improvements in public transportation, established temporary wage subsidies, and created special programs for teen parents (City of Philadelphia 1998). The plan's authors nevertheless acknowledged that, at best, it might locate employment for only 40 percent of the families who needed to find work.[3]

The city's plan relied heavily on private, nonprofit CBOs to deliver support services in a timely and cost-efficient manner. It assumed, and even required, enhanced cooperation and coordination among public and private organizations. The ability of such organizations to fulfill such expectations, however, was complicated by dramatic changes in the TANF population.

By August 1998, when this study began, Pennsylvania's welfare rolls had decreased by nearly one-third, with far more dramatic declines among white women (54 percent) than women of color (~30 percent). Consequently, nearly 80 percent of TANF recipients in Philadelphia and throughout the state were people of color. For the first time, African Americans made up the largest portion of the state's welfare population. Nearly 80 percent of these households had received public assistance for at least two years; half had received assistance for five years or more. Many TANF recipients required extensive job training and education, and had childcare, health care, and transportation needs that exceeded those of average families (East 1999). In sum, welfare reform in Pennsylvania made facts out of long-held stereotypes. The state's Work First strategy, therefore, placed a growing burden on community-based, nonprofit organizations to provide new and improved social services to TANF families.

## Research Focus and Methodology

Our study assessed the extent to which the PRWORA affected the ability of nonprofit agencies to respond effectively to the emerging needs of families receiving TANF and the changing demands of funding sources. Utilizing an action research model, we attempted to promote the empowerment of CBOs by engaging them in identifying the issues to be investigated and their needs for organizational development. The study drew participants from a stratified sample of sixty-four agencies in West Philadelphia that provided a wide range of social services to TANF recipients, including childcare, employment and training, job placement, mental health, and shelter and nutrition. The agencies selected met three principle criteria: (1) they had to be in existence for at least three years; (2) they had to be independent organizations with legal nonprofit (501c(3)) status; and (3) they had to serve primarily the West Philadelphia community.

Forty-two agencies participated fully in the initial one-to-two hour semi-structured interviews, surveys, and focus groups, which took place between August and December 1998; thirty-two participated in the follow-up survey in May and June 1999. The survey instruments focused primarily on changes in agency structure and staffing, client populations, agency programs, funding patterns, and inter-organizational relationships. The surveys also attempted to assess participants' level of preparedness for the March 3, 1999 "cutoff" date, when TANF recipients who had not satisfied the legislation's work requirements would be sanctioned.

The study focused on the following questions:

1.  Had there been changes in the CBOs' missions, their organizational structures and administrative processes, their use of community volunteers, or their staffing patterns as a consequence of welfare reform?

2. Were CBOs finding it necessary to expand or revise services as a consequence of shifting government program emphases?

3. Were CBOs able to locate other resources as substitutes or supplements for government revenues?

4. What changes, if any, had occurred in the nature and size of the agencies' client populations or in client outcomes?

5. What was the impact of devolution and welfare reform on the level of competition and cooperation among CBOs in the community?

6. In what ways had CBOs engaged in collaborative efforts to influence the process of devolution and the state's welfare reform policies and practices?

7. To what extent had CBOs engaged stakeholders such as board members, service recipients, volunteers, community residents, and business leaders in program planning and advocacy efforts?

### Findings

**Impact on Clients**

Ninety-three percent of the agencies[4] reported changes in their client populations as a result of welfare reform. These changes can be broken down into four categories: (1) overall demand for services; (2) client demographics; (3) the nature of clients' needs; and (4) the source of client referrals. Nearly half (48 percent) of the sample reported an increase in the number of clients they served or in the demand for a specific type of service, such as job training, placement, transportation assistance, childcare, and parenting classes. They described substantial increases in the number of younger clients, immigrants, Latinos, males, grandparent caretakers, and parents working fulltime. These overall increases were accompanied by a rise in the number of clients who possessed fewer life skills and lower levels of education.

About one quarter of the agencies also reported an increase in the number of individuals and families with multiple problems and service needs. These clients needed a range of concrete services, such as GED instruction and job placement. Some CBOs expressed a growing need to access subsistence assistance in such areas as food, housing, and utilities. In the follow-up survey, nearly 75 percent of the agencies indicated that the effects of welfare reform had a significant effect on the composition of the clients they served.

### Impact on Services

Nearly 80 percent of the executive directors stated that their program goals and activities had changed during the previous two years; 69.1 percent reported that welfare reform had affected these changes. A similar percentage remarked that the structure of their agency's programs had changed; 42.8 percent attributed these changes to welfare reform. Changes included adding or enhancing programs, particularly regarding the number of hours and range of services the agencies provided. By contrast, more than one quarter of the agencies (27 percent) had reduced or terminated programs because of fiscal pressures and shifting contractual demands.

Virtually all the agencies indicated increased program activity in case and class advocacy, provision of subsistence services, and education regarding eligibility requirements imposed by the new law. They also reported a need to reconfigure existing services through combining concrete and support services.

In the follow-up survey, approximately 59 percent of the executive directors stated that welfare reform had affected changes in their organizations' values and mission. And 83.9 percent reported that welfare reform had affected their program goals considerably or to a great extent. Nearly two-thirds of the agencies stated that welfare changes had significantly affected the specific programs they offered. This indicates that the response of agencies tended to be pragmatic, rather than ideological.

### Program Objectives and Outcomes

Welfare reform produced a clear shift in agency outcome objectives. Nearly 60 percent of the executive directors reported changing program outcome objectives; 43 percent reported an increase in work-related objectives; 38.1 percent indicated that these changes were a consequence of welfare reform. Respondents frequently described a greater programmatic focus on client self-sufficiency and de-emphasis of supportive services. Many spoke about the role that expectations communicated by funding sources, both public and private, played in shaping organizational outcome objectives.

The combined impact of changes in client populations and changes in outcome expectations produced troubling results for a sizable proportion of the CBOs. Two thirds of the organizations stated that their program outcomes had changed; nearly half (47.6 percent) remarked that welfare reform had affected these outcomes. One third of the sample reported increased difficulties in working with clients. They cited such recurring concerns as miscommunication between workers and clients, the presence of more "problem" clients, greater client attrition, and the presence of more clients with complex service needs (e.g., clients with dual diagnoses or families who needed a range of concrete services). An equal number referred to the difficulties caused by growing bias against their clients and the pressures generated by the PRWORA to help clients find employment.

**Staff Changes**

Shifts in the nature of client populations and in the focus of program outcomes also affected agency staff. Nearly 55 percent of the CBOs reported staff changes. Initially, 28.3 percent of the agencies attributed these changes directly or indirectly to welfare reform. In the follow-up survey, the number of respondents who reported that welfare reform had an impact on staffing patterns increased to 48.4 percent.

More than 80 percent of the organizations reported changes in the nature of staff activities, including increased hours, more tasks per worker, revision of assignments, and overall expansion in workload. Nearly three quarters of these respondents attributed the changes directly or indirectly to welfare reform. In the follow-up survey, 64.5 percent of the respondents continued to feel that welfare reform had an important effect on changes in staff activities and responsibilities.

More than 75 percent of the agencies commented that staff experienced increased difficulty in working with families due to a combination of resource deficiencies and environmentally generated stress. For female clients, the impact of economic conditions, such as the lack of employment opportunities and inadequate income, was the most prevalent stress factor. For workers, stress factors included larger caseloads, shifting client demand, staff attrition, changes in job responsibilities (e.g., a greater focus on measurable outcomes), and changes in performance evaluations related to requirements imposed by funding sources and the presence of more families with multiple needs. These factors created lower morale among staff and higher rates of staff turnover.

**Leadership and Communications**

Less than 20 percent of the sample reported leadership changes as a consequence of welfare reform. There were minimal signs of internal dissension despite the obvious strains on staff that welfare reform had produced. In fact, more than 85 percent of the agencies indicated that clients were involved at least "to some extent" in designing programs. Half of these agencies stated that the extent of client involvement had increased in the previous two years. One-third attributed this change to welfare reform.

More than 45 percent of the agencies reported increased communication among workers, clients, and community groups for the purposes of distributing information about the new welfare law, planning new programs, discussing the terms and implications of service contracts, collecting data, and meeting legal requirements. In some agencies, problems like staff morale and high turnover stimulated more discussion, increased board training, and greater attention to funding concerns. Nearly one third of the respondents referred to welfare reform as a precipitant of these changes.

## Resources

More than 45 percent of the organizations reported fluctuations in the size of their budgets during the two years preceding the interviews. Approximately one-fourth of the total sample and more than half of those reporting changes attributed their greater fiscal instability to the onset of welfare reform. This finding was virtually identical in the follow-up survey. Respondents cited such problems as nonpayment of contracts by government departments, fluctuations in funding from both public and private sources, and performance contracting as sources of fiscal instability and uncertainty.

Nearly two-thirds of the agencies indicated the sources of their budget had changed; 19 percent of the total sample, and about one-third of those reporting changes in budget sources, considered these changes a byproduct of welfare reform. In the follow-up survey, the number of respondents who indicated that welfare reform was an important factor in managing change in the source of their agencies' budgets increased to 51.7 percent. Respondents also described an increased reliance on private grants or other targeted funds.

## Inter-Organizational Relationships

Nearly half the executive directors indicated that inter-organizational collaboration had significantly increased since 1995. They described this change as the result of both policy requirements and pragmatic considerations, particularly the need to share scarce resources. The primary types of collaborative activity affected by welfare reform included joint service programs with other community-based organizations or church groups; cooperation around program support, service verification or referrals; information sharing; training; and advocacy.

The follow-up survey, in which nearly two-thirds of the respondents reported changes in the nature of their inter-organizational relationships, confirmed these findings. More than 25 percent of the sample commented that factors influencing their decisions to collaborate with other organizations had changed during the previous six months. The most frequently cited changes concerned the issues around which collaborative activities would be constructed in the future and in the projected outcomes of collaborative efforts.

In the initial interviews, two-thirds of the executive directors commented that competition among service providers for funds and/or clients had increased. Others remarked that welfare reform had prompted changes in their service focus and strategy towards more interdisciplinary, family-centered programs. They indicated that these changes necessitated greater cooperation with other organizations.

More than 25 percent of the respondents to the follow-up survey reported some or considerable change in competition for clients, and nearly 42 percent reported increased competition for resources. Approximately 75 percent of the respondents agreed with the statement "Welfare reform presents opportunities for my organization to work with other organizations to advance a shared vision or service mission." Less than 10 percent disagreed. Only 25.8 percent of the follow-up respondents agreed with the statement "Welfare reform increases conflict and competition between my organization and other organizations." About 55 percent disagreed.

During the initial interviews, more than 60 percent of the executive directors reported changes in their relationship with the Department of Public Welfare due to changes in welfare policy. Increased contacts were required to obtain technical assistance and information and to advocate for clients. While a few respondents noted improved relationships with the department, more than four times as many described the adversarial tone of their interactions with caseworkers, difficulty in reaching department staff, and poor patterns of communication.

### Need for Technical Assistance

Information about the CBOs' technical assistance needs was obtained from the interviews and three focus groups conducted between August and November 1998. Most agencies lacked long-term staff development strategies and sufficient resources to support their staff training needs. Agencies reported a need to spend additional resources on marketing their public image and publicizing existing programs and events.

The interviews revealed several persistent organizational deficits that detracted from agencies' ability to address ongoing community problems. These included an absence of adequate board recruitment and development programs, particularly to provide support for fundraising efforts, and a need for training in management and supervision, because many staff in supervisory or management positions had virtually no educational backgrounds in these areas. Executives also cited their need for additional training in financial management and planning and in the legal aspects of personnel policies. These stemmed largely from the increasing complexity of administrative practice resulting from welfare devolution and its consequences.

Respondents also expressed concern about the need to improve systems of information sharing and communication within the community and among service providers. They referred to a need to establish "true partnerships" between community agencies and the Department of Public Welfare and among community agencies themselves. One of the surprising findings of this research, particularly evident in the focus groups, was the degree to which service providers were unaware of other nonprofit agencies in the community that provided similar or complementary services, even those that were geographically proximate.

## Waiting for March 3, 1999

One of the most striking findings of the study was the agencies' lack of preparation for the consequences of the March 3, 1999, cutoff date. Eighty-one percent had allocated no additional funds for programs designed to respond to the effects of cutoffs. More than 90 percent had not provided any training to staff about welfare reform. As late as November 1998, a comparable number had no plans to hire additional staff for Welfare-to-Work programs. Nearly 80 percent had taken no action to examine how welfare reform had or would affect the structure of their agencies.

### Implications

These findings offer initial insights into the implications of welfare policy change for community-based nonprofit agencies charged with developing and delivering support services in urban neighborhoods. Like the work of Alexander (1999), this research found substantial changes in the client populations agencies served; the goals, objectives, and outcomes of agency programs; staffing patterns; resource acquisition and allocation strategies; and the pattern of inter-organizational relationships. Organizations tended to respond pragmatically, rather than ideologically, to this dramatic shift in public policy. While agencies remained true to their original missions and increased their advocacy efforts, they frequently did so by implementing additional and/or different operating procedures in order to satisfy their survival needs.

The data also demonstrated how little most agencies had prepared for the enforcement of statutory time limits in March 1999. They indicate a need to enhance the CBOs' capacity to achieve program objectives through expanded collaborative service arrangements. The results of the follow-up survey hinted that some nonprofits had begun to move in this direction.

The data also underscored the need for local governments to involve nonprofits more actively in the development of Welfare-to-Work implementation strategies, provide more timely and more coherent information about changes in policy regulations, and to commit to more stable, longer-term funding agreements. At the time of the follow-up survey, there was no indication of any progress in this area.

### Conclusion

These findings indicate a need for enhanced organizational capacity to link TANF recipients to meaningful job training, childcare, and subsistence resources through collaborative service arrangements. Local governments should be more proactive in engaging CBOs in Welfare-to-Work implementation strategies by interpreting plans, regulations, and outcome expectations to CBOs in a timely manner. CBOs, which have become important factors in neighborhood stabilization, require long-term, stable funding commitments and substantial technical assistance if they are to develop culturally competent, effective services that correspond with changing parental roles affected by TANF. Citing conditions of heightened economic uncertainty and shifting client need, nonprofit administrators expressed growing interest in community economic development, strategic and cooperative program planning, and advocacy. They were aware that welfare reform is not occurring in a political or ideological vacuum. Other policy trends such as managed care, devolution, and privatization will shape its development as will the persistence of stereotypes about low-income people and communities.

Despite some sobering findings, there were glimmers of hope. Most agencies reported general stability of leadership during times of policy transition and environmental change. Indicators of positive change included increased client and community involvement in shaping programs and increased communication among workers, clients, and community groups. For some agencies, problems such as staff morale and high turnover stimulated more discussion, training, and greater attention to funding concerns. Welfare reform and its consequences, nevertheless, pose particular challenges for employee retention, job satisfaction, and career development for community-based nonprofit organizations.

In the next decade, the concentration of poverty in inner city neighborhoods is likely to increase (Meyer and Cancian 1998; Abramovitz 2000). Symptoms of economic and social desperation—child abuse, domestic violence, drug and alcohol abuse, for example—will continue to increase (Brandwein 1999; East 1999; Jayakody 1998; Woolis 1998; Murphy 1997). Without well-planned programs of local economic and social development, welfare reform will exacerbate the effects of existing economic realities (Wilson 1997).

History demonstrates that welfare reform will produce a variety of unplanned consequences for communities and organizations. Some consequences may be positive, such as a reconfiguration of public transportation, a process that is beginning to take place in metropolitan areas like Philadelphia, but cannot occur in areas that lack an adequate mass transit infrastructure. Other effects, such as the emergence of new service "industries" that respond to the secondary problems arising from welfare reform—similar to what emerged in response to the growth of homelessness in the 1980s—may be a mixed blessing. There are indications that turning to for-profit organizations to provide TANF-related services exacerbates the plight of TANF recipients who require such services to achieve economic self-sufficiency (Coniff 1997).

At the community level, there is a clear need for greater coordination of services and increased involvement of nontraditional agencies (e.g., churches, feminist organizations, block associations, and cultural groups) in the design and delivery of services (Cnaan, Wineburg, and Boddie 1999; Nichols 1998; Reisch and Jarman-Rohde 1998). There is also a need to initiate more extensive dialogues about the relative distribution of responsibilities among public, nonprofit, and for-profit providers (East 1999; Withorn 1998). Both changes are needed to respond effectively to the monitoring role of government, which is likely to expand, while preserving agencies' missions, program goals, and service integrity. In addition, as clients become increasingly desperate and involuntary in nature, nonprofit organizations, particularly those in low-income neighborhoods, will need to rethink philosophies and program structures that largely assume a voluntary clientele.

Competition for scarce resources among and within nonprofit agencies is likely to increase as for-profit protective services, job training, childcare, and mental health services expand. Under such circumstances, nonprofits will tend to emulate the practices of their for-profit competitors. This includes "lumping together" all TANF families in a "one size fits all" approach to service provision (Nichols 1998; Pavetti 1997). Current policy regulations increase this likelihood, as they contain few provisions that recognize the complexity of working with TANF recipients to achieve economic self-sufficiency.

Ironically, unanticipated fiscal windfalls to the states have complicated the efforts of community-based nonprofit agencies to make welfare reform less punitive for their clients (DeParle 1999). These organizations can play a major role in determining how "successful" welfare reform is defined and whether the voices of community residents will be heard and heeded as dramatic policy changes are implemented (Abramovitz 2000; Fearer 1996). Nonprofit CBOs can influence this highly politicized process, but, as this study demonstrates, only if they make significant intra- and inter-organizational adaptations to the shifting policy environment.

## References

Abramovitz, M. 2000. *Under Attack and Fighting Back: Women and Welfare in the United States.* 2nd Edition. New York: Monthly Review Press.

Alexander, J. 1999. "The Impact of Devolution on Nonprofits: A Multiphase Study of Social Service Organizations." *Nonprofit Management and Leadership* 10 (1): 57–70.

Alexander, J., R. Nank, and C. Stivers. 1999. "Implications of Welfare Reform: Do Nonprofit Survival Strategies Threaten Civil Society?" *Nonprofit and Voluntary Sector Quarterly* 26 (4): 452–475.

Besharov, D.J., P. Germanis, and P.H. Rossi. 1997. *Evaluating Welfare Reform: A Guide for Scholars and Practitioners.* College Park, MD: University of Maryland.

Bloom, D. 1997. *After AFDC: Welfare-to-Work Choices and Challenges for States.* New York: Manpower Demonstration Research Corporation.

Brandwein, R.A., ed. 1999. *Battered Women, Children, and Welfare Reform: The Ties that Bind.* Newbury Park, CA: Sage Publications.

Briggs, R. 1999. "Civic, Church Leaders Map Plans for Welfare Changes." *The Philadelphia Inquirer* (February 8): B1–2.

City of Philadelphia. 1998. *Greater Philadelphia Works – Proposed Plan: Moving from Welfare to Work.*

Cnaan, R., R. Wineburg, and S. Boddie. 1999. *The Newer Deal: Social Work and Religion in Partnership.* New York: Columbia University Press.

Commonwealth of Pennsylvania, Department of Public Welfare. 1997. *Temporary Assistance for Needy Families: State Plan.* Harrisburg, PA: Department of Public Welfare.

Conniff, R. 1997. "Welfare Profiteers." *The Progressive* 61 (May): 32–34.

DeParle, J. 1999. "States Struggle to Use Windfall Born of Shifts in Welfare Law." *New York Times* (August 28): A1–20.

East, J.F. 1999. "Hidden Barriers to Success for Women in Welfare Reform." *Families in Society* 80 (3): 295–304.

Etzioni, A. 1996. "The Responsive Community: A Communitarian Perspective." *American Sociological Review* 61 (1): 1–11.

Fearer, M. 1996. "Welfare Moms Organize." *The Progressive* 60 (February): 18.

Fellin, P., and E. Litwak. 1968. "The Neighborhood in Urban American Society." *Social Work* 13 (3).

Figueira-McDonough, J. 1995. "Community Organization and the Underclass: Exploring New Practice Directions." *Social Service Review* 69 (1): 57–85.

Hassett, S., and M.J. Austin. 1997. "Service Integration: Something Old and Something New." *Administration in Social Work* 21 (3/4): 9–29.

Jayakody, R. 1998. *Mental Health Problems, Substance Abuse, and Welfare Reform.* Chicago: American Sociological Association.

Johnson, A.K. 1998. "The Revitalization of Community Practice: Characteristics, Competencies, and Curricula for Community-based Services." *Journal of Community Practice* 5 (3): 37–62.

Meyer, D.R., and M. Cancian. 1998. "Economic Well-Being Following an Exit from Aid to Families with Dependent Children." *Journal of Marriage and the Family* 60 (2): 479–492.

Murphy, P.A. 1997. "Recovering from the Effects of Domestic Violence: Implications for Welfare Reform Policy." *Law and Policy Journal* 19 (2): 169–182.

Nichols, L. 1998. *Why Welfare Reform Won't Work and What Could: Voices from a Community Program.* Chicago: American Sociological Association.

Pavetti, L. 1997. "New Welfare Reform: One Size Fits All?" *Forum for Applied Research and Public Policy* 12 (4): 18–21.

Perlmutter, F. 1997. *From Welfare To Work: Corporate Initiatives and Welfare Reform*. New York: Oxford University Press.

Philadelphia Citizens for Children and Youth (PCCY). 1998. *Watching Out for Children in Changing Times: The Impact of Welfare Reform on Philadelphia's Children*. Philadelphia: PCCY.

Raffel, J. 1998. *TANF, Act 35, and Pennsylvania's New Welfare System*. Philadelphia: 21st Century League.

Reisch, M., and L. Jarman-Rohde. 1998. "Strengthening Community Advocacy Through Collaborative Cultural Activities and Political Action." Paper presented at the annual conference of the Association for Research on Nonprofit Organizations and Voluntary Action, Seattle, WA.

Reitan, T. 1998. "Theories of Interorganizational Relations in the Human Services." *Social Service Review* 72 (3): 285–309.

Riccio, J., and A. Orenstein. 1996. "Understanding Best Practices for Operating Welfare-to-Work Programs." *Evaluation Review* 20 (1): 3–28.

Roberts-DeGenarro, M. 1997. "Conceptual Framework of Coalitions in an Organizational Context." *Journal of Community Practice* 4 (1): 91–107.

Warren, R. 1983. "The Good Community: What Would It Be?" In *New Perspectives on the American Community*, R. Warren and L. Lyon, eds. Homewood, IL: Dorsey Press.

Wilson, W.J. 1997. *When Work Disappears: The World of the New Urban Poor*. New York: Alfred Knopf.

Withorn, A. 1998. "No Win: Facing the Ethical Perils of Welfare Reform." *Families in Society* 79 (3): 277–287.

Woolis, D.D. 1998. "Family Works: Substance Abuse Treatment and Welfare Reform." *Public welfare* 5: 24–31.

## Notes

[1] Michael Reisch, MSW, Ph.D., is a professor in the School of Social Work at the University of Michigan. He has published and presented extensively on contemporary social policy issues, particularly welfare reform; on community organization theory and practice; and on nonprofit organizations. His most recent book is *The Road Not Taken: A History of Radical Social Work in the U.S.* (with Janice Andrews).

[2] Ursula Bischoff, MSW, JD, Ph.D., is research and planning manager for the County of San Mateo Human Services Agency. She has practiced, taught, and conducted research in the fields of housing, child and public welfare, and human services administration, policy, and planning.

[3] Personal communication from D. Cooper, Mayor's Office, Philadelphia, 1998.

[4] Agencies that participated in the study tended overwhelmingly to be local, community-based organizations. The youngest agency was three years old; the oldest had been providing services to the community for 125 years. Nearly 75 percent had existed for over ten years. They were also predominantly run, staffed, and used by women. Nearly 93

percent reported "most" of their clients came from West Philadelphia. Thus, the study captured the legislation's impact on a clearly defined neighborhood. Reflecting the demographics of the community, 84.3 percent of the participating organizations had staffs that were predominantly African American. Annual agency budgets ranged from under $10,000 to several million dollars. For more information on characteristics of participating agencies, contact Michael Reisch at mreisch@umich.edu. Results of this study are published in the *Journal of Community Practice* 8 (July 2000).

## PART VII

# Conclusion

Joan Acker
Sandra Morgen
Frances Fox Piven
Margaret Hallock

# Toward a New Politics

## Frances Fox Piven, Joan Acker, Margaret Hallock and Sandra Morgen

The chapters presented here contain powerful criticisms of present welfare restructuring and point to the components needed for real welfare reform in the United States. Such reform is theoretically possible in 2002, as Congress considers the abolition, renewal, or replacement of TANF and the PRWORA. We say "theoretically possible" because, as we have shown, politics and ideology shaped the welfare legislation of 1996 more than reasoned social policy following from solid research. We hope that the research of this book's contributors, along with the ideas of clients, advocates, policy makers, and other researchers, will be heard among the many voices in the current debate over a humane agenda for welfare reform.

In support of this agenda, we conclude this volume with policy recommendations that summarize proposals made by participants in the Work, Welfare, and Politics Conference and focus, especially, on the contributions of poverty activists. The most fundamental assumption that guided organization of the conference was that welfare policy should not be taken out of the context of issues concerning the low-wage labor force. The predominant reason that people turn to welfare is that low-wage jobs do not provide enough income to meet a family's needs, especially during a crisis such as illness, divorce, unemployment, lack of childcare, or the need to escape domestic violence. In these situations, people need welfare as a safety net, but "reform" has shredded this net. When clients return to

**349**

work, it is usually to low-wage jobs that still do not give them adequate financial security.

Over the past two decades, much of the job growth in the U.S. economy has been in the low-wage and contingent work sectors. Without policies designed to improve working conditions and wages, welfare reform does little to increase security and alleviate poverty. The vast majority of welfare clients are single mothers with children. Thus, welfare policy should also be considered in the context of the value of women's unpaid caring work, as many of our contributors argue. Present reform policies ignore the value of this socially necessary work and increase the stress of combining work and family for the most vulnerable members of our society.

A significant proportion of welfare clients are women of color. Thus, another facet of welfare policy is racism in society in general, particularly in the labor market and in the construction of welfare programs, as our contributors have shown. TANF reform policies have had a particularly severe impact on families of color. And continuing patterns of racial discrimination in housing, employment, and education position more families of color to need public assistance.

The following proposals are more urgent in 2002 than they were when the Work, Welfare, and Politics Conference was held in 2000. Since then, the booming U.S. economy has slid into a recession, made worse by the shock of the attacks of September 11. The ample supply of jobs that contributed to the decline in numbers of welfare recipients has weakened.

Though some commentators try to reassure us that recession may be short, at this writing we find that unemployment has risen, homelessness is increasing, food kitchens can barely feed those in need, and welfare rolls are rising. Moreover, the specter of a national recession should be a reminder that economic downturns are a persistent feature of economies such as ours, and that even when the national economy is recovering or doing well, localities or states do not share equally in that recovery.

Providing, perhaps, the extreme example, Oregon had the nation's highest unemployment rate of 7.4 percent at the end of 2001. The number of TANF recipients grew by 15 percent between December 2000 and December 2001, and the Food Stamp Program ballooned by 51 percent in the same period, leading to the troubling fact that roughly one in ten residents of the state were receiving this benefit. TANF, based on the idea that finding work is an available solution to financial crisis, simply does not provide a safety net as unemployment rises. Other components of the safety net, such as Food Stamps, Medicaid, and unemployment insurance, also have been weakened, although the Bush administration is taking steps to extend Food Stamps to immigrant groups that had been excluded—a critical policy change. In the economic conditions of 2002, the needs for a comprehensive safety net and improved working conditions and wages are ever more pressing.

Conference participants had many proposals for change, some of which would modify existing programs to increase adequacy and make their administration more humane. Others would create new structures of income and family caregiving support to significantly reduce poverty. We discuss these proposals below.

Political mobilization is the key to turning proposals into programs. Activist Cheri Honkala of the Kensington Welfare Rights Union in Philadelphia underlined the necessity of organizing clients to push for reform, and to give them a voice in deciding what reforms should be. She called for: "Building leadership amongst the poor. Not a leader, but hundreds of thousands of conscious, articulate leaders, who are capable of solving problems by organizing to take back the basic necessities of life." Diane Dujon of Working Massachusetts, a broad multi-issue coalition, argued that effective politics to end poverty require coalitions among low-income organizations, labor unions, religious groups, academics, and community activists. Politics, Honkala, Dujon, and many other advocates point out, means much more than legislative work, such as writing letters or lobbying. Demonstrating, educating, even taking over housing, also are essential tools in the political struggle.

Other activists at the conference were workers at food banks, lawyers representing welfare clients, advocates for higher education for welfare mothers, housing advocates, and researcher/advocates from independent policy centers, such as the Oregon Center for Public Policy and the Economic Policy Institute in Washington, D.C. Also represented were members of the Women's Committee of 100, a group of feminist academics, professionals, and activists who are concerned with the relationship between women, economic survival, and the work of caregiving. Their perspective on the reform of PRWORA, "An Immodest Proposal: Rewarding Women's Work to End Poverty," was widely distributed and discussed during the conference. These proposals are reflected in what follows.

Our policy proposals focus primarily on three large questions: 1) how to repair and strengthen the social safety net; 2) how to reform the low-wage labor market and improve the job prospects of welfare clients; and 3) how to support the family-caring work of low-wage women workers.

## Proposals for Change

### 1. Create a Real Safety Net

PRWORA eroded the previously existing Aid to Families with Dependent Children safety net by ending entitlements to assistance based only on the lack of sufficient funds to support one's family. Under PRWORA, states are no longer required to provide assistance and must enforce a five-year lifetime limit on assistance, regardless of need. A real safety net will require amending PRWORA to ensure assistance to all families who lack the resources to meet their own basic needs. A bill to amend PRWORA and restore the safety net, H.R. 3113, was introduced in 2001 in the House of Representatives by Representative Patsy Mink of Hawaii. If passed, this bill would accomplish our proposals for a new safety net.

**Fundamental changes to the PRWORA should:**

▶ Restore entitlement to financial assistance, or guarantee that those with financial resources below a specified level will get help. Restoring entitlement will probably require that the federal government end block grants and also ensure that states have sufficient funds to meet the needs of poor families. Restoring entitlement will require abolishing PRWORA limitations on eligibility, such as time limits on assistance, demands that applicants identify absent parents for purposes of child support, and denial of assistance for children born while their mother is receiving assistance, also known as "family caps."

▶ Establish a minimum level of cash assistance that is high enough to meet basic needs. This level might be defined as a certain percentage above a revised poverty standard. The minimum assistance level should be pegged to inflation. Establishing a minimum health and decency standard for assistance will also require federal oversight.

▶ Restore Food Stamp cuts, ease income and property eligibility standards for Food Stamps, and abolish time limits and work requirements in the Food Stamp Program.

▶ Provide all benefits to immigrants, including undocumented immigrants. Under PRWORA, immigrants living in the U.S. for less than five years were denied assistance, including Food Stamps and Medicaid, as were all illegal immigrants. This constitutes discrimination against a sizeable group of people. This discrimination may be somewhat reduced with the restoration of eligibility for Food Stamps, as discussed above.

Restoring a "real" safety net also means instituting reforms in other programs, because Medicaid, Unemployment Insurance, Supplementary Security Income, and housing assistance are all resources upon which low-wage families can draw. These programs should be included in debates about reauthorization of PRWORA.

*To weave a true safety net, we should:*

▶ Increase federal and state support for affordable housing, with the goal of providing housing for all, and drastically reducing homelessness.

▶ Extend Medicaid coverage to families with incomes below 200 percent of the poverty line who do not have affordable private insurance.

▶ Reform Unemployment Insurance programs so that part-time and temporary workers, as well as workers with short job tenures, will be eligible, and raise the proportion of workers who can qualify.

▶ Reform the Supplementary Security Income program so that those who are disabled have easier and guaranteed access.

## 2. Reform the Low-wage Labor Market and Improve the Job Prospects of Welfare Clients

To begin to accomplish this Herculean task under the confines of the reform of welfare policy, new legislation must—at the very least— allow education and training to count toward the work requirement that determines eligibility for continuing benefits. Several authors show that higher levels of education are associated both with higher rates of employment and lower rates of poverty. Welfare policies should encourage education and training, in order to better prepare clients for jobs that earn a living wage.

Under the Welfare-to-Work requirements of PRWORA, most states do not count education hours as legitimate attempts on the part of clients to become self-supporting, an effort they must prove in order to qualify for continuing benefits. Such short-sighted rules discourage clients from seeking technical or higher education that would help them exit low-wage work and, thereby, gain true self-sufficiency.

In addition to reforming this aspect of current welfare legislation, more far-reaching reforms are needed to provide better prospects and security for low-wage workers. These include:

▶ raising the minimum wage and tying its level to inflation

- establishing refundable, state earned-income tax credits and federal and state refundable childcare tax credits

- guaranteeing the right to unionize, a right that is fundamental to the ability of workers to organize for and protect all the other rights proposed here

- instituting measures to achieve comparable worth, or equal pay for work of equal value, for jobs held primarily by women or by men of color (e.g., janitors)

- strengthening Affirmative Action to continue to combat discrimination and expand opportunities

- increasing efforts to abolish sexual harassment in the workplace, as well as other forms of discrimination

- enforcing existing labor standards, including prohibitions of involuntary overtime and safety and health standards.

## 3. Provide More Effective Supports for Combining Paid Work and Unpaid Caring Work

Women have the primary responsibility for caring for children and ill or disabled adults. These responsibilities often conflict with employers' demands, particularly for women in low-wage jobs. If single mothers are expected to do paid work, they need resources with which to make possible the combination of labor-market work and care work.

Additionally, policy makers need to give strong consideration to valuing the unpaid work necessary for caring for children and dependent adults, if we are to have family-strengthening social policies.

- End mandatory work outside the home as a condition for receiving assistance for mothers of children under age three, and for mothers who do not have available and satisfactory childcare.

- Subsidize childcare for all low- and moderate-income families.

- Raise subsidy cut-off levels so that childcare does not become too expensive for families as their incomes rise.

▶ Establish quality standards for childcare and enforce these standards.

▶ Raise childcare subsidies to levels that cover costs of high-quality care.

▶ Improve access to transportation between jobs, home, and childcare.

▶ Extend Unemployment Compensation to parents who do not have childcare or who have children who are ill and need care. This would allow parents whose incomes are above welfare eligibility levels to have some wage-replacement while doing essential caring work.

▶ Improve domestic abuse crisis services and ongoing support services to overcome this barrier to successfully combining caring and paid work. Domestic violence disrupts routines of paid work and care, and often results in psychological trauma that impairs women's abilities to cope with complex, daily life arrangements.

### Ending Poverty, Guaranteeing Security

Even if the above reforms were achieved, the United States would still be far from ending poverty and guaranteeing security for all its people. More fundamental changes that bring improvements for moderate as well as low-income families are necessary to achieve that goal.

Middle-class and working-class people face many of the same problems with regard to childcare, income security, affordable housing, and the high costs of higher education. Moreover, both low- and moderate-income families lost ground compared to high-income families over the past two decades. Solutions that apply to all, not just to the poor alone, are more apt to last because they are in the interests of most people and, thus, may attract broader political support than solutions aimed only at the poor.

Among the changes that seem essential now are new ways to guarantee income security to the level of a "living wage"; new forms of support for caregiving that might include paid parental leave or a caregivers' allowance; a national health insurance program; measures to make housing more affordable for those with low and moderate incomes; and new forms of funding higher education that make it accessible to all without imposing huge debts on young people.

## 1. Establish New Ways to Guarantee Income Security to the Level of a Living Wage

▶ Establish a guaranteed minimum income or a "citizen's wage" that would provide a minimum level of living for every individual. Such a solution may never be politically feasible. In its absence, income subsidies such as those that exist in many European countries could be instituted. These include a child allowance paid to parents of all children, and unemployment compensation paid to all those without work, including young people just entering the job world and the long-term unemployed.

▶ Establish new forms of support for caregiving.

▶ Establish universal, publicly supported childcare, with quality standards and professional pay.

▶ Establish a caregiver's allowance, available to all families, that would allow the choice of paid work or family care.

▶ Establish paid leave for all parents at the time of birth or adoption and during the child's infancy. Also establish paid leave for other caregiving responsibilities.

▶ Establish a right to part-time work for parents of young children.

## 2. Transform Wage Work

▶ Establish universal, free higher education and technical training. Provide students with stipends and childcare support. This could be modeled on the GI Bill of Rights of the post-WW II period. Such a provision would solve a problem facing many people—the burden of staggering debt incurred to finance higher education.

▶ Shorten the standard work week with the expectation that people would devote more hours to caretaking of their own families and their communities.

## 3. Establish Other Supports

▶ Establish government support for affordable housing for all. Housing costs are a problem for middle-income as well as low-income people. Measures could include rent control; expanded rent subsidies; increased tax rates on expensive housing; reductions of interest deductions on mortgages for high-cost homes; and subsidies for home purchase.

▶ Establish national health insurance available to all. Middle-income as well as low-income people make up the uninsured who risk going without necessary care or incurring debts they may never be able to pay. Lack of health insurance contributes to income insecurity and poverty.

These proposals for immediate change, if enacted, would give increased protection for the most economically vulnerable families during the present period of recession, and provide a better safety net for the future.

The more fundamental changes we propose require rethinking of policies that have led to the economic polarization that now characterizes U.S. society. The widening gap between the wealthy and the rest of us is responsible for a host of social ills, and threatens the economic future of this country. These more fundamental changes would also reduce poverty and save the United States from the disgraceful distinction of having the highest poverty rate among the rich industrialized countries. However, to turn such proposals from utopian dreams into functioning realities will take powerful social movements, motivated by demands for economic and social justice. We hope that this collection of papers will contribute to such a movement.

# Acknowledgements

It is a rare conference that generates ideas, research and discussion worthy of publication. In February 2000, Frances Fox Piven keynoted such a conference at the University of Oregon on Work, Welfare, and Politics. Professor Piven held the Wayne Morse Chair for Law and Politics in 1999-2000 thanks to Greg McLauchlan of the Sociology Department and the other members of the Morse Chair board. Sponsored by the UO Center for the Study of Women in Society and the Wayne Morse Center for Law and Politics, the conference attracted policymakers and advocates as well as researchers, creating a decidedly spirited and productive atmosphere.

UO President David Frohnmayer noted that universities can act as catalysts for the interactions of people who might not typically come together to discuss and shape vital public policy. Quoting Kingman Brewster, he set the tone for the conference by remarking that "Universities should be safe havens where ruthless examination of realities will not be distorted by the aim to please or inhibited by the risk of displeasure."

We want to thank and acknowledge here the many people who inspired, participated, and carried out the conference. Staff from both the Center for the Study of Women in Society and the (then new) Wayne Morse Center worked diligently and with great dedication to ensure the success of the conference. The conference directors were Sandra Morgen (CSWS) and Gordon Lafer (Labor Education and Research Center). We especially thank Terri Health, Shirley Marc, Beth Hege Piatote, and Nancy Leeper, who were or are CSWS staff and Ina Zucker and Marcy Janes who were Morse Center graduate assistants at that time. Researchers, policy makers, and advocates came to the conference from all parts of the United States, greatly enriching the dialogue. We especially thank the many advocates and activists who brought their truths and visions to the conference and who continue to bring them to other public forums where the voices of the poor must be heard.

It became clear during the conference that we had created something unique that needed to be shared with the larger community of activists and policymakers struggling with welfare reform. Thus began the long process of translating the papers and discussion for publication. This process was aided immeasurably by our colleagues at the UO Press and, in particular, by Cheri Brooks, a fabulous writer, editor, and colleague at CSWS and the Morse Center. Her conscientious and thoughtful editing was a blessing to us all.

During the past two years many of us have worked in our own arenas—as scholars, activists, in advocacy and human service organizations, and in policy arenas—to inform the public that not all was well with welfare restructuring. This book is being published as Congress and the public begin debate about re-authorization of Temporary Assistance to Needy Families. We hope this book will be useful to policy makers, activists, advocates, and researchers serious about meeting the challenge of reducing poverty in this country.

# Index

Page numbers followed by a "t" indicate a table, and page numbers followed by an "f" indicate a figure.

ABAWDs (able-bodied adults without dependents), 302
abstinence education, 101–102
activists
    organizing, 92–93, 351
    resistance, 207–208
    support base, 67
addiction and medical/psychological problems, 61
Adult and Family Services (AFS), 244–245, 255, 322
AFDC (Aid to Families with Dependent Children), 35–38, 40, 96–97
Affirmative Action, 354
AFS (Adult and Family Services), 244–245, 255
agencies
    collaborating, 341–342
    organizations compared, 322–328, 327t
AGI (Alan Guttmacher Institute), 99–100, 101
Aid to Families with Dependent Children (AFDC), 35–38, 40, 96–97
Alan Guttmacher Institute (AGI), 99–100, 101
Alien Nation (Brimelow), 38–39
aliens. See immigrants
Anderson, Martin, 28–29
Anti-Defamation League, 37
ARC (Applied Research Center), 43–44, 49–50
arguments against welfare, 24–26
Arizona. See reform evaluation in Arizona and Oregon
Associated Press, 41
attitudes towards poverty
    causes of, 58–62
    "doing something," 62–65
    dominant view, 55, 117
    language affecting, 65–67

major findings, 56
overview, 56–57, 57t
See also poverty

Bane, Mary Jo, 74, 130
barriers to employment, 41, 248, 249t, 279–280, 282–283
basic-needs budget
    about, 267
    compared to net income, 270–271, 271t, 272t
    county variations, 269–270, 269t
    data sources, 268–269
    living in Multnomah County compared to Union County, Oregon, 271–273, 271t, 272t
Better Chance Program, 99
birth rates, 102–105, 103f, 103t, 104t
Blank, Rebecca, 130, 312
Brimelow, Peter, 38–39
Burstin, H.R., 292
Burtless, Gary, 121, 129–130
Bush, George W., 22, 29, 350
business
    agenda, 22–24
    class politics, 21–24
    corporations contracting work, 281–282
    role of, 187–189

California. See immigrant women affected by welfare reform in Santa Clara County, California; Los Angeles County reform (LA GAIN) study
CalWORKs (California Work Opportunity and Responsibility to Kids), 198–199, 277–278
Cancian, Maria, 130, 131
Canfield, Jack, 204
"capped" child, 97–98
Carter, Jimmy, 22
caseload decline, 116, 243–244, 312–314, 330, 335

CBOs. *See* community-based organizations (CBOs) adjustments to reform
Center for Community Change, 44–45
Center for Law and Social Policy, 98
CETA, 185–186
*Chicken Soup for the Soul* (Canfield), 204
childbearing decisions, 96–98
childcare
    access, 165–166, 283–284
    attitudes toward, 88–89
    reforms needed, 354–356
children in poverty, 290, 290t, 296
child support enforcement and paternity study in Wisconsin
    background, 227–229
    custody/visitation rights of unmarried fathers, 231–232
    economic interests of unmarried mothers, 230–231
    recommendations, 236–237
    risk of domestic violence, 232–233
    tradeoffs, 233–236
Christian Right
    alliance with business, 29–30
    appeal, 28
class politics, 21–24
Clinton, Bill, 29, 39, 74, 96, 125, 227
Cloward, Richard A., 92, 197
Cobb, Roger, 214
Collins, Patricia Hill, 38
Colorado. *See* context sensitivity study in Boulder County, Colorado
communication issues. *See* context sensitivity study in Boulder County, Colorado
community-based organizations (CBOs) adjustments to reform
    background, 333–334
    communication changes, 338–339
    conclusions, 341–343
    funding, 339
    impact on clients, 336–337

    impact on services, 337
    methodology, 335–336
    objectives/outcomes, 337–338
    in Pennsylvania, 334–335
    relationships with other organizations, 339–340
    response to cutoff date, 341
    staff changes, 338
    technical assistance needs, 340–341
comparable worth, 354
Connolly, Laura S., 147
context sensitivity study in Boulder County, Colorado
    background, 213–216
    conclusion, 222–223
    findings, 216–222, 217t, 218t
    Nudist (QSR Nudist), 215, 219–222
    Word Freq, 215, 216–219, 217t, 218t
    words in context by participants, 219–222
CPS (Current Population Survey), 145, 147–148
custody/visitation rights, 231–232

Darity, William, 77
Delgado, Gary, 49–50
Democratic politics, 27–30
democratic rights impacted by social programs, 21
demographic trends, 41, 102–107, 103f, 103t, 104t
Direct Job Placement, 189
discrimination
    of immigrant women, 43–45, 280–282
    outcomes of PRWORA, 41
disincentives to increase earnings, 264–266, 264t, 265t
"doing something," 62–65
domestic violence, 232–233, 285
DSHS Economic Services Administration, 293
Dujon, Diane, 351
Dye, J.L., 100

Earned Income Tax Credit (EITC), 263
earnings and incomes

affected by education, 159
affected by waivers, 148–153,
        149t, 151t
GAIN program, 186–187
gender and wage gap, 247
increase and benefits decrease,
        146–147, 263–266, 264t,
        265t, 266t
leavers in Oregon, 246–247
tax rates, 266t, 267
economic
    boom of 1990's, 23–24, 245, 289,
        302, 312
    interests of unmarried mothers,
        230–231
    policies affecting social policies,
        22–24, 96–101, 302, 341–343
    predictions, 146, 315
Economic Policy Institute, 351
Economic Roundtable, 199
ECONorthwest, 260
education, abstinence, 101–102
education, impact on jobs, 157–163,
167–169, 178
education (postsecondary) in
Michigan
    childcare, 165–166
    importance of, 158–159
    misinformation and harassment,
        167–168
    options limited, 161—162
    policy implementation, 162–163
    reform policies and, 159–161
    student mothers, 163–167
    Work First, 160–165
EITC (Earned Income Tax Credit), 263
election outcomes, 27–30
Ellwood, David, 74, 125, 130
employment barriers, 41, 248, 249t,
279–280, 282–283
Employment Related Day Care
(ERDC), 253, 253t, 262, 263–266
English proficiency as a barrier,
279–280
ERA (Equal Rights Advocates), 278
ERDC (Employment Related Day
Care), 253, 253t, 262, 263–266

Fair Market Rent (FMR), 268
family
    caps, 96–98
    planning, 99–100
    values, 76–78, 88–92
fertility issues, 105–107
FIA (Family Independence Agency),
161, 162, 165, 167
Figlio, David N., 312
Fleming, Patricia L., 102
Florida. See health insurance issues
in North Florida and Oregon
Food Stamp population study
    background, 301–303
    behavior transformations, 310–311
    caseload changes, 301–302, 311–
        314, 312t
    conclusions, 315
    descriptive results, 306
    methodology, 303–304
    regression-adjusted results, 307
    work encouragement policies,
        307–309, 308t, 309t
    work requirement policies, 304–
        306, 305t, 306t
Food Stamp Program (FSP), 244,
245t, 253, 253t, 261, 284
    See also Food Stamp population
        study
future of welfare policy, 30, 48–50

GAIN (Greater Avenues for
INdependence), 177–178, 180–181,
186
    See also Los Angeles County
        reform (LA GAIN) study
gender issues, 247, 247t
Gilder, George, 28–29, 40
Gilens, Martin, 37, 61–62
globalization affecting welfare
programs, 19
Gold, Rachel Benson, 99
good-cause exemption, 233
Gordon, David M., 120
Gordon, Linda, 92
Gottschalk, Peter, 121
Gramm, Phil, 27

Greater Avenues for Independence (GAIN), 177–178, 180–181, 186
Gronbach, L.J., 214

harassment and misinformation, 167–168, 282–283, 354
Harris, Kathleen Mullen, 130
Harrison, Bennett, 120
health insurance issues in North Florida and Oregon
    background, 289–291
    conclusion, 297–298
    leaving welfare, 291–293
    Oregon Health Plan (OHP), 296–297
    poor children's health, 296
    recipients concerns about health, 295–297
    uninsured consequences, 293–295, 294t
health issues
    addiction and medical/psychological problems, 61
    children, 294, 296
    concerns, 284, 295–298
    domestic violence, 232–233, 285
    hunger, 284
    immunizations, 98–99
    insurance, 291–298
    Medicaid, 99–100, 291, 297–298
    uninsured consequences, 293–295, 294t
history of reforms, 39–40, 73–78, 116–122, 129–130, 177
Holmes, Oliver Wendell, 106
Holzer, Harry, 131, 133
Honkala, Cheri, 351
housing costs, 285
Howell, David R., 120
humanitarian rhetoric, 66

ideological campaigns, 24–26
illegitimacy. See out-of-wedlock births
immigrants
    and discrimination, 38–39, 43–45
    legal, 27
    race population control, 38–39
immigrant women affected by welfare reform in Santa Clara County, California
    childcare issues, 283–284
    domestic violence, 285
    English proficiency problems, 279–280
    health and hunger problems, 284
    housing costs, 285
    inadequate information regarding services, 282–283
    job skills and availability, 280–282
    overview, 278–279, 278t
    recommendations, 286–287
    social isolation, 285–286
Immigration and Naturalization Service, 38
immunization requirements, 98–99
income protection programs
    future of, 30
    globalization, 19
    impact on societies, 20–22
    legislation renewal, 29–30
    state-run, 23
    Western countries, 19
incomes. See earnings and incomes
individualist rhetoric, 66
Institute for Women's Policy Research, 116
international comparisons of population issues, 103–107
International Conference on Population and Development, 106–107
interviews on the causes of poverty, 58–67

Jencks, Christopher, 77
Job Club, 199, 201–202
job training
    business lobbies, role of, 187–189
    change in focus, 175–176
    discipline as policy, 189–191
    evaluations, 186–187
    kinds of, 76, 133, 181–182

low wage labor, 118–122, 181–182
mobility, 120–122
motivational training, 179–183
policies, 78–79, 92–93
temporary jobs, 281–282
Workfare, 183–186
Work First model (California), 176–179
JTPA (Job Training Partnership Act), 177

Kaiser/Commonwealth 1997 National Survey of Health Insurance, 293
Kaus, Mickey, 26–27
Kensington Welfare Rights Union, 351
Kirby, Douglas, 102

labor market
    attitudes toward work, 55, 117, 198–199, 203
    education/training, 124
    job insecurity, 26
    low wage labor, 118–119
    segmented, 120–121
    sexual harassment, 354
    standards enforced, 354
    unemployment, 123
LACOE (Los Angeles County Office of Education), 199
LA GAIN. See Los Angeles County reform (LA GAIN) study
leavers. See welfare reform's impact on leavers in Oregon
leaving welfare, 291–293
Lee, Lisa M., 102
legislation, 29–30
Levin-Epstein, Jodie, 97
Loprest, Pamela, 119, 293
Los Angeles County reform (LA GAIN) study
    conclusion., 207–208
    discipline, 203
    incentives, 200–201
    moral control, 204–206
    participants, 198

sanctions, 201–202
work ethic, 198–199, 203
See also GAIN (Greater Avenues for INdependence)
Luker, Kristin, 105

Make the Road by Walking, 44
Manpower Demonstration Research Corporation, 199
Mathematica Policy Research, 130
Mead, Lawrence W., 28–29, 40
Medicaid, 99–100, 291, 297–298
medical/psychological and addiction problems, 61
Mexican immigrants, 279–285
Meyer, Daniel R., 131
Michigan. See education (postsecondary) in Michigan
minimum wage. See wages
misinformation and harassment, 167–168, 282–283
Moffit, Robert, 147–148
moral issues, 24–26
Morris, Lisa A., 130
motivational training, 179–183
Murray, Charles, 28–29, 40, 77
Myers, Samuel, 77

NAALC (North American Agreement on Labor Cooperation), 103
National Longitudinal Survey of Youth, 129–130
National Medical Expenditure Survey (NMES), 268, 291
National Opinion Research Center, 37
National Survey of American Families (NSAF), 293
Newman, Katherine, 121
new welfare regime, 26–27
New York Times, 41
nonprofit organizations. See community-based organizations (CBOs) adjustments to reform
North American Agreement on Labor Cooperation (NAALC), 103
North Carolina. See postexit earnings study in North Carolina
Northwest Job Gap Study, 247
Nudist (QSR Nudist), 215, 219–222

OCR (Office of Civil Rights), 43–44
OECD (Organization for Economic Co-operation and Development), 20, 24
Ohio, Cuyahoga County, 334
OHP (Oregon Health Plan), 253–254, 253t, 254t, 261–262, 296–297
Oregon. See welfare reform's impact on leavers in Oregon; transition to self-sufficiency in Oregon; health insurance issues in North Florida and Oregon; reform evaluation in Arizona and Oregon
Oregon Center for Public Policy, 351
Oregon Coalition of Community Non-Profits, 259, 267
Oregon Health Plan (OHP), 253–254, 253t, 254t, 261–262, 296–297
Organization for Economic Co-operation and Development (OECD), 20, 24
organizing women
    political movements, 92–93
    resistance, 207–208
outcomes affected by agency structure, 322–328, 327t
out-of-wedlock births, 25, 39, 98, 100–105, 103f, 103t, 104t

Parrot, Sharon, 119
paternity establishment. See child support enforcement and paternity study in Wisconsin
Pavetti, LaDonna Ann, 130
Pearce, Diana, 267
Pennsylvania, Philadelphia. See community-based organizations (CBOs) adjustments to reform
Personal Responsibility Act of 1995, 39–40
Personal Responsibility and Work Opportunity Reconciliation Act. See PRWORA (Personal Responsibility and Work Opportunity Reconciliation Act)
policies regarding work
    disincentives, 264–266, 264t, 265t
    incentives, 307–309, 308t, 309t
    requirements, 304–306, 305t, 306t
politics of greed, 22–24

population control policies, 38–40, 105–107
populist rhetoric, 66–67
postexit earnings study in North Carolina
    background, 129–131
    earnings, 136–139, 137t, 138t, 139t
    implications, 139–140
    jobs, kinds of, 133, 133t
    methodology, 131–132
    mobility prospects, 133–136, 135t
poverty
    children in, 290, 290t
    leavers in, 247, 321–322
    line, 122–123, 130, 186, 247t, 289, 290t
    reproductive rights and, 106–107
    solutions to, 124–125, 140, 341–343, 352–357
    working poor and, 140, 321
    See also attitudes towards poverty
Presser, Harriet B., 100
Primus, Wendell, 119–120
Programme of Action, 106–107
Project LIFE (Learning Independence From Employment), 183
Project STRIVE, 183
proposals for reform. See recommendations for reform
PRWORA (Personal Responsibility and Work Opportunity Reconciliation Act)
    abstinence-only education, 101–102
    devolution to the states, 23, 39, 96
    discrimination practices, 40–41
    history of the bill, 39–40, 177
    immigrant policy, 38–39
    marriage policy, 74
    paternity/child support issues, 228–229
    postsecondary education, 159–160
    purpose of bill, 95–96
    work requirements, 37–38, 74, 81, 160–161

psychological/medical and addiction problems, 61
Public Policy Institute of California, 27–28
public support influenced by rhetoric, 65–67

racism. *See* welfare racism
Reagan, Ronald, 22, 77
recidivism, 130–131
recommendations for reform
    agencies collaborate, 341–343
    agency organizations vary, 321–328, 331
    child support and paternity establishment, 227–229, 236–237
    communication/context sensitivity issues, 214, 222–223
    education (postsecondary), 168–169
    evaluation of incomes and earnings, 145, 152–153, 273
    Food Stamp caseload, 315
    good for businesses, 187–191
    health insurance issues, 290–298
    immigrant women, 286–287
    income security guarantee, 355–356
    job prospect improvements, 353–354
    labor market, 122–125, 123t, 140, 256
    overview, 349–351
    reproductive choice, 106–107
    resistance, 207–208
    safety net restoration, 351–353
    support systems improvement, 354–355, 357
    wage work transformed, 357
    women's policies, 78–79
reform evaluation in Arizona and Oregon
    agency organization in Arizona, 324–326
    agency organization in Oregon, 322–324
    background, 321–322

comparisons of agencies, 326–328, 327t
conclusion, 331
*self-sufficiency* defined, 328–330
*work activities* defined, 330–331
reform outcome studies, 45–47, 48
reform study on incomes and earnings
    conclusion, 152–153
    data, 147–148
    methodology, 146–147
    results, 148–152, 149t, 151t
*Regulating the Poor: The Functions of Public Welfare* (Piven and Cloward), 197
reproductive rights, 106–107
Republican politics, 27–30
research topics
    abstinence education, 101–102
    beliefs about poverty, 55–58, 57t
    child support and paternity establishment, 229–236
    context sensitivity, 214, 222–223
    demographic trends, 41, 102–107, 103f, 103t, 104t
    family caps, 96–98
    family planning, 99–100
    illegitimacy bonus, 100–101
    immunizations, 98–99
    population policy, 38–40, 105–107
    problems, 97, 98
    racism, 37, 45–47
resistance, 207–208
responsibility, 204, 206
rhetoric affecting public opinion, 65–67
Rochefort, D., 214
Ruggles, Patricia, 130

safety nets, 253–255, 351–353
S-Chip (State Children's Health Insurance Program), 291
Schram, Sanford E., 47–48, 48
Segal, Lewis M., 147
segmentation theory, 120–121
self esteem training, 179–183
*self-sufficiency*, 328–330

sex education, 101–102
Shor, Ira, 190
SIPP (Survey of Income and Program Participation), 292
social conditioning, 60
social isolation, 285–286
Sonfield, Adam, 99
Soss, Joe, 42–43
State Children's Health Insurance Program (S-Chip), 291
state governments
    devolution of authority to, 23, 39
    education policies, 160–161, 178
    waivers, 96–101, 146–153
sterilization. *See* fertility issues
stigmatization, 204–206, 255
student mothers, 163–167
Sui, Ralph, 214
Sum, Andrew, 120
Supplemental Nutrition for Women, Infants and Children (WIC), 99
Survey of Income and Program Participation (SIPP), 292

TANF (Temporary Aid for Needy Families), 42–43, 81, 98, 99, 188–189
taxes, 262–263, 266t, 267, 354
teenage birth rates, 25, 103–105, 103f
Temporary Aid for Needy Families. *See* TANF (Temporary Aid for Needy Families)
*The Bell Curve* (Herrnstein and Murray), 40
*The New Republic*, 26–27
training, motivational, 179–183
transition to self-sufficiency in Oregon
    basic-needs budget, 267–270, 269t, 270t
    conclusion, 273
    eligibility criteria, 261–263
    income compared to basic-needs budget, 270–273, 271t, 272t
    overview, 259–261
    tradeoffs as earnings rise, 263–267, 264t, 265t, 266t

unemployment
    insurance benefits, 22–23
    levels, 23–24, 26, 123
unions
    impact on wages, 20
    New York Workfare, 185
    right to form, 354
unmarried fathers, 231–232
unwed mothers, 230–231

vaccination requirements, 98–99
Vietnamese immigrants, 279–285
visitation/custody rights, 231–232

wages
    Federal Reserve, impact on, 123
    flexibility, 20–21
    minimum, 22, 61–62, 118–119, 124, 353
    prospects in North Carolina, 133–140
    trends, 118–122, 118f, 136–139, 189, 291–292
    unions, impact on, 20, 185
    workfare, 146
waivers, 96–101, 146–153
Wallace, Geoffrey, 312
Welfare Race and Gender Equity Survey, 43–44
welfare racism
    defined, 36
    demographics, 41
    family caps, 42–43, 96–98
    how to change, 48–50
    ignored, 46–47
    immigrants, 27, 38–39, 43–45, 278–280, 282–283
    poor women of color, 46
    population control, 38–40, 103t
    racial barriers, 41
    in research, 45–47
    role of politicians, 37–38
    sentiments, 37–38
Welfare Reform Review Committee (WRRC), 216–219, 217t, 218t
welfare reform's impact on leavers in Oregon

background, 243–244
barriers to employment, 248, 249t, 291–293
earnings, 246–247, 246t, 247t
employment status, 245–246, 245t, 246t, 310
family wellbeing, 253–255, 253t, 254t
gender issues, 247, 247t
*good jobs* and education, 248–252, 250t, 251t, 252t, 292
health insurance issues, 291–298
recommendations, 256
safety-nets, 253–255
stigmatization, 255
welfare-to-work (WtW)
business lobbies, role of, 187–189
curriculum, 83–84, 297
disincentives to raise earnings, 273
education, impact on, 157–163, 167–169, 178
evaluations, 115, 177–179, 182–183, 186–187
family values, 73, 76–78, 86–87
health insurance, impact on, 291–298
history of, 74, 81–82, 116–117, 176–179, 188
job mobility, 120–122
kinds of jobs, 76, 118–122, 133, 181–182
mothering, value of, 88–92
paid work, 84–86
postexit earnings, 129–131
progressive policies, 78–79, 92–93, 124–125
recession, impact on, 123
recidivism, 130–131
subsidies, 124–125
support inadequate, 74–75, 122, 123f, 160, 163–168
training as discipline, 182–183, 189–191

wage prospects in North Carolina, 133–140
Work First (WF) in Michigan, 160–165
WIC (Supplemental Nutrition for Women, Infants and Children), 99
Wilcox, B.L., 102
Wilson, Pete, 277
Wilson, William Julius, 77
Wisconsin. *See* child support enforcement and paternity study in Wisconsin
women recipients
childcare burden, 61
of color, 46
debt, 294–295
domestic violence, 232–233, 285
health care concerns, 284, 295–298
lack of information, 282–283, 297
organizing, 92–93, 207–208, 351
progressive policies, 78–79
Women's Committee of 100, 49, 351
Word Freq, 215, 216–219, 217t, 218t
*work activities,* 330–331
work ethic, 198–199, 203
Work Experience Program (WEP), 184–185
Workfare, 146, 183–186
Work First (WF). *See* welfare-to-work (WtW)
work incentives, 146, 307–311
Working Massachusetts, 351
working poor, 116–117, 117f, 140, 321
work policies
disincentives, 264–266, 264t, 265t
encouraging, 307–309, 308t, 309t
requirement, 304–306, 305t, 306t
World Health Organization, 101–102
WtW. *See* welfare-to-work (WtW)